VOICES MADE FLESH

Wisconsin Studies in Autobiography

Voices Made Flesh

Performing Women's Autobiography

edited by

Lynn C. Miller,

Jacqueline Taylor, and

M. Heather Carver

THE UNIVERSITY OF WISCONSIN PRESS

The University of Wisconsin Press
1930 Monroe Street
Madison, Wisconsin 53711

www.wisc.edu/wisconsinpress/

3 Henrietta Street
London WC2E 8LU, England

5   4   3   2   1

Printed in Canada

Library of Congress Cataloging-in-Publication Data
Voices made flesh : performing women's autobiography /
    edited by Lynn C. Miller, Jacqueline Taylor, and
    M. Heather Carver.
    p. cm. — (Wisconsin series in autobiography)
    ISBN 0-299-18420-X (cloth : alk. paper)
    ISBN 0-299-18424-2 (pbk. : alk. paper)
    1. American drama—Women authors—History
and criticism.   2. Autobiography—Women authors—
Adaptations—History and criticism.   3. Women and
literature—United States.   4. Women in literature.
5. Women—Drama.
I. Miller, Lynn C.   II. Taylor, Jacqueline.   III. Carver,
M. Heather.   IV. Series.
PS338.w6 v65   2003
812'.54080352042—dc21   2002010200

Contents

Acknowledgments

Lynn C. Miller expresses appreciation to the University of Texas at Austin for a Faculty Research Award in 1998–99, and M. Heather Carver thanks the University of Missouri for a Research Board Grant.

The editors thank Lynda Miller, Carol Sadtler, Bill Horner, Raphael Kadushin and the University of Wisconsin Press, Jill Dolan, Beverly Whitaker Long, Michael Bowman, Lisa Merrill, Paul Gray, Claire Van Ens, Elizabeth Bell, Carol MacKay, Elaine Lawless, Mary Louise and Ronald Carver, Judith and Robert Horner, and the Department of Theatre, University of Missouri at Columbia, without whom this book would not have been possible. Above all, the editors express gratitude for the lives and stories of women who have inspired this collection.

Earlier versions of the following chapters have been previously published and are reprinted here with permission: Lynn C. Miller, "Gertrude Stein Never Enough," in *Text and Performance Quarterly* 20 no. 1 (2000): 43–57; Stacy Wolf, "Desire in Evidence," in *Text and Performance Quarterly* 17 no. 4 (1997): 343–51; Tami Spry, "Tattoo Stories: A Postscript to 'Skins,'" in *Text and Performance Quarterly* 20 no. 1 (2000): 84–96 and "Skins: A Daughter's (Re)construction of Cancer" in *Text and Performance Quarterly* 17 no. 4 (1997): 361–65; Jacqueline Taylor, "On Being an Exemplary Lesbian," in *Text and Performance Quarterly* 20 no. 1 (2000): 58–73; Joni L. Jones, "sista docta," in *Performance in Life and Literature*, edited by Paul H. Gray and James VanOosting, 227–36 (Boston: Allyn and Bacon, 1998).

VOICES MADE FLESH

Editors' Introduction

Lynn C. Miller and Jacqueline Taylor

When autobiography is performed, the immediate confrontation of the live body and voice with the live spectator creates a singular event in time and place. Encounters between live performers and live spectators always have political and social consequences, all the more so for performers whose access to the stage and to authority has been hard won. Such is the case for women, whose autobiographical performances can both resist and transform existing autobiographical traditions. *Voices Made Flesh: Performing Women's Autobiography* explores the theatrical, literary, political, sexual, and cultural impact of a wide variety of autobiographical performance forms that feature women's lives and stories.

In collecting essays and scripts for this anthology, we were motivated by a desire to showcase the proliferation of women's autobiographical practice as it is performed onstage. We wanted to create a collection that examines the links among women's autobiography theory and criticism, feminist performance theory, and performance practice. Other books have amassed texts of women's performance art, much of which draws strongly on autobiographical material, and certainly others have analyzed in depth the complex transaction of self and other; the negotiation of body, spirit, and mind; and the interplay of gender, race, and culture in the construction of autobiography. Our goal has been to produce a text highlighting both the theory and practice of women's autobiographical performance and to include the work of both artist-scholars within the academy and practicing artists in nonacademic arenas.

Creating an autobiographical narrative reconstitutes the self, the audience, and surrounding cultural contexts. It makes sense of the self, gives each part a voice and a body. We can safely say that until a life is shared through writing or performance, it does not exist at all, or at least it does not resonate in the broader realm of public consequence. Jerome Bruner declares in "The Autobiographical Process": "Though it may seem a strange way to put it, we may properly suspect that the shape of a life as experienced is as much dependent upon the narrative skills of the autobiographer as is the story he or she tells about it. It is probably in this sense that Henry James intended his famous remark that adventures happen only to people who know how to tell them" (41).

The story of women's autobiography is the story of resistance to the disembodied, traditionally masculine "universal subject," whose implicit denial of skin color, gender, sexual orientation (other than the heterosexual), and economic disparity constrained many women as "others" with no voices or physicality. One of our primary motivations in compiling this collection is to analyze how the body is reclaimed, celebrated, and complicated in women's autobiographical performance. In "Identity's Body," Sidonie Smith traces the interweaving of text and body that is women's autobiography: "What does skin have to do with autobiography and autobiography with skin? Much I think—as the body of the text, the body of the narrator, the body of the narrated I, the cultural body, and the body politic all merge in skins and skeins of meaning" (267). Smith's thoughtful explications of how women's autobiography subverts the tyranny of the masculine universal subject, in her *Poetics of Women's Autobiography* and *Subjectivity, Identity, and the Body*, influenced the development of this volume. As she states in the latter book: "If the topography of the universal subject locates man's selfhood somewhere between the ears, it locates woman's selfhood between her thighs. . . . There is no isolable core of selfhood there for woman, for in the act of heterosexual intercourse, the female body is penetrated by the body of the other and in the experience of pregnancy, that other that is part of the subject takes up greater and greater space inside until it is suddenly expelled. Inside is outside; outside inside. The cultural notion of autonomous individuality is totally confused, since, as Susan Bordo has suggested, pregnancy is an 'embodiment that houses otherness in the self'" (12).

In this collection, we wish to explore the complexities of the writing and performing female subject, to present what Shirley Neuman has called "a poetics of difference," rather than a "different poetics": "Such a subject is neither the unified subject of traditional theory of autobiography nor the discursively produced and dispersed subject of poststructuralist theory. Nor is it a self 'silenced' by hegemony, an 'empty self,' or a self marked only by its 'difference,' its otherness in relation to a hegemonic subject. It is a complex, multiple, layered subject with agency in the discourses and the worlds that constitute the referential space of his or her autobiography, a self not only constructed by differences but capable of choosing, inscribing, and making a difference" (225). Our book provides fourteen scripts and essays, plus two commentaries, that document the collision of the writing-performing self and the subject of performance, whether in the search for one's own identities or in the struggle to re/present the historical other within the context of one's own identity. As we found earlier in collecting scripts and essays for a special journal issue on autobiography, "[T]hese pieces invite us to consider the paradox of the speaking subject who asserts at one and the same time . . . her rich particularity and abundant connectedness" (Miller and Taylor vi). Each of these fourteen writers takes the reader on a journey as she develops a stance toward her subject, negotiates a model of impersonation as she embodies the subject, and reinvents the context wherein the subject can live and breathe. The process of performing autobiography involves, as Kirk Varnedoe has put it, "a complex mixture of disclosure and disguise" (Bruner 52).

As a means of exploring the theoretical and performative implications of women's autobiography, *Voices Made Flesh* begins with a framing essay that addresses critical concerns of autobiographical practice. "Risky Business: Exploring Women's Autobiography and Performance," by M. Heather Carver, analyzes the risks, power, and agency of autobiographical performance for female readers, writers, and performers. The body of the collection is divided into two sections. The first section, "Women's Historical Auto/biography," consists of seven essays and scripts that portray first-person performances of significant historical or literary figures, what in this collection we are calling *auto/biography*. The second section, "Staging the Self," contains seven essays and scripts that encompass the performance of self; these pieces range from personal narratives performed as lectures, sometimes supplemented with slides and props, to formal staged presentations. Each section concludes with a response essay.

A number of the scripts and performances featured in this collection first came to our attention at communication and theatre conferences over the past decade. The growing body of autobiographical performances created by performance teachers and scholars came, during this time, to occupy more and more program space and more and more critical attention. A number of these performances have toured the country, featured not only at colleges and universities but also at festivals, community centers, and professional theatres. Yet those of us who teach autobiographical performance found that the scripts and essays we were seeing and hearing were unavailable in print. While collections of women's performance art exist (for example, Lenora Champagne, ed., *Out from Under* [New York: Theatre Communications Group, 1990]), as well as collections of performance art scripts that include women (for example, Jo Bonney, ed., *Extreme Exposure* [New York: Theatre Communications Group, 2000]), these works created by performance scholars and independent performers, and marked by a stronger narrative thread than is characteristic of the genre of performance art, remained uncollected. The work we were seeing was rich, provocative, diverse, and ephemeral. Like Toni Morrison, who recounts that she began writing in order to create the stories she wanted to read, we conceived this collection in order to put before our students the essays and scripts we wanted to teach.

The historical denials of women's agency, authority, subjectivity, and bodily integrity combine with the centuries in which women were denied access to the stage and even to public speech to provide the backdrop for these contemporary performances. While many of these barriers have broken down in the face of women's ongoing struggle for equality, the historical legacy continues to exert its influence. Women can now speak publicly and perform, but they do so, still, against considerable odds. The exact nature of those odds is detailed in a variety of ways throughout these pieces.

Yet a facile assumption of common ground and common cause between women has been questioned by scholars. Women are, of course, a large and diverse group of human beings, and early on, feminist scholarship often elided real differences among women in ways particularly problematic for women who were not white and heterosexual. Poststructuralist theory has challenged the very notion of woman as a unifying category. Even narrative, with all its linearity and efforts to order a chaotic world, becomes suspect in the hands of some poststructuralist theorists. Such critiques have resulted in much more careful attempts by performers to situate themselves in this broad category of women and to resist easy assumptions of commonality—moves that recur within the scripts included here. And yet, women, in all our diversity of race, ethnicity, sexual orientation, class, physical and mental ability, age, and circumstance, continue to confront certain common barriers and conditions.

While acknowledging the richness of theoretical contributions to discussions of the category of women and the construction of identity, this collection takes a particular interest in the ways that women, across categories of difference, continue to struggle to find a powerful and embodied voice, one that permits them to function as authors of their own experience. In the introduction to *Sexual Practice, Textual Theory*, Susan J. Wolfe and Julia Penelope wryly note, "Postmodernism gained widespread acceptance among Western intellectuals precisely at the time when those 'constructed' as other by those with power sought liberation. Just as women, lesbians, gay men, and racial minorities rose to challenge their marginalization and to define themselves as subjects, the white male intelligentsia declared that subjectivity was a fiction" (8). Much of what gives this volume unity is the struggle of women, regardless of category, to define themselves as subjects, always against the grain of cultural definitions which deny them the reality of their own experience and integrity. Yet we recognize how any category resists categorizations, particularly ones along the lines of gender, sexuality, and class. Our book seeks to show the self, conceived "not as the product of its different identity *from* others but as constituted by multiple differences *within* and *from* itself" (Neuman 223).

The first section, "Women's Historical Auto/biography," features seven writer-performers who construct a view of a historical figure through the lens of their own autobiographical selves; the section concludes with a critical response. Each piece highlights the writing-performing self in the present as it encounters or struggles with a particular and complex subject of the past; the process of this auto/biographical intertwining shapes and foregrounds the performance. One major challenge of representing the historical figure in the autobiographical mode involves a careful selection process as the writer-performer chooses which layers of a complex, multifaceted persona to weave into the narrative. We label this process *auto/biography*, as this kind of historical presentation represents a negotiation between the autobiographical self of the writer-performer and the biographical record of the historical personage. This kind of performance often involves what Craig Gingrich-Philbrook, speaking of Chautauqua performance, calls "the poignancy and politics of collecting the details of another's life to fashion into the fictive first person address" (viii).

The section begins with a complex example of such a negotiation in "Intimate Partners: A Critical Autobiography of Performing Anaïs," where Elyse Lamm Pineau recreates her collaborative relationship with the author Anaïs Nin during the years of her research and performance of the writer. Their mingling of identities and histories takes place through Pineau's sifting through the legacy of Nin's artistic output in a long series of "meetings" with the famous author. Pineau's journey has been arduous and fulfilling, shaping her as person, artist, and scholar: "I have known Anaïs Nin for close on twenty years. For a full decade of these we have been collaborative partners in our self-making, co-conspirators in 'the necessary [and necessarily intertextual] artifice' of our identities."

The second essay in this section, "Gertrude Stein Never Enough," by Lynn C. Miller, details a performance written and performed in the mode of neo-Chautauqua, which replicates the Chautauqua experience of audiences at the turn of the last century when well-known speakers toured the country bringing culture to small towns across America. In such a first-person performance, "the actor is both a scholar and a performer, essentially 'impersonating' a historical figure for contemporary audiences, attempting to place the figure accurately in her historical time and yet interpreting the character for audiences who may know little about either the cultural milieu or the character." The essay chronicles Lynn C. Miller's quest to discover the many selves of Gertrude Stein in performing the modernist writer for various audiences across the country. Miller explores the transformative aspects of performance in apprehending the selves of Stein, focusing particularly on Stein's multilayered presentation of sexuality and gender.

Another essay detailing a first-person re-creation, "Mule of the World: The Embodiment of Mary Church Terrell," by Eileen C. Cherry, examines representations of identity and otherness in the travel narratives of African Americans, particularly the quest of one woman, Mary Church Terrell. Her essay explores transcultural narratives and the forces of "hybridity, diaspora, and cosmopolitanism" in the performances of both the author and Terrell. Through Terrell, Cherry traces her own nebulous borders: "My body is a crossroads with its four limbs extended like compass points to the four winds. Competing allegiances swirl around me like magnetic fields. . . . Like most travelers, I braved borders to resist typification only to find it."

Stacy Wolf's essay charts a different kind of collision of selves as she tours various biographical and critical sites of knowledge in "Desire in Evidence." In this case, her own encounters with American musical performance filter her interpretation as she charts her attempt to prove that musical star Mary Martin was a lesbian. The essay-performance raises questions about gay and lesbian historiography and the layered tensions of biography and spectatorship. In her textual performance of research, Wolf considers several questions: "What is the difference between a fact and a rumor? Between a quotation made textual and one that is whispered? What is the site of sexual orientation? What is the value of the (textually) visible? What is the difference between outing and getting the facts straight?"

In "Too Wild for Her Own Good: Searching for the Real Calamity Jane," M. Heather Carver confronts a frontier legend, one frequently rewritten and retold in film and popular histories. Interrogating the ways in which the Hollywoodization of social norms has shaped Calamity Jane's performance of gender, her performance grapples with questions of "authenticity, identity, history, reality, and representation" as she strives to discriminate between the many fictionalized accounts of Calamity Jane and the actual woman's history. Carver constructs a narrator who leads the audience on a tour of the multiple selves of the frontier figure, a tour that is contradictory and yet revealing: "[Martha Jane] Cannary's performance when she embodied the role of Calamity Jane propelled her to fame, but her everyday life performances of both masculinity and femininity are what make her an intriguing character to perform."

Playwright Catherine Rogers overtly dramatizes the dual performance of self and other in "Georgia O'Keeffe x Catherine Rogers" as she confronts the task of capturing a visual artist onstage. She finds herself bumping up against her own history in her attempt to detail the "elusive and fragmentary nature" of O'Keeffe's complex personal life, especially her relation to her husband, mentor, and promoter, Alfred Stieglitz. O'Keeffe's artistic inspiration and rootedness in the terrain of Ghost Ranch in New Mexico become keys to Rogers's own journey as an artist. Floating through the text is O'Keeffe's ironic phrase: "Words . . . are like the wind."

Playwright Carolyn Gage's "Last Reading of Charlotte Cushman" creates a text where her own autobiographical self is implicit rather than explicit. Gage's interpretive filter allows her to imagine Cushman performing her lesbianism more openly than her Victorian era would have allowed. In this contemporary reimagining of the legendary actress and platform performer, Gage places Cushman's sexuality center stage as she dramatizes Charlotte Cushman, an aging lesbian dying of breast cancer, performing onstage for the last time. Embattled but triumphant, Cushman engages her audience as she spars with her longtime partner, Emma

Stebbins, and performs her famous rendition of Nancy Sikes from Charles Dickens's novel *Oliver Twist*. Her Dickensian turn is a fitting tribute to Dickens, perhaps the most mythic platform performer of his age:

> And then I went back to the Park Theatre, and I gave them Nancy Sikes. Oh, yes, I gave them Nancy Sikes. Not the whore with the heart of gold, not the feisty little spitfire from the wrong side of town—oh, no—I gave them a prostitute the likes of which they had never seen on a New York stage, even though they passed a dozen girls just like her on the way to the theatre—even though half the men would go home with one of these girls on their arm.
>
> But I gave them a prostitute they could see, not just look at—but really see. I gave them a prostitute that made them weep the tears that no one shed that night at Mother Hennessey's. And weep they did. You see, real life is too painful for most people. That's why they come to the theatre.

Concluding the section, Carol Hanbery MacKay's response, "Performing Historical Figures," critiques and explicates the layers of female identity, representation, and context dramatized by the seven scripts and essays. Her essay provides perspective on these "lives multiply lived, impinging upon one another in constructive, original ways, in scripts of their own making that will be endlessly innovative and self-creating."

In the second section of the book, "Staging the Self," seven performers offer a range of strategies for bringing their own subjectivity and agency into performative focus. A concluding essay traces the implications of these pieces for the practice of women's autobiography and the creation of community. The section opens with Tami Spry's "Illustrated Woman." For Tami Spry, autobiographical performance of "Tattoo" and "Skins" becomes a life-saving exercise: "Although the performative autobiographical location is a space of intense personal and cultural risk, it is simultaneously a space of profound comfort. It has become for me a site of complete narrative authority, offering me the power to reclaim and rename my voice and body privately in rehearsal, and then publicly in performance."

Spry takes the unbearable pain of losing her mother and of her own mental and emotional exhaustion and, through performance, crafts these horrifying experiences into narratives of death and rebirth, growth and healing. The impulse to connect the disconnected, to combine, own, and claim what she has been told cannot cohere, is again evident in this piece.

Jacqueline Taylor's essay, "On Being an Exemplary Lesbian: My Life as a Role Model," turns an alternately serious and comic eye on her various invited appearances/performances "as a lesbian." She considers various aspects of positionality that influence decisions about who gets the microphone. The title, like much of the essay-performance that follows, employs humor as the centrifugal force that seeks to keep the disparate aspects of Taylor's identity from flying off in all directions. For, of course, there is no category for exemplary lesbians, since such a category presumes a sort of lesbian valor that the culture constantly negates and denies. Describing the various situations in which she has appeared as a lesbian role model, Taylor goes on to announce that her upbringing as the daughter of a Southern Baptist preacher provided the perfect education for her role of exemplary lesbian. Yet amidst the humor, Taylor continues to mine the seemingly contradictory and even mutually exclusive aspects of her identity for the connecting veins that allow her to claim a self that is not either/or but both-and.

In yet another performance of testimony, Linda Park-Fuller takes on similarly complex challenges of speaking from and for a large and diverse group of women who both do and do not share common ground. In "A Clean Breast of It," about her experience as a breast cancer survivor, Park-Fuller moves back and forth between the narrative of her particular experience and her role as teacher, reminding the audience of the prevalence of breast cancer and the politics of breast cancer research and treatment. While many of these pieces contain therapeutic elements, "A Clean Breast of It" is the most explicitly therapeutic in the collection. She performs (as do many others here) to facilitate her own healing, but she also performs to bear witness, to reach out to other women and men whose lives have been touched and disturbed by breast cancer, to share strategies for recovery and reintegration. In the incisive framing essay with which Park-Fuller introduces her script, she notes the ways in which this performance reconfigures her own experience: "In the telling of my tale, I attempt to break out of the prescribed, marginalized role of 'patient-victim,' and exercise sociopolitical agency in the world. That exercise of agency, in turn, circles back to transform and constitute me as actor-agent—as *survivor*. In that way, the piece functions performatively to recompose my subjective identity and to influence society." The performative goals Park-Fuller identifies—to exercise sociopolitical agency in the world, to recompose her subjective identity, and to influence society—circulate again and again through the essays and scripts collected here.

In "sista docta," Joni L. Jones situates her performance solidly in the academic setting that functions as backdrop for several other pieces in the book. If academia is a chilly climate for women, it is an arctic one for African American women. "Sista docta" combines poetry, narrative passages, dance, drumming, and music, as the performer enacts the competing demands and relentless assaults on her integrity and humanity that the academic world bestows. Jones is soon dripping with sweat as she moves through the grueling pace of this performance. The audience literally enters into the world she creates by reading the lines she assigns them in the faculty party section of the piece or joining her onstage for improvisational scenes that draw on audience members' own related experiences. Through these strategies she makes concrete a claim implicit in many of the performances collected here: Jones's autobiographical performance taps into shared concerns and struggles of other African American academics. By performing her own story, she also performs a larger story, one that connects her to all the other sista doctas.

Performance artist Terry Galloway deftly alternates comedy and analysis as she makes theatre out of her experience as a swimmer at the Lions Camp for Crippled Children. Galloway's work is remarkable for its unflinching honesty and its ability to move rapidly between multiple perspectives: she sees herself, she sees herself as others see her, she sees others as they dare not see themselves. She manages, somehow, to combine a brutal frankness about the miseries and plain unfairness of life with an open heart. In "The Performance of Drowning," Galloway engages in a dialogue with herself about herself as she explores the moment from her childhood when she simultaneously grasped her own connection to the other crippled competitors, despaired of her position in a ruthless world, and discovered the power of performance to change the course of events.

Pioneering performance artist Linda M. Montano takes on death itself and our culture's colossal denial of death in "Death in the Art and Life of Linda M. Montano." Montano, an experimentalist in being and becoming and long known for employing herself as both subject and object in her performance art works, here combines her past and present selves in discussing a final state of being. Weaving together slides, cross-cultural funeral and mourning rituals, her own performance art, and narratives from her own life, Montano takes on the role of teacher as she performs instructions and advice on how to prepare for and make peace with one's own death.

In "Shaping the World with Our Hands," Laila Farah considers personal narrative of decolonization, legitimacy, and the inheritance of culture in weaving the stories of Lebanese and Palestinian women. Her essay and script theorize and stage the borders of culture and identity. In some ways, the script might seem a surprising choice for a book on performing autobiography, since the script combines Farah's voice and the voices of the Lebanese and Palestinian women she interviews. And yet, we would argue that Farah's piece simply foregrounds the embedded and connected nature of so many of the women's autobiographical scripts featured here. For women, the autobiographical voice is rarely singular but instead exists in chorus with a cluster of other women's voices. In a landscape wracked by war, Farah stitches together narrative accounts of such domestic projects as the making of hommos. The remarkable and ordinary women in Farah's script, who remake the world through acts of raw courage and simple domestic chores, call to mind the lines from Adrienne Rich's "Natural Resources":

> My heart is moved by all I cannot save:
> so much has been destroyed
>
> I have to cast my lot with those
> who age after age, perversely,
>
> with no extraordinary power,
> reconstitute the world. (264)

There are many ways we might trace connections between the scripts in this section, all of which bear witness, tell stories, search for meaning, and seek, through diverse means, to tell a particular woman's truth. In "Orchids in the Arctic," Elizabeth Bell persuasively argues that we can consider these performers through the lens of the scholarly literature on mentoring. She simultaneously attests to the hostile environment the academy offers women and to the power of women performers to mentor one another despite structures that would dispirit and divide.

Autobiographical practice will continue to proliferate. As our daily lives deprive us of the kind of reassuring personal contact that used to be part of community life, we are finding other venues for participation and connection. In "Why Memoir Now?" Vivian Gornick confronts the enormous current popularity of the literary memoir. She writes: "In this culture the idea of the self is vital to the conventional wisdom. Today, millions of people consider themselves possessed of the right to a serious life. A serious life, by definition, is one to which one pays attention; a life one tries to make sense of and bear witness to. The age is characterized by a need to testify. Everywhere in the world women and men are rising up to tell their story out of the now commonly held belief that one's own life signifies" (5).

As the collected essays and scripts in *Voices Made Flesh* illustrate, performing autobiography allows women's life stories "to signify and resonate within multiple layers of consequence: marking the private, spiritual configurations of self in a public arena and creating a space for new possibilities for transformation and communion between performer and audience" (Miller 321).

Works Cited

Bruner, Jerome. "The Autobiographical Process." In *The Culture of Autobiography: Constructions of Self-Representation*, edited by Robert Folkenflik, 38–56. Palo Alto, Calif.: Stanford University Press, 1993.

Gingrich-Philbrook, Craig. "The Personal and Political in Solo Performance: Editor's Introduction." *Text and Performance Quarterly* 20 (2000): vii–x.

Gornick, Vivian. "Why Memoir Now?" *Women's Review of Books* 13 (1996): 10–11.

Miller, Lynn C. "Witness to the Self: The Autobiographical Impulse in Performance Studies." In *Communication: Views from the Helm for the Twenty-first Century*, edited by Judith Trent, 318–22. Boston: Allyn and Bacon, 1998.

Miller, Lynn C., and Jacqueline Taylor. "Performing Autobiography: Editors' Introduction." *Text and Performance Quarterly* 17 no. 4 (1997): v–vi.

Neuman, Shirley. "Autobiography: From Different Poetics to a Poetics of Difference." In *Essays on Life Writing: From Genre to Critical Practice*, edited by Marlene Kadar, 213–30. Toronto: University of Toronto Press, 1992.

Rich, Adrienne. *The Fact of a Doorframe: Poems Selected and New, 1950–1984*. New York: W.W. Norton, 1984.

Smith, Sedonie. "Identity's Body." In *Autobiography and Postmodernism*, edited by Kathleen Ashley, Leigh Gilmore, and Gerald Peters, 266–92. Amherst: University of Massachusetts Press, 1994.

———. *A Poetics of Women's Autobiography: Marginality and the Fictions of Self-Representation*. Bloomington: Indiana University Press, 1987.

———. *Subjectivity, Identity, and the Body: Women's Autobiographical Practices in the Twentieth Century*. Bloomington: Indiana University Press, 1993.

Wolfe, Susan J., and Julia Penelope. *Sexual Practice, Textual Theory: Lesbian Cultural Criticism*. Cambridge, Mass.: Blackwell, 1993.

Risky Business

⤣ Exploring Women's Autobiography and Performance

M. Heather Carver

Women's autobiographical performance is risky business. Autobiographical performance is inherently fraught with the complexities of the relationship between history and representation—between what happened and what is remembered and performed. As the essays in this volume demonstrate, autobiographical performance is a complex multilayering of identity and selves. For women to even begin to write the autobiographical "I" acknowledges that we can be the subjects of our own stories, and thus expands traditional notions of whose voices may take center stage. The many challenges in creating autobiographical works are multiplied as women begin to speak the unspoken and to embody the selves previously unperformed for audiences.

By the very nature of the performance, an autobiographical performer takes an authoritative stance, a literal and figurative space traditionally occupied by men's voices and bodies. As Marilyn Frye writes, "[T]he phallocratic scheme does not admit women as authors of perception," as women's perceptions are seen as "passive, repetitive of men's perception, nonauthoritative." Stepping into the spotlight to perform a woman's life story from a nonmale perspective subverts the Aristotelian concept that "women . . . do not have authority" (165). Jeanie Forte also notes that women's autobiographical stage performance challenges patriarchy by moving female life experiences from the private realm into the public. She writes that women's autobiographical performance is also connected to female sexuality, and that "the challenge presented by women's autobiographical performance gains strength when seen in conjunction with notions of female sexuality arising from the theoretical work of some feminists" (224). The act of women speaking their stories publicly thus radically challenges traditional notions of agency, spectacle, and spectatorship as female performers move their voices and bodies from the background to the foreground.

For the woman engaged in autobiographical performance, notions of the spectator as male and the spectacle as woman are subverted through challenging the power of language itself, as both separate and a part of institutionalized practices. Judith Butler notes: "That gender reality is created through sustained social performances means that . . . a true or abiding masculinity or femininity [is] also constituted as part of the strategy that conceals gender's performative character and the performative possibilities for proliferating gender configurations outside the restricting frames of masculinist domination and compulsory heterosexuality" (*Gender* 141). Butler argues that gender should not be a stable identity, nor be subject to notions of truth or falsehood. Gender is therefore not a noun but a verb, construed through a "stylized repetition of acts" (140). This repeatable series of acts is thus performative. We perform our gender through the series of acts in which we choose to engage. The effect of gender is produced through these stylized acts and "must be understood as the mundane way in which bodily gestures, movements, and styles of various kinds constitute the illusion of an abiding gendered self" (140). Butler asserts that we construct our genders and identities through performative practices that are seen not necessarily as performances but rather as acts which follow common gender norms or beliefs. She notes that the "regulatory norms of 'sex' work in a performative fashion to constitute the materiality of bodies and, more specifically, to materialize the body's sex, to materialize sexual difference in the service of the consolidation of the heterosexual imperative" (*Bodies* 2).

That we perform our gender identity does not mean, however, that we have control over the power of the labels "male" and "female." Indeed, following Butler's line of thinking about stylized and gendered acts, making a spectacle out of oneself is thus a specifically feminine danger. Traditionally it has been permissible for women to control their appearance and not to transgress boundaries of proper public dress and behavior. Women are taught to regulate their physical presentation to "fit in" with standards of mainstream beauty and behavior. Mary Russo discusses her own experience to highlight the way in which radical negation, silence, withdrawal, invisibility, and the bold affirmations of feminine performance, posture, and masquerade have suggested a cultural politics for women. These behaviors of feminine spectacle include proper grooming, neat appearance, and the regulation of fat—namely, no showing of dimpled thighs, bra straps, scars, or body hair. To be unkempt or overweight is to create a spectacle for others to observe as "abnormal" and thus invite ridicule. Russo claims that "women and their bodies, certain bodies, in certain public framings, in certain public spaces, are always already transgressive—dangerous, and in danger" (217). If appearances in everyday life are so easily shameful, then producing autobiographical performances about women's lives challenges patriarchical structures surrounding staging the self.

While such autobiographical performance may be dangerous, many women are brave enough to traverse the territory. This collection of essays seeks to reclaim the voices and bodies that have been silenced. Through performance of both historical women's autobiography and personal narrative, the authors in this volume strive to make the terrain for future performers and scholars more inviting. The scripts and essays that follow illustrate the challenges that today's women performers have faced. Like all risky business, however, there is a history of events, thoughts, and ideas that have helped make these risks possible. I begin my effort to map the terrain of auto/biographical performance by unpacking the various theories of autobiography that have emerged from literary theory. Many of the roots of women's autobiographical performance come from theories of autobiography that explored the nature of subjectivity in writing. To bridge literary and performance theory, I investigate the various theories of the autobiographical self from the perspective of women's life writing. I then trace women's autobiographical research to situate both its history and theoretical implications for performers by exploring the ideas of key theorists that focus on writing, reading, and performing selves.

WOMEN'S LIFE WRITING

Women's autobiographies, argues Shari Benstock, do not fall into what the field of autobiographical studies has traditionally posited as the model of the authoritative self. To follow what Benstock refers to as the male model of autobiography is to see the self as the object of investigation, most notably in that the "first person actually masks the third person" (19). This practice is akin to the practice of a journalist, or even a biographer, writing about her own life as if it were simply another subject to be studied. The result is an autobiography that reads more like an outsider looking in, rather than an insider looking out.

Benstock asserts that this concept is based on the idea that the artist controls "his" subject matter, thus creating a magical effect as "the self appears organic, the present the sum total of the past, the past an accurate predictor of the future" (19). She also notes that this view of what constitutes the autobiographical text is very much grounded in authority. This authoritative stance is not just in the telling of the story, but continues to frame the life story as an important one that *needs* telling. Benstock notes that it is not surprising that those who adhere to this definition are those "whose assignment under the Symbolic Law is to represent authority, to represent the phallic power that drives inexorably toward unity, identity, sameness" (19).

In addition to Shari Benstock, other feminist literary scholars, such as Kim Worthington and Carolyn Heilbrun, have challenged the positioning of an autobiographical self as universally male. George Gusdorf's essay "Conditions and Limits of Autobiography," published more than four decades ago, was hailed as the "seminal" article on the position of autobiography as an important literary genre. Gusdorf's work is also credited with the distinction of an autobiographical self as a constructed self that can never exactly represent the lived self. Gusdorf's concept of an individualistic, "isolated" self has influenced a great deal of scholarship. James Olney's ideas on autobiography draw on the notion of isolation to posit that autobiography stems from "a single, radical and radial energy originating in the subject center, an aggressive, creative expression of the self, a defense of individual integrity in the face of an otherwise multiple, confusing, swarming, and inimical universe" (15).

In "Women's Autobiographical Selves," Susan Friedman argues that the concept of an autobiographical self, based on an individualistic model, is inapplicable to both white and nonwhite women, men and women of color, and many non-Western peoples. This paradigm of the self ignores "the role of collective and relational identities" in the construction of both women and community-based cultures (35). Friedman argues with Gusdorf's notion that autobiography is the "literary consequence to the rise of individualism as an ideology," and notes that Gusdorf's concepts of selfhood are derived from the development of science and the position of "man" in the universe (35).

Kim Worthington notes that "[m]odernity, broadly understood as the past several hundred years in Western history, may be defined by the rise to prominence of the self, or at least the phase in which the concept of the self became fixed in Western culture" (1). This rise to prominence of the self in Western culture developed from the Enlightenment's notions of free thought and the reasoning subject. Transferred into the genre of autobiography, the valorization of the autonomous, predominantly male "I" serves to erase the important complexities of a woman's autobiographical self.

Worthington asserts that feminist theoretical work on concepts of selfhood helps situate historically related differences between women and men. She writes that the application of theories of women's selfhood by scholars such as Sheila Rowbotham and Nancy Choderow to women's autobiographical texts "illuminates the unfolding narratives of women's life writing and thereby revises the prevailing canons of autobiography" (35). Friedman additionally argues that women's autobiographical writing cannot be totally isolated, for her work reflects a group consciousness, an awareness of "the meaning of the cultural category WOMAN for the patterns of women's individual destiny" (41). She notes that Gusdorf's idealization of the autobiographer as a "gatherer of men, of lands, of power, maker of kingdoms or of empires," is not historically congruent with women's experiences. Traditionally, women "have been the gathered, the colonized, the ruled" (55). She continues to argue that "seldom the 'inventor of laws and of wisdom,' they have been born into those inventions—all the more so if their race, religion, class, or sexual preferences also marginalized them" (55).

Friedman is clear, however, in noting that this historical oppression certainly has not "destroyed women's consciousness of self" (56). On the contrary, for women often write their stories as a way to break free from their constraints, although their writing will remain marginalized by critics if evaluated according to the individualistic paradigm of the self. If the woman's autobiographical self is seen contextually, however, her story will reveal the significance of interpersonal relationships and community identification. As Friedman argues, "[T]his autobiographical self often does not oppose herself to all others, does not feel herself to exist outside of others, and still less against others, but very much with others in an interdependent existence that asserts its rhythms everywhere in the community" (56).

The contextualization of a woman's autobiographical self includes the intricacies of race, culture, and class along with gender and sexuality. For example, in discussing the relationship of African American women to what she calls the "condition" of oppression, Fox-Genovese notes that the self "develops in opposition to, rather than as an articulation of, this condition. Yet the condition remains as that against which the self is forged" (64). The context of slavery and other historical forms of oppression, "as much as the representations of self, constitutes an inescapable aspect of the Afro-American female literary tradition, especially of Afro-American women's autobiographies" (64). Elizabeth Fox-Genovese asserts that both the commonality of a shared literary history of slave narratives and lived personal histories produce an important subgenre, "not from the general categories of race or sex, but from a historical experience of being black and female in a specific society at a specific moment over succeeding generations" (65). Fox-Genovese also discusses the importance of looking not only at individual autobiographies but at several works of African American women throughout history. She asserts that these autobiographies, "each of which is necessarily personal and unique, constitute a running commentary on the collective experience of black women in the United States" (65).

Fox-Genovese writes that an African American woman's self cannot be separated from her history, the language through which her self and experience are represented, or the readers of all backgrounds who "not only lay claim to it but who have helped to shape it" (83). Her work indicates the complexity of such self-representation: "[T]o write the account of one's self is to inscribe it in a culture that for each of us is only partially our own. For black women autobiographers, the gap between the self and the language in which it is inscribed looms especially large and remains fraught with struggle" (83). Not only is the gap between the self and the language fraught with struggle, but so, too, is the embodiment of African American women's autobiographical stories in a culture that continues to ignore and suppress their unique experiences.

The role of the self has long been of particular interest to writers, readers, and performers in defining both their disciplines and practices. These three areas of study are important, for the ways in which we relate to texts, as both creators and as audience members, are integral to how the body or self is articulated in performances of women's lives. The long tradition of the "universal self" as male indicates that women's autobiographies have to either position the woman as similar to the male self in

authority, independence, and ambition or find different modes of representation. Some women's biographical performances, primarily those in
film and television, contrast with those about men in that authority, independence, and ambition are represented as vices. Women's autobiographical performance on stage, however, challenges such a traditional
view of women's subjectivity and explores a long history of strong women's
virtues.

WRITING SELVES

Richard Poirier raises several questions about the self and the writer in
The Performing Self. He explores whether the realities writers propose "are
shaped by the exertions of any self or are instead the result of forces existing prior to any individual human presence" (9). This dilemma appears
similar to the philosophical question of whether the individual shapes
reality or outside forces shape the self. Does the writer compose from a
deep inner core unique to her own experiences, or does she solely reflect
her reaction to the society around her? In her autobiography, does Mary
Church Terrell shape reality by sharing her rise to fame, or is she merely
dictating her reaction to the events as they occurred?

Poirier conceives of the very process of writing as a performance of
the self. His concept of the self is important to how one views not only the
writing as a performance but also the self as a *performer.* To write the self
is to perform the self. Poirier cites Norman Mailer's concept of the self:
"When Mailer says that the 'first art work in an artist is the shaping of his
own personality,' he is saying . . . that he cannot take the self in him for
granted and that he cannot look outside himself for an acceptable self-
image. The self is shaped, he says, 'in' the artist, and this shaping he calls
'work'" (103). Mailer is thus performing a self, a writerly self, which man-
ifests itself in his craft. This seems to suggest that there is a self underneath the performing self who is directing the show. Writing as performance in this sense seems to take on a behind-the-scenes and a center
stage duality.

Schweickart argues that for a male reader the text brings together the
self and universal thoughts and actions, but the female reader is continually reminded that such universality is grounded in male experience, and
therefore she is excluded. Thus the woman writer must always write
against the backdrop of a presumed universal, which in fact excludes
much of her experience and perspective. It is, in fact, a false universal. De-

spite the obstacles, women have not hesitated to do this. There is a long history of women's selves in literature. Long before Virginia Woolf there were explorations of the mutable self in writing, in speaking, and in everyday life performance. As Jeanne Perreault notes, "Writing 'I' has been an emancipatory project for women" and the process invests "that individual body with the shifting ethics of a political, racial, and sexual consciousness" (2). Indeed, many women writers have been exploring the structures of writing in order to break free from them.

In *Subjectivity, Identity, and the Body*, Sidonie Smith draws on Woolf's concept of a masculine-dominated *I* in fiction to spark a discussion of women's autobiography. Smith states that the letter has historical baggage, and deems the *I* as a "bar" that dramatically marks the page. Building on this idea of the *I* as a bar, she writes that "for Woolf, the bar that serves metaphorically as site of the universal subject and its normative masculinity, requires barring. It must be crossed, perhaps double-crossed, before it can signal the trace of female subjectivity in an autobiographical text" (2). Smith continues to assert that the autobiographical subject carries a history of the body with her as she negotiates the autobiographical *I* (23). For Smith, this autobiographical *I* is problematic for women writers because of the histories of subjectivity which must be negotiated. Smith notes that such histories "may press her to silence or they may encourage her to cross, crisscross, doublecross that 'I' in order to move from silence to self-narrative" (4).

More recent authors, such as Alice Walker, seem to adhere to Poirier's notion that "[p]erformance creates life in literature in the sense that it is itself the act and evidence of life" (44). Walker has published not only popular novels such as *The Color Purple* (1982) but also personal accounts of the process of her writing and how her words have been interpreted by others. In *The Same River Twice*, Walker describes the experience of seeing her literature come to life on film for the movie version of *The Color Purple*. She also explains how she survived both success and controversy surrounding her work, and how she dealt with both her own illness and her mother's death. Walker writes: "Always with me was the inner twin: my true nature, my true self. It is timeless, free, compassionate and in love with whatever is natural to me. This was the self that came in dreams, to be pursued in the essays I was writing at that time. . . . There were things I just suddenly seemed to know, about life, about the world. As if my illness had pushed open an inner door that my usual consciousness was willing to ignore" (32). For Walker, there seems to be a bifurcated self: one who endures the day to day practical living, and one who lifts her up and gives her the power to write. She describes an inner soul that exposes itself in the writing process and releases her creative energies upon the page. Walker's womanist stance which connects her back to the earth and nature matches her spiritual ideas on writing the self.

Issues of race and the self also have wide implications for writing the autobiographical text. As Elizabeth Fox-Genovese asserts, writing the self for the black woman autobiographer entails many struggles as "the account of the black woman's self cannot be divorced from the history of that self or the history of the people among whom it took shape" (198). In writing the self, one is thus forced to address not just her own personal history but her *cultural* history as well. Fox-Genovese writes that the writing self "cannot be divorced from the language through which it is represented, or from the readers of other classes and races who not only lay claim to it but who have helped to shape it. To write the account of one's self is to inscribe in it a culture that for each of us is only partially our own. For black women autobiographers, the gap between the self and the language in which it is inscribed . . . remains fraught with struggle" (198). Fox-Genovese questions whether the black woman writer is at first a "solitary" self, or first a woman, and notes that "no dilemma could more clearly expose the condition of any self as hostage to society, politics, and language" (198). She asserts that this dilemma of the self deserves more attention, as autobiography raises issues of the historical, racialized, sexualized, gendered, and classed language and context from which each woman writes.

READING SELVES

In *A Room of One's Own*, Virginia Woolf explores the female self as a reader. She also describes her experience when reading certain male writers: "After reading a chapter or two a shadow seemed to lie across the page. It was a straight dark bar, a shadow shaped something like the letter 'I.' One began dodging this way and that to catch a glimpse of the landscape behind it. Whether that was indeed a tree or a woman walking I was not sure" (99). She continues to explore what the presence of this masculine *I* was doing to her view of the characters: "Back one was always hailed to the letter 'I.' One began to be tired of 'I.' Not but what this 'I' was a most respectable 'I'; honest and logical; as hard as a nut, and polished for centuries by good teaching and good feeding. I respect and admire that 'I' from the bottom of my heart. But here I turned a page or two, looking for something or other—the worst of it is that in the shadow of the letter 'I' all is shapeless as a mist. Is that a tree? No, it is a woman" (100). Woolf continues to explain how the overwhelming presence of this *I* made her lose interest in the story. She acknowledges that this masculine dominance of the language excludes women from writing in their own voice.

Toni Morrison raises several questions about the self of the reader, in addition to the writer, in her book *Playing in the Dark: Whiteness and the Literary Imagination.* She says that throughout the history of writing in the United States, regardless of the race of the author, the reading self has been positioned as white. Morrison asks: "When does racial 'unconsciousness' or awareness of race enrich interpretive language, and when does it impoverish it? What does positing one's writerly self, in the wholly racialized society that is the United States, as unraced and all others as raced entail?" (xii). Morrison discovered the racialized ways in which she had been taught to read when she "stopped reading as a reader and began to read as a writer." For Morrison, the self is shaped through a historical racial ideology that permeates the reading experience. Whether, like Morrison, we are acutely aware of not only our own selves but also the "false" selves that have been thrust upon us, or whether we merely read without giving it a second thought, each of us interprets what we read through the filter that is our self. These true and false selves merge to formulate the autobiographical text. The writing process thus becomes part of the author's performance of her self on the page, as she begins to interpret and assign language to her experiences.

PERFORMING SELVES

The performance of the self has inspired a vast amount of performance studies scholarship (see, for example, Corey, Jenkins, Langellier, Lockford, Valentine). While biographical performance has its roots in the Chautauqua tradition dating as far back as early twentieth-century America (Gentile), autobiographical performance has increasingly become an important means of expression and scholarship. *Text and Performance Quarterly* dedicated its October 1997 and January 2000 editions to issues about performing autobiography. Contributing authors in both volumes explored topics such as gender identity construction through autobiographical performance and embodying the "self" on stage.

In "Witness to the Self: The Autobiographical Impulse in Performance Studies," Lynn C. Miller notes that scholars have become more interested in notions of the self through performance: "As the self feels increasingly shattered, we feel more compelled to gather up the fragments to proclaim 'this is the self' for that performative moment or in that particular instance, only to go 'no, not that, this is the self' as we construct another. By creating a performance text around a particular circumstance, we mark that peculiar confluence of time and space with . . . a script, of our emotional/physical/intellectual presence" (318). Performance scholars engaged in this type of research often explore their own selves in transition as they live and then relive particular experiences in front of an audience. Performing autobiography thus becomes an interpretation of one's own life story, with the author functioning in multiple roles of writing, interpreting, and performing the self.

The personal narrative has also become a site for addressing social issues, as shown in Linda Park-Fuller's piece "A Clean Breast of It" about her experience with breast cancer, Craig Gingrich-Philbrook's performance "Refreshment" about gay identity, and Joni Jones's "sista docta" script about her role as a professor who is both a woman and African American. Many performance scholars have also investigated the autobiographical turn in areas such as performance art where artists such as Holly Hughes have used more of a "storytelling" approach in presenting their lives to an audience rather than the explicit body work prevalent in the seventies.

Kristin Langellier's research focuses on narrative strategies and storytelling as a site to study women's lives. Her interest in narrative stems from the idea that "personal narratives participate in the ongoing rhythm of people's lives as a reflection of their social organization and cultural values" ("Personal Narrative" 261). Langellier asserts that "[s]torytelling is embedded within larger social processes, such as the literary practices of preadolescent urban culture, the maintenance of families, and the public and private debates on abortion in the U.S. Studies of the social uses of narrative spring from a variety of disciplines, among them anthropology, sociolinguistics, rhetoric, and communication studies" (261). She investigates personal narratives as a type of community discourse and the social and cultural influences on the use of narrative. She notes that analysis of personal narratives in this context raises questions about "how narratives are used not only *in* talk, but *to* talk, not only to recapitulate past events but to negotiate present and future events" (261).

Langellier also discusses narrative as political praxis, for "narratives make meaning" (267). Humans help us understand important life matters in telling stories, she says, stories that determine our thoughts and actions, and whatever, or whoever, generates narratives assists in defining human thought and behavior. Not that humans are merely empty vessels whose minds are constantly filled by powerful sources, but narrative has an important political function.

WOMEN'S BODIES ON STAGE

In 1985 Sylvia Bovenschen acknowledged that women's art had long been devalued and argued that this oppression can be subverted by valuing women's art and voices, for "feminine artistic production takes place by means of a complicated process involving conquering and reclaiming, appropriating and formulating, as well as forgetting and subverting" (47). While over fifteen years later such appropriation and reclamation are still a function of feminist goals, searching for one particular feminist aesthetic has caused a great deal of controversy. The argument is that such reductionist parameters and borderlines will place feminist performance in a potentially damaging position that would not allow for the many complexities in dealing with issues of race, class, sexuality, and gender in performance. Jill Dolan notes, however, that despite the complexities surrounding the performance of gender, she still finds the act of women occupying center stage extremely compelling: "Even as antimetaphysical theories such as deconstruction and post-structuralism move feminist critics away from their earlier valorizations of the female body onstage, I'm not ready to give up the intense pleasure I find in a powerful female performer" (1). In *Theatre and Feminist Aesthetics*, Karen Laughlin argues against the focus on the "woman performer," writing that feminist aesthetic theoretical discussion needs to move away from an "exclusive focus on the creator or text to encompass theatre's social impact" (18). She explains that feminists need to additionally examine the theatre's structure and critique the hierarchies that exist at various levels.

These arguments about women and performance in the theatre can also be applied to the production of autobiographical works. Many theatregoers might have the same feeling as Dolan about seeing a powerful female autobiographical performance. I must admit that I am often excited by the very notion that a performance is *about* a woman's life, be it based on "fact" or "fiction." But as Laughlin warns, this focus on women can be too easy, too familiar, and too seductive in presenting unchallenged identities. These selves presented on the stage can remain unchallenged as well, as audience members may delight in a performance that focuses on a woman's experience but ignore any wider social or cultural critique of the patriarchical system that continues to suppress women's auto/biographical performances. The performance artist Karen Finley, for example, has become popular both as a performer and as a subject of academic discussion. While her work is exceptionally engaging and powerful in its challenges to the patriarchy, she is by no means the only woman performer taking such risks. To focus the autobiographical performance spotlight only on Finley's work is to deny a necessary critical focus on the variety of women's autobiographical experiences.

The essays in this book reflect a number of diverse voices that rise to the challenge of publicly speaking the unspoken. If the "personal is political" only in written works, then the reality of women's daily performances of self might remain marginalized. To stage the personal, the political, the multiple experiences of a woman's self brings these issues to the forefront of all human experience. When Linda Park-Fuller performs "A Clean Breast of It," for example, the audience is witness not just to her story but to the live body that has been through a battle with breast cancer. Women's autobiographical performance is thus activist in its very nature, as it becomes more of an invitation to share in the experience as a collective audience. The audience is also invited to experience Joni Jones's journey in "sista docta," as she draws upon a collective sense of what constitutes "power" and "privilege." Each of the auto/biographical scripts in this book embark in some way on building a sense of community as they engage in raising questions about identity rather than making authoritative statements about either historical or personal narratives.

Women's auto/biographical performance also challenges notions of an authentic or inauthentic self. No longer is the question of authenticity a focal point of a woman's performance of self. Both "Georgia O'Keeffe x Catherine Rogers" and "My Life with Anaïs," for example, show the intertwining of Rogers's and Pineau's own everyday life performances with their performances of Georgia O'Keeffe and Anaïs Nin. Such plays demonstrate not only the dramatic challenges inherent in scripting women's lives but also the complexities of staging the partnerships they have forged with these historical figures. Following Langellier's concept that "narratives make meaning," in addition to sharing narratives about our lives, women's autobiographical performance gives us new understanding about the importance of recognizing collaboration, multiple selves, and diverse voices.

The creation of performances about women's lives does not mean that women's lives will automatically be represented in all their variety, as theatrical performances that portray women's stories can mirror stereotypical representations. But when women function as true authors and agents, when they speak from the particularity and commonality of their own experiences, the potential for powerful disruptions of hegemonic discourse can occur. The scripts and essays in this book are examples of the ways in which women's auto/biographical performance can break away from stereotypical and predictable representation. Women's auto/biographical performance adheres to Langellier's notion of personal narrative as a "privileged form of expressing embodiment" ("Personal Narrative" 139). The essays that follow diversify the voices heard and the bodies staged.

Works Cited

Benstock, Shari, ed. *The Private Self: Theory and Practice of Women's Autobiographical Writings.* Chapel Hill: University of North Carolina Press, 1988.

Bovenschen, Sylvia. "Is There a Feminine Aesthetic?" Translated by Beth Weckmueller. In *Feminist Aesthetics*, edited by Gisela Ecker, 25–50. Boston: Beacon Press, 1985.

Butler, Judith. *Bodies That Matter: On the Discursive Limits of Sex.* New York: Routledge, 1993.

———. *Gender Trouble: Feminism and the Subversion of Identity.* New York: Routledge, 1990.

Corey, Frederick. "The Personal: Against the Master Narrative." In *The Future of Performance Studies: Visions and Revisions*, edited by Sheron J. Dailey, 249–53. Annandale, Va.: National Communication Association, 1998.

Dolan, Jill. *Presence and Desire: Essays on Gender, Sexuality, Performance.* Ann Arbor: University of Michigan Press, 1993.

Forte, Jeanie. "Women's Performance Art." *Theatre Journal* 40, no. 2 (1988): 217–35.

Fox-Genovese, Elizabeth. "My Statue, My Self." In *Reading Black, Reading Feminist*, edited by Henry Louis Gates Jr., 176–203. New York: Meridian, 1990.

Friedman, Susan Stanford. "Women's Autobiographical Selves: Theory and Practice." In *The Private Self: Theory and Practice of Women's Autobiographical Writings*, edited by Shari Benstock, 34–62. Chapel Hill: University of North Carolina Press, 1988.

Frye, Marilyn. *The Politics of Reality: Essays in Feminist Theory.* Trumansburg, N.Y.: Crossing Press, 1983.

Gentile, John. *Cast of One: One-Person Shows from the Chautauqua Platform to the Broadway Stage.* Urbana: University of Illinois Press, 1989.

Gingrich-Philbrook, Craig, ed. *Text and Performance Quarterly* 20 no. 1 (January 2000).

Gingrich-Philbrook, Craig. "Refreshment." *Text and Performance Quarterly* 17 (1997): 352–60.

Gusdorf, George. "Conditions and Limits of Autobiography." In *Autobiography: Essays Theoretical and Critical*, edited by James Olney, 28–48. Princeton, N.J.: Princeton University Press, 1980.

Heilbrun, Carolyn G. *Writing a Woman's Life.* New York: Ballantine, 1988.
Jenkins, Mercilee M. "Personal Narratives Changed My Life: Can They Foretell the Future?" In *The Future of Performance Studies: Visions and Revisions,* edited by Sheron J. Dailey, 264–71. Annandale, Va.: National Communication Association, 1998.
Langellier, Kristin M. "Personal Narrative, Performance, Performativity: Two or Three Things I Know for Sure." *Text and Performance Quarterly* 19 (1999): 125–44.
———. "Personal Narratives: Perspectives on Theory and Research." *Text and Performance Quarterly* 9 (1989): 243–76.
Lockford, Lisa. "Emergent Issues in the Performance of a Border-Transgressive Narrative." In *The Future of Performance Studies: Visions and Revisions,* edited by Sheron J. Dailey, 214–20. Annandale, Va.: National Communication Association, 1998.
Miller, Lynn C. "Witness to the Self: The Autobiographical Impulse in Performance Studies." In *Communication: Views from the Helm for the Twenty-first Century,* edited by Judith S. Trent. Boston: Allyn and Bacon, 1998.
Miller, Lynn C., and Jaqueline Taylor, eds. *Text and Performance Quarterly* 17 no. 4 (October 1997).
Morrison, Toni. *Playing in the Dark: Whiteness and the Literary Imagination.* New York: Vintage, 1992.
Olney, James. *Autobiography: Essays Theoretical and Critical.* Princeton, N.J.: Princeton University Press, 1980.
Perreault, Jeanne. *Writing Selves: Contemporary Feminist Autography.* Minneapolis: University of Minnesota Press, 1995.
Poirier, Richard. *The Performing Self.* New York: Oxford University Press, 1971.
Russo, Mary. "Female Grotesques: Carnival and Theory." In *Feminist Studies/Critical Studies,* edited by Teresa de Lauretis, 213–29. Bloomington: Indiana University Press, 1986.
Schweickart, Patrocinio. "Reading Ourselves: Toward a Feminist Theory of Reading." In *Gender and Reading: Essays on Readers, Texts, and Contexts,* edited by Elizabeth Flynn and Patrocinio P. Schweickart, 31–62. Baltimore: Johns Hopkins University Press, 1986.
Smith, Sidonie. *Subjectivity, Identity, and the Body: Women's Autobiographical Practices in the Twentieth Century.* Bloomington: Indiana University Press, 1993.
Valentine, Kristin. "Ethical Issues in the Transcription of Personal Narratives." In *The Future of Performance Studies: Visions and Revisions,* edited by Sheron J. Dailey, 221–25. Annandale, Va.: National Communication Association, 1998.
Walker, Alice. *The Same River Twice.* New York: Scribner, 1996.
Woolf, Virginia. *A Room of One's Own.* New York: Harcourt Brace Jovanovich, 1929.
Worthington, Kim. *Self as Narrative: Subjectivity and Community in Contemporary Fiction.* Oxford: Clarendon, 1996.

PART I

Women's Historical Auto/biography

Intimate Partners

✍ A Critical Autobiography of
Performing Anaïs

Elyse Lamm Pineau

Life begets life. A life story begets a life lived. The lasciviously contiguous construct that is the autobiographical subject begets a generational line, a clan of everyday folk made fruitful by this union of selves lived and imagined, of lives actual and possible, of texts intertwined.

I have known Anaïs Nin for close on twenty years. For a full decade of these we have been collaborative partners in our self-making, co-conspirators in "the necessary [and necessarily intertextual] artifice" of our identities (Pineau). Our stories have rubbed up against one another, sometimes lovingly, sometimes with an irritating chafe that rubbed me wrong, rubbed me raw, required the ointment of a critical eye to diagnose and medicate the places where she had erupted under my skin. Places she lives still. Ours is a deep and uneasing partnership, made more so by her ignorance of my presence and by my impersonation of hers.

I first met Anaïs in the *House of Incest*, seven years after her death. Through her legacy of diaries and novels, essays and public lectures, she drew me into intimate conversation, then heated disagreement, and eventually, the rich and layered complexity of longtime companionship. This essay, and the performance script which it contextualizes, use my relationship with Nin to explore the fecundity of autobiographical subjectivities as they are enacted on and off the stage. I want to track some of the shifting configurations that can mark and mar the intimacy between performer and autobiographical other, foregrounding the incorporeality between the lived body and the embodiment of a literary alter ego. My use of the term *autobiography* references three narrative lines: the collected life-stories of Anaïs Nin are situated within, and shaped by, my performance history as a scholar-artist of her work, which is, in turn, situated within the artistic and scholarly workings of my own life. I offer three histories of my partnership with Anaïs. The first history is biographical; it contextualizes the chronology of our relationship within the interpersonal, intellectual, and institutional factors that have shaped its evolution. This biography explores ways in which Nin's work has offered, at critical junctures in my life, a series of performative tropes in which I have alternately "found" and "lost" myself while navigating the contiguity of our selves. The second history is aesthetic. In the performance script, "My Life with Anaïs," I try to evoke the *feel* of our history as storied in a three-day encounter with the Nin archives and the traces of her presence which I encountered there. The third history is genealogical; it explores the ways in which lives, as well as tales, rise up out of encounters with another's storied self. Spinning out of Bryant Alexander's concept of "generative autobiography," I want to theorize the ways in which life-tales perpetually give birth to new persons, both narrative and lived, resulting in a heuristic genealogy of literary and performed kinship.

A PERFORMANCE HISTORY

In 1984 I was accepted into the doctoral program in performance studies at Northwestern University. One of the curricular requirements of new doctoral students was the development of a one-person show that served as a kind of "performance exam" whereby the faculty could assess the literary sensibilities and performative skills of the incoming class. At the time, I was acutely aware of my limitations as a stage performer. My academic background in English had provided more training in literary analysis than in theatrical technique, and I had oft been told that my voice was weak and breathy and my characterization techniques were limited to personae similar to my own vocal and physical mannerisms. Cognizant of the cautionary folklore regarding students who had failed this performative rite of passage, I went in search of literature that would "work": presumably, a collection of texts in the lyric mode whose personae exemplified the ethereal, poetic, metaphor-saturated qualities at which I excelled, without demanding the technical rigor I felt incapable of achieving. I had read Nin's prose-poem *House of Incest* the year I entered graduate school and I returned to it now in the belief that she offered a reasonable chance at performative success by virtue of what I perceived as an incestuous compatibility between my own and her articulated personae. And so our partnership began.

Reading and rehearsing, editing and adapting, improvising and staging, I embarked on a performative mission with acquisition as its goal. "It was magic!" As I began to ease my body into and around Nin's texts in rehearsal, I was struck by how deeply her characters resonated with my own ways of being, ways of thinking and speaking and moving in the world. Like so many young women who had claimed Nin's texts as their own, I felt her words alive within me as if they had grown organically from my own lived experience. "If I could speak," I would say to myself at the end of a rehearsal, "that is what I would say." The fruit of these rehearsals was a compiled script that juxtaposed excerpts from Nin's first adult *Diary* with three psuedo-fictional characters taken from her serial novel, *Cities of the Interior*, and her final novelette, *Collages*. In deference to the means of our meeting, I framed the script with the transformational rebirth-in-water sequence that opens *House of Incest*, the self-referential text that, in the course of rehearsal, had come to seem an intimate allegory for the relationship as a whole. The performance "passed," and with it I passed over into the academic life, a fledgling member of the culture to which I aspired.

Over the next three years of graduate study, I continued to return to Nin as a favored text for course assignments. By 1987 I had written term papers on, and/or performed sequences from, each of the adult *Diaries*, the first childhood volume, *Linotte*, all of the novels, two short stories from the erotica, three essays on the development of a "feminine sensibility," and several snippets from her public lectures. I came to "know" Anaïs intimately, not simply as a resource for my scholarship, but as an interpersonal touchstone whose rites of passage as a young woman-artist seemed to coalesce with my own experiences of interpersonal and intellectual maturation. But intimacy can lead to presumption, and through my now compendious knowledge of her canon, I fancied that I knew how Anaïs would respond to any situation. Surely she had left me a prodigious legacy of herself, and I could cite volume and page number on how she would shape herself around an argument. My staged performances seeped into my everyday performativity such that, on or off the stage, my body could slip in and out of hers with such ease that I had difficulty marking the distinctions between myself and the Nin-in-me who had become a kind of alter ego. Like amiable roommates, we borrowed each other's

clothes—"black, fuschia, aquamarine"—mimicked each other's comport-
ment—"just a lift in the spine, a tilt of the head, a turn of the wrist"—and
spinstoried the twists and turns of our romantic entanglements—"oh, so
you know about our relationship? Well, you would have read about it
in . . ." We were present to one another, Anaïs and I, our voices and bodies commingled through the intimate erotics of extended performance.

But partnerships, and particularly performative ones, rarely remain
congenial beyond the honeymoon of identification. As I began to cut my
academic teeth on feminist and cultural theory, I increasingly found myself shuddering at Nin's insistently apolitical ideology, her lack of reflexivity about her middle-class, white privilege, and her unashamed egocen-
tricity in any and all arenas. "If I could speak," I declared in each seminar
where I invoked her, "this is never what I would say." And as my graduate
study drew to a close, I began to hold my body increasingly apart from
hers, to search out the spaces between, the places where I flinched at her
touch, where, by virtue of our discordant ideologies, my flesh could no
longer cleave to hers. My voice changed. In the classroom and at conferences I began to speak *of* rather than *through* her texts. Whereas the
woman "Anaïs" had been a conversational partner in my self-shaping dialogue, the literary figure "Nin" became the subject of sharp critical commentary. And as the lure of Nin's work shifted from interpersonal touchstone to intellectual whetstone, our partnership grew increasingly
conflicted and alienating.

From 1988 to 1992 I spoke a great deal about Nin, at national conferences, in journal articles, and in the classrooms where I taught autobiographical writing and performance. On each of these stages I began to
juxtapose moments of impersonation with a sharply deconstructive exposé of Nin's presentational strategies. Now, the characteristic "tilt of the
head" was undercut by a cynically raised eyebrow, the "lift in the spine"
coded as a kind of intellectual puffery, and the "turn of the wrist" twisted
by a turn of phrase that mocked the femininity I believed at the time to be
decidedly antifeminist. Again, "it was magic" and within a few years, I had
achieved "the real thing": degree in hand, placement at a doctoral grant-
ing institution, national publications on her work, and permanent membership in the academic community. It seemed I had acquired that original performative goal; I had found a text that "worked." For eight years I
had woven my narrative within and against Nin's tale. I had told her story
from the inside by writing myself in as her main character, telling the
story sometimes more compellingly than she had herself. My own body I

grafted onto hers and I had presumed to assume *her* body like a glove, like a ventriloquist, like a shaman who assumes the materiality of ghosts who are no longer present among us. It was this pervasive, often *invasive* incarnation, finally, that paralyzed me, immobilized at the point where familiarity with another's body feels like foreclosure of one's own. And so, after a long and profitable run, the theatre of our identities went dark for a time.

In retrospect, histories always seem cohesive and purposeful, not because they are so, but because narrative claims them as such. I have configured this summary biography of my Nin performances as an evolution from unreflexive identification to unempathetic critique in order to situate the following performance script as a genesis, a generative trigger for a reconfigured partnership. The shift from performing Nin's autobiographical texts to crafting an autobiographical performance of my relationship to those texts constitutes more than a shift in genre. Rather, it necessitates a teleological turn from representation to reflexivity that exposes the relational ground on which selves are built. This is the terrain of "generative" autobiographical performance (Alexander).

In 1994 I chaired a conference panel that spotlighted scholar-artists working in the genre of autobiographical and autoethnographic performance. After years of studying women's autobiographical writing and encouraging my students to compose and perform their own narratives, this panel was a challenge to put my own body on the autobiographical line, to turn a critical eye toward the relationship that had sustained my scholarship for a decade. Having little else to say *about* Nin, I entered the rehearsal hall prepared, perhaps for the first time, to listen to what she had to say about me, and particularly about the ways in which I had been using and abusing her story over the years. And so it was that our partnership took the stage.

A HISTORY PERFORMED: "MY LIFE WITH ANAÏS"

(A chair sits in the center of a bare stage. Draped across it is an aquamarine scarf; a leather-bound diary rests on the seat, and underneath is an audio-cassette tape. The performance begins down center.)

I want to tell you a true story that never happened.

A story of ten years in three days.

A story of entering the looking-glass house and finding
the real thing.

May 1987. UCLA Special Collections.

When I sign in at the desk I hand over all pens, pencils, and paper clips. I swear that I shall not fold, tear, staple, or otherwise mutilate the evidence I am about to see. I prove that I am carrying no photographic or xeroxing equipment on my person. I sign the forms in triplicate . . . and I am admitted to the inner sanctum.

(I circle the chair slowly and reverently, picking up the diary, stroking it, and eventually beginning to read.)

And there they are! The original manuscripts, the 150 bound journals, 35,000 handwritten pages, the diaries of Anaïs Nin. The real thing.

Trembling with anticipation, I open the first box and, ever so gently, lift out the first childhood diary, begun at the age of eleven on the deck of the emigrant ship *Montserrat*. Opening the cover, I read: "Last look at Barcelona and last thoughts."

And my soul is seized by an instant of perfect understanding.

I thrill to touch the genuine article, the precise moment in time when this artist was born. I delight in the irony that a life's work, eventually spanning six decades, would open with "last look" and "last thoughts." I reach out to this child of eleven, torn from friends, family, father, left to seek refuge in a world of her own making.

But deeper than all this, I feel my empathic body taken up, taken in. I taste words on her tongue. Together we wrap our arms around this child, *this child*, whose only wish was to create a world in which everybody loves her and no one ever leaves.

We are present to one another, she and I. I find sanctuary in this world she has created   just   for   me.

And there is great redemption in that.

(Noticing the cassette under chair, I circle again, greedily, pouncing upon the tape and carrying it downstage to address the audience.)

And then I see them. Cassette tapes. Ninety-seven unedited, unpublished, never-before-touched-by-scholarly-hands audiotapes of Nin in performance and I think to myself: "There's a dissertation in those tapes; there's a book in those tapes; there's tenure in those tapes." *And I wanted them.*

I deserved them. After all these years of reading and writing and performing Nin, who else could understand what they were worth? Who else would know that, for Nin, these performances were "the real thing"!

I had an obligation to the scholarly community to copy and preserve them. It was my privilege—it was my right to possess them!

But I knew I couldn't lay a finger on them without permission. I had to find the right gatekeeper. The one person with the authority. The man with the power to grant me access.

(Pulling the chair downstage, I sit, expectantly, engaged in the game of "password" that will give me access to Nin's executor and, ultimately, her performance tapes.)

So I called up Rupert Pole, Nin's executor and "longtime companion." And I told him of my interest and suggested that perhaps he might give me some insight into her performances, since they had been so . . . close. "Ah, so you know who I am," he said. "Well, of course you would have read about how I met Anaïs and drove her out west in my van. She writes about it in the fifth Diary." "Yes, I remember it vividly," I reply. "Only it was a Ford Model A convertible and the reference appears in the fourth Diary, next to last chapter, May 1947."

He invited me to the house to discuss the project further.

(Throughout this sequence I gradually assume Nin's vocal and physical persona while pacing the edge of the stage.)

Well, I was no fool. I knew that the key to entering Nin's inner circle was in proving that you were already a member. A true believer. A follower of the Goddess of the Eternal Feminine. (You know the story: Woman as Muse, Mother, Mystic.) But you see, I could go one step further. I could "do" Nin. After all those years of performing her, I could call up that voice and body in a heartbeat. An effortless evocation of the Priestess herself.

I mean, let's face it, Nin really isn't all that difficult. Just a handful of phrases: transcendent, ethereal, pre-Raphaelite. A collage of colors: black, fuschia, aquamarine. Nin wasn't a woman so much as an act of construction, a collage of poses and portraits with barely a heartbeat's pause to mark each transformation. She's a lift in the spine, and a tilt of the head. A little more breath in the voice, a turn of the wrist to frame a heart-shaped face of powder and paint. Deliberate and delicate, like a Japanese geisha.

And from the marrow of my bones, I called up just the right touch of that voice and body to seem authentic.   Genuine.   The real thing.

And wrapped in this aura of disguise, I presented myself to Rupert Pole.

It was magic!

Within the hour he had given me his blessing and was sharing witty anecdotes about going on the road with Nin when she was performing the lecture circuit. How they would spend the evenings listening to the tapes of each performance. (You remember the tapes.) And how he would say, "Anaïs, you were so good there, but you must let me write you a great Tchaikovsky ending!" And she would laugh and say, "But Rupert, you know how I much prefer my own Debussy ending!"

Effortless. By the end of the day those tapes were signed, sealed, and delivered. My very own copies of the real thing. So when he invited me back to the house to spend the day with him, of course I said yes. It seemed the least I could do.

On the third day, I entered the looking-glass house.

(I move chair back to center stage and, throughout this sequence, I crisscross the space rapidly, greeting the imagined bits and pieces of her life, recollected from her diaries. Each one invites me like an old friend; there is a frenzy of excitement as I am allowed to view and handle the "real things.")

All around me were dresses and scarves and jewelry and hairpieces. The black velvet she wore to the Dartmouth commencement! The tortoise-shell combs from Bali! There! The floor-length white linen she wore to clean the pool in Schneider's documentary. There was the Thai spirit house! There, the snapshot of Piccolino! A row of paintings. The Varda collage! The piano was covered with first editions, all signed by her hand. And the floor was strewn with box upon box of photographs, playbills, letters, notes to herself.

And at the center of this living gallery was Rupert Pole.

As curator.   And as widow.

(Sitting in the chair, I lean in, reverent again, speaking softly and tenderly with Rupert as he describes his final years, spent nurturing Anaïs until she died. The final lines of the narrative are delivered downstage center, the place of beginning.)

We sat together, he and I, and he spoke to me of Anaïs and of the Debussy ending that he wrote for her. In the last years of her life when her body lay ravaged by cancer, he never left her side. Each morning he would ask her, "Anaïs, what colors would you be today?" And he would sweep up her hair in those tortoise-shell combs and paint the color back into her face. And when she grew too weak to hold the pen, it was his hand that finished the diary. The last diary. The Book of Music. The one manuscript withheld from the Special Collections. And in the last light of that day, ever so gently, he opened that diary and began to read to me.

And when he could no longer speak, he held that diary out to me.

"I thank you. But no. This is one sanctuary I have no right to enter."

And in the space of silence between us, there was a new Presence. Watching me, watching him, looking at her.

Anaïs

The Real Thing.

Alive in the eyes of the man who loved her. And who never left.

And there is great redemption in that.

A GENEALOGY OF AUTOBIOGRAPHICAL PERFORMANCE

In *"Skin Flint (or, The Garbage Man's Kid):* A Generative Autobiographical Performance Based on Tami Spry's *Tattoo Stories,"* Bryant Alexander defines "generative autobiography" as a performative response to a signifying encounter with an autobiographical other. When selves collude in the spectacle and witnessing of autobiographical performance, he argues, a spiral of "sense-[of-self]-making" is triggered that may, when the encounter is genuine and the collaboration rich, give birth to new persons, intertextual identities who subsequently are staged in dialogic response. These autobiographical offspring are conceived of mixed parentage: the "resonant trace of another's lived experience," storied and staged in performance, cleaves to itself the moments of identification in which witnesses are touched and triggered into their own critical memories. These signifying moments, in turn, function as "tropological allusions" that resurrect themselves in the organizational logic, the network of metaphors, or the somatic playfulness of the generated performance. The subject of generative autobiographical performance, then, is constituted between, and stands before, the performance partners, bearing witness to their collaboration. But generative autobiography represents more than a performative record of a partnership, or even the embodiment of a newly configured self. Like a salamander perpetually regenerating its body through newly combined DNA, generative autobiography replenishes the stories of our shared humanity.

Alexander uses generative autobiography to articulate the intertextuality of personhood at three levels. As a compositional logic grounded in Noam Chomsky's theory of generative grammar, Alexander explicates the governing principles, structural features, and attitudinal orientations through which a generated narrative might be crafted in response to the triggering performance. Understood as interpersonal encounter, generative autobiography offers a way to map the intricacies of audience/reader response through the identifications, interpretations, and extrapolations of experience that emerge as reciprocally resonant between performer and witness. As an embodied epistemology, Alexander suggests, generative autobiographical performance narrates the ground upon which a self articulates a vision of itself in relation to the places and persons that have conceived and nurtured it.

I want to extend Alexander's theory from generative to *generational* autobiography by stretching its heuristic potential. I want to stretch it through time to incorporate the multitudinous call and response performances generated by a long-term autobiographical partnership, such as I have experienced with Nin. I want to stretch it also across genres of staged and everyday performance, and across aesthetic and theoretical narratives, each of which offers a unique venue for autobiographical subjectivity. And I want to stretch the generative to accommodate the intergenerational family of persons and tales that spin themselves out from encounters with the storied selves of their kin. I offer, here, a generative response to one of the tropes in Alexander's tale as it has evoked consideration of my collaboration with Nin's texts.

Because generative autobiography is performative, Alexander argues, it originates in an intimate, somatic engagement with the body of another, the touch of whom triggers "goose bumps" of identification. These empathic eruptions stand up and out from the skin of the witness like an intercorporeal braille that codes a story, or series of stories, connecting the life of the performer with the life of the body who watches offstage. Because this empathic projection is visceral as well as attitudinal, the memories which are triggered emerge as embodied moments, fragments of lived experience resurrected in physical sensation. The intercorporeal connectedness that characterizes autobiographical witnessing accounts, perhaps, for the intimacy of the relationship that develops between performer and audience. Autobiographical characters seem to "get under our skin," setting up residence within our own personal histories, as Nin has done repeatedly with me, or as Spry's "garbage man" did for Alexander. For this reason, I think the spatial metaphor of *contiguity*—"being in actual contact along a boundary or a point" (*Merriam Webster's Collegiate Dictionary*, ninth edition)—more aptly describes the commingled subjects of generative autobiography than does the abstract notion of contingency, or even the print-biased term "intertextuality." Contiguous selves "touch" one another literally and metaphorically, and as they move along through space in time, the points of their contact likewise must shift and rotate moment to moment as each supports the other's weight through the dance of identification. It is this movement of bodies, then—or more specifically the movement of *bodies of memory*—that generates new poses and perspectives and, therefore, new subjects who inhabit them.

My decade-long partnership with Nin is not a generative autobiography in the strictest sense of Alexander's definition. I never had the opportunity to witness Nin in performance and my stage work has been primarily performances of or about her texts rather than my own. I am aware that I am stretching Alexander's model considerably by applying it to my situation, yet I would argue that the very longevity of my relationship with Nin, the intensity and breadth of our intercorporeal connection, and the multicontextual nature of my performances exemplify the qualities that Alexander articulates. Further, they open a way to extend the generative to the generational precisely because they allow me to track, in very embodied terms, how my performative responses to Nin's work have evolved over time and across genres. For example, like any performer, I can locate my initial collaboration with Nin in a series of physical negotiations leading from the "discovery" of her body in rehearsal to the representation of her body in the performance of the one-person show. This development of a Nin-in-me, which is the sine qua non of performing autobiographical texts, was formed by the contiguity of Nin's body as present to me in her texts, and my body as present to hers through rehearsal. The character who emerged from these rehearsals, then, might be seen as a kind of generated autobiographical construct, neither wholly Nin nor wholly my experience of her, but something or someone other, continually reconstituted along the moving borders of our respective selves. Because this is a relational construct born of the interaction between two life-texts, the emergent character is never stable but rather shapes and reshapes herself as the relationship between actor and text matures. When a relationship is sustained over many years, the heuristic power is magnified exponentially. In other words, if *generative autobiography* represents a singular performative response to someone else's text, then *generational autobiography* narrates the history of that response *shapeshifting through time*.

In my performance biography and again in "My Life with Anaïs," I tried to explore the twists and turns of my relationship to Nin in terms of how my body constructed itself first *as*, then *against*, and finally *as witness to* Nin's own. At critical points in my life and scholarship, her texts triggered different memories, insights, and orientations, spawning a veritable "family," if you will, of actual and possible personae, all conceived by the interaction of our two life-scripts. More important, my performances were not generated solely for the stage, but incorporated into my written scholarship, my teaching, and my everyday presentation of self such that I might argue my entire scholarly profile as a series of generated autobiographical responses to Nin. This extends Alexander's model by stretching staged autobiographical performance into everyday performativity and accommodating theoretical, poetic, and pedagogical scripts as varying forms of generative response.

Yet, in making such an argument, I am aware of glossing over the uniqueness of a single, staged, autobiographical response which is the heart of Alexander's essay. I want to return, then, to the script of "My Life with Anaïs," locating that performance as a defining moment in the genealogy of my partnership with Nin. Crafting an autobiographical performance necessitates a qualitative shift in perspective. By creating an aesthetic history of my partnership with Nin, the dynamics of the relationship came into sharp focus, enabling a critical rereading of my engagement with her. In the performance script we were present to one another dramatistically, both cast as characters in a meta-narrative about the relationship itself. "My Life with Anaïs" is a generative autobiography in Alexander's sense because it is an accounting of a partnership, in the sense of both adding up the events that comprised our history and holding myself accountable for the positions I assumed in the course of it. The different ways in which I came to know my history as a result of creating that performance form the organizational and thematic structure of the script. The narrative style, recurrent images, and performance choices are all reminiscent of Nin's texts and of different phases in my performances of those texts. I crafted a sense of our history through the narrative patterns and embodied experiences that had emerged over time as the "tropological allusions" binding our respective life stories. "My Life with Anaïs" is, in effect, a story about how I have audienced Anaïs Nin throughout the years and the ways I have felt called to respond to her presence.

But again, I want to extend the generative moment beyond the performed script, locating it doubly in the events being narrated. The kernel story in the script, the experience of "entering the looking-glass house" and engaging Rupert Pole's memory of his beloved partner was itself a triangulated generative performance. Further, it was a performance scripted across three autobiographical texts: my representation of Nin, Pole's narrative of their life together, and the body of Nin herself reincarnated in the collected artifacts that he shared with me. I had entered his home in performance mode, casting before him an image of Anaïs in hope of gaining access to her lecture tapes. As Rupert witnessed my performance, his own memories of her were triggered, giving rise to a series of candid and highly personal narratives that few people outside of their intimate circle had heard. Both performances were enacted against a backdrop of photographs, clothing, and memorabilia, little bits of embodied memory through which Nin herself became present to us both. Through this triangulated performance, each of us was able to witness and to *bear witness* to the others, the simultaneity of it all blurring distinctions between performer and audience, trigger and response, memory of times past and experience of time present. It was as if we three were suspended in a collaborative improvisation, spinning out of the places where our lives and our stories had connected. And by the end of the day, the character generated from this collaboration bore the traits of each of our bodies, shaped her voice from each of our stories, and carried the memories of each of our histories. Our shared performance gave birth to a new entity: "Anaïs, the Real Thing," a generative, performative construct whose complex genealogy was a testament to our kinship and the narrative bloodlines through which our histories entangled.

Life begets life. A life story begets a life lived. Generative autobiographical performance begets a generational line whose heritage is mingled from all the bodies of memory we have touched and incorporated into our own. The power of autobiographical performance, I believe, is in evoking moments of embodied subjectivity in a witness by calling narratives forward out of an audience's individual and collective histories. When we witness autobiographical performance, perhaps more so than any other genre, we respond through the dense ensemble of sensate memories whereby our own identities are continually (re-)storied. We are present as persons bearing the genes of our histories, which are the nearly infinite combination of our own and others' incorporated experiences. Autobiographical performance does not call selves into existence so much as it calls them into *significance* in a moment remembered and a memory embodied. When those memories take the stage in a generative performance, Alexander tells me, our sense of ourselves is enriched through the artful articulation of how we came to be who we are, because of the touch of another along our body of memory. These fertile bodies, I respectfully reply, are made endlessly fruitful as the ghosts of many "generations" resurrect themselves as witness to our shared ancestry. And the redemption in that is altogether Real.

Works Cited

Alexander, Bryant Keith. *"Skin Flint (or, The Garbage Man's Kid):* A Generative Autobiographical Performance Based on Tami Spry's *Tattoo Stories." Text and Performance Quarterly* 20 (2000): 97–114.

Pineau, Elyse Lamm. "A Mirror of Her Own: Anaïs Nin's Autobiographical Performances." *Text and Performance Quarterly* 12 (1992): 97–112.

———. "A Necessary Artifice: A Phenomenology of the Performing Self Explored in the Life-Text of Anaïs Nin." Ph.D. diss., Northwestern University, 1990.

Spry, Tami. "Tattoo Stories: A Postscript to 'Skins.'" *Text and Performance Quarterly* 20 (2000): 84–96.

2

Gertrude Stein
Never Enough

Lynn C. Miller

INTRODUCTION

In June 1993, I began touring a solo performance about the life and work
of Gertrude Stein. The project was first developed for the Tulsa Chautauqua in Tulsa, Oklahoma, for a two-week program entitled "Americans
Abroad," where my Stein presentation found itself in the colorful company of other scholars portraying Dorothy Parker, F. Scott Fitzgerald,
Ezra Pound, and Isadora Duncan. Since that first Oklahoma tour, I have
performed "Gertrude Stein as Gertrude Stein" across the country for a
variety of audiences.[1]

In the Chautauqua style of performance, the actor is both a scholar
and a performer, essentially "impersonating" a historical figure for contemporary audiences, attempting to place the figure accurately in her historical time and yet interpreting the character for audiences who may
know little about either the cultural milieu or the character. Delivered
in the first-person, in words characteristic of the historical figure, the
performance is followed by two question-and-answer sessions, in this
case first with the character, Miss Stein, and then with the scholar, myself,
about my construction of the performance of Stein. The typical time constraints for a Chautauqua performance are approximately forty to forty-
five minutes for the monologue, followed by twenty to thirty minutes of
questions.

As most contemporary Chautauquas are funded directly or indirectly
through the National Endowment for the Humanities, the focus of these
presentations is educational, and, essentially, this mode of performance

teaches the audience, as in a seminar, why a historical figure is important or memorable, in both the figure's context and ours. The ground of the context—the point of view the performer takes toward personal characteristics, professional achievements, or intellectual and social background, for example—can vary widely. Therefore, as this essay points out, the politics of interpretation and representation figure heavily in the construction (and reception) of the performance.

As a scholar of Stein, as well as an adapter and director of her works for the stage, I am only too aware of the burdens of encapsulating one of the more complex and multifaceted figures of the twentieth century (indeed a woman who saw herself as one of the creators of the twentieth century, as she says in *Paris France*) in a performance of forty-five minutes.[2] And, as in any historically based solo production, there is an equally pressing temptation—and thus danger—to reduce a human being to a neatly packaged "authentic" or "essential" self. Stein, both in her work and in her life, resists tidy packaging.

Performing one's own autobiography places the performer in the interesting position of being both subject and object, both writer and reader. Sidonie Smith delineates these dual positions in *The Poetics of Women's Autobiography* (19). Performing the life of another as autobiography adds another level to the multilayered configuration of reader/text/performer/audience. The performer not only creates the lens through which to view another's life but becomes actively engaged with that life (critiquing it, interpreting it, transforming it into the vocabulary of another era), and so builds a dynamic and living new persona. The performance, then, necessarily becomes an amalgam or merging of the body, voice, and intelligence of the performer with those of the person portrayed.

Stein displayed, of course, many selves: the great modernist genius who allied herself primarily with other, male geniuses like Picasso and Whitehead; the inquisitive, lovable youngest child who reveled in all forms of play and craved attention; the linguistic innovator who experimented with bringing back "vitality to the noun" (Wilder 26) in works like *Tender Buttons*; the vulnerable young woman who allowed her older brother Leo to shape her life and opinions; the sensual partner of Alice B. Toklas who created a language for female sexuality as in her works "Lifting Belly" and "As a Wife Has a Cow, a Love Story." The aforementioned constitute a few of the obvious roles Stein played in her life. In creating my Stein performance, I knew that I was committed to showcasing Stein as a working artist, as so many other representations of her life (for example, Pat Carroll's performance of Marty Martin's *Gertrude Stein Gertrude Stein Gertrude Stein*) had focused on her as a personality, friend to the famous, the High Priestess of Montparnasse. Yet Stein always wanted "gloire" not merely for her persona but for her art. As she said in *Everybody's Autobiography:* "It always did bother me that the American public were more interested in me than in my work" (50).

During my work with Stein, I have come to see how performance itself becomes a method through which to understand and appreciate Gertrude Stein, as woman and as artist. In my research and staging of Stein, I have identified four major areas of her work that performance illuminates:

1. Much of her writing can be seen as a *performance of conversation* as, through the repetitions and associations of fairly simple words, she places human conversation, particularly the process of listening and speaking, into a psychological context.[3] Her theories (and subsequent practice) of listening and speaking originated in her studies in psychology and philosophy at Radcliffe with William James in the late 1890s. Adapting James's notion of selective attention, Stein used repetition and conversation to demonstrate character or, in her parlance, to reveal the "bottom nature" of a person.

2. Over the course of Stein's thirty-nine years with Alice Toklas, the two performed a *poetics of collaboration*, reading aloud, editing, and shaping Stein's compositions. Their partnership is most easily seen in *The Autobiography of Alice B. Toklas*, where Stein speaks in Toklas's voice. Appropriately, Toklas's books *The Alice B. Toklas Cook Book* and *What Is Remembered* reveal a voice similar to that of the narrator of *The Autobiography*. Many of Stein's other works, word portraits like "Miss Furr and Miss Skeene" and "Ada," for example, also are easily adaptable into dialogue. The conclusion of "Ada," which Stein wrote for her partner, reflects Stein's collaboration (as well as highlighting the act of conversation) with Toklas, as it shows two people, clearly lovers, both listening and telling:

> That one being loving was then telling stories having a beginning and a middle and an ending. That one was then one always completely listening. Ada was then one and all her living then one completely telling stories that were charming, completely listening to stories having a beginning and a middle and an ending. Trembling was all living, living was all loving, some one was then the other one.

Certainly this one was loving this Ada then. And certainly Ada all her
living then was happier in living than any one else who ever could,
who was, who is, who ever will be living. (*Geography and Plays* 16)

3. Stein's creation of a new literary genre, the word portrait, resulted in
a *performance of cubism*, as she attempted to use words to replicate the process
of living and being which the cubist painters explored visually on canvas. In
these works, Stein's repetitions and associations create a spatialization of language similar to cubist painting. Marjorie Perloff has described the word portraits: "Like a Cubist collage, Stein's composition creates its effect, not by
representing the external event but by, so to speak, pasting up metonymically
related items that . . . spatialize the narrative and make it what Stein calls a
'continuous present'" (149). Stein's repetitions, a device she used to make the
language new—as she said, "to bring back vitality to the noun"—evoked
from her critics many disparaging references, like the appellation "The
Mother Goose of Montparnasse."[4]

4. Stein created new connotations and contexts for words and an an-
tipatriarchal language which allowed her to write about her lesbianism in a
time when lesbian sexuality was entirely absent from public (and largely even
from private) discourse, constituting a *performance of sexuality*. As Catharine
R. Stimpson says, "She disguised her own lesbian experiences by projecting
them onto others or by devising what William Gass, one of her most scrupu-
lous and sensitive critics, has called her 'protective language'" ("Somograms" 72). Using the repetition of ordinary words and phrases, Stein created a context that, upon close reading, described an action without naming
it. For example, in the above excerpt from "Ada," simple phrases like "telling
stories" and "completely listening" represent giving and receiving within a
relationship through a whole complex of practical, affectional, and sexual
behaviors.

In the following discussion, I touch on all four of these aspects, with
particular attention to the difficulties in presenting the last, the performance of sexuality. In creating this historical autobiographical performance, I believed that representing Stein's sexuality and the embodiment
of her particular femaleness, especially the embodiment of her physical
presence, was paramount in bringing this key modernist figure alive to a
contemporary audience. Many scholars have written about ways to read
Stein on the page;[5] I primarily discuss reading/performing Stein off the

page, onstage, using my performance as a text. After summarizing the key considerations forming the process of creating my interpretation of Stein for "Gertrude Stein as Gertrude Stein," I detail the many audience readings, both of Gertrude Stein and of my characterization, which reveal the various public perceptions of Stein the woman and artist. I conclude by exploring the transformative role of performance in apprehending Stein.

THE STRUCTURE OF THE PERFORMANCE

One of the major challenges in a Chautauqua performance, which traditionally dictates a direct address to the audience, lies in creating a believable context for addressing an audience. Clarifying the context allows the audience to firmly have an identity in relation to the speaker. In this detail, my task was simplified by the events of Stein's life. I decided to frame this performance as one of Stein's "Lectures in America," delivered in 1934–35 during her actual, and triumphant, lecture tour of America, which followed the great success of her 1933 memoir, *The Autobiography of Alice B. Toklas*. After decades of laboring in relative obscurity, known principally only by other working writers and artists, Stein became a celebrity at the age of sixty. Urged by her publishers and friends to undertake an American tour, she returned to her beloved America for the first time in thirty years. She had refused such a trip many times. Two events finally convinced her to attempt an American tour: an extraordinarily successful production in 1934 of *Four Saints in Three Acts*, Virgil Thomson's opera based on Stein's libretto, which put Stein's name in lights in New York for the first time; and assurances that the trip would be orchestrated comfortably. These assurances came from both her dear friend (and chief promotor) the writer Carl Van Vechten and from one of her "military godsons," William Rogers, whom she had "adopted" during the Great War.

She and Alice B. Toklas arrived in New York harbor in October 1934 to a barrage of publicity. The revolving lighted sign in Times Square pronounced that "Gertrude Stein has Returned to New York"; major dailies punned in such headlines as "Gerty Gerty Stein Stein Is Back Home Home Back" and "Gertrude Stein, Stein Is Back, Back, and It's Still All Black, Black." Photographers and reporters followed her avidly, wanting to present to a greedy public the eccentric, "difficult," and obscure Sybil of Montparnasse. Having heard the popular line that Stein's work was inscrutable, a reporter expressed astonishment during his interview at her easy conversation: "Miss Stein, why don't you write the way you talk?" to which Stein replied: "Why don't you read the way I write?" (Hobhouse 177).

Given the complexity and scope of Stein's life, as I was initially crafting the script, I kept seeing the question-and-answer period as my safety net. As I left things out—her ambivalent feelings about her parents; her struggle with her homosexuality; the myriad reasons for the deterioration of her relationship with her brother Leo, which next to that with Alice, was perhaps the most formative intimate relationship of her life; her constant craving for recognition (all things she would not talk about in a lecture to the public)—I would think, well, that will come up in the question-and-answer and I can really clarify it then. But that still left me with the task of presenting an enormously rich and nuanced life and a wide-ranging, often difficult, body of work. I was determined to keep my performance accessible to a general audience, and yet was equally determined to educate the audience about her multilayered life, particularly her scientific education at Radcliffe and Johns Hopkins, her theories of writing and poetics, her importance in the collecting and promotion of key modernist artists such as Picasso and Matisse, and her full life with Alice B. Toklas.

Again, issues of sexuality formed the core of my dilemma: Many feminist critics have written about Stein's obscure style as a screen for her explorations of female sexuality.[6] While only fully explored in the past twenty years, this supposition is not new. Edmund Wilson, writing in 1951, discerned that the "vagueness" and "masking" that obscured Stein's writing from 1910 on came from a need "imposed by the problem of writing about relationships between women of a kind that the standards of the era would not have allowed her to describe more explicitly" (Mellow 167). However, this "coding" of Stein's style was more than masking or deliberate obfuscation. As Stein became more comfortable and secure in her partnership with Toklas, her play with language became a way to explore—and playfully enjoy—her sexuality. As Stimpson says, "Given this [Stein's later pleasure in her sexual/emotional life], Stein's coding of sexual activities ceases to be a suspect evasion and becomes, instead, a privileged, and a distinguished, 'anti-language'" ("Somograms" 75–76).

In 1910, Alice B. Toklas permanently moved into the rue de Fleurus, giving Gertrude Stein her first experience of a stable romantic relationship (one that was to last more than thirty-eight years, until her death) and enabling her for the first time to accept her own lesbianism. Stein's sexuality was a source of great conflict in the early part of her life, as she was solidly entrenched in the bourgeois values and patriarchal traditions of her upper-middle-class, German Jewish roots. So homophobic was Stein that when she initially met and grew attracted to Toklas, she distanced her feelings by writing in her journal that Alice "'was an old-maid mermaid who dressed like a whore'" (Wineapple 272). The relationship prospered despite this early impression. In addition to providing stability and emotional and erotic fulfillment, Alice also steadfastly believed in Gertrude when she had no fame or prospects of fame. Her support enabled Stein to keep believing in herself.

Much has been made of what seems now to be the stereotypical role behavior of Stein the husband, the genius and creator, and Toklas the wife, who managed the couple's domestic sphere. For me, this public observation of their roles masks the complexity of their relationship. Toklas was a writer herself and definitely a collaborator in Stein's own writing, as Benstock, as well as Gilbert and Gubar, have pointed out. And Stein's references to herself in poems and letters as "baby" certainly undercut this dominant public persona. The youngest of five children, Stein was accustomed to being coddled and flattered. Her delight in the new, her extravagance and huge persona, her precocity in discerning trends and perceiving talent, all stem from her childlike self. To create, she had to feel the security of being at the center, petted and cared for. She adored being adored, as she might have said herself, and the couple's "structure" probably revolved around this need as much as any other. "One should always be the youngest member of the family," she wrote later in life. "It saves you a lot of bother, everybody takes care of you" (*Everybody's Autobiography* 70).

While I was not able to articulate the subtle ambivalences of Stein toward her sexuality or toward her relationship with Toklas in the monologue, I was able to create a persona who entertained as well as educated her audience, much as I imagined Stein herself did on her celebrated Saturday evenings in Paris. I made fairly sharp distinctions between quoting from her texts as illustrations and speaking improvisationally about her life as she herself might have done.

In the performance, I ration examples of her denser style carefully, using them merely to garnish the main body of the performance. For example, using a passage from Stein's *Lectures in America*, I summarize her work with William James at Radcliffe by talking about her experiments in automatic writing that constituted her very first publication in the *Harvard Psychological Review* in 1898: "I was supposed to be interested in their reactions, but soon I found out I was not but instead that I was enormously interested in the types of their characters that is what I even then called the bottom nature of them, and when in May 1898 I wrote my half of the report of these experiments I expressed these results as follows: 'In these descriptions it will be readily observed that habits of attention are reflexes of the complete character of the individual'" (137–38).

This "bottom nature" forms a key concept in Stein's process of writing as talking and listening. After attending medical school at Johns Hopkins (at William James's suggestion), Stein returns to her earlier observations on people's behavior. After I describe her (by her admission, deliberate) failure in her fourth year of medical school, I adapt a statement she makes in *Lectures in America*: "After I left the medical school, I began again to think about the bottom nature of people. I became enormously interested in how everyone said the same thing over and over again with infinite variation but over and over again so that if you listened with great intensity you would hear it rise and fall and tell all that there was inside them not so much by the actual words they used or the thoughts they had but the movements of these thoughts endlessly the same and endlessly different."[7]

Stein frequently refers to modernist and cubist painters (Picasso, Matisse, Cezanne, Juan Gris, among others) in her writings. Clearly, she was influenced by their use of color, line, and composition. Her own use of the "continuous present," which she says she discovered while writing the story "Melanctha" in *Three Lives*, captured the immediacy of much visual modern art. As mentioned earlier, she declares that she invented the literary word portrait (works like "Miss Furr and Miss Skeene" and "Mabel Dodge at the Villa Curonia") as an attempt to replicate in language the process of living, the illusion of three-dimensional simultaneity, that the cubists presented on canvas (in works like Picasso's "Les Demoiselles d'Avignon"). In the monologue, as I present her discussing the public's rejection of Matisse's portrait "La Femme au Chapeau," I include a comparison of her work to this artist as a way of showing this strong, visual influence on her composition process: "Their [the public's] anger disturbed me just as it disturbed me when the public did not understand my work and mocked it when to me it was so clear and natural. What Matisse was doing was using layers of paint and brush strokes to create movement and emphasis, just as later in my work I would use the repetition of words and rhythm like brush strokes to create movement and emphasis."

A theme throughout Stein's writing, in portraits like *Picasso*, memoirs like *Paris France*, and her essays *Lectures in America*, was her pride in discerning a twentieth-century sensibility, of going beyond the nineteenth-century beliefs of "progress, science, and 'character'" (Ruddick 1) that had once fascinated her during her apprenticeship at Radcliffe with her mentor, William James. In her thirties and forties, these were the beliefs that now repelled her as she realized how they had shackled her creatively and sexually. To create as a woman, particularly as a woman with erotic feelings for other women, Stein had to renounce the patriarchy. As Lisa Ruddick says in *Reading Gertrude Stein*, Stein killed off not only the nineteenth century but the patriarchy as well, the traditionally masculine center of what that century stood for. As Stein said herself in *GMP*, "[F]athers are dead" (Ruddick 3).

This part of Stein's life—her early work with William James, the development of her writing career and style, her discoveries of a twentieth-century sensibility—I trace clearly in my performance, creating a first-person account using language characteristic of Stein's speech, and intercutting my interpretation with passages from her works. This "public" Stein, hugely confident, demanding, and charming, I found quite "clear and natural," as Stein herself said of Matisse's controversial Fauvist paintings when she first saw them.

As I have said, much more difficult to depict in a Chautauqua performance are issues of her sexuality. Stein would never have discussed her lesbianism publicly, even though it was acknowledged among the circles she and Toklas frequented in Paris. In fact, during their celebrated tour of America, Alice B. Toklas's chief worry "was the way the public would respond to them as lesbians. . . . Still afraid of slander, Alice defined her role on this tour as that of Miss Toklas, secretary. Never before, and never afterward, did she play such a part" (Wagner-Martin 208–9).

Gertrude Stein was public about her work and her opinions, but not about her private life. There were many homosexual artists who frequented the Saturday evenings at the rue de Fleurus; Picasso was particularly puzzled by many of these young American women in attendance, remarking: "They are not men, they are not women, they are Americans!" (Stein, *Autobiography* 60). During my "lecture," then, I had the task of referring to Alice quite often and quite comfortably but not in a romantically intimate way. Of course, Stein did not refer to Alice in her lectures of 1934–35, which are collected in *Lectures in America*, but I had taken on the task of introducing Stein to contemporary audiences in the 1990s and

Alice had to be included. Stein's sense of humor is a saving grace and I retold stories about why she wrote *The Autobiography* for Alice, adding to the portrait the kind of teasing that characterizes long-term relationships ("for years I told her, you should write your autobiography, it would be fascinating, everyone would want to read it, you could call it *My Twenty-Five Years with Gertrude Stein* or *Wives of Geniuses I Have Sat With*"). I expanded upon an anecdote from *The Autobiography*, explaining how she and Alice felt upon meeting each other, to more clearly state their attraction for one another: "We liked each other immediately. . . . I invited her to come and see me the very next day. She did come, but she was thirty minutes late. I forgave her and that was the beginning of our long relationship. When I wrote *The Autobiography of Alice B. Toklas* for Alice, because she would not write it for herself, I described how she felt when she met me, that a bell within her rang. She told me later I was struck by something very strong also. I was certainly struck by her."

As a lesbian, I was somewhat uncomfortable having to walk this line about Stein's intimate life, as she too must have been. I tried to arrange my script to pique the audience's curiosity so that they would ask me more detailed questions when I returned to the role of scholar of Stein at the end of the question-and-answer and would be more freely able to address questions about Stein's personal life. The lack of detail about Stein's performance of sexuality is partly a context issue (I wished to emphasize the public Stein and one that she herself might have presented in her lifetime), partly a matter of time constraints, and partly a limitation of Chautauqua-style performance, which privileges a more declamatory, rather than intimate, style of performance. I would be tremendously interested in building a performance that focuses on the nuances of sexuality in Stein's life and work; of necessity, such a presentation would demand an indirect address to the audience or a construction of an intimate listener. Perhaps most effective would be the combination of a private address to self (self=Stein), using letters and diaries, and an address to an "intimate other." The following explores some of the reactions to my portrayal of Stein.

AUDIENCE READINGS OF "GERTRUDE STEIN AS GERTRUDE STEIN"

I will not attempt to discuss all of the audience reactions to my performing Stein, but instead will focus on my construction of a performance around the issues of Stein's sexuality and physicality. Therefore, I have deliberately selected responses that reflect the literal body (both of Stein and of myself as I portray Stein) and, by extension, the body of her work. As I chronicle in this section, the corporeal body of Gertrude Stein occupies a strong presence in history and in the current conception of Stein. So strong is this image of massiveness and masculinity, in fact, that it obscures the person, the artist, and the art of Gertrude Stein.

My first "exposure" to audiences came during the auditions in June of 1992 and during the rehearsal weekend the following January. The Chautauqua selection committee was composed of educators and business leaders in Tulsa, an informed and interested group. As I was to find out, however, they were like most contemporary Americans—they knew virtually nothing about Gertrude Stein. Some of them knew that she was a large woman; one of them had heard she was quite imposing. One said, after informing me that I had been selected as a performer, "Of course you're much prettier than Gertrude Stein," in a consoling voice, almost as if I had lost a close relative. I received this news with great puzzlement, uncertain how to respond.

Another said, "You make Gertrude Stein sound so charming, so much fun, shouldn't you make her more forbidding, more severe?" At least I had an answer to this: I assured the woman that Stein's sense of humor and enjoyment of life were legendary and that everyone came to her salon because she was an eloquent conversationalist. "People enjoyed being around her," I added as two committee members appeared dubious. Perhaps they hadn't paid attention in my audition when I read from *The Autobiography* about Stein's failing a course in medical school (she had a penchant for not taking her professors seriously): "but Gertrude Stein always laughed and this was difficult." Apparently they had missed this anecdote, because they persisted: "But have you listened to her voice?" I assured them that I had, that it was an educated, vaguely East Coast voice, well modulated, but unfortunately in public readings and lectures (her biographers confirm this) she would read in a monotone which simply wouldn't do in the performance, didn't they agree?

During the rehearsal weekend, the five of us who were part of "Americans Abroad" were introduced. The public accepted without comment the Isadora Duncan who was played by an actress clearly in her sixties (Isadora died at fifty) and extremely thin compared with the voluptuous Isadora; they accepted an Ezra Pound much larger, much younger, and more robust than Pound had ever looked in pictures. But after I was introduced, a woman, a complete stranger, came up to me and said archly,

"I'll have to loan you my feather pillows. You're too thin. You just won't do." At dinner that evening, the person I'd found to be the most literary and discerning of the Chautauqua committee leaned over and confided to me: "Of course you have the hardest task of the five of you." "Oh?" I said, dreading what he was going to say next. "You have to gain fifty pounds by June!" he said smiling the same self-satisfied smile as the woman earlier. Other comments about my weight became commonplace. When I recounted this story later to a good friend, a poet, a very large woman herself, and I said, "Well, I know I don't look like Gertrude Stein but . . ." even she interrupted me with "Thank God."

At this point, I talked to a Chautauqua expert who had traveled with the Great Plains Chautauqua for years. He was then in his late fifties, a tall, thin, Anglo-American man with a professorial air. I asked him if he'd ever played a character he didn't look like. He assured me that he had played short, portly characters, characters with hair, without hair—"in fact, I've never played anyone I remotely resembled and no one's ever said anything," he said. How interesting, I thought. Here we have the only really famous woman modernist of the Paris arts renaissance, one renowned for discovering and entertaining other artists, an artist who had amassed a huge and valuable art collection, a woman who in 1935 represented to the world the very archetype of bohemian Paris. Not even considering her own voluminous literary output, she was a well-to-do, brilliant, charismatic, and decidedly *powerful* woman. But in contemporary America, mention of her name evoked only vague notions of an appearance that didn't fit the standards of traditional femininity. I wasn't sure if this obsession with Stein's looks, particularly her weight, was a way to dismiss her significance, or if these opinions reflected discomfort with Stein's lesbian sexuality, or possibly the unease engendered by the combination of her ambiguous (in terms of masculinity/femininity) appearance with a body of work even more difficult to categorize and even to understand.

Clearly, the *body* of Stein, both in and out of the text, was troubling, and a source of contention. Given Stein's project of challenging gender roles, and her desire to develop new methods of writing about female sexuality, I think this continuous questioning of the signification of her own body would have pleased her in some ways. However, I can imagine that (what she would have seen as) the displacement of interest away from the body of her work and instead toward a fascination about her own physical body would have puzzled her and most likely displeased her. In her own time, particularly in Europe, the standards of body image for women were not nearly so narrow. While friends and acquaintances commented on Stein's physical appearance, their observations frequently indicated their admiration. As James Mellow points out: "People who met Gertrude Stein for the first time were usually impressed with her remarkable head; the broad, smoothly modeled brow, the full, straight nose, the deep-set, candid, and sometimes mischievous eyes, a mouth that was generous but uncompromisingly straight. Some likened it to the head of a Roman emperor—but carved from American granite. Others were charmed by the lightness and suavity of her voice, by the irresistible fullness of her laughter. It was a laugh, one of her friends remarked, 'like a beefsteak'—juicy and solid" (26).

Stein's physical self became a magnet for a host of problematic considerations (in her life and in my performance), and I contend that it is easier for audiences to dismiss her as a woman because she does not fit the contemporary, mediated image of female attractiveness or femininity than to wrestle with her significance as a sensual being and an artist. As a person and as an artist, Stein resists categorization, requiring audience members to configure her as a unique being; some spectators resist this engagement with the subject by ridiculing or overemphasizing her physical person.

Stein's sexuality was often rejected along with her physicality. I was occasionally asked in the question-and-answer whether Stein had married, despite what was to me an obvious presentation of her life partnership with Alice B. Toklas. As I mentioned earlier, I talk in my performance about their "momentous meeting" (aided by the San Francisco earthquake of 1906) and I mention Alice's "twenty-five years with Gertrude Stein" when Stein tells how *The Autobiography* came to be written.

When the question about heterosexual marriage came up, directed to the character of Stein, I would answer something to the effect that "my sister-in-law Sally Stein has always been after me to marry, settle down, and have children, but that was not the life I imagined for myself. Of course, I have lived with Alice Toklas for twenty-five years; she goes everywhere with me." As the scholar Lynn Miller I would always get back to that questioner and state that the relationship with Toklas was indeed a marriage.

In Austin, I had a question that I had been waiting for since I'd begun the project. During the questions I fielded as a scholar, a young woman who had been scowling at me throughout the performance, said, "How can you present this woman and not talk much more about her lesbianism?" "*I* talk about it," I replied, "in this part of the question-and-answer, but she never would—the lecture is set in 1935; confessions about sexuality were not part of the public discourse then." "But what about all of the other lesbians in Paris?" she persisted. "You mention Picasso and Matisse more than you do them." I imagined Gertrude in her lecture extolling the virtues of lesbians in Paris as if describing a musical review. Aloud, I replied: "Matisse and Picasso were her artistic peers—the other geniuses of her time who served as benchmarks for her success." "Well, of course," my interrogator continued, "she was butch. Butch women always have a lot of men friends." Could this possibly be true, I thought? And why was she calling Stein butch? Because she was large with short hair? Many accounts of the time by both men and women stress Stein's physical charisma and sensuality. I then mentioned to the young woman Djuna Barnes, Nathalie Barney, Una Lady Trowbridge, Radcliffe Hall, and other celebrated lesbians of the time who frequented Paris—women who were not part of Stein's inner circle—but I could see that somehow she thought I was destroying a personal icon of hers, a woman who was big and butch and proud of it and who lived in a mythical lesbian Parisian utopia circa 1920. Her Gertrude Stein was not the great thinker and artist I had presented her as; she was simply the lesbian mother of us all. Period. Nothing I could say would ever be enough.

For many, Gertrude Stein the person has transformed into "Gertrude Stein" the myth, a woman whom people create to suit their own particular view of her time and of themselves as they might exist in some idyllic bohemian paradise. This was true even in her lifetime: The anecdote in my monologue that always gets the most audible response is the story of Picasso painting his famous 1906 portrait of Stein: "Finally after eighty or ninety sittings he painted out the head of the portrait, 'I can no longer see you when I look at you,' he said and then he left the country—he went to Spain for the summer. When he returned he painted the head back in without seeing me and the portrait was complete. He was pleased with it and I was very pleased. But our friends would always look at it and say: 'But Gertrude does not look like this picture.' And Pablo would always shrug and say, 'She will.'" In one question-and-answer session, I was telling the audience about some of the difficulties of doing this performance. "One is that I know I don't look like Gertrude Stein . . ." I began. At this point the local theatre reviewer called out, "Oh, but you will!" evoking the spirit of Picasso's delightfully paradoxical remark from the early years of the century.

THE TRANSFORMATIVE EFFECTS OF PERFORMANCE

The Picasso anecdote emphasizes a central facet of Gertrude Stein's personality: ever-mindful of her reputation, particularly her literary reputation, Stein was constantly engaged in the process of creating and recreating herself. She believed in the future, continually anticipating a time when her work would be understood; she invested much of her time in members of younger generations (artists and of course multitudes of American GIs from both world wars). Both her great invention of the continuous present and her use of associative language to create context and to make language new emphasize her belief in process, in the circular, repetitive expression of life and character. Not only did Stein strive to reveal the "bottom nature" of her subjects by showing the way they talked and listened, but she sought to make literature as vivid a sensory experience as a painting. As Donald Sutherland points out about her use of language: "You must also be aware of the most notorious sentence of Gertrude Stein: a rose is a rose is a rose is a rose. In this case, we have not a consecutive counting but a moment by moment insistence on the rose, and each moment of insistence is a heightened and refreshed recognition of the rose, not merely a prolongation of the rose, as could perfectly well be done in another era" (10).

While every human being is a somewhat fragile construction of selves, and consciously or unconsciously experiences shifts in identity over the course of a life, Stein in particular celebrated in her writing the interplay of voice and identity. The word portraits ("Picasso," "Matisse," "Mabel Dodge at the Villa Curonia") exemplify the layering and repetitions, small movements and tiny details that the performance of character entails. Her poems and prose works reflect the ongoing struggle during her life over gender and genius, which caused her to redefine what it meant to be identified as a woman in an age where few acknowledged geniuses were female. Gender and sexuality emerge as less absolute categories in the writings and life of Stein, who referred occasionally to herself in her notebooks as "he," and to her role in her marriage, occasionally, as "husband."[8] She wrote once, referring to the critical reaction to her literary experiments: "'They needn't be so afraid of their damn culture. . . . It'd take more than a man like me to hurt it'" (Pierpont 80). Her abandonment of nineteenth-century notions of character and plot underscores her desire to freely create personae who resist traditional bound-

aries of place and time. One of her chief modernist successes was her abil-
ity to evade rigid or simple classification in her creative and personal lives.
Only her mode of living, characterized by a prescribed schedule of meals,
work time, and socializing, was "regular" (and of course she and Miss
Toklas, as she says in "Miss Furr and Miss Skeene," "were regularly gay.
They were gay everyday" [*Geography and Plays* 18]).

A Chautauqua colleague, after watching my performance at the
Rocky Mountain Book Fair in Denver and hearing me tell the audience as
a scholar that my not resembling Stein had created some problems, com-
plimented me by saying, "After seeing you perform, I've decided Stein
should have looked like you." While his was a humorous observation, it
made me realize again that space exists for the presentation of Stein in
many guises and in many shapes and embodiments.

Despite the resistance of some members of my Chautauqua audiences, performing Stein allows us not to be limited to the one corporeal
body of Stein. Only through performing Stein, through staging the many
voices and permutations of meaning imbedded in her poems and word
portraits, through experimenting with meanings, connotations, and spatial arrangements, and through presenting the many selves of Stein the
person, the artist, the woman onstage, can we give her texts and per-
sona(e) the multiplicity of bodies they suggest. For Stein, the concrete
bodies of her texts exist in language as much as in nature, as Marjorie
Perloff explains: "The paradox, then, is that Stein practices what William
James called, with reference to *Three Lives*, 'a fine new kind of realism,'
even as she resolutely opposes mimesis, the notion that the verbal or visual construct can replicate the external world of nature" (148).

Throughout my solo performances of "Gertrude Stein as Gertrude
Stein," I have been gratified to have audience members tell me that they
could, after seeing and hearing me, read Stein. Having heard Stein orally
they began to comprehend her playfulness with language, as well as her
significance in dramatizing our perceptions of language and our process
of listening and speaking. The potential of performance, which displays
for the audience the oral and spatial dimensions of a text as well as recreating the embodied voice of the writer, allows Stein to be accessible to
contemporary readers. In addition, although performance has a strong visual component, placing Stein's words in acoustic space allows her words
to transcend her person. I extend an earlier-mentioned quotation from
Everybody's Autobiography to underscore her belief that the work remain
primary: "It always did bother me that the American public were more in-

terested in me than in my work. And after all there is no sense in it because if it were not for my work they would not be interested in me so why should they not be more interested in my work than in me" (50). Stein's concept of the continuous present coexists nicely with her own continuous living through an oral tradition.

EPILOGUE

This brings me to the title of this essay, "Gertrude Stein Never Enough." As I performed this piece I was told:

>   that I wasn't large enough
>   that I wasn't short enough
>   that I wasn't old enough
>   that I wasn't serious enough
>   that I took myself too seriously
>   that I didn't laugh enough
>   that I was far too humorous enough
>   that I wasn't arrogant enough
>   that I was more than confident enough
>   that I wasn't butch enough
>   that I wasn't voluptuous enough
>   that my language wasn't dense enough
>   that my language wasn't conversational enough
>   that I was not simple enough
>   that I wasn't abstract enough
>   and there's always the question, was I Jewish enough?

On behalf of myself and Gertrude Stein I would like to say, enough is enough is enough is enough.

Notes

1. Performances of "Gertrude Stein as Gertrude Stein" include: Chicago House Upstage, Austin, Texas, 14–21 October 1993; Vortex Theatre and Albuquerque Museum, Albuquerque, New Mexico, 13–14 April 1994; Eastern Communication Association, Washington, D.C., 30 April 1994; Rocky Mountain Book Festival, Denver, 28–29 October 1994 and 13–14 October 1995; Indiana State University, Terre Haute, 16 February 1995; University of Colorado, Colorado Springs, 12 October 1995; Northern Illinois University, DeKalb, 9 November 1995; DePaul University, Chicago, 10 November 1995; University of North Dakota, 12 April 1996; Texas Speech Communication Association, Dallas, 30

September 1999; Oklahoma Celebration of the Book, Tulsa, 2 October 1999; Indianapolis Art Museum, 23 March 2000; University of Texas at Austin, 15 September 2000; High Plains Chautauqua, Greeley, Colorado, 9 August 2002.

2. "Three Americans in Paris: Gertrude Stein, Ernest Hemingway, and Sherwood Anderson" (University of Texas at Austin, October 1985); two distinctly different productions of "Miss Furr and Miss Skeene" (one performed at the University of Texas at Austin and at Southwest Missouri State University in 1986, and the other performed at Hyde Park/Frontera Theatre in September 1994 and at the University of Tulsa in October, 1994); and "As a Wife Has a Cow, a Love Story" (University of Texas at Austin, September 1995, and the national meeting of the Speech Communication Association in San Antonio, November 1995).

"So Paris was the place that suited those of us that were to create the twentieth century art and literature naturally enough" (*Paris, France* 2).

3. See my essay "Writing Is Hearing and Saying."

4. "If she was 'The Mother Goose of Montparnasse,' as someone said . . ." (F.W. Depee in Van Vechten ix).

5. An excellent guide to Stein's texts is Ruddick's *Reading Gertrude Stein*.

6. See, for example, Gilbert and Gubar, *No Man's Land*; DeKoven, *A Different Language*; Stimpson, "The Somograms of Gertrude Stein"; Benstock, *Women of the Left Bank*.

7. Unreferenced excerpts that I discuss in this section are from my performance script, "Gertrude Stein as Gertrude Stein."

8. For example, in "As a Wife Has a Cow, a Love Story," the presence of a "wife" in the lesbian couple implies a husband. For discussions of Stein's adoption of masculine roles at points in her life, see also DeKoven, *A Different Language*, and Stimpson, "Gertrude Stein and the Transposition of Gender."

Works Cited

Benstock, Shari. *Women of the Left Bank*. Austin: University of Texas Press, 1986.

DeKoven, Marianne. *A Different Language: Gertrude Stein's Experimental Writing*. Madison: University of Wisconsin Press, 1983.

Gilbert, Sandra M., and Susan Gubar. *No Man's Land: The Place of the Woman Writer in the Twentieth Century*. Vol. 1, *The War of the Worlds*. New Haven: Yale University Press, 1988.

———. *No Man's Land: The Place of the Woman Writer in the Twentieth Century*. Vol. 2, *Sexchanges*. New Haven: Yale University Press, 1989.

Hobhouse, Janet. *Everybody Who Was Anybody: A Biography of Gertrude Stein*. New York: G.P. Putnam's Sons, 1975.

Martin, Marty. *Gertrude Stein Gertrude Stein Gertrude Stein: A One Character play*. New York: Random House, 1980.

Mellow, James R. *Charmed Circle: Gertrude Stein and Company*. New York: Avon, 1974.

Miller, Lynn C. "Gertrude Stein as Gertrude Stein." Unpublished monologue.

———. "Writing Is Hearing and Saying: Gertrude Stein on Language and in Performance." *Text and Performance Quarterly* 13 (1993): 154–67.

Perloff, Marjorie. *Poetic License: Essays on Modernist and Postmodernist Lyric*. Evanston, Ill.: Northwestern University Press, 1990.

Pierpont, Claudia Roth. "The Mother of Confusion." *New Yorker,* 11 May 1998, 80–89.

Ruddick, Lisa. *Reading Gertrude Stein: Body, Text, Gnosis*. Ithaca, N.Y.: Cornell University Press, 1990.

Smith, Sidonie. *The Poetics of Women's Autobiography: Marginality and the Fictions of Self-Representation*. Bloomington: Indiana University Press, 1987.

Stein, Gertrude. *The Autobiography of Alice B. Toklas*. New York: Random House, 1933.

———. *A Book Concluding with As a Wife Has a Cow, a Love Story*. Barton: Something Else Press, 1973.

———. "Composition as Explanation." In *What Are Masterpieces*, 23–38. New York: Pitman Publishing, 1940.

———. *Everybody's Autobiography*. New York: Random House, 1937.

———. *Geography and Plays*. Boston: Four Seas, 1922.

———. *GMP, or Matisse, Picasso, and Gertrude Stein with Two Shorter Stories*. New York: Something Else, 1972.

———. *Lectures in America*. Boston: Beacon Press, 1957.

———. "Lifting Belly." In *The Yale Gertrude Stein*, 4–54. New Haven: Yale University Press, 1980.

———. "Miss Furr and Miss Skeene." In *Geography and Plays*, 17–22. Boston: Four Seas, 1922.

———. *Paris France*. New York: Liveright, 1940.

———. "Picasso." In *Selected Writings of Gertrude Stein*, edited by Carl Van Vechten, 333–35. New York: Vintage Books, 1972.

———. *Tender Buttons*. New York: Claire Marie, 1914.

———. *Three Lives*. New York: Random House, 1909.

Stimpson, Catharine R. "Gertrude Stein and the Transposition of Gender." In *The Poetics of Gender*, edited by Nancy K. Miller, 1–18. New York: Columbia University Press, 1986.

———. "The Somograms of Gertrude Stein." *Poetics Today* 6 (1985): 67–80.

Sutherland, Donald. "Gertrude Stein and the Twentieth Century." In *Gertrude Stein Advanced: An Anthology of Criticism*, edited by Richard Kostelanetz, 4–17. Jefferson, N.C.: McFarland, 1990.

Toklas, Alice B. *The Alice B. Toklas Cook Book*. New York: Harper and Row, 1954.

———. *What Is Remembered*. New York: Holt, Rinehart, and Winston, 1963.

Van Vechten, Carl, ed. *Selected Writings of Gertrude Stein*. New York: Vintage Books, 1972.

Wagner-Martin, Linda. *"Favored Strangers": Gertrude Stein and Her Family*. New Brunswick, N.J.: Rutgers University Press, 1995.

Wilder, Thornton. "Four in America." In *Gertrude Stein: Modern Critical Views*, edited by Harold Bloom, 25–45. New York: Chelsea House, 1986.

Wineapple, Brenda. *Sister Brother: Gertrude and Leo Stein*. New York: G.P. Putnam's Sons, 1996.

3

Mule of the World

⌁ The Embodiment of Mary Church Terrell

Eileen C. Cherry

CONSTELLATING THE MULE

My body is a crossroads with its four limbs extended like compass points to the four winds. Competing allegiances swirl around me like magnetic fields. My travels have heightened my awareness of the forces of hybridity, diaspora, and cosmopolitanism performing in my life. I am concerned about representations of Africans and all other marginalized people in the Western imagination and the particular impact those representations have on our psyches and identity concepts as embodied in travel practice. Naturally, this emerges from my own local and global travel experiences as "a colored woman in a white world."

Like most travelers, I braved borders to resist typification only to find it. I struggle with the silence that has come over me regarding my travel experiences. But not too hard. There are times it must be honored. Silence has often served the role of protective cloak in the flight to freedom. Since I was not prepared to tell my own travel tale as directly and honestly as I wanted, I drew upon the legacy of Mary Church Terrell. A woman of great wisdom, polish, and decorum, Terrell was a champion of civil rights and feminism at the turn of the twentieth century. An educator, civic leader, and the first African American woman to serve on a board of education in Washington, D.C., she passed away in 1954 at the age of ninety-one. I perform her to signify the African American woman's search for accommodation in the Euro-American cultural landscape. Her travels through Europe and the United States as recorded in her autobiography, *A Colored Woman in a White World*, chronicle an African American woman's struggle for healthy self-definition in the face of cultural erasure. As Terrell I could produce a variously positioned native who was trying to resist typification as well—one who claims a wider range of identity by challenging audience conceptions regarding the African American women they meet in everyday life.

How Terrell and I negotiate the zones of cultural polarization and our historical context are major factors affecting our style of transcultural performance. That style mirrors what we feel is our relationship to hegemonic power, which is represented in the following folktale gathered by a fellow intrepid, the venerable Zora Neale Hurston:

> Ole feller one time had uh mule. His name wuz Bill. Every mornin' de man go tuh ketch 'im he say, "Come 'round Bill!"
>
> So one mornin' he slept late, so he decided while he wuz drinkin' some coffee he'd send his son tuh ketch ole Bill.
>
> Told him say, "Go down dere, boy, and bring me dat mule here."
>
> Boy he sich a fast Aleck, he grabbed de bridle and went down tuh de lot tuh ketch old Bill.
>
> He say, "Come 'round, Bill!"
>
> De mule looked round at 'im. He tole de mule, "Tain't no use you rollin' yo eyes at me. Pa want yuh dis mawnin'. Come on round and stick yo' head in dis bridle."
>
> Mule kept on lookin' at 'im and said, "Every mornin' it's 'Come round, Bill!' Don't hardly get no rest befo' it's 'Come round, Bill!'"
>
> De boy throwed down dat bridle and flew back tuh de house and told his Pa, 'Dat mule is talkin.'" (172)

By identifying myself as the Mule, I am constellating those parts of myself as an African American woman that are contradictory and complex: the traveler, the restless one society tries to master who is untamable and, in the eyes of many, unlovable. Constellating the Mule also recognizes that marginality in this culture comes with the two faces of a hybrid or a half-breed. One face may "affirm the values and precedence of the centre" (Thomas 6), while the other expresses a kind of transgressive freedom practice. So the self-fashioning maneuvers of marginalized subjects evoke and perform this dualism in their quest for an accommodating space.

There is more to this barnyard scenario, but for now let it serve as an allegory on Euro-American cultural power and the autobiographical practice of African American women like Mary Church Terrell. I am borrowing Hurston's vignette to illustrate what Michael Omi and Howard Winant call an "interlocking system of race, gender and class oppression" that keeps the Mule in check (quoted in Collins 78). The figure of the Mule has been ever-present in African American folklore; one of its primary uses has been to denigrate African American women. The Mule represents the contradiction between the dominant cultural ideology of womanhood and black women's devalued status which has been a source of wonder and frustration for me and other African American women. Ironically, it also stands with a pantheon of "Idealized Others" as described by Patricia J. Williams: "The Noble Savage . . . the Great White Father, the Good-Hearted Masses, the Real American, the Rational Consumer, and the Arms-Length Transactor are all versions of this Idealized Other whose gaze provides us either with internalized censure or externalized approval: internalized paralysis or externalized legitimacy, internalized false consciousness or externalized claims of exaggerated authenticity" (9).

As a performer, I see the travel narratives of African American women as speech acts of self-reclamation that critique the expansionist ideology of texts by European imperialist envoys. They have, however, in the course of their development, internalized European Africanist discourse and other forms of oppression. The African American envoy in the contact zone finds an almost endless metropolitan culture fraught with the continuities and mutations of imperial imagery (Pratt 6). These narratives "give witness" to the peculiar difficulty of black women in patriarchal worlds (Mason 341). Terrell's autobiography offers abundant examples of such, as in the following passage, which candidly describes her positionality in the heart of American democracy in the early decades of the twentieth century:

> As a colored woman, I might enter Washington any night, a stranger in a strange land, and walk miles without finding a place to lay my head. . . . Indians, Japanese, Chinese, Filipinos and representatives of other dark races can find hotel accommodations, as a rule, if they can pay for them. The colored man or woman is the only one thrust out of hotels of the National Capital like a leper. As a colored woman I may walk from the Capitol to the White House ravenously hungry and supplied with money to purchase a meal without finding a single

restaurant in which I would be permitted to take a morsel of food if it was patronized by white people, unless I were willing to sit behind a screen. And in some places I would not be allowed to do even that. I am almost ashamed to admit that more than once I have been downtown attending a meeting or transacting business and have been hungry and weary, I have stood in front of a restaurant or a cafeteria in the National Capital looking with longing eyes at a special menu offered for that day at a price I could afford to pay, and have been unable to summon the courage to go in and get what I needed. . . . I was not always in the frame of mind that I felt I could stand a slap in the face. Sometimes when I am provoked with colored people who are too timid to insist upon their rights as citizens, I remember those lapses of my own when I have lost my nerve. But I have never stopped trying to get what I knew was just and right for me to have. (383–84)

As one of the black people living in the center of the Western world, Terrell finds she represents the paradox in a culture where so much is invested in pedigree and unvaried ideas of "us" and "them." For the white dominants in power as well as for the black subjugated, her marginality and transcultural performance reshuffle whatever dogmatic concepts there are of distinct borders. Yet she must be resigned to wander as an outsider. Throughout her autobiography, Terrell's efforts to get to her destination and find accommodations are continually thwarted by a number of factors, most evolving out of issues of race and social class. However, as demonstrated in the following episode, these issues drive Terrell to exercise a particular "privilege" of her birth unavailable to most African Americans:

It was irritating and nerve-racking to be obliged to stand at the ticket window and wait till all the people in the white waiting room had purchased their tickets, before the agent would sell me mine, no matter how early I would come to the station. It was hard to exercise self control and banish from my mind such thoughts as I would be ashamed to acknowledge as my own. When I first filled lecture engagements in the South, I traveled with a trunk, and several times I barely secured my ticket in time to have it checked. . . . How self-respecting colored people can patiently endure such treatment year in and year out without getting desperate is difficult to understand. (306–7)

Terrell became adept at maneuvering within the realms of misguided authority. Classified as a Negro in the New World and the Old World, she had to engage in duplicitous tactics to circumvent the bigotry leveled against what she often refers to in her text as her "drops of African blood." Terrell, with discretion, could "pass" for white. Recognizing her location in the asymmetry of racism makes her the consummate "Trickster." She is essentialist/pluralist: sister, spy, and envoy. Here she explains the nature of her Trickster practice while traveling in Europe:

> Everywhere I went in Europe I received a cordial reception and made a host of friends. My nerves were not on edge, neither was my heart in my mouth because I feared I would be persona non grata to people I met abroad, if perchance they happened to discover I was of African descent. I did not attempt deliberately to deceive these new friends concerning my racial identity. To be sure I did not wear a placard on my back announcing in big black letters, "I am a colored woman from the United States, BEWARE!" But after our relations of friendship were close enough to justify it, I told some of those belonging to the social circle in which I moved that I had African blood in my veins. . . . I felt that I could not be loyal to my race if I did not pursue such a course. (97–98)

This is one of a series of experiences Terrell recounts in a thematically rich chapter entitled "Traveling under Difficulties." The chapter is a minibiography of her travel perils in America from youth to maturity, when she became in demand as a speaker on race and women's issues in the early part of the twentieth century. As background, Terrell writes about her life occupying two realms. One I will call "Paris, France," a place of enchantment, idealism, and possibility—away from racist America; the other "Paris, Texas," a place of debasement, narrowness, and terror, the native land. She says of France:

> How I love France and the French people! To be sure, they have faults like other groups, but with all their faults I love them still. Goethe says that everybody has a fatherland and a motherland. The country in which I was born and reared and have lived is my fatherland, of course, and I love it genuinely, but my motherland is dear, broadminded France in which people with dark complexions are not discriminated against on account of color. (209)

But of America she writes after an extensive European tour:

> [T]he time had come for me to return to my native land, and my
> heart ached when I thought about it. Life had been so pleasant and
> profitable abroad, where I could take advantage of any opportunity I
> desired without wondering whether a colored girl would be allowed
> to enjoy it or not, and where I could secure accommodations in any
> hotel, boarding house, or private home in which I cared to live. I
> knew that when I returned home I would face again the humiliations,
> discriminations, and hardships to which colored people are sub-
> jected all over the United States. (98)

On one train trip in the United States, Terrell is stranded one night
between Shreveport, Louisiana, and Paris, Texas, and takes the risk of
checking into the only hotel available—the one for white people. She
fears being recognized by the waiters:

> I remembered that I had written my full name quite legibly in that
> register, and a great fear suddenly took possession of me. I had been
> filling engagements in that part of the South for three or four weeks,
> and it was quite possible that some of the waiters in the hotel had
> read the colored newspapers which gave rather full accounts both of
> my career and of my speeches. What if they should see my name and
> recognize who I was? If they did and should tell the management of
> the hotel, what would happen? I trembled with apprehension and
> fear. What a fatal mistake I had made by not registering under an as-
> sumed name! I tried to allay my alarm as best I could and retired. Fi-
> nally I fell asleep. I had been in bed about two hours, perhaps, when
> a loud noise at my door awoke me out of a sound slumber. "Your time
> has come," was the first thought that popped into my head. (301)

What she does is envision her own lynching. She contemplates possible
ways of escape. Her turmoil expresses a form of internalized racism in
which the basis of her terror is the image of herself imposed by the racism
of the dominant group's system of ideas, thus making her moment of terror the odd consummation of a transcultural act. There came a second,
then a third knock at the door. Finally the voice on the other side speaks:
"Did you ring for a pitcher of water?" The threat was not actual at that
particular moment, but very real if her secret had ever been discovered.

The question we must ask is why, with all of the options available to her, would Terrell as a vibrant and intelligent young woman decide to return from Europe to such a place to struggle and make a life for herself? She writes of a fated meeting with a woman in Europe not so unlike herself:

> The day I was to take the steamer home I saw a colored woman who had married an Englishman who belonged to a good family and was well-to-do. She had been living happily near London with a devoted husband and several children for years. Would such an existence appeal to me? I was perfectly certain it would not. I knew I would be much happier trying to promote the welfare of my race in my native land, working under certain hard conditions, than I would be living in a foreign land where I could enjoy freedom from prejudice, but where I would make no effort to do the work which I then believed it was my duty to do. I doubted that I could respect myself if I shirked my responsibility and was recreant to my trust. (99)

Terrell recognized that her world is like Michael Taussig's "Canal Zone," a cosmos "stitched together by white-defined dictates of work, discipline and efficiency" in which blacks represent all that is clumsy and inept. The racist aim is to achieve a society that is ordered and racially engineered and so the black nature is something that is in the way. The white canal has to "bore through [it] to join oceans for commercial might" (145). But what is actually achieved and what Terrell represents is the merger and consequent fecundity of African European cultures. She is the continuation and transformation of the African and the European in a newly synthesized form. Terrell's special qualities place her in the position to exchange knowledge between segregated communities. This includes "details, facts, observations, psychoanalytic readings of the Other" (hooks 38) that stimulate a special black women's perspective as described by Patricia Hill Collins: "Threatened with isolation and real physical harm, she begins hammering out a black woman's standpoint, developing Afrocentric feminist views that discover, interpret, and analyze the world—a process which is the heart of a Black feminist literary tradition and political thought which challenges the very definition of discourse" (13–15). Collins acknowledges the impact of economic conditions and who controls them. They not only determine the "shape" of black women's subordination but give birth to their particular style of activism. What she calls a "subjugated knowledge of resistance" is crafted and passed on by these women because of their location at the very crossroads of race, gender, and class (10, 18).

Adapting Terrell's transcultural performance text for the stage was my way of laying hands on this subjugated knowledge and constellating the Mule. Configured as the body of Mary Church Terrell, the Mule is a catalytic site for the dialogue on difference. We can see this in many recent examples of ethnographic performance work in which the performer, while enacting interethnic conflict, speaks words and embodies gestures that inhabit the spaces between herself and her Other. Kobena Mercer looks to Mikhail Bakhtin's concept of dialogism to describe the movement that takes place when the master codes of the dominant culture are made "one's own." He describes the subversive, destabilizing might that is unleashed from the mouth of the dispossessed, exposing and illuminating the "diverse social forces always represented by the monologism of discourses of domination" (59).

In Hurston's collected folktale, the master's words "Come 'round, Bill" are parodied in the mouth of the Mule as a means of gaining some degree of mastery of its location—its marginalized circumstance (57). For Terrell, the bridle had been placed on her at birth, but she denied it until she could see herself mirrored in the eyes of her audience: the racists and ethnic essentialists she encountered on her journeys. As a result, she became angry, resigned, then determined to have that bridle removed. The result is a text that clearly defines the location of the "colored woman" in the white world of her period. That bridle also became a badge of honor—an identifying mark which she was determined to wrest from the demeaning interpretations of her race fostered by white Euro-Americans. She transforms the denigration by waging an investigation of the facts, connecting with those "like" herself and devoting her text to making a fervent argument against the misrepresentation of Africans in the diaspora.

Because she is in a position to acquire knowledge with the "authority to offer that knowledge to others," as "a traveling woman [she] is a disorderly woman" (Tsing 219). For example, when Terrell arrives at the train station in another strange city in Delaware, not knowing the address of a contact, she is accosted and threatened with arrest by a white man serving as a ticket agent when she asks him for a phone book. He tells her to sit down and wait to be arrested. When she protests and declares that she is a "busy woman" and will not wait, and will leave the train station, he shouts at her to take her seat. "You are disorderly. You know you are" (312). Later the men sent to arrest her at the theatre where she was speaking refused to do so because she spoke in sympathy of Ireland's struggle against England, among other topics, demonstrating her knowledge of the arresting officers' "plight." However, she was arraigned on charges of disorderly conduct, which were later dismissed. Terrell got an out-of-court settlement of one dollar for her abuse providing she did not sue the railroad company for the conduct of its agent.

I wanted my performance of Terrell's transcultural experiences to performatively exemplify the concepts of hybridity, diaspora, and cosmopolitanism that show us two things: the variable influence that the conceptual dyad of essentialism/pluralism had upon her and the degree of her marginality in relation to the prevailing authority on both shores. As a sister, she projects a domestic identity that is essentialist—as envoy, the borders extend and finally give way as she represents the pluralist by fashioning a more globalized persona. The essentialist identity appears to be the most diasporic in nature. As essentialist, she recognizes that she can not escape the facts of her existence in relation to the European, which she shares with other black Africans the world over; she understands that her "freedom" is relative and that she can learn from the courage, craft, and momentum of the fugitive slaves. Her essentialist identity grows out of her subjection to checkpoints and sanctions and second-class citizenship, the driving currents of race and racism in her life; it feeds her claims to have never betrayed that race and her willingness to intervene and sacrifice personal advantage for the cause of freedom and justice, to be a symbol of black progress, to be a black feminist thinker.

On the other hand, Terrell's pluralism, not surprisingly, embodies a bit of all three indicators—hybridity, diaspora, and cosmopolitanism. The diasporic performer in this context sees her privileges against the stark contrast of others of her kind living under some vicious variation of colonial rule. The hybrid actualizes herself as a crucible among the three worlds of Europe, America, and Africa, understanding her body as the location for their reconciliation. But the prominent cosmopolitan—a bright, confident voice that seems to flavor the whole text—has a sense of borderlessness and expansiveness, even loneliness. The cosmopolitan identity has self-respect and a sense of social order. It is transnational and crosscultural in its vision and practice. It seeks independence and transparency. Between the essentialist and pluralist, Terrell, of course, seemed to enjoy the latter more because transparency was the desired condition she wanted to achieve. But she was subjugated in either role. Transcultural performance was never a matter of cultural "tourism" for her but a critical survival strategy. Location taught her body the intersecting maneuvers of essentialism, where she epitomized a particular ethnicity and pluralism, where, as described by Paul Gilroy, she is perceived as complex and her blackness as an open signifier.

PERFORMATIVE CHOICES

In *A Colored Woman in a White World*, Terrell clearly focuses on her seemingly endless transcultural journey from her birth in the year of the Emancipation Proclamation, 1863, in search of an accommodating space for herself. In one recorded episode, while conferring with the literary godfather of her autobiographical work, H. G. Wells, she sees the major complication in her quest:

> I confided to Mr. Wells that some day before I passed out I wanted to write the story of my life and call it "The Confessions of a Colored Woman." "I like the title," he said immediately. "It will be widely read in England. But write it dispassionately." I tried to follow the advice of this distinguished author as best I could. I am well aware, however, that what the victim of race prejudice would call a "dispassionate" account of her life might be called by another name by the dominant group. (351)

Throughout her life and journeys, Terrell was continually warned not to subvert the controlling discourse that was persistent in denying her reality. Even Wells was aware that the highly controlled discourse on race and gender was already established to silence Terrell and deny credence to the very sound of her voice. It would take tremendous courage and communicative skill to overcome this.

We can get a sense of how Terrell negotiated borders and positioned herself in the world by studying the elegant photograph of her in the front of the latest editions of her autobiography. The book was first published in 1940 when Terrell was seventy-eight. She appears in the photo as a "dowager" in evening dress—a dignified, fair-skinned black woman of medium build with silky white hair. I share neither Terrell's upper-class background nor her appearance. I was raised in public housing. I am cocoa and stocky with dark wooly hair. But like Terrell, I learned in my travels that the black woman traveler projects a power and authority. I think the only way I come close to her physical likeness is through my carriage. In

my performance I present Terrell as an energetic, elderly woman in conservative dress in the style of the 1930s.

As her autobiography was published at the dawn of the Second World
War and the European Holocaust, I thought it timely for Terrell to reflect
on her links with the German Fatherland, as she calls it in her narrative
(she spoke fluent German from an early age), and on her own encounters
with patterns of intolerance as she toured that country in the 1880s. By
talking about these experiences Terrell indirectly addresses the currents of
intolerance active in our society as we enter the new millennium. The
twenty-minute monologue I perform is the first installment of what I am
envisioning as an extended performance work.

My aim was to provide what I knew to be a mainly white audience a
different view of black women and to enrich the view of those who share
my racial and cultural background. Both "views," I felt, were shaded by
dominating images of what is assumed to be our location and thus our
stagnation. The prevailing view assigns the production of "real" knowledge only to sites dominated by white, European males. Women and persons of color are not generally perceived as knowledge producers but as
conditioned, defined, localized, and disorderly. Black women are forced
to live in a cultural establishment that denies their presence but supports
the continuing domination of white males and their narratives. So the
prevailing beliefs regarding the transcultural and travel practices of
African American women are, at best, limited and distorted.

Indeed, the African American woman traveler is a representative
questing figure in the Western myth who reflects the shifting character of
what has long been known in our cultural tradition as "heroic" terrain:
the domain of the European and masculine. Although the marginality of
black female bodies in the West determined the degree and character of
their participation in the mainstream of travel discourse, it never pre-
cluded the range of these women's travels or the scope of their vision. The
visionary texts of women like Terrell show their situated bodies infused
with knowledge of hybridity, diaspora, and cosmopolitanism. They represent the bodies of African American women not as stagnant and localized but traveling between what Edward Said describes as "nations and
narrations" (xiii).

My performance depicts Terrell focused on the practicalities of
African American struggle and survival within a racist, capitalist system.
My monologue is adapted from her chapter "In Europe with Mother and
Brother," which I feel encapsulates her intercultural experience. (Page

numbers after the following passages from the monologue refer to Terrell's *Colored Woman in a White World*.) Boundaries annoy her, inconvenience her—"handicap" her—as she was prone to use the word. They confine her all too often to what she sees as some very tight spaces, among them, the maze of definitional restraints imposed by the Euro-American imagination.

IN PERFORMANCE: AN AMERICAN "SCHÖN SCHWARZ"

(As the lights rise on the darkened stage, we hear the rolling mezzo-soprano of the African American diva Jessye Norman, renowned for her renditions of German art songs, singing Schubert. We see a small table covered with an intricate white lace cloth, an elegantly gleaming sterling silver tea service with a single white china cup and saucer. Next to the table setting is an Edwardian-style chair and on the floor to the right of the chair is an open, rustic travel valise full of old stuff.

Terrell enters the space from the audience. She is wearing a calf-length navy blue day dress with a white collar with a sprig of violets at her breast. Her shoes are black, elegant and sturdy. She pours herself tea before seating herself to examine the array of items in the valise — old souvenirs, framed photographs, maps, postcards, letters, brochures from the Hamburg-American line and Marrietta College, a small journal which remains on her lap, and a wallet from which she carefully extracts a lottery ticket that reminds her of the lucky one that sponsored her mother and brother's tour of Europe in September 1889. Terrell's wealthy father had sent her there previously to study and she was eager to see family. She sips her tea, then acknowledges the audience of visitors to her sitting room.)

Just before Mother started for Europe, she enjoyed a rare visitation of good fortune. A plumber who happened to be working for her one day persuaded her to buy a ticket in the Louisiana lottery, which at that time flourished like the proverbial green bay tree, but has since been out of commission altogether. She paid a dollar for it, then threw it aside and forgot all about it, as she had done many times before. After a while this plumber, whom Mother had neither seen nor heard from since he sold her the ticket, came to the house to tell her that the number on the ticket she had bought had won the first prize and she was entitled to $15,000. My mother thought the plumber was joking until he showed her the number of the ticket, which he had carefully preserved.

But where in the world was that valuable ticket? Who knew? (81)
*(Terrell details for the audience the comic search the family waged for the
ticket and how it was recovered in the trash by Anna, a German immigrant
girl who had been working for her mother for several years.)*
Mother gave the plumber who notified her of this good fortune $1,000.
She gave Anna $300 for finding the ticket and sent me $300 to buy a fur
coat. I was in Lausanne at the time and put this money into the bank, re-
solving not to touch a penny of it till Mother could help me select whatever I bought. The good fortune enabled Mother to travel in Europe
with her son and daughter without being worried about financing the
trip. (82)
*(She discusses her visit to the Paris Exposition of 1889 and then on to
Berlin, leaving her mother and brother behind. She could never avoid in-
terrogation about her identity or its consequences. Despite her idealism,
Terrell soon learned that Europe offered no psychological Promised Land.
She had to continually take precautions against the intrusion of American
racism abroad.)*
When I reached Dresden I was glad I decided to study in Berlin. The city
was full of Americans and English. Wherever I turned in the streets, I
heard my mother tongue. I knew that a foreign city full of my white coun-
trymen was no place for a colored girl. I was trying to flee the evils of race
prejudice, so depressing in my own country, and it seemed very stupid indeed for me to place myself in a position to encounter it abroad. (73)
*(There were times, however, when it could not be avoided. She falls ill in
Berlin and is visited by a well-meaning white friend from Oberlin College
in Ohio, who insists she move into her pension. But Terrell is cautious.)*
I protested vigorously against doing so, because I did not want to live
among English-speaking people, since it would tempt me to use my
mother tongue too much. Way down deep in my heart I feared to board
in a house where there are many Americans. I felt I would get into some
kind of trouble on account of race prejudice. (84)
*(At this point, my performance of her text focuses on two such encounters
while staying at a pension run by a Fräulein von Finck at the insistence of
her Oberlin friend. It begins with her experience with the Spanish wife of
a German general, who identifies herself as a "woman of color.")*
I had been in Fräulein von Finck's pension but a few days when I observed
that a woman whose complexion was quite swarthy fastened her eyes
upon me every time I came into her presence. Finally, she accosted me

one evening when we were both in the reception room, and asked me to what nationality I belonged. "I have heard that you are an American," she said, "but you are rather dark to be an American, aren't you?" I laughingly replied that I was a "dark American." "And I am dark like you, too, you observe," she said. "I am a Spaniard and my husband is German. Every time I see a woman who is not fair, I become interested in her indeed." . . . Through my Spanish friend I was introduced into several distinguished social circles into which few Americans had entree. And this opportunity came to me because my complexion was dark! It was indeed a rare experience for a colored girl hailing from the United States. (84–85)

> (*Terrell learns from this milieu that although she is educated, wealthy, and American, as a black she is considered among the degenerate whose presence an imperialized world finds troubling. Among the issues she faces are the proscription of her womanly virtues because of her racial status [Washington xxiv], and other challenges to her categorization based on class and national affiliation.*)

After I had been in Fräulein von Finck's pension a short time, I saw two young American men eying me as though they were anything but pleased to behold me in their midst. These two students were studying medicine. One was from Baltimore and the other hailed from Washington, D.C. I observed that Fräulein, who was literally fair, fat, and forty, quite loquacious, and especially catered to Americans, held long conversations with these two medical students, who could neither speak nor understand German very well. But Fraulein could speak English and enjoyed practicing it on Americans who would let her do it.

One day she called me and told me she would like to see me in her room that afternoon at two o'clock. When I entered, Fräulein appeared embarrassed, and it was evident she did not know how to say what was on her mind. "To what nationality do you belong, Fräulein Church?" she began. "I am an American," I replied. "But you are darker than the average American aren't you?" She flushed a deep red when she asked this question. "Yes, I am darker than some Americans," I admitted. "Can you go to a hotel in the United States?" I knew by that question that somebody had explained to her the disabilities under which colored people labor in the United States. "I certainly can," I assured her. "I have been going to good hotels with my father ever since I was a little girl. But why do you ask me these questions, Fräulein von Finck? What difference does it make what my nationality is . . ." (85–86)

(Yet it has made all the difference. Due to the presence and "intervention"
of white nationals from her homeland who explain to von Finck their spe-
cial rules of engagement regarding blacks, Terrell is forced to leave the pen-
sion.)

This incident proved to me that among some Americans race prejudice
is such an obsession that they cannot lay it aside even in a foreign land,
where there is no danger they will be pestered to any appreciable extent
by the objectionable Negro. When these young men saw a colored girl
trying to cultivate her mind in a foreign land, the chivalry of southern
gentlemen snapped. They did not hesitate to humiliate me and disturb
my peace by attempting to persuade my landlady to put me out of the
house. (87)

(An embittered Terrell later finds lodging in the home of a Fräu Ober-
prediger, a Berlin widow with two daughters her same age. She seizes the
opportunity to perfect her language skills and to learn more about ominous
developments in the German way of life. In the Oberpredigers' younger
daughter, Terrell must confront the bigotry not aimed directly at her person
but at her sensibilities. Ironically, in the face of the young Oberprediger's
venomous anti-Semitism, she finds her own physicality being made an issue
once again.)

In Fräu Oberprediger's home I spoke German all the time and was never
tempted to lapse into English. I enjoyed the mischief and fun of the
younger daughter, but the bond of union between us would have been
closer if she had not hated the Jews so fiercely and bitterly. . . . It amazed
me to see how a girl so young could hate so deeply a race, no representative of which had ever done either her or any member of her family any
harm. . . . Her attitude toward the Jews irritated and annoyed me greatly.
I would never laugh at her stories in which the Jews were made the butt
of ridicule, no matter how funny they were. And she had a remarkable
sheaf of them, to be sure! I could not help thinking how the race with
which I am identified is misrepresented, ridiculed, and slandered by
people who feel the same animosity against it as the young German girl
manifested toward the Jews. . . . I told her also that if she lived in a certain section of the United States she could not eat at the same table with
me, would not even allow me to sit beside her in the street car or in the
railway coaches, and that her mother would not give me room and board
in her home.

But my young German friend did not understand this at all. She was
sure I was exaggerating the facts. She could not believe that any human

being could object to another solely on account of the color of his skin.
If a race had all the vices and defects which she insisted were characteristic of the Jew, she could understand why people would not want to come
in close contact with such a group, but for the life of her she could not
comprehend why anybody would object to another human being because
he happened to be a few shades darker then himself. . . . My young German friend admired my type very much. She had never seen a colored
woman before. She used to pat my cheek and say, "You are so *schön
schwarz* (so beautifully dark) and your hair curls so prettily." (90)

    *(The monologue ends as Terrell wisely observes, "It is always difficult for one
prejudice-ridden human being to understand why his brother should be obsessed by a prejudice which differs from his own" [90]. The lights lower. The
voice of Jessye Norman swells once again and Terrell graciously takes her
leave from the audience.)*

CONCLUSION

As Mary Church Terrell I can resist typification and claim a wider range
of identity not only within the world of the staged performance but in
challenging audience theories regarding the African American woman
they meet in everyday life. I wanted the audience to see and understand
her resistance to the dominant cultural ideology of the black woman's devalued status. I wanted the audience to see her body as the site for the dialogue on difference, for Terrell's positionality made her astutely aware of
the plight of the marginalized and the traps of reflexive intolerance (Karttunen 289). I wanted the audience to see her struggle to come to terms
with the demands of domination, particularly the provocation of totalizing discourse in the United States and abroad. And finally, I wanted the
audience to see her recognition of her identities, ambiguities, and ambivalence. Terrell's loyalties are complex but they assure her continuation.
I wanted this audience to learn a way to travel by my "imitative assertion"
of this figure (States 157–58) who, as characterized in my earlier discussion of the Mule, is so often maligned and localized.

    She demonstrates great mobility—moving quickly from space to
space in the course of her autobiography, facilitated by a sophisticated
network. Who she knows seems more important than where she is or has
been. She sketches in events. There is little detailed description of landscapes, settings, or even people's expressions—but an abundance of cari-
catures. She outlines the influential people in her life by representing

their voices and presences—their roles and functions. In a sense, Terrell seems disassociated from the landscapes in her narrative. In discussing her relationships with the various locations in her life, her narrative also reflects her manner of engaging the process of self-creation—her style of renewing her commitment to life and her ideals. We see that her spatial practice is the actualization of her questing hybridity and of her ideal that the world fully accommodate the facts of her being.

Her autobiography's table of contents reads like the résumé of a plucky, ambitious woman—a public life with a public voice: the consummate Negro club woman and social advocate addressing authorities, particularly the authority of the Euro-American dream-makers who subjugate her image. Her journeys, therefore, are an assertion of personal authority that faces off the influences of white supremacy and black subjugation. But what Terrell learns is that the issue is not just whether the journey was taken, but also who will listen to the "intelligence" gathered and whose authority will be honored, believed, or discounted. The issue is: Does Terrell's presence—her return from the journey—count? Is it of "general" interest? Is the knowledge gathered worth respecting?

In this study, Terrell's encounter with "insider" figures, such as the "Hurston boy," the various gatekeepers, conductors, ticket agents, and innkeepers, represents the European imagination she takes utterly by surprise. The boy finds it normal for the Mule to be silent and under restraint. The Mule has long symbolized the restrictive life offered to blacks in the United States. Selecting and debasing imagery has been an instrument of suppression and conquest in the polemics of Western domination. The Mule glares back at the boy with the bridle. Its reversed gaze becomes an expressive methodology that embodies the imagined terrain between itself and its Other.

Formerly voiceless women are ending their private soliloquies and engaging their "unknown other" in the field of public discourse (Trinh 8). Terrell did so through both her travel and her published account of those travels. Through my performance, which I entitled "In the Body of Mary Church Terrell," I attempted the same. As an African American woman traveler in my own right, and one struggling with silence, I can speak with and through the performed autobiographical voice of Terrell. The ensuing performance becomes a site of transcultural tension that calls into question old, damaging representations. As the Mule, Terrell and I challenge the audience to reconceptualize power and powerlessness, "heroism, . . . symbolic landscapes and ritual grounds" (Washington 403).

Works Cited

Bakhtin, Mikhail. *The Dialogic Imagination: Four Essays*, edited by Michael Holquist. Translated by Caryl Emerson and Michael Holquist. Austin: University of Texas Press, 1981.

Collins, Patricia Hill. *Black Feminist Thought: Knowledge, Consciousness, and the Politics of Empowerment*. New York: Routledge, 1990.

Gilroy, Paul. *The Black Atlantic: Modernity and Double Consciousness*. Cambridge: Harvard University Press, 1993.

hooks, bell. "Representing Whiteness in the Black Imagination." In *Cultural Studies*, edited by Lawrence Grossberg et al., 338–46. New York: Routledge, 1992.

Hurston, Zora Neale. *Mules and Men*. New York: Harper Perennial, 1990.

Karttunen, Frances E. *Between Worlds: Interpreters, Guides, and Survivors*. New Brunswick, N.J.: Rutgers University Press, 1994.

Mason, Mary G. "Travel as Metaphor and Reality in Afro-American Women's Autobiography, 1850–1972." *Black American Literary Forum* 24 (1990): 337–56.

Mercer, Kobena. "Diaspora Culture and the Dialogic Imagination." In *Blackframes: Critical Perspectives on Black Independent Cinema*, edited by M. Cham and C. Andrade-Watkins, 50–60. Cambridge, Mass.: MIT Press, 1988.

Pratt, Mary Louise. *Imperial Eyes: Travel Writing and Transculturation*. New York: Routledge, 1992.

Said, Edward. *Culture and Imperialism*. New York: Alfred A. Knopf, 1993.

States, Bert O. *Great Reckonings in Little Rooms: On the Phenomenology of Theater*. Berkeley: University of California Press, 1975.

Taussig, Michael. *Mimesis and Alterity: A Particular History of the Senses*. New York: Routledge, 1993.

Terrell, Mary Church. *A Colored Woman in a White World*. Washington, D.C.: Ransdell, 1940.

Thomas, Nicholas. *Colonialism's Culture: Anthropology, Travel and Government*. Princeton, N.J.: Princeton University Press, 1994.

Trinh, T. Minh-ha. *Woman, Native, Other: Writing Postcoloniality and Feminism*. Bloomington: Indiana University Press, 1989.

Tsing, Anna Lowenhaupt. *In the Realm of the Diamond Queen*. Princeton, N.J.: Princeton University Press, 1993.

Washington, Mary Helen, ed. *Invented Lives: Narratives of Black Women, 1860–1960*. Garden City, N.Y.: Doubleday, 1987.

Williams, Patricia J. *The Alchemy of Race and Rights*. Cambridge: Harvard University Press, 1991.

4

Desire in Evidence

꿍

Stacy Wolf

Postmodern writer Kathy Acker writes that "*Peter Pan* is proof that only girls exist" (17). As a girl-performer turned lesbian-performance scholar, I understand in some visceral way what she means. I played Peter Pan in third grade, barely understanding that I was following in Mary Martin's illustrious footsteps (illustrious hung-wires?). But by the time I was eight and dressed from head to toe in green felt, I already knew countless musicals by heart. I stared at the record cover of *The Sound of Music*, aching to be a British-accented, corkscrew-curled blonde in a sailor suit. At twelve, I played Marta (not the youngest daughter but the one who "is going to be seven on Tuesday and I'd like a pink parasol") for three months in a dinner theatre production of *The Sound of Music*.

I grew up on musicals and pretended (like any good feminist) to reject their heterosexism and misogyny by the time I got to college. My recent work on musicals is motivated by a desire to recuperate this form from a lesbian and feminist perspective; motivated, that is, by a "political" and "academic" desire. I did not expect that one particular research project, specifically the performances of Mary Martin, would so thoroughly entrance me. I did not expect my desires to shift so strikingly to the "personal." I did not expect to desire Mary Martin.[1]

Mary Martin occupies a singular, almost legendary place in American musical theatre history. She created some of the most well-known and best-loved roles on Broadway, including Maria in *The Sound of Music* (1959), Nellie Forbush in *South Pacific* (1949), and her signature role—Peter Pan (1954). Martin also had a successful touring career, which included an extended run of *Annie Get Your Gun* and *Hello, Dolly!* She performed on radio, television, and in films, and continues to be associated

with the era in Broadway history of lavish musicals with outstanding female characters.

ᥣᥩᥩᥩ

What is the difference between a fact and a rumor? Between a quotation
made textual and one that is whispered? What is the site of sexual orientation? What is the value of the (textually) visible? What is the difference
between outing and getting the facts straight?

ᥣᥩᥩᥩ

In the spring of 1995, I agreed to write an essay about Martin for a book
about gay and lesbian theatre workers. Some subjects were known to be
gay, and others' homosexuality needed to be "discovered." The anthology
would render theatre history more accurate by documenting the significant contributions of American gay and lesbian actors, directors, play-
wrights, designers, and producers and by demonstrating the artistic relevance of one's sexual orientation. The editors required a theorized
historiography, a historically accurate definition of sexuality, and academ-
ically acceptable proof of each subject's sexual orientation.

I was already interested in Martin, and I was already interested in lesbians, as I was working on a book that was then about *The Sound of Music*
and *Funny Girl* and lesbian spectatorship. But at that point, I wasn't very interested in biography, in part because I was suspicious of intentionality as
an analytical tool. I was even less interested in sexual biography, which
seemed predicated on ahistorical interpretations of a given person's life
or relationships. By acknowledging that sexuality is historical, that sexual
practices must be analyzed in context, and that the very definition of lesbian continues to be a site of theoretical and material debate, I occupied
too skeptical a position to furrow willingly for clues about Martin's sexuality. I had no desire to participate in that debate. No desire. Or so I thought.

Yet, I was titillated; I was downright excited, curious, and confused.
Was Mary Martin, of *South Pacific* and *The Sound of Music* fame, really a
lesbian? Did the body in green tights that flew across the television screen
each year as Peter Pan want other women? It was inconceivable to me.

Once it was suggested, I couldn't stop thinking about it. I found an old
copy of her autobiography, *My Heart Belongs* (1976), in a used bookstore
in Madison, Wisconsin. The photograph on the back cover shows Mar-

tin astride a horse in a large, open, sunlit meadow. She looks to be in her fifties, wears a checkered blouse and a bandanna around her neck. One hand holds the horse's reins, the other hand waves joyfully into the camera. I stared at this picture, trying to examine it with an innocence I'd already lost. I smiled and opened the book. On the dedication page was a black and white close-up of Martin and Richard Halliday, her second husband and manager. He holds her closely; neither one looks to the camera; he looks down at her, and she just looks down. It seems to be a moment of intimacy, caught by the camera's watchful eye. It looks as if he's suffocating her.

Knowledge is irresistible. Or is it gossip that is irresistible?

cᘓ෯Ꮆ෯

Born in Weatherford, Texas, in 1913, Martin was supposed to be a boy, as she writes in *My Heart Belongs*. A tomboy with a gift for dancing and an inability to read music, Martin portrays her childhood as one full of adventures and promise. She notes that she read *The Well of Loneliness*, a classic of lesbian fiction, at age eleven. She married Benjamin Hagman at sixteen to avoid staying in a girls' finishing school. Her mother raised Martin's son, the well-known actor Larry Hagman; Martin and Hagman divorced, and she opened what became a lucrative dancing school in Texas.

Martin left for California with Mildred Woods, her "friend, companion, chaperon, boss, [and] secretary," to pursue a career in acting and singing, and was "discovered" by Oscar Hammerstein II, and then by Jerome Kern, who urged her not to be a prima donna but to "find and perfect" her own style (47). Laurence Schwab helped her land a small part in Cole Porter's *Leave It to Me* (1938), in which she made one of the most stunning debuts in Broadway history with "My Heart Belongs to Daddy." Martin's rendition of the song was not the expected striptease at all, but a tongue-in-cheek dance in which she wore a fur coat and took off nothing. She made a number of films in the 1940s but did not become a film star, in part because Paramount could not successfully mold her into a glamour girl. Martin's "style" was characterized by warmth and honesty, in contrast to both the glamour girls of the 1940s and '50s and the belting bravado of Ethel Merman.

Although in her autobiography Martin thanks her second husband, Richard Halliday, for taking care of her personally and professionally, she in fact managed her own career, pursuing the projects that interested her, working with whomever she chose, getting consistently rave reviews, and breaking records for Broadway ticket sales. Throughout her life, Martin had close working and personal relationships with many women, including Cheryl Crawford, Jean Arthur (an earlier Peter Pan), and Janet Gaynor, all of whom were known or assumed to be lesbians.

The tomboy image dominated Martin's public self, emanating from a physical and "personal" presence that rejected typical femininity but relied on it for meaning. Significantly, Martin's body was not "mannish" but rather "tomboyish" or "butch," and her personality was "charming and friendly"; thus, her boyish qualities were not threatening but simply noted throughout her career. That she was "not pretty" and "not seductive" implied that Martin lacked feminine wiles and coyness, and such perceptions added to her aura of sincerity. In the early 1940s, for example, journalist John Rosenfield dubs her "a friendly, gabby West Texas girl with an entirely universal enthusiasm for a new and pretty (her word) husband and a new and very pretty Bel Air house." Irving Stone writes in 1956, "She has no mask to take off. She is enchanted with life."

I searched gay and lesbian history and biography for theoretical and methodological models to interpret the "facts" of Martin's life and career. Martha Vicinus, for example, argues that defining lesbian as a woman nurtured and supported by other women both broadens the notion of lesbian identity and lessens the significance of actual sexual practices. Leila J. Rupp analyzes "a broader category of women-committed women who would not identify as lesbians but whose primary commitment, in emotional and practical terms, was to other women" (408). It's difficult to identify Martin's "primary commitment." She eschewed politics, feminist or otherwise. When pressed, her politics were extremely conservative, and perhaps explicitly racist. Martin also relied on many men to work creatively, and to some observers, was anything but independent. She was happily married for many years to a man whom she most certainly loved. She enjoyed the privileges of money and fame.

These essays, while fascinating, seemed to offer no ways into Martin's life and sexuality. I kept telling myself that I hadn't known before that she was a lesbian, trying to ensure myself of the secret's secrecy. I imagined that if I *had* known, I could have succeeded in this scholarly project. I fantasized that prior knowledge would have made the scholarly task easier. I stumbled over language, even to myself. What exactly was I looking for? Martin's "sexuality," "sexual orientation," "sexual preference," "affectional preference," "sexual practices"?

But soon, this unnameable search led me to new and different places, strange and exciting. I remembered: Martin was a performer, a star, a singer, dancer, actress. Perhaps she would perform lesbian in music, in dance, on a publicity photo. I listened to cast recordings of her shows. Martin sings, "Let's start at the very beginning, a very good place to start." Her voice is richer and thicker than most Broadway performers today and very distinctive, as she slides up to notes and then lets the notes slip away through vibrato. Is this what a lesbian sounds like?

In the Billy Rose Theatre Collection of the New York Public Library, I waited all day for a file of Cheryl Crawford's letters. Crawford, one of the women who ran the Group Theatre, produced many plays, including *One Touch of Venus*. A supporter of Martin's, a friend, and a known lesbian, Crawford insisted that Martin play the title role. Crawford's considerable correspondences, I eventually found out that day, were being refiled and would not be available for the foreseeable future. For many days after, I was absolutely certain that Crawford's file of letters contained the truth, the answer, the evidence, the proof.

But in one of several "Mary Martin" files, I found a clipping from a 1939 *King Feature Syndicate*. Ann Pichot, the journalist, writes: "Using men for stepping stones is a dirty feminine trick. She hasn't had time for beaux yet. . . . She used to wear her stockings rolled like any subdeb, but now that her legs are a precious commodity, in the Dietrich class, she dares not mar them with rings, so she wears garter belts. And black satin brassieres. . . . The hit of the show, she has never seen a Broadway production; nor has she gone through a serious love affair" (21). Pichot characterizes Martin in terms typical of a Hollywood starlet in the late 1930s. Because of Martin's west Texas origins and her buoyant personality, she was frequently described (and of course, constructed by Hollywood's vast publicity machine) as innocent and "gabby." Although I'd read similar descriptions of other film stars, I noticed the possible signs of Martin's lesbianism and Pichot's attempt either to deny them or to hint at them. I wondered if she'd ever have "time for beaux" or if she'd ever go through a serious (heterosexual) love affair; I smiled at her legs being compared with those of Marlene Dietrich, a known lesbian.

Part of my anxiety, of course, was uncertainty about Martin, her life, gay gossip, and homophobia in and around the theatre collection at the New York Public Library. I never knew whether to come right out and ask the person at the desk if he or she knew anything about Martin being a lesbian. I feared the answer's obviousness either way: either Martin was a lesbian and I was the only one who didn't know it and so actually felt compelled to prove it; or she wasn't one (or no one knew she was) and I would get arrested for slandering her name. I wondered if the lesbian files had been intentionally destroyed. I wondered if there ever were any lesbian files.

I tried to imagine how "lesbian," "lesbian desire," or anything related to "lesbian" might be mentioned, named, or noted during Martin's career as a Hollywood actress and Broadway star in the 1940s and 1950s. At the same time, I felt a clear and deep suspicion that I wouldn't find it. Not only that—I didn't know what I was looking for. I knew of "the smoking gun"—the undeniable evidence of presence and practice on which the value of the work of detectives and scholars who do evidence-based work depends. And I knew that the notion of "evidence" is hotly contested in current historiography. As W. J. T. Mitchell asserts, "Evidence is a set of facts that have been mustered and put into an interpretive context and are no longer raw material. Of course, then there's a question of whether the facts are raw material" ("Status" 22). Blanche Wiesen Cooke once laughed out loud at the suggestion that one might locate the smoking gun of sexuality. Her assertion that there is no historical evidence for sexuality, performed with the comfort of one who helped to invent the field of lesbian and gay history, made me feel somewhat better about my inability to find "it" and more committed to a responsibly creative bio-historiography.

I kept going back to what was accessible: the videotape of *Peter Pan*, for example. I looked at Martin's tight little body, her characteristic gestures that never denied her female form but imbued it with boyishness. Because the habits of close reading were failing me, I thought a kinesthetic interpretation might yield meaning. I tried on her gestures myself, singing, "I Gotta Crow," imitating her steps, following her on the videotape, trying to memorize her movements onto my body.

There is a photograph in her autobiography that typified her countenance for me. She's flying on wires that are unseen in this picture. Her right leg is extended behind her, the left toe pointed at the right knee. Her arms are spread and she looks blissfully free.

So consumed was I with understanding her life, discovering her desires, that I imbued every image of my daily life with her significance. I started living with Mary Martin. She was in my dreams. She accompanied me on the bus ride into Manhattan and up Madison Avenue to the Museum of the City of New York; I stared out the window at the dog-walker with ten tangled leashes, and Martin sent me teasing glances, laughing that I'd never pin her down.

I read queer theory to find models to analyze Martin's (and my) performative desires. Valerie Traub writes that "lesbian" is "less a person than an activity, less an activity than a modality of pleasure, a position taken in relation to desire . . . better used as an adjective ('lesbian' desire) than a noun" (131). Traub's invocation of the adjective "lesbian" struck me because I could never know Martin's "person," yet I undeniably desired her. As I continued to search for the unrecognizable clues, I felt Martin's sweet, ghostly, and thoroughly bemused (lesbian?) presence all around me.

Martin's "papers," held by the Theatre Collection of the Museum of the City of New York, are photos, letters, and scraps of paper housed in numerous huge, numbered boxes. Some are loosely organized by date. I combed through the boxes one by one. I took notes but often didn't really know why I found an article compelling. I tried to take notes about identity, about references to Martin's femininity. The curator kept asking me what I was looking for. I hesitated, thinking at once that either I'd get kicked out for trying to prove that Martin was a lesbian or that he'd know that she was and would find the "lesbian" box for me. The first day I told him that I was trying to find out about "Martin's women friends." The second day I asked him if he'd ever heard that Martin was a lesbian. He said he hadn't heard it directly but come to think of it he was sure she was, and that explained all kinds of things, such as why Ethel Merman (who was straight but so butchy and terrified of lesbians) hated her, and why Larry Hagman was openly bisexual and admitted that his stepfather, Richard Halliday, was gay but guarded his mother's memory.

I sneezed over interviews in crumbling newspapers from the 1940s, handled publicity photographs with cotton gloves, chuckled over fan letters from lovelorn girls, and tried to decode a note written in September of 1960. On ivory stationery embossed with the initials B. T. in navy blue from an Upper East Side address, a Bea Traub wrote, "Dear Mr. Halliday, I am delighted that the black 'bras' arrived. I do hope Janet enjoys them."

"Janet?" I thought. "Janet Gaynor? Martin's 'lifelong best friend' with whom she had a 'uniquely close friendship'?"

It thrilled me to think about Halliday buying bras for Martin's best friend and possible lover. Married to the famous costume designer Adrian (who was closeted as a Jew and as a gay man), Gaynor was actually known to be a lesbian (known?). Gaynor won the first Academy Award for Best

Actress and retired from filmmaking in her early thirties. She and Adrian bought a ranch in Brazil, where she also later lived with her second husband (after Adrian's death), Paul Gregory. Martin and Halliday bought the adjacent property, and the couples spent much time together. Throughout their lives and more frequently in later years, Gaynor and Martin traveled together. They were in a car accident in 1982 in which Gaynor sustained injuries from which she never completely recovered. Knowing that Halliday bought bras for Gaynor placed the women intimately together.

As I continued to find no "proof," I felt increasingly defensive. I told myself firmly, I was never really a fan of Mary Martin's. I knew Maria in *The Sound of Music* as Julie Andrews, Annie Oakley in *Annie Get Your Gun* as Ethel Merman, Nellie Forbush in *South Pacific* as Mitzi Gaynor, Dolly Levi in *Hello, Dolly!* as Carol Channing. And Peter Pan? That was me. I played Peter Pan in third grade. My best friend Marcie Pachino played Wendy. When I watched and rewatched the videotape of Martin's performance, I tried to remember my own. But of course Martin seemed closer to me now than to my third grade child-self.

As Elspeth Probyn writes, "Desire points us not to a person, not to an individual, but to the movement of different body parts" (14). I tried again to position myself as Martin in her roles, laminating my body onto her poses. There's an image of her as Nellie Forbush in *South Pacific*. She's cross-dressed in a man's sailor suit, balancing on one leg with the other one lifted behind her in a kind of donkey-kick. In another, she's dressed in Bermuda shorts and a blouse tied at the waist. Her head covered with lather, she's "Washin' That Man Right Outta My Hair."

Terry Castle writes, "[T]he fact that the body is female, the voice is a woman's voice, remains inescapable. The effect (on this listener at least) is both stirring and paradoxical—like something out of a dream" (230). Castle writes of women-as-boys in opera but I came to believe that Martin's underlying (essential?) boyishness somehow rendered all of her roles as women in drag. I listened intently to Martin singing, "I'm as corny as Kansas in August, high as a flag on the Fourth of July. . . . I'm in love with a wonderful guy." Did I hear ironic self-consciousness in her voice? I stared at the photo on the back of her autobiography. Day by day, Martin's lesbianism seemed more and more obvious to me.

In a photograph from *One Touch of Venus*, Martin stands, planted solidly, her weight equally distributed on both feet. She wears a long, flowing, wind-blown, sheer chiffon gown. Martin's legs are parted and her bare arms raised in an extremely feminine costume and a conventionally sexy picture. A few months earlier, I might not have paused over this picture, but now I saw this image differently. I gazed at it through lesbian desire.

In the early 1950s, Martin performed in a television special with Noel Coward. Their coupled interactions seemed to me to mock heterosexuality. Love songs sung in Coward's fey and Martin's gawky styles sent up their implied romantic seriousness. Martin singing Cole Porter's "I Get a Kick Out of You" is shot in an extreme, almost grotesque close-up. Her voice is lovely, as she uncharacteristically varies her tempo and volume, makes her breath audible, caresses the notes. Her expression entranced me, with one eyebrow raised, half-smiling; she looked at once deliciously sexy and supremely, self-consciously amused. Judith Mayne writes that "a confusion is made between spectatorship and identification, in that pleasures taken in watching are assumed to be fully of a piece with projected ideals" (163). In other words, just because I love watching Mary Martin doesn't mean that she was a lesbian.

I was clear where I needed to go: the gay male subculture, musical theatre mavens. A gay male friend took me to lunch with another gay man who worked at Applause Books. My treat. Over pasta and white Italian bread, he named so many names I couldn't keep up, much less take notes. I soon stopped asking, "Who's she?" as it became clear that I knew nothing about musical theatre.

Andrea Weiss writes, "Rumor and gossip constitute the unrecorded history of the gay subculture" (283). Had I no access to rumor and gossip?

The questions that I kept asking myself: What is the difference between a fact and a rumor? Between a quotation made textual and one that is whispered? What is the site of sexual orientation? What is the value of the (textually) visible? What is the difference between outing and getting the facts straight?

But, as we all know, the difference is evidence. At this point, I could summarize the "evidence" I'd acquired. One: Martin had very short hair. Virtually every picture of her shows a short haircut. Two: Martin had VERY short hair. More pictures. Three: Martin, on and offstage, performed herself with a boyish quality. She was referred to as butch, boy, tomboy, unfeminine, or what Ethel Merman called her—fey. There's a photograph of her as a teenager in jeans and a shirt tied at the waist, standing with feet planted and looking, well, butch. Four: Martin had many well-publicized close friendships with women. Five: Martin had even

MORE close friendships with women. I have pictures of her with Janet Gaynor, Jean Arthur, and one of my favorites, her arms draped around and over the real Maria Von Trapp. Six: Martin's marriage to Halliday (her second) featured excessive displays of affection in the early years. All of the pictures of them show him holding her extremely closely and protectively. The lady doth protest too much. Seven: Martin was positively obsessed with Peter Pan.

"Evidence is rhetorical," Antoine Compagnon asserts ("Status" 22). But sometimes I couldn't tell which pieces of evidence were about Martin and which were about me. I listened to Martin singing from *Peter Pan* and sang with her: "Never gonna be a man [. . .] I won't grow up!" Terry Castle writes of opera: "To 'come out' as the fan of a great diva is always an embarrassing proposition—as difficult in its own way, perhaps, as coming out as a homosexual. For what can be more undignified than confessing one's susceptibility to a thrilling female voice?" (200).

I played the tape of *The Sound of Music*, the wedding march when the nuns sing, "How Do You Solve a Problem Like Maria?" and I heard the song to mean that Maria's getting married would hardly solve the problem of her really being a lesbian.

My search for "evidence," then, became intimately linked with my desire—my desire for knowledge, answers, and proof, and my desire to see a lesbian presence in musicals and to see "lesbian" on Martin's body, to hear it in her voice, to read it in her self-presentations. That I heard the chorus of women's voices singing, "How do you find a word that means Maria?" as an allusion to lesbian identity marks the tension among necessary but perhaps contradictory methodologies: historically specific definitions of lesbian, contemporary "queer" reading practices that resist heteronormativity, and an undeniably personal and idiosyncratic investment in the feminist potential of mid-twentieth-century American musicals.

As I searched for evidence based on assumptions about history and facticity, I learned that research requires and is a performance. Along the way I got caught in my own history, my own desires, and in Martin's unexpected seduction of me. My desire fueled my readings of Martin's self-performances, on and off stage, in her autobiography and interviews. My desire encouraged and necessitated active, transgressive readings, which always happen in historical work but which are denied, masked, or naturalized. My desire produced a biographical, critical, spectatorial performance of Martin, her career, her life, her performance.

Notes

1. This essay is in conversation with the research project described: see Wolf, "Mary Martin." Some of this material is differently configured in my book, *A Problem Like Maria*.

Bibliography

Acker, Kathy. "Statements on the Nature of Musical Comedy, Especially on Peter Pan." *New Theatre Review* 10 (spring 1994): 17.

Castle, Terry. *The Apparitional Lesbian: Female Homosexuality and Modern Culture*. New York: Columbia University Press, 1993.

Doty, Alexander. *Making Things Perfectly Queer: Interpreting Mass Culture*. Minneapolis: University of Minnesota Press, 1993.

Martin, Mary. *My Heart Belongs*. New York: William Morrow, 1976.

Mayne, Judith. *Cinema and Spectatorship*. New York: Routledge, 1993.

Peck, Seymour. "They Made the Sound of Music." *New York Times*, 15 November 1959.

Pichot, Ann. "Mary Martin." *King Feature Syndicate* (1939): 21.

Plum, Jay. "Cheryl Crawford." In *Passing Performances: Queer Readings of Leading Players in American Theater History*, edited by Robert A. Schanke and Kim Marra, 239–61. Ann Arbor: University of Michigan Press, 1998.

Probyn, Elspeth. "Queer Belongings: The Politics of Departure." In *Sexy Bodies: The Strange Carnalities of Feminism*, edited by Elizabeth Grosz and Elspeth Probyn, 1–18. New York: Routledge, 1995.

Roof, Judith. *Come as You Are: Sexuality and Narrative*. New York: Columbia University Press, 1996.

Rosenfield, John. "'Howyah, Hon?' or Merely Mary Martin: The Studio Can't Understand It, but Her Heart Belongs to Daddy." Mary Martin Collection, Theatre Collection, Museum of the City of New York.

Rupp, Leila J. "'Imagine My Surprise': Women's Relationships in Mid-Twentieth Century America." In *Hidden from History: Reclaiming the Gay and Lesbian Past*, edited by Martin Bauml Duberman, Martha Vicinus, and George Chauncey Jr., 395–410. New York: New American Library, 1989.

"The Status of Evidence: A Roundtable." *PMLA* 111 (January 1996): 21–31.

Stone, Irving. "Mary Martin's Marriage." *Life*, 8 January 1956, n.p.

Straayer, Chris. "The Hypothetical Lesbian Heroine in Narrative Feature Film." In *Out in Culture: Gay, Lesbian, and Queer Essays on Popular Culture*, edited by Corey K. Creekmur and Alexander Doty, 44–59. Durham, N.C.: Duke University Press, 1995.

Traub, Valerie. "The Ambiguities of 'Lesbian' Viewing Pleasure: The (Dis)Articulations of Black Widow." In *Out in Culture: Gay, Lesbian, and Queer Essays on Popular Culture*, edited by Corey K. Creekmur and Alexander Doty, 115–36. Durham, N.C.: Duke University Press, 1995.

Vicinus, Martha. "'They Wonder to Which Sex I Belong': The Historical Roots of the Modern Lesbian Identity." In *The Lesbian and Gay Studies Reader*, edited by Henry Abelove, Michele Aina Barale, and David M. Halperin, 432–52. New York: Routledge, 1993.

Weiss, Andrea. "A Queer Feeling When I Look at You: Hollywood Stars and Lesbian Spectatorship in the 1930s." In *Stardom: Industry of Desire*, edited by Christine Gledhill, 283–99. New York: Routledge, 1991.

Wolf, Stacy. "Mary Martin: Washin' That Man Right Outta Her Hair." In *Passing Performances: Queer Readings of Leading Players in American Theater History*, edited by Robert A. Schanke and Kim Marra, 283–302. Ann Arbor: University of Michigan Press, 1998.

——. *A Problem Like Maria: Gender and Sexuality in the American Musical.* Ann Arbor: University of Michigan Press, 2000.

——. "The Queer Pleasures of Mary Martin and Broadway: The Sound of Music as a Lesbian Musical." *Modern Drama* 39 (spring 1996): 51–63.

5

Too Wild for Her
Own Good

☙ Searching for the Real
Calamity Jane

M. Heather Carver

When I was nine I had a role in the ensemble cast of the musical *Calamity Jane*. The experience piqued my interest in her life. I remember singing songs from the show with my sister during our family vacation to South Dakota one summer. Every time we stopped at an "authentic" Wild West spot, we would interrogate the guide about Calamity Jane. The answers we received were typical of much of the biographical information on Jane; she was daring, spunky, and unusual for her time.

A few years ago I decided to create my own one-woman show about Martha Jane Cannary, better known as Calamity Jane. While researching and creating my play, I realized the multiple layers of performativity that her life story entails. Cannary's performance when she embodied the role of Calamity Jane propelled her to fame, but her everyday life performances of both masculinity and femininity are what make her an intriguing character to perform. The central problem in my play thus became the problem of women's representation, authority, and agency. Performing Calamity Jane's multiple selves, as depicted in history, enabled me to wrestle with this problem throughout the play. The audience is left to decide for themselves who Jane was, and who she continues to represent.

In researching material for my performance, I found that many historical works on the Wild West make passing references to her, but few writers of the Wild West genre have focused their attention solely on Calamity Jane. She has not been ignored by all writers, however, as historical fiction novelists such as Mrs. George E. Spencer (1887), Duncan Aikman (1927), Glenn Clairmonte (1959), and Ron Fontes and Justine

Korman (1992) have written tales about Calamity Jane by drawing on documentation of her activities in the Dakota Territory. Edward Wheeler (1885) cast her as a heroine of the *Deadwood Dick* dime novel series, and a more modern writer of Wild West tales, Larry McMurtry, made Calamity a leading character in *Buffalo Girls* (1990). In fact, there are more "fictionalized" accounts of Calamity Jane than attempts to chronicle her life story in a more traditional biography. In terms of so-called nonfiction, Roberta Beed Sollid's book, *Calamity Jane: A Study in Historical Criticism,* is positioned alongside Martha Cannary's autobiography, *The Life and Adventures of Calamity Jane by Herself,* and the diary Jean Hickok McCormick produced, now published as *Calamity Jane's Letters to Her Daughter.*

In creating an auto/biographical performance of Calamity Jane, I realized that it would be problematic to use any one of these texts as the sole resource. Questions immediately emerged about authenticity, identity, history, reality, and representation and made it difficult to determine who was the "real" Calamity Jane. I quickly found that an attempt to answer this question became counterproductive, for in this postmodern world of multiple identities it is more important to show the complexities of the self in performance. I therefore chose to include the problems of authenticity, representation, and identity, as they relate to autobiography and biography, in my performance of Calamity Jane.

WILL THE REAL CALAMITY JANE PLEASE STAND UP?

(A table occupies the center of a smoky room. There are several chairs around the table, each with various clothing items, hats, and props. One woman, JANE THE NARRATOR, *sits at the table, her face shrouded in shadows. A spot hits* JANE THE NARRATOR *in the face. She looks up and talks directly to the audience.)*

JANE THE NARRATOR: Hello everybody! I'm a loose woman! I'm a mother! I'm a hero! I'm a troublemaker! I'm a lover! I'm a prostitute! I'm sexually confused! I'm an oddity! I'm a drunk! I'm angry! I'm . . . oh hell, I'm whatever they say I am.

*(*JANE THE NARRATOR *sits down at her place and the spotlight goes out. Lights come back up on the table, and* JANE THE PARTY GIRL *stands up and stumbles slightly. She wears a feather boa and matching headband around her forehead. She picks a book off the table and wanders downstage toward the audience.)*

JANE THE PARTY GIRL: Who the hell am I? Who the hell's business is it, any-
how? Is it Miss Roberta Beed Sollid's business? I don't tootin' think so.
She called me a loose woman, says, "No career is so elusive to the historian as that of a loose woman. Calamity Jane was that sort of woman, and
known details about her life are hard to find. Like most prostitutes and
drunkards she left little behind in the way of tangible evidence which
could be used by historians to reconstruct the story of her checkered career." (*She snorts.*) Checkered career? Who the hell does she think she is?
Busybody. At least I had a career. Ain't it just like people to take a famous
gal like me and try and exploit 'em for their own gain? And to do it by
callin' 'em names? That's the worst kind of dirty, low down deal. (*Clears
throat.*) Now, here's the parts Ms. Roberta Beed Sollid did git right. I was
born in the Midwest, in the late 1840s. Course, she weren't good enough
to be any more detailed than that. She knows I liked to keep company
with miners, soldiers, and railroaders, but she looks at that as some kind
of character flaw. Those are the best people I ever knowed. (*Making an
angry face.*) All that ain't so bad, though. It's calling me a liar that gets me
riled. She says that I wrote a autobiography that's nothin' but lies. Who
does she think she is? And no, Ms. Roberta Beed Sollid, I didn't die a
lonely, broken old woman.

    (JANE THE PARTY GIRL *harrumphs and stomps back to the poker table.
The lights dim and then come back up on* JANE THE WESTERN HERO. *She
is wearing a red bandanna, duster coat, and an enormous cowboy hat.*)

JANE THE WESTERN HERO: Howdy, folks! I guess you could 'pose that I'se got
it easier than some of these other girls. (*She gestures toward the table.*) I'm
the Disney-ized Calamity Jane, and I'm a red-blooded American heeero!
To most folk, I'm a genu-wine legend, just like Pocahontas and Saca-
jawea and my good friend Annie Oakley. I'm part of the "American Frontier Series," whatever the heck that is, ladies and gentlemen. Watch
this . . . (JANE THE WESTERN HERO *ties a bandanna over her face and pan-
tomimes driving a stagecoach, running around in circles on the stage, cracking a
whip.*) Wee-hah, we're coming home!

    (JANE THE NARRATOR *alternates her lines with* WESTERN HERO —
shown by removing her hat.)

JANE THE NARRATOR: This is the main street of Piedmont, in Wyoming Territory. Jane the Western Hero is drivin' her coach, behind six sweaty
horses, drivin' 'em hard. There are cowpokes all around. There are fancy
ladies doin' their shopping, gettin' dust on their silk dresses. "My goodness, what a young man to be driving such a dangerous route," one fancy

lady is heard to remark, as she exits the coach. Well, before you could spit or swaller, Jane the Western Hero drove that coach right up the stairs into the Silver Dollar Saloon.

(Puts the hat on.)

JANE THE WESTERN HERO: Whoa, boy! Wee-hah!

(Removes hat to become JANE THE NARRATOR.*)*

JANE THE NARRATOR: And much to the surprise of all the gamblers and menfolk half in the bag, that weren't a young man at all . . . it was Jane the Western Hero.

(Puts the hat on.)

JANE THE WESTERN HERO: I'm Martha Jane Cannary! Let 'er rip!

(Removes hat, JANE THE NARRATOR *takes over.)*

JANE THE NARRATOR: 'Course, Ms. Beed Sollid wasn't the only one who thought she could make a penny off my hide. No, there've been others. One damn fool writer of fictions even tried to argue I's a hermaphrodite, whatever the hell that is.

*(*JANE THE NARRATOR *fades into the background and another Jane emerges. It is* JANE THE WOMAN'S WOMAN. *She wears blue jeans, a red flannel shirt, and two enormous guns in a belt around her waist.)*

JANE THE WOMAN'S WOMAN: There's this one lady, a historian for *Time* and *Life*, who says I couldn't get along with so-called proper women. Well . . . *(She slowly smiles.)* I'll allow there might be some truth to that. I worked as a bartender in Deadwood, South Dakota . . . that's where I met my one true love, but we'll get back to that . . . one of us will. Anyway, I worked as a bartender and I did run into trouble with the women of virtue. They wanted to run me out of town, they wanted to bullwhip me and shave me bald. Oncest, they came for me in the saloon and I had to knock 'em ass over teakettle to git away. I done what I wanted, when I wanted. I worked as an army scout, a wagon freighter, an Indian fighter, and yes, when I felt like it, a woman of pleasure. And I liked a nip on the bottle oncest in a while, but anyone who says they don't is a damnable liar, I say. I shore enough wasn't the only woman in the West, and they weren't all, or nearly all, as independent minded as me but, by gawd, we all worked to make the world a better place for us and ours.

(She raises her fist in salute and fades into the shadows. JANE THE NARRATOR *re-emerges.)*

JANE THE NARRATOR: We had us a daughter. It's our progeny we count on to defend us when we're gone, ain't it? We did all right with ours, I dare say.

(She steps into the shadows and is replaced by JANE THE WRITER. *She has*

a woolen shawl around her shoulders. She's carrying a lantern, a tablet of paper, a pencil, and a Bowie knife. She sets everything but the pencil and the knife down on a small table. She puts her foot on the chair in front of the table and leans in toward the audience.)

JANE THE WRITER: I've got to tell the real story, 'cause I'm the only one who can. I wrote it all down. (*She taps the tablet of paper with the point of the knife. She begins to sharpen the point of the pencil with the knife.*) I left this diary for my daughter. I had to give her up, you know. The plains were no place to raise a little girl, you know. It weren't easy . . . givin' her up, I mean. I was married twice, once to Wild Bill Hickok. That's right, the very one and the same Bill Hickok, met his terrible end at Deadwood. I's eighteen at the time. Bill was thirty-one. We was married by the Reverends W. F. Warren and W. K. Snipes. I never did know what the W's were for. I felt a powerful love for that man. I wrote about him, of course. (*Flips open the tablet and reads.*) We met one day, and we both found we still love each other better than ever. I forgot everthing when I was near him. No one else ever knew—if anyone hinted such to me, I hauled off and knocked them down . . . we both lived a life of lies. (*She looks sad, then she smiles, remembering.*) My daughter, my little girl, Jean , was from Bill's seed. She was born in September, back in 1873, I recall, in Livingston, Wyoming. Bill was already gone when she came along, and I was befriended by an Englishman—a sea captain for the Cunard line. We went to Omaha, then all the way back east to Virginny, where I gave up my rights to my little girl. (*She looks up and out at the audience, reflecting on her life.*) Losing Bill and my little girl. That's a powerful lot of loss. My little girl found out about me when the captain died, which was, of course, long after I died. They buried me next to Wild Bill, out at Mount Moriah Cemetery. He, meaning the captain, left my papers to her, including the diary. Her husband left her when he found out who her momma was. Damned men.

(*She shakes her head. She steps into the shadows and* JANE THE WOMAN'S WOMAN *steps forward, laughing.*)

JANE THE WOMAN'S WOMAN: We know what they're worth, don't we?

(JANE THE WOMAN'S WOMAN *steps back into the shadows and* JANE THE WRITER *reemerges.*)

JANE THE WRITER: My little girl moved back to the States after I died and she appeared in the rodeos and the western shows, tellin' how she was my daughter. I didn't leave her much. I hope she gets somethin' outta bein' my kin. Well, we're gonna share a little more of our story with you now.

(She stands up and walks into the shadows, leaving the lantern burning on the table. JANE THE NARRATOR *reemerges.)*

JANE THE NARRATOR: My maiden name was Martha Cannary, was born in Princeton, Missouri, May first, 1852. Father and mother natives of Ohio. Had two brothers and three sisters, I being the oldest of the children. As a child I always had a fondness for adventure . . .

*(*JANE THE NARRATOR *wanders into the shadows.* JANE THE PARTY GIRL *reemerges.)*

JANE THE PARTY GIRL: That fondness for adventure took me to the Indian fighters, where I hid my sex and joined up with General Custer as a scout at Fort Russell, Wyoming, in 1870. I soon felt right at home in men's clothes.

*(*JANE THE PARTY GIRL *turns and walks back into the shadows and* JANE THE WOMAN'S WOMAN *appears.)*

JANE THE WOMAN'S WOMAN: Was in Arizona up to the winter of 1871 and during that time I had a great many adventures with the Indians. I was considered the most reckless and daring rider and one of the best shots in the western country.

*(*JANE THE WOMAN'S WOMAN *smiles, points at her chest with her thumb, and walks into the shadows.* JANE THE WESTERN HERO *comes out.)*

JANE THE WESTERN HERO: 'Twas during this campaign that I was christened "Calamity" by Captain Egan. 'Twas on Goose Creek, in Wyoming. When we returned to the post one time we were ambushed about a mile and a half from our destination. Egan was shot. I galloped back with all haste to his side and got there in time to catch him as he was fallin'. On recoverin', he said, "I name you Calamity Jane, the heroine of the plains."

*(*JANE THE WESTERN HERO *stands up, raises her arms in victory, and walks into the shadows.* JANE THE WRITER *emerges and sits down at the table.)*

JANE THE WRITER: Well, folks, us girls is just about out of time. So, you tell us, who is the real Calamity? Are we a loose woman? Are we a mother? Are we a hero? Are we a troublemaker? Are we a lover? Are we a prostitute? Are we sexually confused? Are we an oddity? Are we a drunk? Are we angry? We're . . . oh hell, are we whatever they say we are? Could there be some of all of those in us? Would that make us so different from y'all? *(She looks toward the table, shrouded in shadows.)* Will the real Calamity Jane please stand up? *(Beat.)* Will the real Calamity Jane please stand up?

*(*JANE THE WRITER *looks around and smiles. After a beat, she reaches out and turns out the lantern. The stage is dark.)*

Bibliography

Aikman, Duncan. *Calamity Jane and the Lady Wildcats*. New York: H. Holt and Company, 1927.

Cannary, Martha Jane. *The Life and Adventures of Calamity Jane by Herself.* N.p., 1896.

Clairmonte, Glenn. *Calamity Was the Name for Jane*. Denver, Colo.: Sage, 1959.

Hickok, Martha Jane Cannary. *Calamity Jane's Letters to Her Daughter*. San Lorenzo, Calif.: Shameless Hussy Press, 1976.

McMurtry, Larry. *Buffalo Girls*. New York: Simon and Schuster, 1990.

Paine, Clarence. "Wild Bill Hickok and Calamity Jane." In *The Black Hills*, edited by Roderick Peattie, 151–76. New York: Vanguard, 1952.

Peattie, Roderick, ed. *The Black Hills*. New York: Vanguard, 1952.

Rafferty, Terrence. "Larger Than Life: Walter Hill's Wild Bill." *New Yorker*, 4 December 1995, 115–18.

Reiter, Joan Swallow. *The Old West: The Women*. Alexandria, Va.: Time-Life, 1978.

Rosa, Joseph. *They Called Him Wild Bill: The Life and Adventures of James Butler Hickok*. Norman: University of Oklahoma Press, 1964.

Sollid, Roberta Beed. *Calamity Jane: A Study in Historical Criticism*. Helena: Western Press, Montana Historical Society, 1958.

Spencer, Mrs. George E. *Calamity Jane: A Story of the Black Hills*. New York: Cassell, 1887.

Wheeler, Edward L. *Calamity Jane: The Heroine of Whoop-Up*. New York: Beadle and Adams, 1885.

6

Georgia O'Keeffe x Catherine Rogers

e&

Catherine Rogers

An earlier version of *Georgia O'Keeffe x Catherine Rogers* was presented at the CMA Theatre, University of Texas, Austin, on 18 October 1999. Director was Ted Altschuler. Solo performer was Catherine Rogers. Sound designer was Esther Regelson of RegelSound. Recorded pianist was John Gaffney.

to Miriam

(*There's a red bentwood chair stage left. There are three empty music stands center stage. From stage right to stage left, music stands are A, B, C. There is a work table upstage right.* SOUND: *Beethoven's "Appassionata."* GEORGIA O'KEEFFE *wears black coat and hat, carries black suitcase, walks to chair. Dusts off chair with her glove. Sits. Opens the book she carries.* SOUND: *Airport ambiance.*)

O'KEEFFE: Words . . .

AIRPORT ANNOUNCER (*tape*): Attention Albuquerque passengers. Attention Albuquerque passengers. Flight 242 is now boarding at gate two for New York LaGuardia Field. Flight 242 for New York now boarding at gate two.

(*Reads through the book. It is the biography* A Woman on Paper: Georgia O'Keeffe, *by Anita Pollitzer.*)

O'KEEFFE: Words . . .

AIRPORT ANNOUNCER (*tape*): Attention, Albuquerque passenger Georgia O'Keeffe.

(O'KEEFFE *reads. Mutters.*)

O'KEEFFE: Words . . .

AIRPORT ANNOUNCER (*tape*): Georgia O'Keeffe, please report to gate two for
   boarding . . .

O'KEEFFE: Words . . . are like the wind. "[T]he man who works in my garden
   said a few days ago, 'Words are like the wind.'—He only speaks Spanish—I only speak English."[1]

AIRPORT ANNOUNCER (*tape*): Albuquerque passenger, Georgia O'Keeffe.
   (O'KEEFFE *hears the announcement. Shakes it off.*)

O'KEEFFE: New Mexico
   "Anita Pollitzer
   419 West 115th Street
   New York, New York

   Dear Anita:

   I read your manuscript some time ago and it has lain on my table—probably because you are an old friend I do not like to say to you what I would
   say to someone else. . . .
       You write of the legends others have made up about me—but when
   I read your manuscript, it seems as much a myth as all the others.

       (SOUND: *Phone rings.* CATHERINE ROGERS *as* O'KEEFFE *glances fur-
       tively at the audience. Has someone left a cell phone turned on?*)

   I really believe that to call this my biography when it has so little to do
   with me is impossible."[2]

       (SOUND: *Phone rings.* CATHERINE *steals a glance at audience. What is
       that phone?* CATHERINE *realizes where the ringing phone is. Sheepishly
       extracts a bright red cell phone from her bag.*)

   Hello?

       (*Apologetic gesture to the audience. Eek, it's my mother. I'll just be a
       minute.*)

   Mom . . . Hi Mom, hi Mutti . . . (*Mom talks.*) um . . . Mom . . . Mom . . .
   Mom! yeah . . . I can't talk right now, I'm doing a performance . . . a performance . . . now. . . . Yeah, the people are here now. . . . In Texas, at the
   university.

AIRPORT ANNOUNCER (*tape*): Attention Albuquerque passengers . . .

CATHERINE: Huh? Georgia O'Keeffe . . . you know Georgia O'Keeffe the
   artist. You don't? Why not? They look like what? Well, she painted a lot

of things besides flowers. How's your own painting going? Dab by dab, yeah I know what you mean. There's the announcement. I gotta go. Good-bye.

AIRPORT ANNOUNCER (*tape*): Attention Albuquerque passengers. Attention Albuquerque passengers. Flight 242 is now boarding at gate two for New York LaGuardia Field. Flight 242 for New York now boarding at gate two.

> (CATHERINE *becomes* O'KEEFFE *again. Grabs her stuff. Goes for the plane.*
> SOUND: *Phone rings.* CATHERINE *drops her stuff in the middle of the stage. Dives for the phone. Takes most of this call at table right.*)

CATHERINE: Hello? Mom I . . . My job? This *is* a job . . . yes they're paying me. . . . Yes, I'm in it. Yes, I wrote it. . . . Telemarketing? I haven't had to do telemarketing for four years now. . . . Actually, Mother, I wrote it when I was working on the child abuse hotline. . . . No . . . did you know I'm teaching at NYU, by the way . . .

> (CATHERINE *puts the phone down. Finishes setting up. Keeps picking up the phone saying "Mm-hm, yup, I agree," et cetera.*)

Yes, Mom, you're right . . . I mean, no! I don't take all my clothes off. No . . . that was a different show. Yes, she did. I am perfectly aware of that. Georgia O'Keeffe did pose nude for Alfred Stieglitz. Mother, I am not going to pose nude. No, I don't use chocolate. There are no yams, no vegetables. Mother, there is no food whatsoever in this piece. Flowers. Yes, I know what flowers look like.

> (SOUND: *"Appassionata."*)

OK, there's the music. Bye. Yes, it's John playing "Appassionata." She used to listen to Beethoven all the time. John, my little brother? You remember him? Sorry, I know it's painful, Mom. I gotta go.

> (CATHERINE *hangs up.*)

All right, where were we. I'm sorry. I know I should not let her cross my boundaries like that. My therapist is working with me on that. She says my identity is too tied up with my mother's. Is she here? Is my therapist here? Tell you what, can we start again? Let's start again . . . Never mind the first sound cue, Allison (*names sound technician*).

> (CATHERINE *performs a fast forward version of the first scene.*)

So I'm over here. Pretend I have the suitcase. La da da da da da da da . . . dum da da dum da da dum da da da . . . I walk on. Dust chair. Sit. Suitcase. Dream . . . "Georgia O'Keeffe please report." Wake up startled . . . Reach in . . . Anita Pollitzer biography. *What the hell is this about* . . . it's certainly not my biography . . . and . . . Roll sound cue 2!

> (SOUND: *Phone rings.*)

Mom? Well, apparently these people *would* want to pay to see me. But
they probably don't want to pay to see me talking to you all night. . . . I'm
sorry . . . OK, OK, yes I gotta go. Yes, you break a leg too . . . Oh, I
mean . . . Good-bye. Say hi to Dad for me . . . no . . . no . . . Mom . . .
Dad! Hi, I'm in Texas doing a performance.

> *(This call is going to be longer than expected.* CATHERINE *pulls out some
> Georgia O'Keeffe paraphernalia from her bag: books, a calendar, a diary.
> "Show and tell." Hands out to the audience. Look at these pictures. Com-
> pare and contrast. Discuss among yourselves. Places a stack of "paintings"
> on music stand A showing* Special No. 4, 1915. *Turns music stand B to
> face upstage and places a stack of "paintings" on it. Places the old-fashioned
> phone on stand B. Stand C remains empty.)*

Georgia O'Keeffe. Yeah, a good Irish girl. Like you . . . well, you're not
a gir— . . . *(Passes book to audience.)* Here look at this . . . No, no jokes,
Dad! I heard the one about the nuns and the station wagon . . . no I heard
a frog goes into a bar . . . no . . . Dad . . . . the snail? Oh, I love the snail.
OK you can tell the snail. Wait. We have to tell everybody. My dad wants
to tell us a joke. OK, a man hears a knock . . . let's make it a woman,
Dad . . . A woman hears a knock at the door. She opens the door. It's a
snail. She picks up the snail and throws it across the road into the bushes.

> *(Listen to Dad.)*

Ten years later. OK, ten years later the woman hears another knock at the
door. Opens the door. It's the snail. The snail says, "What the hell was
that about?" *(To audience.)* Thank you, thank you. *(Back to Dad.)* It's the
timing, Dad. OK, thanks, Dad. Yeah, bye. I lo[ve you].

> *(Return to chair just in time as airport announcement runs.)*

AIRPORT ANNOUNCER *(tape)*: Attention Albuquerque passengers, now boarding . . . Chicago passengers . . . at gate two for New York LaGuardia . . .
Chicago passengers at gate two for Austin, Texas . . . Attention passengers, will Georgia O'Keeffe . . . will Catherine Rogers please report . . .
Attention Chicago passengers, now boarding for Austin, Texas.

CATHERINE: Words are like the wind.

> *(Pulls out letter. Reads.)*

Dear . . . Chicago was beautiful . . . when will I see you again . . . oh,
wait, that's not her . . .

> *(Wrong color letter.* CATHERINE *tries to get rid of it.)*

AIRPORT ANNOUNCER *(tape)*: Final call for passenger Georgia O'Keeffe.
Mrs. Georgia O'Keeffe please report to gate two, Mrs. O'Keeffe . . .

O'KEEFFE: Mrs.!?

(O'KEEFFE grabs her bag and marches off left in search of the offending announcer. Reenters, crossing from up left to table up right. Drops bag. She is a young art student. All she wants to do is get to the work. But she has to put the groceries away. Plums in a bowl? O'KEEFFE draws on a yellow legal pad, rips off page after page, throws pages on the floor through the following. Slow. Concentrating.)

O'KEEFFE: "At the moment I am very annoyed. — I have the shapes—on yellow scratch paper—in my mind for over a year—and I cannot see the color for them—"

(She searches the easel upstage center for answers to the color.)

"I've drawn them again—and again—it is from something I have heard again and again till I hear it in the wind—but I can not get the color for it—only shapes."[3]

(Looks up. Scans the audience. Points. Accuses.)

You want to know about Stieglitz, dontcha?

(O'KEEFFE refuses to "tell." Resumes where she left off.)

But I can't get the color for it. Only shapes.

(O'KEEFFE climbs on the table.)

O'KEEFFE: "Dear Anita—Did you ever have something to say and feel as if the whole side of the wall wouldn't be big enough to say it on and then" *(O'KEEFFE jumps down into the studio. Crawls among the papers.)* "sit down on the floor and try to get it on to a sheet of charcoal paper . . . I've been crawling around on the floor till I have cramps in my feet— . . .
I always have a hard time finding words for anything . . .
I wonder if I am a raving lunatic for trying to make these things—
You know—I don't care if I am—but I do wonder sometimes."[4]
I cannot get the color for this.

(Sees audience. They are no help.)

You want to know about Stieglitz, dontcha.
(O'KEEFFE takes a stack of "paintings" from the suitcase. Tucks the paintings under her arm, and climbs the stairs to Stieglitz's gallery at 291 Fifth Avenue. Strides into the gallery, hand outstretched to Alfred Stieglitz.)
Good afternoon, Mr. Stieglitz. Georgia O'Keeffe. I'd like to know, Mr. Stieglitz, what my drawings are doing on your wall. Without my per-

mission? Yes, my friend at art school—Anita Pollitzer—told me she brought you my drawings, but I didn't give her perm—. . . and then I heard there was an exhibit by "Virginia" O'Keeffe down at 291. Imagine my surprise. Virginia? I am Georgia, another state altogether. I will thank you very kindly, Mr. Stieglitz, to take these down at once.

My private life? Is private, Mr. Stieglitz. You may not hang me on your wall and you may not . . . oh, these, well, I do have some new . . .

(O'KEEFFE *places her "portfolio" on music stand C. On top is* Blue No. IV *which she "shows" to Stieglitz.*)

You may not ask me about my private—oh, yes I like it, too. Not my private life. Good day!

(*She holds out her hand for a stiff handshake. He turns it to kiss.*)

The blue is something I'm trying to say about . . . private life, Mr. Stieglitz . . . Alfred . . .

(O'KEEFFE *is in a pose resembling Stieglitz Plate 4.*)[5]

(SOUND: *Camera click #1.*)

(*24 seconds: Music stand A. Moves* Special No. 4 *to behind. Reveals Stieglitz Plate 4.* O'KEEFFE *shyly, slowly unbuttons her coat and folds it over the chair. She wears a long black skirt and a black blouse with a white collar. She assumes the pose of Stieglitz Plate 2.*)

(SOUND: *Camera click #2.*)

(*10 seconds: Moves around music stand B. Turns stand around to reveal Stieglitz Plate 2.*)

(SOUND: *Camera click #3.*)

(*21 seconds:* O'KEEFFE, *less shy, more engaged in the act, takes off her hat, her collar. Unbuttons her blouse. Under the blouse is a black close-fitting T-shirt. She turns upstage and drops the blouse to the floor. Still facing upstage she loosens her hair and stretches her arms upward as in Plate 9.*)

(SOUND: *Camera click #4.*)

(*21 seconds: Music stand B. Drops Plate 2 to the floor, revealing Plate 9.* O'KEEFFE, *now thoroughly engaged in the act, unbuttons her skirt and lets it drop. Music stand C. Drops* Blue No. IV *to the floor revealing Plate 7.*)

(SOUND: *Camera click #5.*)

(SOUND: *Phone rings.*)

(CATHERINE *looks over her shoulder, deer in the headlights. She quickly grabs the nearest item and slaps it over her body. It's the Georgia O'Keeffe calendar with the flaming Red Poppy strategically placed in the "fig leaf" position. She hobbles over to chair and answers the phone.*)

CATHERINE: Hello? Mom, this is a bad time. . . . They are not *off!* This is just pretend. I have tights on. See, these are clothes. . . . Yes, Mom, you're right . . . I mean, no! I don't take all my clothes off. . . . No *that was a different show*. That was my piece about therapy, my hair, Einstein, sleeping with married men. . . . This is performance art, it's about the body . . . it's not like posing for *Playboy*. . . . I use my body as . . . Yes, she did pose nude for him. They got married, OK? Does that make it better? I know, they weren't married when she posed nude. (*Joke to audience.*) But *he* was married. . . .

STIEGLITZ (*tape*): What do you want to do more than anything?

(CATHERINE *hands phone to audience member.*)

CATHERINE: Here, would you talk to her? . . . Is my therapist here? Doctor, are you here? I thought she would be here.

(*Stieglitz's voice on tape jolts* CATHERINE *into dressing* O'KEEFFE.)

STIEGLITZ (*tape*): What do you want to do more than anything? (O'KEEFFE *smoothes her hair and puts it up again, seductively.*) More than anything . . . To teach art?

O'KEEFFE: I would like a year to paint.

(O'KEEFFE *looks to Stieglitz expecting an answer. After a little silence,* CATHERINE *breaks the* O'KEEFFE *character.*)

CATHERINE: I think that can be arranged. That's what he said. (*Wistfully.*) A year to paint! When we lived in Texas, my husband—my *ex*-husband— worked so I could have a year to write. What I wrote got me a fellowship to write this.

(CATHERINE *becomes* O'KEEFFE *again. Performs a "Year to Paint Dance." She juggles the photos and the paintings in the Georgia O'Keeffe Calendar as her work is constantly interrupted by the "clicks" of Stieglitz's camera.*)

(SOUND: 6 *camera clicks.*)

(*At last she drops all the photos to the ground.* O'KEEFFE *tries a self-portrait of her face. It doesn't work. Walks on top of mirror, looks down. Smiles. Paints radically.* O'KEEFFE *turns music stands around to display paintings as in a gallery:*

Music stand A: *White Trumpet Flower.*

Music stand B: *Radiator Building—Night, New York.*

Music stand C: *Grey Line with Black, Blue, and Yellow.*)

O'KEEFFE: "[M]y year on the wall."[6]

(Grey Line *painting is upside down.* O'KEEFFE *goes to music stand C, rights the painting. The exhibit is hung. She surveys the work triumphantly. Runs for the newspaper. Reads.*)

O'KEEFFE: *New York Herald*, February 4, 1923.

CATHERINE: A year to paint? That was five years.

O'KEEFFE: February 4, 1923.

CATHERINE: My birthday . . . ahem . . . oh . . . sorry . . .

O'KEEFFE: *New York Herald*, Henry McBride on One Hundred Pictures by Georgia O'Keeffe: "Georgia O'Keeffe is . . . a B. F. [before Freud] . . . She became free without the aid of Freud . . . There was another who took the place of Freud. . . . It is of course Alfred Stieglitz."[7]

> That's hilarious, Henry.

CATHERINE: January 7, I go to the shrink. 1989. Oops.

> *(CATHERINE also reads the paper.)*

CATHERINE: December 11, 1924, Georgia O'Keeffe marries Alfred Stieglitz.

O'KEEFFE: I felt as if I had lost a leg.

CATHERINE: Oh, dear. How's my mom?

> *(CATHERINE retrieves the phone from audience member.)*

Mutti? Mom? How do you like it so far? What's not to get? She met Stieglitz. He brought her to New York from Texas. He housed her at his studio so she could paint. She painted the One Hundred Pictures exhibit. She married Stieglitz. What do you mean it's not about her? It's all about me. It doesn't paint the picture. What can I do? Mom, I have forty-eight minutes; she lived for ninety-eight years, do the math. How am I supposed to . . . get the whole picture. Part of it? Part of the picture. OK. What part do you want to see?

> *(Music stand B. Photo of O'Keeffe in hat and coat. Steiglitz Plate 36.*
> CATHERINE *tries to become the photo through the following. Still on phone with Mother.)*

Her first big sale. That figures. OK. Her First Big Sale: 1928. She's forty. Twenty-five thousand dollars—what's that, half a million dollars today—to an anonymous buyer in France. Yes, Mutti . . . technically Stieglitz sold it. But she painted it. What? Oh, it was lilies, the *Calla Lilies*. Mutti, would you get off the flowers?

What? I don't have to worry it's all about me. The half a million dollars is definitely not about me. Yeah, Mom, you're right. It's nothing like me. Thanks for the help.

> *(CATHERINE puts the phone down, but doesn't hang up. Shouts at phone.)*

Did you know I'm teaching at the Parsons School of Design? Teaching artists to use words . . .

> *(CATHERINE finishes her attempt to look like the photo. Does eyebrows with a pencil.)*

How am I supposed to be her? Who do I think I am? I don't look like her.
(Shouts at phone again.)
She's gorgeous. She looks like Dad. All right. The *Calla Lilies.*
(CATHERINE becomes O'KEEFFE again. Takes the Calla Lilies *painting. Walks slowly across the stage. Silent. Then breaks into a Groucho Marx stride.)*

O'KEEFFE: Wanna buy a painting?

CATHERINE: Hey!

(CATHERINE stops abruptly. Looks out into the audience.)
I'm sorry. This is getting to be a mess. I'm sorry, Lynn *(names producer).* What made me think I could do this. What was I thinking . . . Georgia O'Keeffe. This isn't her . . . it's the "All about Me Show."

And I haven't had the time. . . . I mean I work nine hundred day jobs just to pay an exorbitant rent. . . . Not to mention my mother interrupting . . . well, my therapist is trying to work with me on that. . . . Is she here? Is my therapist here? Doctor? I thought she was going to be here.

What am I supposed to do . . . to "perform" O'Keeffe? Move my hand like I'm painting a painting? I'm not a painter, I'm a writer. . . . This room is a mess. Georgia O'Keeffe would never have such a mess.

(She picks up the bowl of plums.)
Food! I told my mother no food.

(CATHERINE tries to tidy up the space. She starts packing to leave.)
Look at this . . . it's not her painting . . . it's some plastic stuff I got from Superior Copy. These clothes? The Gap! They are my clothes. To "perform" Georgia O'Keeffe? I should take you to the museum and walk through it with you . . . her work . . . her work speaks for itself . . . ninety-eight years of her work . . . she doesn't need some "performahnce artiste" to justify her existence . . . who the hell do I think I am . . .

Let's just call it a night . . .

(CATHERINE begins to pack and can't help telling things about O'Keeffe until she has resumed the identity of O'KEEFFE. Put on the hat, the body, the voice . . . As CATHERINE packs the calendar, she finds The Lawrence Tree. *She sinks to the table holding the calendar in the air above her. She lies on her back under the "tree.")*

Oh, look at this. Isn't this beautiful. Even the cheap imitation on my calendar . . . is beautiful. I know, you're not supposed to say "beautiful" about art in the twentieth century. But . . .

O'KEEFFE: "Filling a space in a beautiful way—that is what art means to me."[8]

"I had one particular painting—that tree in Lawrences front yard as you see it when you lie under it on the table—with stars—it looks as tho it is standing on its head."[9]

"Taos, August 1929. . . . It is 5 A.M.—I have been up for about an hour—watching the moon grow pale—and the dawn come—. . . one bright—bright star—so bright that it seems like a tear in its eye—The flowers are so lovely—. . . I wanted you to see it."[10]

(O'KEEFFE *pulls* White Flower *from behind* Grey and Blue *on music stand C and places on music stand A. The "Passion for Whiteness Cantata."*)

"The large White Flower with the golden heart is something I have to say about White—quite different from what White has been meaning to me."[11]

I have a passion for whiteness in all its forms.

I have a passion for whiteness in all its forms.

(CATHERINE *finds a note among the photographs.*)

CATHERINE: "I have a passion for whiteness in all its forms," Alfred Stieglitz![12]

(O'KEEFFE *rushes to music stand C, pulls down* Grey and Blue *to reveal* Red Canna.)

O'KEEFFE: "*Color* is one of the great things in the world that makes life worth living to me."[13]

(*There is squawking from the phone.* CATHERINE *grabs it.*)

CATHERINE: Mom! . . . Mom, that's what flowers look like!

(CATHERINE *opens the book* Georgia O'Keeffe, *by Nancy Frazier, to various O'Keeffe paintings. She holds the phone, making the phone "look" at the paintings.*)

She painted a lot of other things besides flowers. Have you seen her New York paintings? Or her New Mexico . . . skulls and bones. Occult? What about the hills, the Badlands, the . . .

A lesbian? So what if she was . . . and so what if she wasn't? That's not the point . . . Mom, is it just that any single, independent woman for you has to be a lesbian . . . or crazy?

What's the difference? Mother, I cannot continue this conversation. I will call you after the show. Good-bye.

(CATHERINE *hangs up the phone.*)

O'KEEFFE: "Anita—You are a bit off about my mother. We had violent differences—. . . When I was near her I tried to do what she expected—when I was alone I did as I pleased . . .—I was not with her very much."[14]

(O'KEEFFE *hangs nude pictures of herself.* CATHERINE *finds a page in her own journal,* Georgia O'Keeffe: One Hundred Flowers, 1989 Engagement Calendar.)

CATHERINE: January 2, 1989. Low key day. In Chicago: I go to the Field Museum to see Gods and Spirits with (*pause, guilty look*) "X." I ask him what faith is. X tells me about his life and I begin to understand him. I tell him what I want him to hear, to know.

Austin, Wednesday, January 4, 1989. X takes me to the airport in the morning. B . . . (my husband) picks me up. John is back from Paris . . . for good. Good to be home in Texas. John says Mom is worried about him. I say don't worry, Mom is worried about all of us. I read all my letters from X.

"Where, dear and lovely lady, do I begin this letter that should have been written months ago . . ."

(O'KEEFFE *rises in indignation.*)

O'KEEFFE: "Im full of furies today—I wonder if man has ever been written down the way he has written woman down—I rather feel that he hasn't been—that some woman still has the job to perform—and I wonder if she will ever get at it."[15]

CATHERINE: All right, O'Keeffe. I'll get at it. I'll write it down.

(CATHERINE *starts to make two piles: O'Keeffe's, Catherine's. She builds the piles into a line of demarcation, a wall between herself and* O'KEEFFE.)

I'll write a piece about me. If you want a piece about you, you do it. Over there.

(CATHERINE *searches through the rubble for clues. She throws things to* O'KEEFFE*'s side of the line.*)

"Words are like the wind—"[16] Yours.

"Words and I are not good friends."[17] Yours.

"Did I know about your feelings? Of course I knew . . ." Mine.

"The meaning of a word—to me—is not as exact as the meaning of a color." Yours.

"Just as you knew" Just as you knew? "Admit it, my dear, you knew." Mine.

(O'KEEFFE *butts in.*)

O'KEEFFE: Such odd things have been done about me with words. I have often been told what to paint. I am often amazed at the spoken and written word telling me what I have painted.

CATHERINE: Get back on your side. This is my part now!

(O'KEEFFE *reads the paper.*)

O'KEEFFE: Henry McBride, 1926: "There were more feminine shrieks and screams in the vicinity of O'Keeffe's work this year than ever before. . . . I begin to think that in order to be quite fair to Miss O'Keeffe I must listen to what women say of her—and take notes."[18]

(SOUND: *Phone rings.*)

CATHERINE: Oh, no. (*Speaks into phone.*) Mother! I have had it with you! I told you I would call you after the show, and yet you insist on calling me. I have tried to be polite, but I am now yelling at you in front of a theatre full of people: Have some respect for my boundaries, and do *not* call me here again!

Hello? (*Gasps.*) Doctor? An appointment? Now? I have an appointment with you? I forgot. Wait, wait I can explain. See, I'm in the middle of a show and I forgot to . . . yeah . . . cancel . . . and . . . Don't hang up; I need to talk to you . . . (*To audience.*) It's my therapist. (*To therapist.*) Doctor . . . um . . . Doctor K? Why am I calling you Doctor K . . . just to protect your identity; we're on stage. You don't think it's a good idea to do our session in front of other people. I know, it's not, but I need to . . . Look. Doctor, um, K, every time I come to see you you are at work. Right? So once in my lifetime, could you do me the same favor. You come and see me while I'm at work.

GOLF ANNOUNCER (*tape, sotto voce, like a "golf announcer."*): We are in New York with Michael Gold, the editor of *New Masses*, and Georgia O'Keeffe, American artist.

CATHERINE: Hang on, hang on, I just have to do this scene and then I'll be right back with you . . . (*To audience.*) 1930, New York, Hotel Brevoort. (*To therapist.*) You'll like this. It's very, um, feminist.

(O'KEEFFE, *carrying her coat, enters the hotel room for the interview. Carefully drapes her coat on the chair. Sits.*)

GOLF ANNOUNCER (*tape*): "Her face, unadorned by cosmetics, with its flash of intelligent arched eyebrows, her severely simple silk dress, her tapered, sensitive, ivory-colored hands, merged quietly into a whole, utterly simple, utterly poised . . ."[19]

O'KEEFFE: Shall we begin?

GOLD (*tape*): The biggest struggle of the age is that of the working class. The oppressed! If art is alive, the oppressed is the only possible subject.

O'KEEFFE: When you name the oppressed, do you include women?

GOLD (*tape*): Only working-class women. I'm afraid it doesn't seem very important to me if the pampered bourgeoisie in her rose-colored boudoir gets equal rights or not.

o'keeffe: Oppressed women of all classes are important. In my case I've been forced to look to male artists for models because social oppression has made for a paucity of female painters in history. Before I put a brush to canvas I question, "Is this mine? . . . Is it influenced by some idea which I have acquired from some man?" . . . I am trying with all my skill to do a painting which is all of women as well as all of me.

Is it necessary to paint realistic, glorified cartoons of women's struggles?

Form, color, and pattern are more important than subject matter. Beauty enriches everyone's existence.

golf (*tape*): Abstract issues of technique are little tinkerings, the psychological mewings of a bunch of ingrown decadents, prettified, artified evasions that are fit only to decorate the drawing rooms and boudoirs which hold the drunk parties and *kept women* of the rich . . . Gosh, I hate to argue with a woman. You have to be polite.

o'keeffe: Why do you have to be any more polite to me than to a man?

gold (*tape*): Sorry. Didn't mean it that way.

o'keeffe: You don't like flowers, do you, Mr. Gold?

gold (*tape*): Sure I do.

o'keeffe: Well, I don't really see how you can approve them since you want all things to be useful. . . . You know, I think you're a nice boy all mixed up by a lot of prejudices, defenses and hatreds. We haven't talked half enough about this. I think I'll take you to see my show, and then bring you home to Stieglitz and dinner!

> (o'keeffe *puts on her coat. Walks Gold through her show. Stops first at music stand A. Shows* White Flower.)

That is me. On the wall.

> (*Shows photo under it, Stieglitz Plate 4.*)

That is me. *Was* me.

> (*Shows* Trumpet Flower. *Removes* Trumpet Flower *to reveal photo of Catherine Rogers, but* o'keeffe *does not see photo. She has moved on to music stands B and C. She carelessly drops* Red Canna *to reveal* Georgia O'Keeffe, 1920? *and she becomes* catherine *bringing a man home to dinner.*)[20]

catherine: Hi honey we're home what's for dinner? Honey? . . . Hello . . . Honey? Hon, X is here . . . for dinner.

> (catherine *finds a note. Speaks to X.*)

He's . . . not here. . . . Look, it's really not such a good idea for us to be here when he's not here.

(CATHERINE'S *coat comes off, as if X is taking it off. She sinks into the chair.* CATHERINE *grabs her coat and enters psychiatrist's office.*)

Hello, Doctor.

(*Long pause.* CATHERINE *squirms in the chair, trying to speak. Finally . . .*)

I slept with a married man. . . . I know it's against feminism; you said that last time. What? Why did I sleep with my friend's husband? Who said I slept with my friend's husband. I said I slept with a married man . . . I don't even know . . . I mean he's married but I don't know his wife, she's certainly not my friend. How could she be my friend if I don't know her, and now that I've slept with her husband, forget it. We'll never be friends. How awful. Who would sleep with their friend's husband; that's a terrible thing to do I would never . . . well, never say never . . . but I *didn't* sleep with my friend's husband. I slept with somebody's husband, Doctor, but she's not my friend.

Wait a minute. Why did *you* say I slept with my friend's husband? Maybe somebody in this room slept with their friend's husband, but it wasn't me . . . Doctor?

(CATHERINE *picks up phone, talks to Doctor.*)

Doctor? No, that wasn't you. That was the performance. That was from the past. I mean it's fictional. I never slept with X. No, I slept with someone, but it wasn't X. But the part about you is real . . . I mean you really did say . . . whoa, look, this is her, this is me, this is her . . .

(CATHERINE *puts on coat and leaves Doctor. Arrives as* O'KEEFFE *into Stieglitz's gallery. Paces slowly around the two photographs of women, Georgia O'Keeffe and Catherine Rogers. Points first to one, then the other. Ends by standing center in the dramatic hair-slicked-back haughty pose of Georgia O'Keeffe, 1920?*)

O'KEEFFE: This is her, this is me, this is her, this is me, this is her, this is . . .

Who the hell is this. (*Points to photo of Catherine.*) No, I know Dorothy Norman when I see Dorothy Norman, I mean what the hell is Dorothy Norman doing hanging on my wall. Alfred, no. I know you photograph all of us . . . What *about* Rebecca Strand? There's a difference and you know it. This is disgusting. I will not play second fiddle to this who[re] . . . this . . . this . . . kept woman!

(*At the end of this tirade,* O'KEEFFE *rips down the photo* Catherine Rogers *from music stand A. She picks up* Georgia O'Keeffe, 1920? *from music stand C and waves it as she cries out.*)

I'm first. First. I was born first. I will always be first. I am first . . .

(o'KEEFFE *changes from black clothes to white linen pajamas. Now on music stand A there is Stieglitz Pate 24. On music stand C there is* Jimsonweed. o'KEEFFE *takes her hair down.* SOUND: *"Moonlight" Sonata.)*

o'KEEFFE (*tape*): To Henry McBride, New Mexico, July 1931, 2:45 A.M.
   "A night when I can not sleep— . . . bright moonlight on my door— . . . I wonder what painting is all about What will I do with those bones and sticks and stones— . . . I will be going East soon."[21]

(o'KEEFFE *goes to "the door." Pulls* Calla Lilies *down from music stand B to reveal* Horse's Skull with White Rose. *She sits downstage. On "going East" she wraps her arms around herself as if in a straitjacket.*
   Through the following she stretches out as if asleep. Awakening from dreams, she laughs, sighs.)

o'KEEFFE (*tape*): Lake George 10 January 1934.
   Dear Jean Toomer—"I waked this morning with a dream about you just disappearing— . . . you sat on the side of my bed the way you did the night I went to sleep and slept all evening in the dining room— . . . when someone came for you—I wasn't quite awake yet—seemed to be in my room upstairs—doors opening and closing . . . —whispers—a woman's slight laugh—a space of time."[22]

(CATHERINE *goes back to journal. Finds an old, folded-up slip of paper. Unfolds it. Reads.)*

CATHERINE: That Night There Was Jasmine, by Catherine Rogers.
   That night there was jasmine in the house
   Not you but you are never there
   Sweet potatoes
   And ravioli for Easter dinner
   Emilia told stories of *registi*
   And *fascisti*
   A dog named Mussolini
   and the prospective mother-in-law
   Who bartered for Emilia
   like a cow

   That night there was jasmine in the house
   I kissed you for the first and only time
   And you kissed back

Didn't you
After forty years
Did I ever say you
look like that movie star
and who do I look like to you

There was jasmine in the house
And I loved you
And I married you
And we named our dog Fido
Forgetting our allegiance
to the State

there was jasmine I was wearing it in my hair
I kissed you long and hard
For the first and second time
(today) you kissed back
Someone played Vivaldi in the other room

One Easter became another
you grew older than me
the jasmine melted our eyes
down to tea
I left my heart under the covers
all morning
In the afternoon you walked in the park
drank too many portions
and I grew less like myself

There was jasmine
Do you remember
None of our friends do

Under a hundred trees
We spread our silverware
Picnicking on vows
monogrammed into our napkins

Tell me you remember jasmine
Even when it's less a reminiscence
More a flower

O'KEEFFE (*tape*): "I have a passion for whiteness in all its forms." Alfred Stieglitz.

CATHERINE: January 4, 1989. I take John to the doctor. John practices "Appassionata" until I'm crazy.

(CATHERINE *picks up the newspaper from the O'Keeffe pile.*)

O'KEEFFE (*tape*): Henry McBride: "In health she has always seemed so unearthly and so unphysical as to be quite without the range of the slings and arrows that attack us lesser mortals. . . . The illness, if illness it be, must be pure illusion."[23]

(CATHERINE *reads from journal.*)

CATHERINE: January 5, 1989 Thursday

I go to the office. John and I make potato carrot soup for supper. I talk on the phone to X.

(CATHERINE *picks up old-fashioned phone, thinking it's X on the line. Sexy voice.*)

Helloo-o-o? Oh! Mutti . . . hi. OK. Oh, fine, John and I had potato carrot soup for supper. B? I don't know. Working late. Huh? I don't know where his is. Ma, he's my husband, he's not my . . . leg. How's your painting class? You didn't go? You went to church? With Dad.

January 6, 1989

I make feeble New Year's resolutions.

(CATHERINE *reads from journal, compares Pollitzer biography to journal.*)

On train from New York to Texas, 1917.

To Paul Strand:

"I saw my brother in Chicago—He has enlisted in the officers camp of engineers at Ft. Sheridan—is hoping to be one of the first from there to go to France—and doesn't expect to return if he goes. . . . —He was the sort that used to seem like a large wind when he came into the house."[24]

May 22, 1989

John's birthday. John back in Paris. Sick. I'm afraid. Divorce filed 5/18.

(CATHERINE *dials the old-fashioned phone.*)

Hello? Mutti? . . . I'm OK. No, he isn't here we're getting div—. . . What

do you mean does he have a girlfr— . . . Do I have a boyfr— . . . *Mom.*
You may not ask me about my private life. Mutti? Mommy?

O'KEEFFE: "[I]n spite of all my tearing about[,] many things that had been ac-
cumulating inside of me for years were arranging themselves—and rear-
ranging themselves—The same thing had been happening to Stieg—"[25]

(She cuts herself off.)

CATHERINE: In 1990, John died. Of AIDS. Before he died he said to me, "I always wondered what I was going to do with my life. This is my life."

O'KEEFFE *(writing a letter)*: I wish I could tell you how important these months
have been to me— . . . I knew I would have to go back to my Stieglitz—
but I didn't want to go till I was ready and today I am ready— . . . I am
anxious to get to work for the fall—it is always my best time."[26]

(CATHERINE writes in her journal.)

CATHERINE: 8/23/90 Starting again. There's never a day fresh enough to start
one of these. So today is today and today I start. I'm going back to school
this fall. Most of all I want to write. Mom says when she paints everything
else goes away.

(CATHERINE reads from the Pollitzer biography.)

"All the earth colors of the painter's palette are out there in the many miles
of bad lands. . . . You may not have seen it, so you want me always to paint
flowers."[27]

O'KEEFFE: "I hate flowers. I paint them because they're cheaper than models
and they don't move!"[28]

(CATHERINE looks up sharply.)

CATHERINE: O'Keeffe. You're back.

O'KEEFFE: "I painted the flower big to give the feeling I had in me when I
looked at it. . . . And when the bloom came out, I felt as though a sky-
scraper had gone up overnight."[29]

CATHERINE: You painted skyscrapers too.

(CATHERINE flips through the Frazier book.)

You painted skyscrapers. You painted the desert. You painted Texas. You
painted bones. It doesn't mean she's occult. You painted flowers. You
painted the sky above clouds. You painted the Great American Painting
(red, white, and blue). You painted the road far away. You painted, uh . . .
shapes . . .

O'KEEFFE: I find that I have painted my life—things happening in my life—
without knowing. "Making your unknown known is the important
thing."[30]

(CATHERINE and O'KEEFFE make beginnings to break down the wall.)

CATHERINE: Still wrestling with . . .

(O'KEEFFE *moves books.*)

O'KEEFFE: "You'd push the past out of the way if only you could."[31]

CATHERINE: . . . the damn O'Keeffe!

(O'KEEFFE *removes the images from music stands A, B, C to reveal: Music stand A*, Special No. 4; *Music stand B, Stieglitz Plate 40; Music stand C*, Winter Road I)

O'KEEFFE: 1946, Henry McBride: "The name Georgia O'Keeffe goes up in lights . . . at the Modern Museum. . . . Stardom at last! . . . Security. . . . The top position among women artists."[32]

CATHERINE: What about man artists? Stardom . . . due to the serenity and extreme finish of her style . . . style? Due to your style? What about your genius?

O'KEEFFE: Genius? What about work? Hard work.

(CATHERINE *and* O'KEEFFE *pack up through the following.*)

"One works because I suppose it is the most interesting thing one knows to do. The days one works are the best days. . . . You get the garden planted. You get the roof fixed. You take the dog to the vet. . . . You hunt up photographs for someone who thinks he needs them." (*Packing up the Stieglitz book.*) "Never mind whose photographs. *He* isn't the only photographer in the world.

"You certainly have to do the shopping. . . . But always you are hurrying through these things . . . so that you can get at the paintings again. . . . The painting is like a thread that runs through all the reasons for all the other things that make one's life."[33]

"Ya see, a painter is one thing and a person in a way is another thing."[34]

(CATHERINE/O'KEEFFE *surveys the photos, the journal, the biography, the letters, the paintings.*)

CATHERINE: What other thing? Is a person?

O'KEEFFE: "I wonder who that person is. It is as if in my one life I have lived many lives. If the person in the photographs were living in the world today, she would be quite a different person—but it doesn't matter—Stieglitz photographed her then."[35]

CATHERINE: Alfred Stieglitz, photographer, art dealer. Little Galleries of the Photo Secession, 291 Fifth Avenue, New York.

O'KEEFFE: If you must know.

CATHERINE: If you must know.

AIRPORT ANNOUNCER (*tape*): Final call all passengers. This is your final call, all passengers.

CATHERINE: Wait, there's so much more to say . . .

(O'KEEFFE *hands* CATHERINE *a letter.*)

O'KEEFFE: Here.

CATHERINE (*reads date*): Christmas?

O'KEEFFE: Read it.

CATHERINE: Dear Catherine,

"All I have to say is this—"

O'KEEFFE: "Making an object look like what you see is not as important as making the whole square you paint it on feel like what you feel about the object."

CATHERINE (*reads*): "Don't worry about it— . . . I think you are grand . . . You just go ahead working."[36] December 25, 1928. Letter to Catherine O'Keeffe. (*To* O'KEEFFE.) Thank you, I . . .

O'KEEFFE: Don't get sentimental.

(CATHERINE *picks up calendar. Sees* A Black Bird with Snow-Covered Red Hills. *That reminds her . . .*)

CATHERINE: Oh, 1946, Stieglitz died.

O'KEEFFE: And I lived forty more years.

AIRPORT ANNOUNCER (*tape*): This is your final call.

(SOUND: *"Appassionata" plays.* CATHERINE/O'KEEFFE *picks up the suitcase. Walks to the bentwood chair, stage left as at the beginning.*)

CATHERINE/O'KEEFFE: "'Words are like the wind'—Circumstances make us not have many."[37]

(*Holds calendar open to* Red Hill and White Shell. *As the lights fade,* CATHERINE *softly talks on phone.*)

CATHERINE: Knock, knock. Hi, Dad. It's the snail. The show's over. Yeah . . . it was OK . . . OK, thanks, Dad . . . Mutti? I lo[ve you]. . . . G'night, now.

(*"Appassionata" plays to the end. In the last bars of the music, the light fades.*)

Notes

1. O'Keeffe to John I. H. Baur, 8 May 1957, Estate of Georgia O'Keeffe and Whitney Museum of American Art (in Cowart et al. 267).

2. O'Keeffe to Pollitzer, 28 February 1968, Yale Collection of American Literature (hereafter cited as YCAL), Beinecke Rare Book and Manuscript Library, Yale University (in Giboire 320).

3. O'Keeffe to Baur, 22 April 1957, Estate of Georgia O'Keeffe and Whitney Museum of American Art (in Cowart et al. 267).

4. O'Keeffe to Pollitzer, 13 December 1915 (in Pollitzer 39–40).

5. Throughout the script, "Stieglitz Plate" refers to the plates in Alfred Stieglitz, *Georgia O'Keeffe: A Portrait*.

6. O'Keeffe to Dorothy Brett, February 1932, Harry Ransom Humanities Center, University of Texas at Austin (in Cowart et al. 206).

7. Henry McBride, "Curious Responses to Work of Miss Georgia O'Keeffe on Others," *New York Herald*, 4 February 1923 (in Lisle 138).

8. Kotz 37.

9. O'Keeffe to Mabel Dodge Luhan, August 1929, YCAL (in Cowart et al. 192).

10. O'Keeffe to Luhan (in Cowart et al. 191–92).

11. O'Keeffe to William M. Milliken, 1 November 1930, Cleveland Museum of Art (in Cowart et al. 202).

12. Stieglitz to Mitchell Kennerley, 9 September 1923, Kennerley Collection, Manuscript Division, New York Public Library (in Lisle 141).

13. O'Keeffe to Milliken (in Cowart et al. 202).

14. O'Keeffe to Pollitzer (in Giboire 323).

15. O'Keeffe to Sherwood Anderson, September 1923?, YCAL (in Cowart et al. 174).

16. O'Keeffe to Baur, 8 May 1957 (in Cowart et al. 267).

17. O'Keeffe to Stieglitz, 1 February 1916, YCAL (in Cowart et al. 150).

18. Henry McBride, "Modern Art," *Dial*, May 1926 (in Lisle 162–63).

19. Gladys Oaks, "Radical Writer and Woman Artist Clash on Propaganda and Its Uses," *New York World*, 16 March 1930 (in Lisle 237–38). This quotation and the following material through "and dinner" are taken from Oaks. The text has been paraphrased or rearranged.

20. Alfred Stieglitz, *Georgia O'Keeffe, 1920?*, National Gallery of Art (in Greenough, plate 41).

21. O'Keeffe to Henry McBride, July 1931, YCAL (in Cowart et al. 202–3).

22. O'Keeffe to Toomer, 10 January 1934, YCAL (in Cowart et al. 217).

23. Henry McBride, "Star of an American Place Shines in Undiminished Luster," *New York Sun*, 14 January 1933 (in Lisle 260).

24. O'Keeffe to Strand, 3 June 1917, Center for Creative Photography, University of Arizona, Tucson (in Cowart et al. 161).

25. O'Keeffe to Luhan, September 1929, YCAL (in Cowart et al. 196).

26. O'Keeffe to Luhan, August 1929 (in Cowart et al. 192).

27. Georgia O'Keeffe, catalog statement 1939 (in Pollitzer 229).

28. Emily Genauer, "Art and Artists: Arts and Flowers Theme of New Show," *New York Herald Tribune*, 18 April 1954 (in Lisle 177).

29. Pollitzer 224.

30. O'Keeffe to Anderson (in Cowart et al. 210).

31. *Georgia O'Keeffe*, Adato.

32. Henry McBride, "O'Keeffe at the Museum" *New York Sun*, 18 May 1946 (in Lisle 334).

33. Lee Nordness, *Art USA Now* (Lucerne: Switzerland: C. J. Bucher, 1962) (in Lisle 398).

34. *Georgia O'Keeffe*, Adato.
35. Georgia O'Keeffe, introduction to *Georgia O'Keeffe: A Portrait* by Stieglitz, n.p.
36. O'Keeffe to Catherine O'Keeffe Klenert, 25 December 1928, Estate of Georgia O'Keeffe (in Robinson 310).
37. O'Keeffe to Baur, 8 May 1957 (in Cowart et al. 267).

Bibliography

Beethoven, Ludwig van. Sonata no. 14 in C-sharp minor, op. 27, no. 2 ("Moonlight"). Performed by John Gaffney.

————. Sonata no. 23 in F minor, op. 57 ("Appassionata"). Performed by John Gaffney.

Callaway, Nicholas, and Alexandra Arrowsmith, eds. *Georgia O'Keeffe: One Hundred Flowers, 1989 Engagement Calendar.* New York: Knopf, 1988.

Castro, Jan Garden. *The Art and Life of Georgia O'Keeffe.* New York: Crown, 1985.

Cowart, Jack, Sarah Greenough, and Juan Hamilton, eds. *Georgia O'Keeffe: Art and Letters.* Washington, D.C.: National Gallery of Art, 1987.

Frazier, Nancy. *Georgia O'Keeffe.* Greenwich, Conn.: Brompton Books, 1990.

Georgia O'Keeffe. Television documentary directed by Perry Miller Adato. WNET/Channel 13, New York. 1977.

Georgia O'Keeffe: 1989. Calendar. New York: Metropolitan Museum of Art, 1988.

Giboire, Clive, ed. *Lovingly, Georgia.* New York: Simon and Schuster, 1990.

Greenough, Sarah, and Juan Hamilton, eds. *Alfred Stieglitz: Photographs and Writings.* Washington, D.C.: National Gallery of Art, n.d.

Kotz, Mary Lynn. "Georgia O'Keeffe at 90." *ARTNews,* November 1977.

Lisle, Laurie. *Portrait of an Artist: A Biography of Georgia O'Keeffe.* 1980. New York: Washington Square Press, 1987.

Pollitzer, Anita. *A Woman on Paper: Georgia O'Keeffe.* New York: Simon and Schuster, 1988.

Robinson, Roxana. *Georgia O'Keeffe.* New York: Harper and Row, 1989.

Rogers, Catherine. "That Night There Was Jasmine." Unpublished poem. 1999.

Stieglitz, Alfred. *Georgia O'Keeffe: A Portrait.* New York: Metropolitan Museum of Art, 1978.

7

The Last Reading of Charlotte Cushman

❧

Carolyn Gage

Cast of Characters
CHARLOTTE CUSHMAN: A large woman in her late fifties.
STAGE MANAGER: A man or woman of any age.

Scene
(The scene for the reading is the actual theatre where the play is being produced. The stage is set for a public reading, with a small table, chair, books, and water.)

Time
(The present.)

ACT I

(SETTING: Lighting is set at pre-show levels. An antique table and chair are center stage. On the table is a pitcher of water with a glass, and next to them is a stack of old books with markers in them. An elegant vase with an arrangement of flowers graces the table.
AT RISE: The STAGE MANAGER enters, uncomfortable to be addressing an audience.)

STAGE MANAGER: Could I have your attention please? I've been asked to announce that the reading tonight has been canceled. It seems that the performer is ill, and she won't be able to appear—
CHARLOTTE (*from the wings*): Just a minute! Just a minute!

(CHARLOTTE CUSHMAN *enters. She is a tall, white-haired woman in her late fifties. She has a square jaw and muscular arms, and she wears her hair pulled back off her forehead. Her outfit is unorthodox, but it suits her well. She wears a man's tailored jacket and tie from the 1870s over a long, full skirt of dark color. A lesbian, she is decidedly butch in appearance and manner.*

CHARLOTTE CUSHMAN *is a proud woman, fiercely in control of her own destiny. Her life has been the theatre, and her relationship with her public has always taken precedence over her relationships with lovers or friends.*

CHARLOTTE *is dying, and she knows it. This will be her last stand, and she pulls out all the stops.*)

CHARLOTTE (*entering, out of breath*): What do you think you're doing?

STAGE MANAGER (*turning in surprise*): Miss Cushman—

CHARLOTTE: Who told you to cancel my reading?

STAGE MANAGER: They said you had collapsed in the dressing room.

CHARLOTTE (*enraged*): Yes, and I have expanded again. I want to know whose idea it was to cancel the reading.

STAGE MANAGER: It was Miss Stebbins, your . . . your . . .

CHARLOTTE (*a challenge*): My wife?

(*Enraged, she turns toward the wings to confront Emma.*)

Yes, well, Emma tends to overreact sometimes.

(*To Emma.*)

Don't you?

(*To* STAGE MANAGER)

I'm sure Emma told you all about my cancer, didn't she? My *breast* cancer?

(*To Emma.*)

Yes.

(*To* STAGE MANAGER.)

And did Miss Stebbins tell you that it was my cancer that brought me out of retirement four years ago? And did Miss Stebbins tell you that in these four years of touring, I have performed hundreds of readings and plays?

(*To Emma.*)

No?

(*To* STAGE MANAGER.)

And did Miss Stebbins tell you that in all these years, I have never missed a single performance? *Never?*

(*To Emma.*)

No?

(To STAGE MANAGER.*)*

But, if you and Emma feel that it would be better for me not to go on, I will be happy to withdraw . . .

(Scooping up her books.)

. . . *after* I have collected my full fee, of course.

STAGE MANAGER *(an agonizing pause, during which the* STAGE MANAGER turns first to Emma and then back to CHARLOTTE*)*: Miss Cushman, if you're willing to—

CHARLOTTE *(dropping the books)*: Thank you, I am. Now, if you'll just introduce me, I think we can get on with our evening.

(She hands her/him a card and turns her back.)

STAGE MANAGER *(glancing in Emma's direction before reading the card)*: "Ladies and gentlemen, it is my privilege tonight to present the greatest English-speaking actress on two continents, a performer who has entertained for three presidents and the crowned heads of Europe, an American artist whose interpretations of Shakespeare's tragic heroines are legendary, and a leading lady for four decades . . ."

(With a flourish.)

". . . Ladies and gentlemen—Miss Charlotte Cushman!"

(The STAGE MANAGER *exits, and the lights come up on the set.* CHAR-LOTTE *turns to acknowledge the applause. She is still stung by Emma's interference.)*

CHARLOTTE: Well . . . *(picking up the books)* I was preparing to read a little Tennyson for you . . . and a little Bobby Burns . . . and some of Mrs. Browning's poetry tonight, but since Miss Stebbins has taken it upon herself to select a theme for this evening—death—I am afraid that the readings I had prepared are no longer suited to the occasion. Well . . .

(Pushing the books to one side.)

I shall just have to improvise. Death . . .

(She crosses to the table and takes a drink of water.)

The first time I encountered death, I was twenty-three years old and in bed with a prostitute.

(Sitting, she turns to the audience.)

That got your attention, didn't it?

(Turning toward Emma in the wings.)

See what you've started?

(To audience.)

This is all Emma's fault.

(A long look at Emma before she turns back to the audience.)

So—where was I? Ah. In bed with a prostitute.

Well, I was twenty-three years old and living in New York. I was what they called a "walking lady," which is the actor who takes the roles too large for the chorus and too small for the leads. This was at the Park Theatre. And it was excellent training, too. Everything was repertory in those days, and during my three years as a "walking lady," I performed over 120 different roles. But what does this have to do with a prostitute?

I'm getting to it. The Park Theatre was managed by one Stephen Price, and it is an understatement to say that Mr. Price and I did not get along. You see, Mr. Price resented any actor who was more handsome than himself.

(She laughs.)

He saw it as his personal mission in life to drive me out of the company, and in February of 1839, it looked as if he just might succeed.

The Park Theatre was going to produce *Oliver Twist*, and there is a part of a prostitute in the play, Nancy Sikes. Well, in my day, no actress with any kind of reputation would touch a role like that, and Stephen Price knew it. So, naturally, he assigned it to me. If I took the part, I would be professionally ruined, and if I refused, I would be fired. Yes, Mr. Price finally had me where he wanted me.

And to tell you the truth, I considered quitting. It was quite an insult to be cast as a prostitute, and of course, he had done it in front of the whole company. But I had seen too many talented women lose out to temperament in this game, and I was determined not to be outmaneuvered. If there was a way to play Nancy Sikes without damaging my reputation, I was going to find it. And I was equally determined to see Stephen Price hoist on his own . . .

(Pausing to consider.)

. . . *tiny* petard.

(Laughing, she rises.)

So I accepted the part—graciously. And then I took myself down to Five Points. That was the area just east of Broadway—the worst slum in New York. And I rented myself a room at Mother Hennessey's, which was the cheapest and dirtiest rooming house I could find. That was where the streetwalkers and the drunks stayed, when they could afford a roof for the night. And it was there, at Mother Hennessey's, that I began to study the role of Nancy Sikes.

During the day, I went out on the street and watched the old women pick through the garbage, and then I watched the young women pick through the old men. I watched their hands, their hips, their elbows, their mouths, their teeth, their eyebrows. I watched them flirt, I watched them joke, I watched them steal—I watched the things that no one else was watching.

And at night, I went to the saloons, and I studied the women there.

(Smiling.)

And sometimes the women studied me. On the third night, a young prostitute came into the bar. She was very sick, shaking all over, and she asked for water. They gave her a glass of whiskey, and she got sick all over the floor. The men thought this was funny.

(A long pause.)

I went to help her, and it turned out she didn't have any place to stay for the night, so I took her up to my room at Mother Hennessey's, I undressed her, I helped her to bed . . .

(Pausing.)

And then she died.

(She sits.)

That's it. That's the story. No last words, no touching prayers, no anxious faces hovering over the bed, no final embrace. A convulsion and she died. That was it.

(Reflecting.)

> ". . . Out, out, brief candle!
> Life's but a walking shadow, a poor player,
> That struts and frets his hour upon the stage,
> And then is heard no more. It is a tale
> Told by an idiot, full of sound and fury,
> Signifying nothing."

What did I do? I took her clothes.

(Rising with mock indifference.)

Of course, I took her clothes. I had a show to open, and they fit me . . .

(With anger.)

And then I went back to the Park Theatre, and I gave them Nancy Sikes. Oh, yes, I gave them Nancy Sikes. Not the whore with the heart of gold, not the feisty little spitfire from the wrong side of town—oh, no—I gave them a prostitute the likes of which they had never seen on a New York stage, even though they passed a dozen girls just like her on the way to the theatre—even though half the men would go home with one of these girls on their arm.

But I gave them a prostitute they could see, not just look at—but really see. I gave them a prostitute that made them weep the tears that no one shed that night at Mother Hennessey's. And weep they did. You see, real life is too painful for most people. That's why they come to the theatre.

So—would you like to see Nancy? You would? All right. This is from the third act, where the boy Oliver has been kidnapped by Nancy's pimp, Fagin. Her boyfriend, Bill, is threatening to turn his dog loose on Oliver, and Nancy is determined to stop him. Here's Bill:

(Turning away to get in character as Bill Sikes.)

"I'll teach the boy a lesson. The dog's outside the door—"

(As Nancy.)

"Bill, no! He'll tear the boy to pieces."

(As Bill.)

"Stand off from me or I'll split your skull against the wall!"

(As Nancy.)

"I don't care for that, Bill. The child shan't be hurt by the dog unless you first kill me."

(As Bill.)

"Shan't he? I'll soon do that if you don't keep off."

And here comes Fagin:

(As Fagin.)

"What's the matter here?"

(As Bill.)

"The girl's gone mad."

(As Nancy.)

"No, she hasn't."

(As Bill.)

"Then keep quiet."

(As Nancy.)

"No, I won't . . . Now, strike the boy, if you dare—any of you! Don't 'dear' me! I won't stand by and see it done! You have got the boy, and what more would you have? Let him be then, or I will put that mark on you that will bring me to the gallows before my time! Oh, yes, I know who I am and what I am. I know all about it—well—well! God help me! And I wish I had been struck dead in the streets before I had lent a hand in bringing him to where he is. Ah, me! He's a thief from this night forth—and isn't that enough without any more cruelty? Civil words, Fagin? Do you deserve them from me? Who taught me to pilfer and to steal, when I was a child not half so old as this?—You! I have been in the trade and in your service twelve years since, and you know it well—you know you do!

And, yes, it is my living! and the cold, wet, dirty streets are my home! and you are the wretch who drove me to 'em long ago, and that'll keep me there until I die—"

(She lunges, as if to strike Fagin.)

"Devil!"

(The gesture tears open CHARLOTTE'*s mastectomy scars, and she freezes in pain, her hand covering the place. Glancing toward the wings,* CHARLOTTE *holds up her hand to prevent Emma coming onto the stage.)*

No! I'm all right, Emma. I'll be fine—

(Turning her attention toward the table.)

I just need a little water . . . and I'll be fine.

(Sitting, she concentrates on pouring the water. She gestures toward the wings, in order to divert attention from her condition.)

Emma. Emma Stebbins, my wife.

*(*CHARLOTTE *forces a laugh.)*

Emma and I have been together—what?—twenty years now?

(She looks toward the wings, in need of Emma's support.)

Nineteen?

(Relieved at Emma's response, she turns to the audience.)

Nineteen years. Emma's counting. Emma Stebbins, the world-renowned sculptor. We met in Rome. Emma was living with Harriet Hosmer—

(She turns toward the wings. Emma has apparently said something.)

What? Oh, it's all right. They don't care.

(To audience.)

Do you? I didn't think so.

(To Emma.)

See? They don't care.

(To audience.)

Emma was living with Harriet Hosmer. She is a sculptor, too. An excellent sculptor. Harriet Hosmer—Hatty.

(To Emma.)

May I tell them about Hatty? I know they want to hear about her. Everybody wants to hear about Hatty. May I?

(Emma has said something.)

What?

(Defensive.)

What about Rosalie?

(Pause.)

All right, I will . . . *after* I tell them about you and Hatty.

(To audience.)

Emma's a little touchy about Hatty. Well—Hatty Hosmer. Hatty's not speaking to me now. Something about our hunt club in Rome. Hatty didn't think it was fair that they never gave the tail—the fox tail—to the Americans. Of course, she's talking about herself. Hatty's always talking about herself. But I have to admit, she can ride the pantaloons off the Italians. But there was no need to blow the whole thing into an international incident, which is what she did. Well, apparently she felt I didn't give enough support to her cause. So now she's not speaking.

But it's not really about fox tails. It's about death. I know Hatty. She lost practically her whole family before she was twelve. Her mother died when Hatty was six, and then she lost her two brothers, and then her sister. I just don't think she can take anyone else dying on her. So, you see, she's decided to kill the friendship instead.

But you want to hear the scandal. Well, I met Hatty Hosmer in 1851. I was thirty-five, and she—bless her heart—was just twenty-one. And a cuter little tomboy you never saw. Oh, she was a wild thing! Reminded me of myself. Anyway, I was touring in Boston, and she had just come back from medical school. She had been taking anatomy courses for her sculpting. Of course, she was the only woman they let in the school. That was Hatty.

(Rising.)

Well, she came backstage to see me, and, frankly, she was quite smitten. And, to tell the truth, I was rather dashing in those days—prancing around in tunics and tights . . . I had good legs. Still do.

(She shows us.)

Anyway, Hatty started coming backstage after every performance—and bringing me flowers.

(She shakes her head at the memory.)

It was very sweet.

But I was married at the time—to Matilda Hays, and Matilda did not think it was so sweet. Matilda and I were having some problems. Oh, Matilda . . .

(She sits.)

She had shown up at my door in London—not unlike the way Hatty was showing up in Boston—asking me for acting lessons. It has always amazed me how many young women seem to be in need of my instruction.

Well, as luck would have it, I had just lost my touring partner, and I was in the market for a new Juliet for my Romeo. How's that for a line?

(Laughing.)

Worked, too. Matilda auditioned for me, and I cast her, and we became lovers on and off the stage. It was all very daring and very romantic, and we were so pleased with ourselves, we got married. That's right. We had a ceremony and exchanged vows of celibacy—referring to men, of course—and promised to be faithful for eternity.

(Laughing.)

And it *was* an eternity.

(Another burst of laughter.)

It turned out that Matilda was not really up to the demands of a touring performer, and she retired from her public role as Juliet, but she continued to accompany me as my wife. She told me she was happy, and I believed her. I have never understood a woman who is actively miserable and not doing anything about it—but that was Matilda. And such was the state of our affairs when Hatty Hosmer knocked on my stage door in Boston.

(She is about to proceed with more confidences, when she sees Emma give her "the look." She assumes an air of wounded dignity.)

But there's no point in boring you with the details. One thing just led to another, and the next thing you know, Hatty was joining Matilda and myself in Rome that winter—

(To Emma.)

To study sculpting.

(To the audience.)

The whole thing was very innocent.

(Protesting to Emma, who has said something.)

It was!

(She starts to speak to the audience, but turns back to Emma.)

How would you know? You weren't even there.

(She rises, laughing. The joke has been on Emma.)

Where was I? Rome . . . Yes, well, there had been one slight obstacle. Hatty's father, Hiram—but we all called him "Elizabeth." I can't remember now why we did that.

(Laughing.)

Well, anyway, "Elizabeth" was terrified at the thought of his daughter leaving him. I never met a more possessive man in my life. He had even built a little studio on the back of his house, just so that Hatty could stay home and be a little "sculptress."

(Soberly.)

Don't ever call Hatty a sculptress.

(She laughs.)

Well, her father made us all promise that we would send Hatty back at the end of a year. That was twenty-five years ago, and Hatty is still in Rome. Well, Hiram had a fit and he cut off all the money. But Hatty had her revenge. Oh, yes, she had her revenge.

What she did was, she designed a monument in honor of a girl who had murdered her father—Beatrice Cenci. You don't know who that is, but, believe me, everybody in Rome knew about Beatrice Cenci. Her father had locked her up and raped and beaten her for years, and then she finally hired someone to murder him. Well, they arrested her, of course, and sentenced her to die—she was only seventeen—and the whole city was in an uproar, especially the women.

Well, Hatty's statue of Beatrice was something else. It was the most exquisitely beautiful female form I have ever seen—and I've seen a few. She has the girl lying on the stone slab of her prison cell, looking for all the world like an angel on a cloud—sleeping unmolested at last. And she has the sweetest little smile on her face. Hatty's statue of Beatrice has gone around the world now. Yes, it even went back to Boston, where Elizabeth could see it. Oh, yes, Hatty had the last word. She always does. . . . She always does.

(Rallying.)

But the point of this whole story is how I met Emma.

(Turning toward the wings.)

You were hoping I'd forget.

(To audience.)

So, anyway, Matilda and Hatty and I moved to Rome. And then Hatty did what most young women do to older women who have helped them unstintingly and from the pure goodness of their hearts—she dumped me. And didn't Matilda just love that! Poor Matilda. She never could do anything on her own. She had to let Hatty use her in order to hurt me. So the two of them got together to act out their little melodrama for my benefit.

(Reflecting.)

I have a horror of amateur theatricals, and so I booked a tour of England, leaving my little semi-retired Juliet to her understudy of a Romeo back in Italy. And, of course, after I left, there wasn't much point in the whole thing for Hatty, so she dumped Matilda. And then Matilda came running up to London, her little tail tucked between her legs, to see if I would take her back. I did, of course, but nothing could be the same between us— thanks to Hatty. But I had my revenge—

(Toward the wings.)

Didn't I?

(To audience.)

This is the good part. Emma came over from the States to study sculpting, and of course, she met Hatty. Everybody who came to Rome had to see the Pope and Hatty. Not necessarily in that order. So, Emma met Hatty, and Hatty can be very persuasive when she wants to be. She talked Emma into living with her, and the next thing you know she was going all over Rome introducing Emma as her wife. Her wife! Hatty was about as domestic as her horse.

But she made the fatal mistake of introducing Emma to me, and as Rosalind would say:

(Crossing seductively toward Emma.)

"No sooner met, but they look'd; no sooner look'd but they lov'd; no sooner lov'd but they sigh'd; no sooner sigh'd but they asked one another the reason; no sooner knew the reason but they sought the remedy."

That was twenty years ago—

(To Emma.)

Excuse me, Emma—nineteen . . .

(To audience.)

. . . and she is still with me.

Poor Hatty . . . But we're all friends now. Hatty even came and lived with us for six years.

(To Emma.)

Yes, we're all friends now . . .

(To audience.)

Except now, of course, with this death business.

Funny how everyone else is more upset about it than I am. They should know better. The only thing that kills an actor is a bad review. Audiences will forgive you if you die, but they will never forget a bad performance.

No, I have already died once in this lifetime, and once is enough, thank you. It was in New Orleans, the winter of 1835. I died every day for five months. Every single day. I'll never forget it. Nineteen years old, away from home for the first time—singing opera. You didn't know that, did you? Well, that's how I got started—and nearly how I got finished.

Yes, I was an opera singer. And I could have been a very good one, too, if my teacher hadn't insisted I sing soprano when it should have been obvious I was a natural contralto.

Well, the critics were brutal. Absolutely brutal. Would you like to hear what they said? Of course you would. There are few things in this life which give us as much pleasure as other people's bad reviews. Well, let's see . . . "Seldom in tune, she possesses neither taste nor skill." You like that? Or, "we would as soon hear a peacock attempt the carols of a nightingale as to listen to her squalling caricature of singing"?

Oh, I died a thousand deaths that winter. A thousand deaths. I had left Boston with such high hopes, and now it looked as if my life was over before it even started. I would go back to Boston, back to my mother's wretched little rooming house, back to a life of drudgery, back to Charlie Wiggins—the driveling little store clerk who was always pestering me to marry him. And wouldn't Mother have loved that! Yes, my life was over.

(*As Wolsey.*)

> "Farewell? a long farewell to all my greatness!
> This is the state of man: to-day he puts forth
> The tender leaves of hopes, to-morrow blossoms,
> And bears his blushing honours thick upon him;
> The third day comes a frost, a killing frost,
> And when he thinks, good easy man, full surely
> His greatness is a-ripening, nips his root,
> And then he falls, as I do. I have ventur'd,
> Like little wanton boys that swim on bladders,
> This many summers in a sea of glory,
> But far beyond my depth. My high-blown pride
> At length broke under me, and now has left me,
> Weary and old with service, to the mercy
> Of a rude stream, that must forever hide me."

Cardinal Wolsey, *Henry VIII.* Charlotte Cushman, New Orleans.

But I never gave up. As long as I was still under contract, I would perform—no matter how vicious the critics, no matter how rude the audiences, no matter how unkind my fellow performers. No, when that curtain went up, I was always in my place. Dying every second, but *in my place*.

Well, finally, one of the critics took pity on me. He suggested that I might be successful in a nonsinging role. That was it. That was my break.

I took the notice to the manager of the company, and I begged him to give me a speaking part. Well, he didn't have much to lose, because I was still under contract for another month, and, heaven knows, my notices certainly couldn't be any worse. So he told me the role of Lady Macbeth was mine if I wanted it. I wanted it.

Lady Macbeth. In two weeks. Now, bear in mind I was still just nineteen years old, and I had never performed a play in my life—much less a Shakespearean play, much less a lead role. But this was it—my one chance, and *I could not fail.*

What did I do? I made a plan. I would impersonate a famous actor who had been a success in the role. Not a bad plan—except that the actor I chose was Sarah Siddons.

Sarah Siddons. "The" Sarah Siddons. England's greatest tragedienne. Lovely Sarah Siddons. Petite Sarah Siddons. Charming, seductive, gracious, vivacious, flirtatious, *feminine* Sarah Siddons.

(She nods.)
Yes, Sarah Siddons . . .
(A damsel in distress, veddy proper accent.)
"Alack, I am afraid they have awak'd,
And 'tis not done; th' attempt, and not the deed,
Confounds us. Hark! I laid their daggers ready,
He could not miss 'em. Had he not resembled
My father as he slept, I had done't."
(Laughing.)
The director was concerned. He told me to be more passionate.
(Properly petulant.)
"Go get some water,
And wash this *filthy* witness from your hand.
Why did you bring these daggers from the place?
They must *lie* there. Go *carry* them, and *smear*
The sleepy grooms with blood."
Oh!
(A feminine cry of exasperation.)
"Infirm of purpose!
Give me the daggers!"
(A long pause.)
We were days from opening. The director was tearing his hair out. Finally he stopped the rehearsal. He told me I had no talent, that I was wasting my time, that I would never have a career on the stage, and that all my dreams were ridiculous.

Well, I might have accepted that I couldn't act. I might even have accepted that I didn't have a future—but that my dreams were ridiculous . . . ? What did he know about the dreams of a nineteen-year-old girl? What did he know about my wanting to hold another woman in my arms, to feel her soft breasts pressed against mine, to kiss her on the lips, to wake up in the morning with her head resting tenderly on my shoulder? What did he know about my dreams of having enough money so that the woman I loved could live with me for the rest of my life, so that I could travel anywhere I wanted, dress any way I pleased, do anything I liked with anyone I chose? Ridiculous? No, my dreams were not ridiculous. They were beautiful, and this man had no right to make fun of them.

What did I do? I reared up on my hind legs like a beast who has been cornered. I showed him my fangs, and I showed him my claws. I backed that poor fellow into a wall, my fists waving in his face, and I tore into him. I let him know exactly what I thought of his arrogance, of his conceit, and of his "Shakespe-ah." I don't know what all I said, but I know that I said it. And when I was all through, shaking from head to toe, tears running down my face, waiting for him to fire me—do you know what he did? He clapped. The son-of-a-bitch stood there and clapped. And then he said:

(Whispering.)

"Do it just like that."

(Smiling.)

And I did.

(She turns her back, for a moment to get into character. During this speech, CHARLOTTE *directs rage toward her body and the disease which is ravaging it — alluding to the mastectomy at the end.)*

    "The raven himself is hoarse

    That croaks the fatal entrance of Duncan

    Under my battlements. Come, you spirits

    That tend on mortal thoughts, unsex me here,

(Clutching her breast.)

    "And fill me from the crown to the toe top-full

    Of direst cruelty! Make thick my blood,

    Stop up th' access and passage to remorse,

    That no compunctious visitings of nature

    Shake my fell purpose, nor keep peace between

    Th' effect and it! Come to my woman's breasts,

    And take my milk for gall, you murth'ring ministers,

    Wherever in your sightless substances

    You wait on nature's mischief! Come, thick night,

>   And pall thee in the dunnest smoke of hell,
>   That my keen knife see not the wound it makes,
>   Nor heaven peep through the blanket of the dark
>   To cry, 'Hold, hold!'"
>   *(She collapses in the chair, out of breath and panting.)*
> I stopped the show. . . . Stopped it cold . . .
>   *(Struggling for breath.)*
> They loved me. . . . They loved me!
>   *(Unable to rally, she signals toward the wings.)*
> I think this would be a good time . . . for us to take a break . . .
>   *(Lights fade, as* CHARLOTTE *rises with extreme difficulty to exit. Blackout. End of act 1.)*

ACT 2

>   *(*SETTING: *Lights come up on the same set.*
>   AT RISE: CHARLOTTE *enters. She has rallied during the intermission, and she paces the stage like an animal in a cage. Conscious that her time is running out,* CHARLOTTE *plays with a feverish energy bordering on delirium.)*
>   "'Tis now the very witching time of night,
>   When churchyards yawn and hell itself breathes out
>   Contagion to this world. Now could I drink hot blood,
>   And do such bitter business as the day
>   Would quake to look on."
>   *(Smiling.)*
> Hamlet. . . . Emma didn't think I'd make it back for the second half.
>   *(To Emma.)*
> Did you?
>   *(To audience.)*
> She didn't think I'd recover from my surgery either. I had a breast removed four years ago. One of the first operations of its kind ever performed . . .
>   *(Pausing.)*
> . . . a distinction which was not without disadvantages. *But,* I survived.
>   *(To Emma.)*
> Didn't I?
>   *(To audience.)*
> And here I am.
>   *(Turning suddenly to Emma.)*

I'll tell you what, Emma—I'll make a bet with you. If I don't finish the
show tonight, I'll cancel the rest of the tour and go home with you. How's
that?

(To the audience.)

She likes that.

(To Emma.)

But, you have to agree, if I *do* finish the show, you will go with me to San
Francisco.

(To the audience.)

I've always wanted to go there. They'd love me in San Francisco, don't
you think?

(To Emma.)

Well, what do you say? Is it a deal?

(Rallying, she turns to the audience.)

You are the witnesses! Miss Emma Stebbins has just agreed to accompany
Miss Charlotte Cushman on a tour to California and points west.

(Turning toward Emma, who has apparently interrupted her.)

What?

(Irritated.)

Of course, I'm going to tell them about Rosalie. I said I would, didn't I?

(To the audience.)

You want to hear about my first girlfriend, don't you? I thought so.

Rosalie . . . Rosalie Sully. I was twenty-six and she was twenty-two.
Would you like to know how I seduced her? Well, I sat absolutely mo-
tionless for hours at a time and never said a word. You don't believe me?
Her father was painting my portrait.

(She laughs.)

Rosalie Sully . . .

(Sitting.)

Well, Mother thought the whole thing was disgusting. She presented me
with an ultimatum: Give up Rosalie or move out of the house . . .

(Defensive.)

What could I do? I was young, and I had no one to advise me. I did what
I thought was the right thing. I felt I had no choice at the time . . .

(With mock contrition.)

I rented an apartment, so Rosie could sleep with me.

(Laughing heartily, she rises and crosses downstage.)

Oh, we were in love. We were so in love—and I had waited so long! Is
there anything like that first girlfriend? It was sweet and tender and pas-

sionate and everything I had ever dreamed it would be. And more. And better. Rosalie Sully. My Rose.

She died while I was over in England. Died at twenty-six. . . . Beautiful Rose.

(Changing the subject abruptly.)

But that reminds me—we were doing death this evening, weren't we? I suppose you want to see me die. That's what they pay me for. So—what's your pleasure? Suicide? Sword wound? Musket ball . . .? How about poison? Poison is good.

This is Hamlet's mother, Gertrude. She has to die in front of both her husband and her son, but without upstaging either one of them. Needless to say, this is a role which presents a challenge for many women.

(CHARLOTTE, *a vapid expression on her face, lifts the glass and sips from it as if it were wine. She suppresses a series of coughs, rises in alarm, only to lose her balance, and waves to Claudius to indicate that he is not to worry. Attempting to sit, she falls out of the chair and lies panting on the floor, but still indicates that there is nothing wrong. Pulling at the neck of her dress and gasping for air, she crawls painfully toward the front of the stage. She rejects an offer of help.)*

"No, no,

(Gesturing toward the table.)

"the drink, the drink—O my dear Hamlet—
The drink, the drink! I am pois'ned."

(A final suppressed gasp — and a wave to her husband to indicate that he is not to worry — and Gertrude expires.)

And then there's Queen Katharine. She dies of a broken heart. Henry the Eighth has divorced her, and this is her way of getting even. It takes her eight pages to die.

(Moving the chair center stage.)

I'll just hit the highlights.

(She positions herself by the chair.)

"My legs like loaden branches bow to th' earth,
    Willing to leave their burthen.

(Snapping her fingers.)

"Reach a chair.

(She sits.)

"So; now, methinks, I feel a little ease.

(She begins to sink, but rouses herself, irritably snapping her fingers.)

"Patience—"

(Coming out of character.)
Patience is her maid.
(Katharine again, snapping again.)
       "Patience, be near me still, and set me lower;
       I have not long to trouble thee. . . .
(Rousing herself and snapping her fingers.)
       "Cause the musicians play me that sad note
       I nam'd my knell, whilst I sit meditating
       On that celestial harmony I go to.
(She sinks, but, irritated, she rallies for another snap.)
       "Bid the music leave,
       They are harsh and heavy to me."
(Coming out of character and rising.)
Here's Patience:
(A long scream.)
       "How pale she looks,
       And of an earthy cold? Mark her eyes!"
(Another scream, and then she is Katharine again, rolling her eyes. She starts to die, but rallies.)
       "Patience, is that letter
       I caus'd you write yet sent away? . . .
       Sir, I most humbly pray you to deliver
       This to my lord the King. . . .
       Say his long trouble now is passing
       Out of this world; tell him in death I blest him,
       (For so I will.) Mine eyes grow dim. Farewell, . . .
(Rallying.)
       "Nay, Patience,
       You must not leave me yet. I must to bed . . .
(She rises and falls back.)
       "Call in more women . . .
       Embalm me,
       Then lay me forth: although unqueen'd, yet like
       A queen, and a daughter to a king, inter me.
("To hell with it.")
       "I can no more."
(Katharine dies, and CHARLOTTE *rises to replace the chair.)*
Needless to say, Henry had the rest of his wives beheaded.
    But you want to know about my most famous dying scene, don't you?

It was in *Guy Mannering.* You've never heard of it, of course. One of those Sir Walter Scott potboilers.

I played Meg Merrilies, Queen of the Gypsies. And do you know my whole part was less than twenty minutes long—*and* at the end of the last act—and *still* this is the role everyone remembers? Not Lady Macbeth. Not Rosalind. Not Gertrude. No, Meg Merrilies, Queen of the Gypsies. It is one of the cruel ironies of the theatre, that an actress who has distinguished herself in some of the greatest classical roles in dramatic literature, can go down in history for twenty minutes of the worst applesauce ever written. Well, I have no intention of doing Meg Merrilies here tonight . . .

(She begins to thumb through one of the books.)

Still . . . she *did* sell out every performance . . .

(Still thumbing.)

. . . and that was even during the war . . .

(More thumbing.)

. . . lines all the way around the block . . .

(Looking up suddenly.)

But you don't want to see it, do you? You do . . . ? All right, but don't say I didn't warn you.

(CHARLOTTE *turns her back, musses up her hair, and whirls around with a wild leap. This speech is delivered with a thick Scottish burr. A critic of her day described this scene thus: "She stood like one great withered tree, her arms stretched out, her white locks flying, her eyes blazing under their shaggy brows. She was not like a creature of this world, but like some mad, majestic wanderer from the spirit-land.")*

"The tree is withered now, never to be green again; and old Meg Merrilies will never sing blithe songs more. But I charge you . . . that you tell him not to forget Meg Merrilies, but to build up the old walls in the glen for her sake, and let those that live there be too good to fear the beings of another world; for if ever the dead come back among the living, I will be seen in that glen many a night after these crazed bones are whitened in the mouldering grave!"

(Jumping back to play the villain.)

"Hark ye, Meg, we must speak plain to you! My friend Dirk Hatterick and I, have made up our minds about this youngster, and it signifies nothing talking, unless you have a mind to share his fate. You were as deep as we in the whole business."

(As Meg.)

"'Tis false! You forced me to consent that you should hurry him away, kidnap him, plunder him; but to murder him was your own device! Yours! And it has thriven you well!"

(As the villain.)

"The old hag has croaked nothing but evil bodings these twenty years; she has been a rock ahead to me all my life."

(As Meg.)

"I, a rock ahead! The gallows is your rock ahead."

(As the villain, pulling an imaginary gun.)

"Gallows! You hag of Satan, the hemp is not sown that shall hang me."

(As Meg.)

"It is sown and it is grown, and hackled and twisted—"

(CHARLOTTE is indicating a noose, when suddenly she makes the sound of a pistol shot and clutches her heart. A critic of her day has described her death in these words: "When Hatterick's fatal bullet entered her body, and she came staggering down the stage, her terrible shriek, so wild and piercing, so full of agony and yet of the triumph she had given her life to gain, told the whole story of her love and revenge." She screams and staggers downstage.)

"I knew it would be like this!"

(Collapsing on the floor, CHARLOTTE crawls the entire length of the stage to snatch victory from the jaws of defeat. She speaks her dying words to Dirk.)

"It has ended as it ought."

(After dying a lugubrious death, CHARLOTTE rises and dusts herself off.)

Meg Merrilies, Queen of the Gypsies . . .

But I didn't just play queens. I played princes and kings, too. Breeches parts. That's what they called it when we took the men's roles. And why shouldn't we? They had all the lines.

I played Aladdin, and Oberon—King of the Fairies. . . . And two cardinals—Richelieu and Cardinal Wolsey. I was the first woman to play Cardinal Wolsey. And, of course, Hamlet. I borrowed Edwin Booth's costume.

(Remembering.)

Filled it out better than he did, too.

(She laughs.)

But my most famous breeches part was Romeo. Oh, Romeo! How I loved to play that boy! Mad, passionate, tempestuous Romeo. I loved him! I *was* Romeo!

(Shaking her head.)

All those years of pent-up passion for my girlfriends. . . . All those long nights of fantasy—and frustration! I felt as if I had been rehearsing for Romeo all my life.

And Susan was my first Juliet. My baby sister Susan. You didn't know that, did you? Yes, my sister and I acted together for ten years. And those were the best years of my life. Especially, *Romeo and Juliet*, and especially when we took the play to London. Yes, Susan and I were a team. Top billing: "Charlotte Cushman and her sister."

Well, Mother had a fit. It was bad enough that *I* was in the theatre, but Susan! Oh, no, not Susan!—not her precious little blue-eyed baby girl! No, Mother had it all planned out that her *beautiful* daughter was going to marry a rich man, and that he was going to support the whole family, and then she and Susan would never have to work again.

(A bitter laugh.)

And Mother was in such a hurry to spare Susan a life of drudgery, she forced her into marriage at the age of thirteen. Thirteen. How did she get Susan to go along with it? Well, she told her that the man was sick and going to die soon—which is what he had told Mother—and that the whole thing was just a legal formality so that Susan could inherit his property. Well, needless to say, the scoundrel was lying about the state of his finances—*and* his health! One year later, there was Susan, my baby sister, fourteen-year-old Susan—pregnant, abandoned, and being hounded by an army of creditors. Well, I came to the rescue, of course. I was already supporting Mother and both my brothers.

But I'll tell you something—the day—the very *day* that baby was weaned, I marched Susan down to the Park Theatre and got her an audition. My baby sister was *never* going to have to depend on a man again—not if I could help it!

Well, they cast her, and then Susan and I started working together. You know, the women didn't usually team up—but *we* did. We knew each other's timing, we knew each other's business—There was no one in the theatre who could beat us! And we played everything—*everything:* Mistress Page and Mistress Ford in *Merry Wives*, Gertrude and Ophelia in *Hamlet*, Oberon and Helena in *Midsummer Night's Dream*, Lydia Languish and Lucy in *The Rivals*, Desdemona and Emilia in *Othello*, Lady Macbeth and Lady Macduff, and then—our most daring—*Romeo and Juliet*!

In 1846 we took the show to London. Oh, that was a story! But first we thought it would be a good idea to try it out in Scotland. Well, we managed to scandalize the entire population of Edinburgh. For weeks rumors were flying that Susan was an unwed mother, and that I was . . . well, what I am!

Of course, none of this would hurt our reputations in London. No, what almost stopped us there was a dead actor. That's right, a dead actor. His name was David Garrick.

It seems that Mr. Garrick had taken it upon himself to improve on Shakespeare's plays—which meant, of course, writing longer scenes for himself and cutting the women's lines. Oh, do I know David Garrick! He may have died before I was born, but I know him. I have been sharing the stage now for forty years with the David Garricks of this world, and they are no different now than they were a hundred years ago.

Well, Mr. Garrick had done such an excellent job of promoting himself, that his version of *Romeo and Juliet* had become more popular than Shakespeare's. When Susan and I got to London to rehearse with the company at the Haymarket, there was not a single actor who knew the original version. Furthermore, they absolutely refused to learn it. No, they were not about to let two Americans teach them their Shakespeare—much less two women, much less a woman who intended to dress like a man and make love to her sister!

(Laughing.)

Well, Susan and I had no intention of performing the Garrick butchery—so there we were, on the verge of an actors' strike. Then, at the eleventh hour, the manager of the Haymarket stepped in. He posted a modest notice in the Green Room, to the effect that any actor who was not willing to cooperate with the Misses Cushman would be free to seek employment elsewhere.

And so we opened. December thirtieth, 1846. And we were an immediate sensation. I have always maintained that only a woman can play Romeo with any credibility. The male actors with the maturity and experience to handle the role are obviously too old to be boys. On the other hand, an experienced actress can impersonate a young man well into her forties—provided, of course, she has the right "attitude."

(To Emma.)

Then, too, there are those things that only a woman can know about what pleases a woman.

(To the audience.)

Apparently the critics agreed. They wrote that I put their gender to shame with my lovemaking. Yes, rumor had it that "Miss Cushman was a very dangerous young man."

(Laughing.)

So, Susan and I were a sensation. We ran for eighty consecutive performances at the Haymarket—which was a record. And then we went on tour to the provinces. And then Susan had to go and ruin it all. She got married . . . again!

(CHARLOTTE *begins to pace.*)

Helena, *Midsummer Night's Dream.*

> "Injurious Hermia, most ungrateful maid!
> Have you conspir'd, have you with these contriv'd
> To bait me with this foul derision?
> Is all the counsel that we two have shar'd,
> The sisters' vows, the hours that we have spent,
> When we have chid the hasty-footed time
> For parting us—O, is all forgot?
> All school-days friendship, childhood innocence?
> We, Hermia, like two artificial gods,
> Have with our needles created both one flower,
> Both on one sampler, sitting on one cushion,
> Both warbling of one song, both in one key;
> As if our hands, our sides, voices, and minds
> Had been incorporate. So we grew together,
> Like a double cherry, seeming parted,
> But yet an union in partition,
> Two lovely berries molded on one stem;
> So, with two seeming bodies, but one heart . . .

(With sudden fury.)

> "And will you rent our ancient love asunder,
> To join with men in scorning your poor friend?
> It is not friendly, 'tis not maidenly.
> Our sex, as well as I, may chide you for it,
> Though I alone do feel the injury."

Yes, Susan got married. She got married and gave up acting. Or I should say, she gave up the stage. Her whole marriage was a performance, if you ask me. We were never close again after that.

(Agitated by her memories.)

Yes, Susan betrayed me. Just like Matilda. Just like Hatty. Just like all the women I have tried to love—they always leave me. I don't understand it. I have never abandoned a woman in my life.

(Turning with irritation toward Emma who has interrupted her.)

What?

(In a threatening tone.)

What about Rosalie?

(Pause.)

I told them she died.

(Bullying the audience.)

Didn't I? I told you she died while I was in England, didn't I?

(To Emma.)

See? I told them . . .

(She starts to address the audiences, but turns back to Emma with sudden ferocity.)

But you want me to say I murdered her, don't you? Stuck a knife in her heart like Iago—don't you? That I betrayed her, because I told her I would only be gone for six months, and instead, I stayed in England for three years.

(With rising anger.)

Yes, I did stay. Because for the first time in my life I was a leading lady. For the first time in my life the managers were coming to *me*. And for the first time in my life, money—*real* money—was finally coming in. And wasn't that the whole point? To make enough money so that Rosie and I could live together for the rest of our lives? Yes, I stayed, and I would do it again.

(To Emma.)

But you want me to say that I killed her.

(To audience.)

Do you know that Rosalie wrote to me every single day of those three years? Every single day—and sometimes twice a day! What was I supposed to do with all those letters? Drop everything to answer them? Was I supposed to apologize to her, because my life was full of excitement and glamour, while she had nothing better to do than clean her father's paintbrushes—and write me those interminable letters? Was that my fault? Was I supposed to give up my life and live hers, because she couldn't live mine?

(Enraged, she turns toward Emma.)

Is that what I was supposed to do? If Rosie killed herself, it wasn't my fault!

(Turning back to the audience with manic intensity.)

So—would you like to see some of my Romeo? Let's see . . . this is the scene at the end of the play where Romeo is entering the vault of Juliet's tomb. He thinks she has died, but she is really just asleep—and he is going there to kill himself.

(She attacks the scene with Romeo's frenzied desperation.)

"Give me the light. Upon thy life I charge thee,
What e'er thou hearest or seest, stand all aloof,
And do not interrupt me in my course.
Why I descend into this bed of death
Is partly to behold my lady's face,
But chiefly to take thence from her dead finger
A precious ring—a ring that I must use
In dear employment—therefore hence be gone.
But if thou, jealous, dost return to pry
In what I farther shall intend to do,
By heaven, I will tear thee joint by joint,
And strew this hungry churchyard with thy limbs.
The time and my intents are savage-wild,
More fierce and more inexorable far
Than empty tigers or the roaring sea . . .

(Turning suddenly, she confronts the body of Juliet. Exhausted, CHAR-
LOTTE *drives herself to finish the monologue.)*

"O my love! my wife!
Death, that hath suck'd the honey of thy breath,
Hath had no power yet upon thy beauty:
Thou art not conquer'd, beauty's ensign yet
Is crimson in thy lips and in thy cheeks,
And death's pale flag is not advanced there. . . .
Ah, dear Juliet,
Why art thou yet so fair? Shall I believe
That unsubstantial Death is amorous,
And that the lean abhorred monster keeps
Thee here in dark to be his paramour?
For fear of that, I still will stay with thee,
And never from this palace of dim night
Depart again: here, . . .

(She falters.)

"here will I remain
With worms that are thy chambermaids; O! here

(She falters again.)
"Will I set up my everlasting rest,
And shake the yoke of inauspicious stars
From this world-wearied flesh.
(She has difficulty going on.)
"Eyes, look your last!
Arms,
(Faltering.)
"Arms, take your last embrace!"
(As she reaches out her arms for Juliet, she breaks down and turns her back to the audience. Racked with sobs, she collapses in the chair, her face in her hands.)
I'm sorry. I can't finish it.
(She takes out a handkerchief, breaks down again, and then collects herself.)
I'm sorry. . . . This has never happened before. I . . . was just . . . remembering Rosalie.
(Taking another moment.)
Yes, I did betray Rosie. There was another woman. Of course there was another woman. I was only thirty, and I was the toast of London. Of course there was another woman. I know Rosalie heard the rumors. Mother would have told her.
(Weary, but without bitterness.)
Yes, Mother would have enjoyed that.
And Rosie began writing me desperate letters. And I wrote angry letters back, denying everything. So then, of course, she knew.
The truth was, I had outgrown Rosalie. How could I tell her that? But I never should have lied to her. That was the betrayal. Rosie deserved the truth. We all deserve the truth.
(Looking at Emma.)
Well, Emma . . . it looks like you've won the bet.
(She begins to gather the books.)
You know, the great tragedy of *Romeo and Juliet* is that Romeo doesn't know that Juliet is still alive. He puts himself through all that agony for nothing. All the time Juliet is just waiting for him . . . waiting for him, and he doesn't have the sense to know it.
(A long look at Emma.)
Well—
(She rises. This is her farewell to forty years in the theatre.)

"Our revels now are ended. These our actors
(As foretold you) were all spirits, and
Are melted into air, into thin air,
And, like the baseless fabric of this vision,
The cloud-capp'd tow'rs, the gorgeous palaces,
The solemn temples, the great globe itself,
Yea, all which it inherit, shall dissolve,
And like this insubstantial pageant faded
Leave not a rack behind. We are such stuff
As dreams are made on; and our little life
(Pausing to smile.)
"Is rounded with a sleep."
(To Emma.)
Let's go home, Emma. I'm tired.
(To the audience.)
Goodnight.
(Exiting with tremendous dignity. Blackout. The End.)

8

Performing Historical Figures

✍ The Metadramatics of Women's Autobiographical Performance

Carol Hanbery MacKay

Having just encountered, through various degrees of direction and indirection, the preceding seven "historical" figures, the reader might be willing to join me in invoking the spirit of Caryl Churchill's *Top Girls*, which transported into its early 1980s setting several historical and fictional women. Putting these five women (Patient Griselda, Lady Nijo, Pope Joan, Isabella Bird, and Dull Gret) into juxtaposition as they help the heroine, Marlene, celebrate her promotion to an executive post at a temp agency allows Churchill to explore the range and limits of female freedom, to burst many of the myths we hold about these heroic women while forging new truths informed by the promise of feminism.[1] Although bringing together the seven figures who constitute the performance subjects of part 1 of this book might serve a similar purpose, they would also complicate the picture by injecting multiple layers of complexity into key questions of identity, history, authenticity, reality, and representation—questions explicitly raised by M. Heather Carver in her introduction to her performance script of "Calamity Jane." Much of that complexity can be addressed by recognizing the metadramatic qualities of the preceding essays and scripts. For although these historical figures presumably take center stage, they in fact compete with their authorial personae, who frequently turn them into reflections of themselves in order to expand their territory beyond traditional boundaries of gender and sexuality.

Perhaps it is not too surprising that little purpose is served by merely calling up these seven figures and ranging them across a chronological spectrum. Most of what we learn is that they are more immediate to our time than Churchill's collection, spanning as they do just 174 years: Charlotte Cushman (1816–76), Martha Jane Cannary (1848–1903), Mary

Church Terrell (1863–1954), Gertrude Stein (1874–1946), Georgia O'Keeffe (1887–1986), Anaïs Nin (1903–77), and Mary Martin (1903–90). What is interesting to us as readers and potential spectators is not just the historical personages per se but *how* they are rendered and represented by the writer-performers who act as mediators for us. And this point leads to one of the most telling aspects of this particular collection: these historical figures variously float in and out of focus, depending on the degree to which their writer-performers come to the fore. We might expect that the four essayists—Elyse Lamm Pineau on Nin, Lynn C. Miller on Stein, Eileen C. Cherry on Terrell, Stacy Wolf on Martin—would necessarily provide less vivid depictions because they are engaged in acts of framing and analysis, not reproducing their own performance scripts. Yet Stein and Terrell emerge fairly clearly from these pages, while O'Keeffe, who is enacted by Catherine Rogers in her own script, purposefully becomes conflated with the character of the writer-performer much of the time. Meanwhile, Pineau confounds the reader by triangulating herself with Nin and Nin's longtime partner Rupert Pole, and Wolf never really brings Martin "onstage" as she immerses herself in a protracted performance of biographical research that is essentially autobiographical. The two remaining scripts disperse their subjects as well—Carver by featuring multiple facets of Calamity Jane as if they were separate individuals, Gage by stretching Cushman between her own time as a nineteenth-century actress and our present in an open acknowledgment of her lesbianism.

So what is the logic of presenting the various essays and scripts in their current order? Because all of the texts raise issues pertinent to the subjects of autobiography, performance, and feminism, the order could be reconfigured in numerous ways to emphasize a particular argument.[2] And I suspect that the editors recognized this fact by not treating their chronology as an ironclad sequence. Instead, what we have here is the opportunity to witness some key issues about women's autobiographical performance explored and exemplified. Increasingly, what emerges from these pages is a kind of living theory about how one-woman shows are born, developed, and continually reborn.

What better place to start interrogating the relationship between the writer-performer and her subject than with the first essay, Pineau's investigation of Nin, whom she considers a "collaborative partner" and "co-conspirator"? By tracing for us her route back to her first reading of Nin, Pineau articulates the subjective experience of almost merging with her subject. But the act of writing about that experience also brings clarity to her vision: Pineau can thereby recognize and explain her own "evolution" as ranging between "unreflexive identification to unempathetic critique." In a sense, we could say that the writer-performer looks for surrogate selves in order to play out aspects of her personality and then gain insight into them.[3] Surely this is partly the case for Cherry, who admits, "Since I was not prepared to tell my own travel tale as directly and honestly as I wanted, I drew upon the legacy of Mary Church Terrell." The choice of subject for a one-woman show may be inherently autobiographical, and the essayists in this section are fairly explicit about their relationships with their subjects. As for the scripts themselves, the reader can only speculate about the connections between playwright and star-vehicle, but of the three in this collection, Rogers provides us with the most tantalizing material because she freely alternates between her performer persona and her subject, even to the point of setting her two "selves" in dialogue with each other. As we witness the collision of the life of the writer-performer and that of her subject, we would do well to recall the editors' terminology of "auto/biography," which signals "a negotiation between the autobiographical self of the writer-performer and the biographical record of the historical personage."

On a very basic level, the relationship of the writer-performer and her subject involves a physical component. The external world is pertinent to the performer when we are talking about matters of setting, actual props, and technical support. By definition, the performer of a one-woman show is alone on stage, yet like any performer she usually has collaborators (however few) in the wings helping her to create the illusion of bringing her subject to life. But it is the interior, more intimate element that is both the challenge to and measure of success for the performer. Pineau actually speaks of experiencing "empathetic eruptions" when she performs as Nin; she acknowledges the visceral, contiguous factors that constitute "bodies of memory," even stretching the concept to embrace a kind of "intercorporeal connection" with her subject.[4] In the case of performing Stein, however, Miller informs us that many prospective audience members were not even able to get past the question of external appearance, thus prematurely almost foreclosing the performer's opportunity to invoke a more internal correlation. Matters of appearance, and especially physical size, seem more readily open to critique for women performing women, and Miller found herself constantly replaying the same argument before the fact of her performance, finally declaring "enough is enough is enough is enough." In contrast, Cherry as an African American is appar-

ently granted a certain entrée to performing the African American Terrell, but as she informs us, lacking other features of similarity, she opted
primarily for conveying her character through her carriage.

Behind the physical is the more subtle realm of the psychological elements that need to be employed to link the writer-performer with her
subject. Getting into the subject's historical context is one step, and finding a method of "inhabiting her skin" is another, but entering her mental-
emotional universe is a much more tricky and ineffable affair. According
to this collection of "case studies," projection, loss of interpersonal
boundaries, psychosomatics, even dissociation can occur. At their extreme edge, these performances suggest that walking the line between
sanity and insanity is part of the challenge that most woman performance
artists are willing, nay desirous, to invite. Questions of emotional stability and sanity are fundamental to the study of women's lives as lived in
every culture and historical period that we have studied, and these writer-
performers all recognize that finding the means to raise and explore these
questions is equally fundamental to the success of their enterprise.

Once again Pineau's case is instructive. She candidly assumes a cautionary tone as she informs her reader that she reached a point of believing she could understand anything Nin might have thought or done. At
the same time, as she warns us, "intimacy can lead to presumption." After
experiencing a kind of alter-ego slippage as she moves back and forth between herself and Nin, Pineau achieves the questionable state of a "pervasive, often *invasive* incarnation." This self-insight is turned to constructive purpose, however, for eventually Pineau can sift through "the Real
Things" of Nin's personal effects and discover for herself that she must establish limits. Thus it is that she can refuse Pole's well-intentioned gesture of offering her access to the one diary that had been held back from
the official depository of the Nin special collections: "This is one sanctuary I have no right to enter."[5] Such self-knowledge empowers Pineau to
write for us her critical autobiography of performing Nin and to extend
Bryant Alexander's terminology of "generative autobiography" to give
name to her own long-term relationship with Nin as an experience of
"generational autobiography."[6] Ultimately, Pineau can engage in acts of
"shape-shifting through time" without fear of getting stuck in the Nin
persona, and the result is a performance text that is all the richer for its
ability to move back and forth between empathy and critical acumen.

Yet separating the writer-performer from her subject is not important
just to the artist; it can be almost as informative for the reader or spectator

to go through the process of discerning the various distinctions. Miller's Chautauqua performances of Stein have provided her with an eminently practical forum for establishing levels of persona discreteness.[7] Having steeped herself in Stein's language as it has appeared in numerous autobiographical accountings, and giving nuance to the written script by suffusing it with the conversational patterns she has further deduced, Miller is able to create a "natural" performer-spectator arena in the lecture platform. Maintaining the historical persona of Stein during her first question-and-answer period puts both Miller and her audience to the test: she must draw from her scholarly knowledge of Stein while improvising in character, and questioners must suspend their disbelief long enough to establish a conversational model that has no real-life concomitant. By the time questioners are addressing Miller in her own persona, they have begun to sort out the elements of Stein's style and character that Miller has chosen to emphasize. Furthermore, as she explains, this last shift in persona can open up for consideration the heretofore private role of Stein's lesbianism, a subject that Miller adroitly maneuvers to the fore at this stage.

But for sheer bravado on the topic of subject-object conflation we need only turn to Rogers on O'Keeffe. Right from the start Rogers gives herself equal billing with her choice of historical figure, openly calling her production "Georgia O'Keeffe x Catherine Rogers." Speaking for itself—that is, not introduced or framed by critical commentary—this script switches back and forth between Rogers's performance of O'Keeffe and her performance of herself as writer-performer. As she proceeds, Rogers gradually reveals through one-sided telephone conversations with her "mother" her persona's insecurities about her chosen field and her family relations, reaching a kind of climax when she addresses Miller as her producer at the University of Texas performance: "This isn't her. . . . It's the 'All about Me Show.'" At this point, the script overtly introduces the topic of therapy by having the Rogers persona talk with her "therapist" on the telephone. Therapy is here a tool to help Rogers explore her problems with boundaries, but by implication the reader/spectator could apply it to reexamine O'Keeffe's life. So the playing back and forth continues, with a variety of different parallels emerging from the myriad vehicles cited to convey the multiplicity of a woman's life—journal entries, letters to and from others, biographical or autobiographical tidbits detailing many different relationships. Finally, Rogers and O'Keeffe engage in dialogue with each other, this self-debate signaling the potential for an actual breakdown. Yet what ultimately develops is an equally strong possibility that this script may be celebrating a psychological breakthrough, for both subject and object. "They make beginnings to break down the wall," declare the stage directions as the performance approaches its crescendo, with O'Keeffe eventually testifying for herself and Rogers, "It is as if in my one life I have lived many lives."

By now it should be clear that the performances described or reproduced in this collection are transgressive in nature. They all raise issues about going too far, crossing indistinct and problematic boundaries, getting too close, imposing one's sexuality on one's subject. Perhaps Pineau best sums up this tendency by talking about it as "invasive." But how else could she have evolved through the stages of constructing her body "first *as*, then *against*, and finally *as witness to* Nin's own"?[8] Inevitably, when women study their own lives and those of other women, they encounter issues of containment and regulation, and in order to expose those restrictions they necessarily breach boundaries and create their own rules.[9] Moreover, the subjects these seven authors chose were themselves egregiously transgressive in outlook and behavior. Gage rather neatly brings to the fore one of the major ways in which women who pursued the acting profession were immediately judged sexually suspect, for the Victorian era in general equated actresses with prostitutes. Thus Gage doubly critiques nineteenth-century hypocrisy when she has Cushman relate how dangerous it was for an actress to play a prostitute and then not only describes the impact of her portrayal of Nancy Sikes from *Oliver Twist* but also enacts it for our confirmation of her power to transcend petty limitations.[10] No wonder Cherry herself, surrounded as she is by "competing allegiances," her "body . . . a crossroads," chooses to embody Terrell, a representative of the cosmopolitan, the transnational, the cross-cultural. For in all these aspects Terrell takes on the role of the heroic questor previously assumed to be male and white and apparently makes it her mission to cross boundaries. Out of resistance and rebellion emerges the new order: Cherry believes that in performing Terrell she has created a synthesis between herself and Terrell that captures the historical feminism inherent in a "transformation" that is also a "continuation."[11]

What these seven writer-performers produce is essentially metadrama. They consciously craft their essays and their scripts to embody the creative tension inherent in one artist attempting to depict another. Sometimes, as in the case of Rogers on O'Keeffe, the *mise en abyme* is almost dizzying; at other times, as in the case of Miller on Stein, it is more implied or can only surface in the final question-and-answer period.[12]

Perhaps metadrama is also especially appropriate for a woman trying to express what it is like to be another woman, all the more so if one or both are lesbian. Sexuality is not something that female performance artists shy away from; rather, they find ways of addressing it, perhaps even imposing it at turns, in order to free it up as a subject for more open discussion. Wolf's essay at first reading may seem rather anomalous, but its metadramatics ultimately represent the kind of relentless honesty involved in all the one-woman shows discussed and reproduced in this collection. From the outset, Wolf makes this her-story, her scenario about her fascination with the breeches parts women have often performed, Mary Martin in particular. But as Wolf's desire for Martin commingles with her search for Martin's lesbian identity, the two stories cross paths. "[S]ometimes I couldn't tell which pieces of evidence were about Martin and which were about me," she admits. The upshot is an essay that is both Wolf's autobiography and Martin's biography, tellingly encapsulated by Wolf as "spectatorial performance of Martin, her career, her life, her performance."

The metadrama of Gage's script of "The Last Reading of Charlotte Cushman" serves its subject extremely well. Like Miller, Gage adroitly treats the present-time stage as a stand-in for the historical one, even introducing a stage manager who might be dismissing both audiences when he (or she) starts to announce that the performer is ill and won't be able to appear. This ploy is Gage's cue to have Cushman wrest the stage from him and start a one-sided dialogue with her unseen, protective lover lurking in the wings. The "absent" Emma Stebbins thereby becomes the means by which Gage brings to the fore Cushman's lesbianism, something the actress would never have directly addressed on the public stage of the nineteenth century. So Cushman turns her reading into a kind of improvisational set-piece which is a pastiche of her accounts of her love relationships with other women and the dying speeches she has performed from Shakespeare. Gage makes explicit her protagonist's lesbianism for a contemporary audience that is relatively comfortable with the subject, reinforcing for us the point that Cushman's own period was not. Yet Cushman played both male and female roles rather regularly in her own time, most notably cross-dressing as Romeo to her sister Susan's Juliet. The tension that emerges between the level of awareness implied by the two time periods comments doubly on them: we can derive the homophobia and hypocrisy of the Victorians from making the distinction, but with any degree of honesty we can also recognize the parallels to them in our own time.[13]

In many respects, these seven essays and scripts raise for us the epis-

temological issues unleashed by postmodernism. Seeing the self as re-
fracted and multiple is both freeing and disturbing, and our seven writer-
performers know how to work with the exhilaration and anxiety induced
in performance-subject and spectator alike.[14] On the one hand, Miller
speaks of the transformative effects of Stein creating and recreating herself, using her multiple performances of Stein to reflect that multiplicity.
Carver, on the other hand, makes multiplicity frighteningly explicit as she
gives us a series of personae—Jane the narrator, Jane the party girl, Jane
the western hero, Jane the woman's woman, Jane the writer—almost as if
Calamity Jane were indeed a multiple personality. In fact, the narrator's
opening monologue compounds the possibilities even further: "Hello
everybody! I'm a loose woman! I'm a mother! I'm a hero! I'm a troublemaker! I'm a lover! I'm a prostitute! I'm sexually confused! I'm an oddity!
I'm a drunk! I'm angry! I'm . . . oh hell, I'm whatever they say I am." In
the interplay of "multiple levels of performativity," Carver acknowledges
both the usefulness and ultimate impossibility of answering the question
posed by the title of her script, "Will the Real Calamity Jane Please Stand
Up?" She thus spotlights the very dilemma most women find themselves
in, namely, being stretched and torn among multiple roles and relationships. But as women's autobiographical theory elucidates, that multiplicity is a power tool in the hands of a woman who is self-conscious of her
complexity. And a performance artist like Rogers knows how to display
that self-consciousness in a way that transcends self-indulgence by discovering its potential to create the self anew.

Finally, the range of methodologies employed by our seven writer-
performers is itself educative, especially for other performance artists in
the reading and/or dramatic audience. At one end of the spectrum is
Miller's scholarly, conscientious, yet creative reproduction of Stein at a
specific historical period; at the other end is a text like Wolf's, whose Martin remains an elusive, often virtually absent figure. In between exists an
intriguing mixture of autobiographical texts bodied forth in the present
and imaginative speculation about "what might have been." Cherry, for
example, incorporates large swaths of Terrell's actual autobiography, *A
Colored Woman in a White World* (1940), introducing and framing them
with her own rendition of some key incidents in Terrell's life story, creating what she calls a synthesis of herself and her subject, even interpolat-
ing a folktale to help make a key point. In a similar yet different way,
Pineau creates her brand of merging with her subject, but over the years
her rendition of Nin has subsumed one or the other to secondary, maybe

even tertiary, status. Meanwhile, Carver gives us a series of individuated monologues, all based on discrete aspects of Calamity Jane that the writer-performer has invented by reading autobiographical, biographical, and fictional accounts of her enigmatic subject. As for Gage's version of Cushman, choosing to present the actress as she confronts her own mortality lends a dramatic verisimilitude to an otherwise fictional scenario. And Rogers continues to maintain her precarious balance between subject and object, curiously enough turning that tightrope act into a form of self-excavation for each of them. Let me hasten to add that no value judgment is implied in describing this range, for each presentation is successful in its own right.

Harkening back to the beginning of my essay, I suspect that my reader would now agree that putting our seven historical figures onstage together would create a fascinating but hardly containable dramatic production. And if we factored in the writer-performers—as we must, given their intimate relations with their subjects as we have recently encountered them—we'd have more metadrama than any single stage could rightfully claim. At the same time, however, the prospect is tantalizing, not the least because I can imagine many of the writer-performers willingly collaborating on such a project. For what they all have in common is a fervent desire to tell a woman's story as many stories, as lives multiply lived, impinging upon one another in constructive, original ways, in scripts of their own making that will be endlessly innovative and self-creating.

Notes

1. Griselda is the patient wife in Chaucer's "Clerk's Tale"; Lady Nijo was a Japanese emperor's courtesan and later a Buddhist nun; Pope Joan is speculated to have been a ninth-century woman disguised as a man; Isabella Bird was a well-known Victorian traveler; and Dull Gret is taken from a painting by Breughel.

2. For an example of a collection of essays that displays this awareness, see Warhol and Herndl's anthology, *Feminisms*. The editors actually suggest several alternative arrangements of the essays, based on shuffling their own categories, as a coda to their text.

3. I argue the case for surrogate selves in autobiographical performance in "Both Sides of the Curtain," about the actress-playwright-novelist Elizabeth Robins (1862–1952), particularly with respect to the Ibsen roles for women at the turn of the nineteenth century.

4. Gage's Cushman serves as an example of an early method actress ("I gave them a prostitute they could see, not just look at—but really see"), while Pineau's playing of Nin makes her a contemporary exemplar.

5. This boundary-setting is probably the experience of most scholars working closely

with the intimate manuscript material available to them in special collections around the world; it may be a necessary stage, in fact, to achieving critical distance, yet it is not easy to put the enticements of collapsed boundaries to regular scrutiny. For a satiric exposé of obsessive desire aroused by the scholarly study of private papers, see Byatt's best-selling novel *Possession*.

6. See Alexander's article on Tami Spry for a more thorough discussion of "generative autobiography." This coinage (as well as Pineau's in response to Alexander's) recalls the excitement of 1980s feminist critiques as they simultaneously came up with similar yet critically distinct terminology which was used to help forge the new theory of women's autobiographical writing and, by implication, performance.

7. Terrell, too, performed on the Chautauqua circuit. Now that more of her "platform speeches" are coming into print, they invite analysis and (ideally) reenactment.

8. Notably, at this point Pineau has stopped referring to her subject with the given name she still evokes in the title of her performed script, "My Life with Anaïs." A valuable inquiry in itself would be a comparative analysis of the use of first names in critical and biographical studies of men and women.

9. The motif of crossing boundaries occurs in autobiography theory in general. See especially Bell and Yalom, Brodzki and Schenck, Friedman, and Smith.

10. Charles Dickens's own portrayal of both Sikes and Nancy in his public reading (derived from his own novel) was adjudged by many as primarily responsible for his death.

11. I respectfully disagree with Cherry's reading of Terrell's life, for the autobiography bears witness to frequent instances of accommodation and conformity, leading me to read it as a highly conflicted self-portrait. I trust, though, that recent efforts (1980; 1996) to get the autobiography into reprint will promote more lively debate about this African American proto-feminist.

12. Fleishman presumes that the self-referentiality of *mise en abyme* as it occurs in certain autobiographical texts makes them more valuable than others, most notably the memoir, which he relegates to a lower status, in turn associated more often with the self-writing of women than that of men (*Figures of Autobiography* 37). Besides taking issue with that hierarchical assessment (essentially a dismissal), I also argue that women's autobiographical texts invoke his coveted *mise en abyme* with relative ease, as examples in this volume show.

13. This is, of course, the primary point in Foucault's *History of Sexuality* in relation to Victorian England, by now an accepted stand-in for nineteenth-century America as well. Incidentally, although Cushman was American born, she settled in England in 1849 and launched her farewell tour of the United States in 1874 (within two years of her death).

14. From its inception, women's autobiography theory has recognized women's especial propensity to be fragmented and hence to create a different kind of self-writing from that of most men. Always already self-divided, women performing other women's lives will perforce multiply that multiplicity. This observation is one I develop in *Creative Negativity*.

Bibliography

Abel, Elizabeth, Marianne Hirsch, and Elizabeth Langland, eds. *The Voyage In: Fictions of Female Development*. Hanover, N.H.: University Press of New England, 1983.

Alexander, Bryant Keith. *"Skin Flint (or, The Garbage Man's Kid):* A Generative Autobiographical Performance Based on Tami Spry's *Tattoo Stories." Text and Performance Quarterly* 20, no.1 (2000): 97–114.

Aston, Elaine. *An Introduction to Feminism and Theatre.* London: Routledge, 1995.

Belenky, Mary Field, Blythe McVicker Clinchy, Nancy Rule Goldberger, and Jill Marruck Tarule. *Women's Ways of Knowing: The Development of Self, Voice, and Mind.* New York: Basic Books, 1986.

Bell, Susan Groag, and Marilyn Yalom, eds. *Revealing Lives: Autobiography, Biography, and Gender.* Albany: State University of New York Press, 1990.

Benstock, Shari, ed. *Feminist Issues in Literary Scholarship.* Bloomington: Indiana University Press, 1987.

Brodzki, Bella, and Celeste Schenck, eds. *Life/Lines: Theorizing Women's Autobiography.* Ithaca, N.Y.: Cornell University Press, 1988.

Bunch, Charlotte. "Introduction." In *Building Feminist Theory: Essays from Quest,* xv–xxiii. New York: Longman, 1981.

Butler, Judith. "Conclusion: From Parody to Politics." In *Gender Trouble: Feminism and the Subversion of Identity,* 142–49. New York: Routledge, 1990.

Byatt, A.S. *Possession: A Romance.* London: Chatto and Windus, 1990.

Caine, Barbara. *Victorian Feminists.* Oxford: Oxford University Press, 1992.

Case, Sue-Ellen. *Feminism and Theatre.* London: Macmillan, 1988.

———, ed. *Performing Feminisms: Feminist Critical Theory and Theatre.* Baltimore: Johns Hopkins University Press, 1990.

Case, Sue-Ellen, and Janelle Reinelt, eds. *The Performance of Power: Theatrical Discourse and Politics.* Iowa City: University of Iowa Press, 1991.

Chodorow, Nancy. *The Reproduction of Mothering: Psychoanalysis and the Sociology of Gender.* Berkeley: University of California Press, 1978.

Churchill, Caryl. *Top Girls.* London: Methuen, 1982.

Cixous, Hélène. "The Laugh of the Medusa." Translated by Keith Cohen and Paula Cohen. *Signs: Journal of Women in Culture and Society* 1, no. 4 (1976): 875–94.

Cook, Blanche Wiessen. "Female Support Networks and Political Activism: Lillian Wald, Crystal Eastman, Emma Goldman." *Chrysalis* 3 (1977): 43–61.

Davis, Tracy C. *Actresses as Working Women: Their Social Identity in Victorian Culture.* London: Routledge, 1992.

Dolan, Jill. *The Feminist Spectator as Critic.* Ann Arbor: University of Michigan Press, 1991.

Felski, Rita. *Beyond Feminist Aesthetics.* Cambridge: Harvard University Press, 1989.

Fleishman, Avrom. *Figures of Autobiography: The Language of Self-Writing.* Berkeley: University of California Press, 1983.

Flynn, Elizabeth A., and Patrocinio P. Schweickart, eds. *Gender and Reading: Essays on Readers, Texts, and Contexts.* Baltimore: Johns Hopkins University Press, 1986.

Foucault, Michel. *The History of Sexuality.* Vol.1. Translated by Robert Hurley. New York: Pantheon Books, 1978.

Friedman, Susan Stanford. "Women's Autobiographical Selves: Theory and Practice." In *The Private Self: Theory and Practice of Women's Autobiographical Writings,* edited by Sheri Benstock, 34–62. Chapel Hill: University of North Carolina Press, 1988.

Gardiner, Judith Kegan. "On Female Identity and Writing by Women." *Critical Inquiry* 8, no. 2 (1981): 347–61.

Gilligan, Carol. *In a Different Voice: Psychological Theory and Women's Development.* Cambridge: Harvard University Press, 1982.

Gilmore, Leigh. *Autobiographics: A Feminist Theory of Self-Representation.* Ithaca, N.Y.: Cornell University Press, 1994.

Greene, Gayle, and Coppélia Kahn, eds. *Making a Difference: Feminist Literary Criticism.* London and New York: Methuen, 1985.

Gubar, Susan. "'The Blank Page' and the Issues of Female Creativity." In *New Feminist Criticism: Essays on Women, Literature, and Theory*, edited by Elaine Showalter, 292–313. New York: Pantheon Books, 1985. First published in *Critical Inquiry* 8 (1981).

Heilbrun, Carolyn G. *Writing a Woman's Life.* New York: W.W. Norton, 1988.

Jacobus, Mary. "Is There a Woman in This Text?" *New Literary History* 14, no. 1 (1982): 117–41.

Klein, Julie Thompson. *Crossing Boundaries: Knowledge, Disciplinarities, and Interdisciplinarities.* Charlottesville: University Press of Virginia, 1996.

Laughlin, Karen. "Introduction: Why Feminist Aesthetics?" In *Theatre and Feminist Aesthetics*, edited by Karen Laughlin and Catherine Schuler, 9–21. London: Associated University Presses, 1995.

Lionnet, Françoise. *Autobiographical Voices: Race, Gender, Self-Portraiture.* Ithaca, N.Y.: Cornell University Press, 1989.

Lorde, Audré. "The Master's Tools Will Never Dismantle the Master's House." Remarks at "The Personal and Political Panel," Second Sex Conference, New York, 29 November 1979. Reprinted in Lorde, *Sister Outsider: Essays and Speeches*, 110–13. Freedom, Calif.: Crossing Press, 1988.

MacKay, Carol Hanbery. "Biography as Reflected Autobiography: The Self-Creation of Anne Thackeray Ritchie." In *Revealing Lives: Autobiography, Biography, and Gender*, edited by Susan Groag Bell and Marilyn Yalom, 65–80. Albany: State University of New York Press, 1990.

———. "'Both Sides of the Curtain': Elizabeth Robins, Synaesthesia, and the Subjective Correlative." *Text and Performance Quarterly* 17, no. 4 (1997): 299–316.

———. *Creative Negativity: Four Victorian Exemplars of the Female Quest.* Stanford, Calif.: Stanford University Press, 2001.

Mason, Mary G. "The Other Voice: Autobiographies of Women Writers." In *Life/Lines: Theorizing Women's Autobiography*, edited by Bella Brodzki and Celeste Schenck, 19–44. Ithaca, N.Y.: Cornell University Press, 1988.

McMurtry, Larry. *Buffalo Girls.* New York: Simon and Schuster, 1990.

Miller, Nancy K., ed. *The Poetics of Gender.* New York: Columbia University Press, 1986.

Nalbantian, Suzanne. *Aesthetic Autobiography: From Life to Art in Marcel Proust, James Joyce, Virginia Woolf and Anaïs Nin.* London: Macmillan 1994.

Olsen, Tillie. *Silences.* New York: Delacorte Press, 1978.

Postlewait, Thomas. "Autobiography and Theatre History." In *Interpreting the Theatrical Past: Essays in the Historiography of Performance*, edited by Thomas Postlewait and Bruce A. McConachie, 248–72. Iowa City: University of Iowa Press, 1989.

Prose, Francine. "Scent of a Woman's Ink: Are Women Writers Really Inferior?" *Harper's Magazine*, June 1998, 61–70.

Russ, Joanna. *How to Suppress Women's Writing*. Austin: University of Texas Press, 1983.

Sellers, Susan, ed. *Feminist Criticism: Theory and Practice*. Toronto: University of Toronto Press, 1991.

Shires, Linda, ed. *Rewriting the Victorians: Theory, History, and the Politics of Gender*. New York: Routledge, 1992.

Showalter, Elaine. *The Female Malady: Women, Madness, and Culture in England, 1830–1980*. New York: Pantheon Books, 1985.

Singley, Carol, and Susan Sweeney, eds. *Anxious Power: Reading, Writing, and Ambivalence in Narrative by Women*. Albany: State University of New York Press, 1993.

Smith, Sidonie. *A Poetics of Women's Autobiography: Marginality and the Fictions of Self-Representation*. Bloomington: Indiana University Press, 1987.

Stephens, Autumn. *Wild Women: Crusaders, Curmudgeons and Completely Corsetless Ladies in the Otherwise Virtuous Victorian Era*. Berkeley: Conari Press, 1992.

Stern, Carol Simpson, and Bruce Henderson. *Performance: Texts and Contexts*. New York and London: Longman, 1993.

Terrell, Mary Church. *A Colored Woman in a White World*. Washington, D.C.: Ransdell, 1940.

———. "The Progress of Colored Women." Address before the National American Women's Suffrage Association. Washington, D.C.: Smith Brothers, 1898.

Wagner-Martin, Linda. *Telling Women's Lives: The New Biography*. New Brunswick, N.J.: Rutgers University Press, 1994.

Warhol, Robyn, and Diane Price Herndl, eds. *Feminisms: An Anthology of Literary Theory and Criticism*. New Brunswick, N.J.: Rutgers University Press, 1991.

Woolf, Virginia. *A Room of One's Own*. New York: Harcourt, Brace and World, 1929.

Catherine Rogers
as Georgia O'Keeffe
(photo by Tom Bloom,
used by permission)

Debra Wright as Charlotte Cushman (© Pamela Newman Photography, used by permission)

Engraving of Charlotte Cushman, "From the original painting by Chappel, in the possession of the publishers," 1872 (used by permission of the Harry Ransom Humanities Research Center)

Graphic of Tami Spry's
tattoo (courtesy of Tami
Spry and Tattoos by Kore)

Jacqueline Taylor with parents and sister, 1958 (courtesy of Jacqueline Taylor)

Jacqueline Taylor preparing for "sword drill" (courtesy of Jacqueline Taylor)

THE BEACON

FIRST BAPTIST CHURCH
ELDRED M. TAYLOR, Pastor
28 NORTH MAIN   SOMERSET, KENTUCKY

**GETTING READY FOR THE STATE
TRAINING UNION CONVENTION**

Talking about the State Finals of the Junior Memory Work and Bible Drill are, left to right above, Ann O'Bryan, Rebekah Correll, Jackie Taylor, and Roy Thompson. Jackie has earned the privilege of participating in the State Finals by her showing in the Church Drill, the Pulaski Association Drill, and the Regional Drill. Ann and Becky have been practicing with Jackie to help her prepare for the Finals. Roy Thompson has directed this phase of the training program for Juniors.

The State Finals Drill will be held on Wednesday, April 17, during the Opening Session of the State Training Union Convention. Everyone is invited to attend the Convention sessions which will be held in our church next week. We especially want to commend Jackie for her fine work, and promise her our support in the Final Drill.

VOLUME VI   APRIL 14, 1963   NUMBER 15

Linda Park-Fuller addressing an audience after "A Clean Breast of It" (© Chuck Giorno Photography, used by permission)

*Joni L. Jones and Alli
Aweusi in "sista docta"
(© 2002 Lynda Miller,
used by permission)*

Performance artist
Terry Galloway
(photo by Alan
Pogue, used by
permission)

PART II

Staging the Self

9

Illustrated Woman

❧ Autoperformance in "Skins:
A Daughter's (Re)construction of Cancer" and
"Tattoo Stories: A Postscript to 'Skins'"

Tami Spry

A piece of paper, whatever the reason, can't carry the weight of a
body.
> —Elyse Lamm Pineau, "Nursing Mother"

The story comes, after the accident, to identify the body.
> —Craig Gingrich-Philbrook, "What I 'Know' about the Story
> (For Those about to Tell Personal Narratives on Stage)"

I know I am an un/learning body in the process of feeling. You too.
> —D. Soyini Madison, "Performing Theory/Embodied Writing"

The comments of Pineau, Gingrich-Philbrook, and Madison help me
make sense of why I bring my body up on stage and explicate the accidents
of my lived experience. As I constitute myself first and foremost as a performer, I often find my writer's "un/learning body" crashing clumsily
through paper, landing in a heap on the stage. As I lift my head up from
the pains of falling and make eye contact with audience others, I feel the
joining of voices in my body with other bodies on the ground(ing) of that
staged social space. Like Madison, when it comes to performance, "I am
guilty of gluttony. I have taken Performance for myself. . . . I want to hold
on to her, not wanting her to be with anyone but me and my kind; because
we've known her for a longer time—who she is and how to treat her"

(108). And it is she, Performance, who helps me up from a heap on the stage "to know myself more, to know you, more." "Yes," Madison whispers to me, "vulgar performacism," but understandable, I think, in a time when performance is bandied about by those who have never heard the tear of the paper resisting the weight of their body, or later, after looking back upon their body, wondered where the bruises came from. The story comes then, after these accidental fallings, to identify the body. And so here, on the page, I will present a discursive composite of my body through "Skins: A Daughter's (Re)construction of Cancer" and "Tattoo Stories: A Postscript to 'Skins,'" first offering some brief thoughts on the composition of autobiographic and autoethnographic performance.

PERFORMING "SKINS"

The debut of "Skins: A Daughter's (Re)construction of Cancer" in 1994 at the Speech Communication Association convention in New Orleans marked the beginning of my journey into performing autobiography;[1] it also marked the seventh year since my mother's death from ovarian cancer. I was confused and devastated at her death and tried numerous times to compile a script that would offer others and myself some clarity and insight into this complex experience. Each time I began to research the experiences of motherless daughters, however, I would become emotionally paralyzed and artistically bereft. This, of course, only exacerbated the confusion and devastation.

Then, in 1993, a close friend and colleague who possesses a witchy sixth sense asked me to contribute to a panel on autobiography. She said, "It's been six years, Tam. Talk about your Mom." I did. In my twenty years of performance experience, I had never felt so terrified before a performance. An hour before "curtain" I was in my hotel room sobbing in the arms of two dear friends after I had tried in vain to run the show. These women knew my mother, Belle; they knew how she had notarized herself upon my body and knew how I had struggled to be a reliable narrator to her text all of my life. Performing the highly contested relationship between Tami/Belle/Little in the intimacy of our hotel room was more than I could bear. However, I later realized that the public performance of "Skins" would have been impossible without the private cradling by these women as I wept.

Although the performative autobiographical location is a space of intense personal and cultural risk, it is simultaneously a space of profound comfort. It has become for me a site of narrative authority, offering me the power to reclaim and rename my voice and body privately in rehearsal, and then publicly in performance. The process enables me to speak about the personally political in public, which has been liberating and excruciating, but always in some way enabling. Performative autobiographies are, as Dwight Conquergood might say, "enabling fictions."

In the process of performing autobiography, the performer concentrates on the body as the site from which the story is generated. She seeks to read what she and others have written on the pulpish hides of her skins. The autobiographical performance process turns the internally *somatic* into the externally *semantic*. I try to coax words out onto the surface of my body. Words write themselves on and in the layers of my skins, introducing me to myself. My reading of those textual pelts becomes the semantic interpretation of my own somatic experience.

In "Skins" and "Tattoo Stories" I use the body's skin as a unifying and fracturing metaphor for the cultural narratives played out upon bodies. Sidonie Smith articulates the corporeal and conceptual complexity skin suggests when trying to semanticize one's autobiographic experience: "Skin is the literal and metaphorical borderland between the materiality of the autobiographical 'I' and the contextual surround of the world. It functions simultaneously as a personal and political, psychological and ideological boundary of meaning. . . . Skin has much to do with autobiographical writing, as the body of the text, the body of the narrator, the body of the narratee, the cultural 'body,' and the body politic all merge in skins and skeins of meaning" ("Bodies" 127–28). Smith suggests further that the autobiographical subject can find herself outside of her skin, homeless inside her own body. This is certainly an experience I lived after my mother's death. In "Skins" I use my mother's full-length mink coat as a symbol of her sociocultural identity, one that was often illustrated upon my body:

> *(Crossing to mink coat and clutching it, the daughter is afraid, angry, confused.)*
> I clung to these dead skins. But they kept drying up and flaking off. These new ones would appear, but she's not here to initialize them.
> *(Desperately indicating initials in the coat.)*
> Look. BMS. Belle Marie Spry.
> *(Indicating self.)*
> Who is this woman? Who is this woman whose skins are not notarized by Belle Marie Spry?

My life had been largely built around emulating my mother, grafting her skins upon mine. This bodily construction fit the social and ideological specifications of my surround. But a person cannot grow within the hide of another. I was not-me and not-not-me simultaneously (Schechner). "Tattoo Stories" charts the sloughing and tearing off of layers of hide as I tried desperately to find a home of my own making.

In performing "Skins" my hide became a corporeal semaphore signaling to myself and others that I was the agent and author of these embodied illustrations. After three decades of reading my body according to my mother's authorship, autobiographical performance has been a central tool in the reconstitution of my identity. The performing body offers a thick description of an individual's engagement with cultural codes and expectations; it is an ancient scroll upon which is written the stories of one's movement through the world.

PERFORMING "TATTOO STORIES"

"Tattoo Stories: A Postscript to 'Skins'" emerged about two years after I began performing "Skins." My experience and explication of the autobiographical performance process began to merge with my work in ethnographic fieldwork and performance, informed by the rhetorical and performative turn in anthropology articulated by Victor Turner, Clifford Geertz, Dwight Conquergood, Kristin Langellier, and others.

I found the dynamic and dialectical relations of the text and body to be a major theme in autoethnographic praxes (Anzaldúa, Crawford, Denzin, Ellis and Bochner, Ellis and Flaherty, Goodall, Neuman). In the fieldwork, writing, and performing of autoethnography, text and body are redefined, their boundaries blurring dialectically. The researcher, in context, interacting with others, becomes the subject of research, thereby blurring distinctions of personal and social, self and other (Conquergood, Ellis and Bochner, Richardson). Trinh Minh-ha writes, "Experience, discourse, and self-understanding collide against larger cultural assumptions concerning race, ethnicity, nationality, gender, class, and age" (157). For me, plaiting ethnography with autobiography emphasizes the cultural situatedness of the autobiographic subject.

Autoethnographic texts reveal the fractures, sutures, and seams of the text's generation of self—interacting with others in the context of researching lived experience. In interpreting the autoethnographic text, readers sense the fractures in their own communicative lives and, as described in Gramsci's notion of the organic intellectual, create efficacy and healing in their own communal lives. Barbara Jago writes of her autoethnographic work with family stories: "Because we tell our stories within the frames of dominant cultural myths, the aspects of our experience we can include are limited. Once such myths are identified and externalized, people can begin to rewrite alternate life stories outside of the dominant cultural narrative, reselecting elements of their experience to support a new and more satisfying vantage point" (507). Thirteen years after I was sexually assaulted, profound healing came when I began to rewrite that experience as a woman with strength and agency rather than accepting the victimage discourse of sexual assault embedded in our phallocentric language—and, thus, value systems (Spry "In the Absence").

As I continue to write and perform autoethnography, I believe I exist somewhere amid the sociopolitical narratives written on my body. My body is a cultural billboard advertising the effects of selves/others/contexts interacting with and upon it. Identity exists in a constant flux of interpreting self's interactions with others in sociohistorical contexts (Trinh; Smith "Performativity"). Autoethnography—with its body in the borderlands of autobiography and ethnography—is a narration signifying at least one interpretation of ever-fluctuating identity. And since the autoethnographic story is a discursive act, it is always turning back upon itself, affecting a continual praxis of identity tangled in the reifications and resistances of other(ed) bodies in the body politic. The autoethnographic "I," then becomes a plural pronoun with the constant refraction of selves in disparate locations (Smith "Bodies"; Perreault).

Performance presents another location, as I/we constitute selves in the staged moment of performance. Working off Jacques Derrida's "law of genre," Caren Kaplan argues that this plural "I" constitutes an "out-law" genre in its resistance to master genres in autobiography. Out-law genres in autobiography reveal the "power dynamics embedded in literary production, distribution, and reception" (208). Kaplan maintains that these emerging out-law genres "are more closely attuned to the power differences among participants in the process of producing the text. Thus, instead of a discourse of individual authorship, we find a discourse of situation; a 'politics of location'" (208). The postcolonial ethnographic and performance theory imperative of contextualizing the subject and the subjective researcher creates a tight theoretical weave with Kaplan's discourse of situation.

Kaplan illuminates the epistemological processes that guide my work in autoethnography, specifically in "Tattoo Stories." Her focus on power dynamics in literary production, distribution, and reception is the theory link to my lived experience of generating, rehearsing, and debuting "Tattoo Stories" at the Otis J. Aggert (OJA) Festival in 1996. Using the dancing/kicking/falling figures on my newly minted tattoo as a metaphor, this performed autoethnography monographed my experiences between sanity and mental illness. Before the OJA Festival, this particular all-too-lived experience was not one I had shared with anyone but intimate friends. I felt like a madwoman debutante presenting my psychotic selves at the Performance Studies Society Ball. The people assembled at this festival are often faculty of prestige in performance studies, some of whom I believe I know well, others who believe they know me well. This gathering was no different. As I constructed this performance, the dynamics of professional status and impression management caused weird collisions with the already personally and culturally fractured self—created out of notes and memory of going mad. Here, the "distribution" and "reception" of the text is performance, and packed with power differences.

Kristin Langellier's recent writing on "performativity" helps me make further sense of these collisions in the performance of personal narratives. She writes, "Approaching personal narrative as performance requires theory which takes context as seriously as it does text, which takes the social relations of power as seriously as it does personal reflexivity, and which therefore examines the cultural production and reproduction of identities and experience" ("Personal Narrative" 128). The "social relations of power" in the *context* of that debut performance were as constitutive of the autoethnography's literary production as the personal relations of power entangled in my alliance with my mother articulated in the *content* of "Tattoo Stories."

And again, it is the verisimilitude of the "'un/learning body' crashing clumsily through paper and landing in a heap on the stage" in performance that critically illuminates particular social relations of power between an academic community and myself. In "Dancing Bodies and the Stories They Tell," Ann Cooper Albright writes: "In performance, the audience is forced to deal directly with the history of that body in conjunction with the history of their own bodies. This face-to-face interaction is an infinitely more intense and uncomfortable experience which demands that the audience engage with their own cultural autobiographies" (121).

The verisimilitudinal stakes are vastly different when I perform "Tattoo Stories" for a Women's Center audience than when I perform this work for a scholarly convention audience. The meanings and desires of myself and the audience are terribly transformed due to the personal and professional expectations, ideologies, and politics inherent in these grossly different contexts. Albright continues, "Thinking of autobiography as a performance . . . helps us to keep the physical body in mind yet paradoxically refuses any essentialist notion of bodily experience as transparent and unmediated by culture" (120). Ethnographer Ruth Behar asserts that autoethnography brings the researcher "so disturbingly present" (25) to the audience, creating a context whereby meanings and interpretations are created between the participants in a flesh-to-flesh theorizing.

But theorizing "flesh to flesh" amidst the OJA audience brought to bear the histories of our flesh that, too ironically, contributed to the break(through)down described in "Tattoo Stories." Smith suggests that communal discourses and practices determine how the body is called together as a "unified or coherent material reality with specific identity constructions" ("Bodies" 128). The OJA audience represented for me a reified and hegemonizing communal narrative—a mini version of the wider communal narrative of academe, highly determinant in the "calling together" of the material body "with specific identity constructions."

Up until five years ago, my performance of self in academe was an exhausting artifice. Beginning with my first years in graduate school I carefully observed the social constructions of "scholar" performed at academic conventions. I watched, listened, and sought to construct a believable version of "successful academic." As a woman, I gendered myself in a costume of heels, hose, suit, and power hair. I networked, performed intellectual-white-middle-class-liberal-feminist, and was wounded and inflicted wounds in the competitive battlefield of the academy. I used my body as a billboard, advertising all of the insightful thoughts and attractive personal attributes required for full membership into the academic fraternity. I distorted my scholarly voice into a distanced, disembodied, phallocentric mimicry. I dissertated, published, tenure-tracked, nursed a dying mother, birthed a child, maintained a troubled marriage, and finally, inevitably, thankfully, had a mental breakdown. "Tattoo Stories" is the story of that breakdown. So, I would be debuting an autoethnographic performance in a context that helped cause the mental rupture described in the performance.

Strangely (or maybe quite ordinarily), performing that narrative in that context to that audience created for me a profound emancipation from the coherent material realities called together upon my body in a communal narrative of the academy. The performance was, for me, a "coming out ball." (Read within that phrase the [extra]ordinary mix of queer theory with bourgeoisie gender presentation; it was all part of the sociopolitical mix of identity construction I was experiencing.) Not only was I tearing off the skins of my mother "in" performance, I was also breaking out of an academic communal narrative that I had long used as a corset restricting the breath and breadth of my personal/professional body. Furthermore, "Tattoo Stories" describes the experience of a "Hysterical Woman," a bodily experience grotesque to the Mind of the Academy. Smith writes, "The body categorized as abnormal becomes associated with those forces threatening the stability of the body politic. It becomes a pollutant, a grotesquerie." Smith adds that while the autobiographical subject "finds herself subjected to the social meanings of bodies, she can find ways to resist the kind of body pressed upon her through the body politic" ("Bodies" 130). I cannot stop the modernist mediated profiles of identity scripted upon my body, but because identity exists amidst discursive profiles, I can change the way I dialogically engage these stories; for me, this change is most profound through performance.

Performing autoethnography has motivated an intense shift in the shape of my life. It has been a vehicle of resistance and emancipation from cultural and familial identity scripts that have governed the size and shape of my body and identity personally and professionally. The point of my work is to express scholarship in ways that mirror the passion, pain, and hope of lived experience. This work has literally saved my life by providing me the means to claim reflexive agency in my interactions with others in contexts. My body is still a cultural billboard, but its advertisements promote the "insightful thoughts and attractive personal attributes suggested for full membership" into a life of hope and renewal.

I began creating a self in and out of academe that allowed an expression of passion and spirit I had long suppressed. Although expressing passion and spirit within the communal narrative of academe seemed more like heresy than successful scholarly practice, in going mad, I had learned that heresy is greatly maligned and, when put to good use, can be the music that begins a robust dance of agency in one's personal/political/professional life.

"Skins" was about dancing and kicking.

"Tattoo Stories" is about falling through paper and landing in a heap on a bare stage.

SKINS: A DAUGHTER'S (RE)CONSTRUCTION OF CANCER

(A plain straight-backed wooden chair is placed center stage. The rest of the stage is bare. Carefully placed over the back of the chair is an opulent full-length mink coat. The chair and coat are prelit in a wide dim spot; all else is dark.

The daughter enters slowly from left. She is dressed in a classic, basic black dress and heels. As she enters, the spot level increases. She very tentatively enters the space delineated by the spot, then walks slowly toward the coat. She circles the coat, touching it gingerly. She picks the coat up to put it on. The coat is heavy in the daughter's hands and she is conflicted about donning the coat.

Finally, she puts it on and is transformed into a caricatured model on a runway. The daughter/model smiles garishly, walking briskly downstage center as if modeling and selling the coat; she speaks to the audience.)

Skins
Dead skins
Skins of mothers:
   (As mother.)
"Little . . . Tami? . . . Little? . . ."
Skins of daughters:
   (As daughter.)
"Oh, mom . . . where are you? . . ."
   (Daughter enacts the action of the narrative as she speaks it.)
Do you remember the commercial where the model strides down the runway, takes a big turn at the end of the runway, and as she turns blood comes out of her fur coat
and splatters
the faces
of the audience?
I remember that.
I also remember this:
   (In a bright and emotionally distanced tone.)
A small hunched woman whose skin is falling from her face and her neck and her body. She is wrapped in these very skins
   (Indicating the coat.)
On one elbow is a daughter, on the other is a husband.

They help her to the car in the middle of a cold January Michigan winter and whisk her off to the hospital where she dies four days later. After the four days, the daughter wraps herself in these skins. She leaves the hospital, goes to the mother's house, up the stairs into the mother's bedroom, goes into the closet,

(The daughter now begins to embody the described experience as her own.)
parts the clothes, and slides down the wall with the clothes around her.

(Crouched downstage center.)
I wrapped these dead skins tight around me and cried for my mother's death, and mourned my life. How would I ever grow new skins now? And I feel the blood tears on my face as the skins whip around on the final turn of the runway.

(She stands and crosses upstage center.)
And I remember this:

(As the mother.)
"Now, Little, you need some new clothes. So, you and Mumma will go to lunch and go shopping.

Oh, Little, that is absolutely darling. Well, you have to have that."

(As saleswoman.)
"Oh, Mrs. Spry, your daughter is a perfect size seven."

(As mother, scrutinizing the daughter.)
"Gads, she really is."

(As daughter to audience.)
Did you see the dignity and power and grace?

(As mother.)
"Little, that is abso*lute*ly darling."

(As daughter to audience.)
My mother died of ovarian cancer when I was twenty-six years old. And I look just like her—so much so that my grandfather, her father, would not be in the same room with me for two months after she died. My father would come visit us in southern Illinois and would stand at the door for the first five minutes weeping at the sight of me.

(Crossing upstage of chair and draping coat over chair.)
She wrote herself all over this body.
And the cancer did some writing of its own.
I remember this:

(The daughter experiences the narrative action as she speaks it.)
Bang bang bang.
I remember waking up in the middle of the night to a

Bang bang bang.
It was faint but *very* direct.
My father and I were light sleepers during this time
because my mother had to sleep downstairs in a hospital bed.
She was too weak to climb the stairs.
Bang bang bang.
I went to the top of the stairs and looked down into the darkness. Mom
was having trouble sleeping and wanted all the lights off.
I went down the stairs and flipped the hall light on and
Bang bang bang . . .
there was my strong, powerful, beautiful mother
banging on the bed stand with a brush
because she was in too much pain to cry out.
And I remember:
    (As mother.)
"Little, you need some new—"
    (As if the sound is going off in the daughter's head.)
Bang bang bang
    (As mother.)
"Little that looks absolutely—"
    (As daughter, sound building.)
Bang bang bang
    (As saleswoman.)
"Mrs. Spry, your daughter is a perfect size—"
    (As daughter, sound building and reaching a crescendo.)
Bang bang bang.
    (Crossing to coat and clutching it, the daughter is afraid, angry, confused.)
I clung to these dead skins. But they kept drying up and flaking off. These
new ones would appear, but she's not here to initialize them.
    (Desperately indicating initials in the coat.)
Look. BMS. Belle Marie Spry.
    (Indicating self.)
Who is this woman? Who is this woman whose skins are not notarized
by Belle Marie Spry?
    (The daughter crosses and places the coat on the chair.)
A few weeks after her death, the Black Hole Dreams began.
    (She crosses downstage center and intimately tells the story to the audience.)
The Black Hole Dreams went something like this:
I would come home after a long time at college or a long theatre run. I

would come in the back door where Mom would be standing at the top
of the stairs. She would say, "Hi, Little!"
Well, in the dreams, I was at the top of the stairs looking down at a black
hole. From the hole would come my mother's voice,
"Little . . . Tami . . . Little . . ."
I could never see her,
but I imagined her reaching for me.
And I was too afraid
to go into the black hole
to help her.
Now,
on a bad day,
I cry, "Oh, Ma, come out of there."
   (Crossing upstage to coat and placing hands on coat.)
But on a good day . . .
on a good day I say,
"Oh, Ma, come out of there and be with me."
And she does.
   (Crossing center stage.)
And she seeps into, through, and all around this body.
And the hunched woman,
and the daughter sinking into the closet,
and Little
and Belle
and Tami
all work to reweave and remake these live skins.
And on a very good day,
you can hear them singing:
"Little . . . Tami . . . Little . . . ."

TATTOO STORIES: A POSTSCRIPT TO "SKINS"

   (Performer stands downstage center. She is wearing a sleeveless funky-chic
   flowing dress that highlights the tattoo on her upper left arm. She wears a
   shawl animated with suns, moons, and stars. She is barefooted. A straight-
   backed chair with no arms is placed center stage. The stage is otherwise bare.)
But
on a good day . . .
on a good day I say,

"Oh, Mom, come out of there and be with me."

And she does.

And she seeps into, through, and all around this body.
(The performer enacts the following images through movement.)
And the hunched woman,
and the daughter sinking into the closet,
and Little
and Belle
and Tami
all work to reweave and remake these new skins.

And on a *very* good day,
you can hear them singing:
"Little . . . Tami . . . Little . . . ."
So ended a performative autobiography that I first performed in 1994,
at SCA New Orleans, called "Skins: A Daughter's (Re)Construction of
Cancer." I wore heels, hose, and a tailored black dress imported from
Italy. It was the dress that I wore to my Mom's funeral.
This autobiographical performance is called "Tattoo Stories,"
and is just one continuation
of "Skins."
(Performer crosses up left and reenters the stage powerfully and playfully
singing a funky rhythm. Throughout this play with the audience, she some-
what coyly flashes her tattoo hidden by her shawl. Finally with great flour-
ish, she reveals the tattoo on her upper left arm and makes a muscle for the
audience. She then crosses to the chair and lays her shawl across it.)
My mother died ten years ago last month.
She cut a beautiful,
dignified,
and dominating
figure.
She wore a full-length mink coat;
it was iconic of who she was.
It symbolized her struggle from poverty
into a life of comfort,
a journey from a family of chaos
into our family's regimented control.

And Mom
was the overseer,
the sergeant,
and the sage.
     (Performer engages movement reflecting the following images as she speaks.)
It has taken me these ten years to shed that coat,
     (She begins taking it off slowly, tentatively, with difficulty.)
to peel off those skins,
     (The coat becomes harder to take off, she peels it off her arms.)
and to find out who else
she and I are
     (The coat is off; she is tentative but anticipatory.)
underneath.
One year ago January,
another layer of skin fell away
and underneath was this.
     (Gesture to tattoo.)
It just
emerged one day.
The artist
who happened to be there
when it happened
said that she could
feel it writing itself
as if it were surfacing
from a space
in my body
dark
and
deep.

The outer design is the Celtic symbol for the Tree of Life. In Pagan spir-
itualities, the tree is a sacred symbol of life, circularity, fertility, and creativity. Inside the body of the tree are two women dancing—something
like this.
     *(She lifts her right arm over her head and lifts her left leg; she then leans
     back gracefully.)*
But as the tattoo continued to grow out of me,
writing itself from that dark and deep space,

I became more and more unclear
as to whether the women were dancing,
> *(She enacts the above movement.)*
or kicking,
> *(From the dance position she uses her left leg to angrily kick.)*
or falling.
> *(The kick causes her to fall off balance; she catches herself before falling to the floor.)*
Now, I rather like this ambiguity
because I am never quite sure if *I*
am dancing,
or kicking,
or falling.

But up until a couple of years ago,
I was *very* sure.
In my family growing up,
one must always at least *appear*
as if
she were dancing.
> *(During the next passages the performer confidently and proficiently enacts complicated formal ballet movements and positions.)*
One must always be
in control—
always disciplined.
One could kick if she were angry;
but it was always understood
that this was just a different kind
of control.

In my family,
if you were not in control,
you risked people seeing your weaknesses and vulnerabilities.
And that was *never, ever*
appropriate.
So I worked very hard
to make everyone   believe
that I was always dancing,
always   in   control.

(The dancing stops.)
Two and a half years ago,
after thirty-four years of disciplined dancing
and angry kicking . . .
I finally fell.

Two and a half years ago
I had a mental breakdown,
a breakthrough,
a deconstruction
and reclamation
of the most intimate kind.
It was a most terrifying,
ecstatic,
                  and euphoric
                           dance of selves.

The process of falling was slow,
    (She begins walking in a large circle center stage; she seems worried and unable to stop her movement.)
but not gentle.
It was punc
    (Her torso spasms and contracts forward and backward.)
tuated with
fits
    (Again.)
and   starts,
    (Again.)
far from the disciplined dance that I was used to.
    (Performer shifts to a flashback of the breakdown. She is walking/stumbling in a circle on stage, talking on the phone.)
Um, um . . . Deb . . . ah, um, I, um . . . Deb?
    (Performer shifts back to present time.)
During those last days, I saw many faces.

Some were the faces of my Mom:
    (Performer sits and talks with a fictional other using off stage focus. She tells the story as if it is humorous, as if it is "no big deal.")

Um, Marla, did I ever tell you about this one thing my Mom used to tell me? When I was little, like three, and four, and five, up until I was a teenager, my Mom used to tell me that I wasn't really hers, that I wasn't really her child and that my real father was the garbage man and that he might come to get me someday. And she would go on to say that she found me one day in the garbage can . . . and that she took me in. And it was like this family joke, that she wasn't really my real mom, and that I was the garbage man's kid and that he could show up any day. It was supposed to be this funny joke. And when I was very young—before I had learned that it was funny—my mom would go on about it until I started to cry. And then she would laugh and say, "Oh, no. Not really, not really." But even though it was supposed to be this family joke . . . um . . . she was usually the only one there . . .

Isn't that funny?

(Back to present audience.)

And my friend Marla said, "Oh, Tami."

And my friend Laila said, "Oh, honey."

And I was surprised by their somber reactions.

Well, I told my therapist, Carole, this story because she seemed really interested in my mom. Even though I kept telling her that my mom was this wonderful person, she kept asking me about my mom. And since she had diagnosed me as severely clinically depressed I thought I should give her something, so . . .

I told her.

And

as I told her . . .

I started to sob.

I started to sob

those deep gut-twisting sobs.

And I couldn't stop.

And she put her hand on my knee

as I fell

and fell

and fell.

(Flashback to breakdown. Again on phone.)

Um, um, um, Carole? Um . . . I . . . I . . .um, I . . . I don't know. Carole? Um . . .

(Back to present.)

And on the way down,
I saw the face of my grandmother.
(As Mother talking to performer. Use onstage focus.)
"Little, Little, come on. Come on, wake up."
(Performer as younger, just waking up.)
What? What's the matter? What time is it?
(As mother.)
"It's 2:00 A.M. Come on you have to come with Mumma. Grandma's hav-
ing one of her spells again. We need to get to Aunt Judy's. Come on."
(Still as mother. Flashback to Gram on couch.)
"Mumma? Mumma, it's Belle. Mumma? Come on, Mumma, you need to
get up.
(Sternly.)
"Mumma!
Mumma come on now, you need to get up.
(Mother waves her hand in front of Gram's face. She becomes fearful.)
"Mumma? Mumma?!"
(As performer in present time.)
When I was around twelve, and fifteen, and seventeen, my mom would
be summoned in the middle of the night to go to one of my aunt's houses
because my Gram was having one of her "spells." My mom would wake
me up to go with her. And during these times I remember opening my
eyes and seeing the uncharacteristic fear in my Mom's face.
(Cross quickly to stage left — the aunt's house.)
We would drive quickly in the dark, get to my aunt's house, and there
Gram would be,
(Sees grandmother.)
lying on the couch
stiff,
still,
paralyzed,
her jaw locked,
her eyes half open.

I remember watching my mother
try to coax,
cajole,
and command

her mother
back into her body.

But something inside Gram would just   go off . . .
and she would leave us,
leave us her cracking shell,
her dry limbs brittle
from droughts of loneliness,
family chaos,
and—at that time—
the death of four children.

Sometimes Gram would   moan
through her clenched teeth
      (Performer enacts the following.)
and we would all rush over
leaning close
trying to hear,
all of us leaning over her,
my Mom,   my three aunts,   and me,
all of us
leaning over
watching bits
and pieces of ourselves   breaking
in Gram's
distorted face.

We stood there,
witches
over an ancestral cauldron
trying and trying
to incantate ourselves
out of the fear
and familiarity
of that face.
      (Back to present time. Performer gradually becomes confused and angry.)
She lay there
captive of a stingy

shaming
Catholic
god
who required that she be either
Virgin Mary
or Magdeline the repenting whore.
Unwilling or unable to embody either,
 (Performer turns upstage and begins walking in a circle.)
Gram looked back on her options,
and decided instead to turn to stone
like Sister Sara.
 (Flashback to breakdown. Sitting and swaying in a circle.)
I . . . I can't, I can't, um, I . . . no, I have to . . . Deb? Carole? Oh . . .
I, um . . .
 (Back to present.)
And the last faces I saw
on the way down
were the faces of others,
others who found comfort
in the splitting of selves.

It was finals day in my Interpersonal Communication course. The last group had just finished a thorough and sensitive presentation on gendered reactions to sexual assault. And in the middle of the ensuing discussion I noticed Karen—
 (Gesture toward chair.)
usually a very active student in discussion—
 (Cross to chair.)
was slumped in her chair with her head on her desk. Her eyes were partially opened, extremely dilated, and tears were running down her face into a puddle on the desk.
 (Flashback.)
"Karen? Karen?"
 (Present time.)
I couldn't rouse her. She was catatonic . . . stiff . . . brittle . . . a stone of salt . . .
 (Flashback as Mom.)
"Little, Little, come on, wake up. Grandma is having one of her—"
 (Back to performer within the story.)

I quickly dismissed class and called for the secretary to call nine-one-one
and my friend Nancy who worked at the Sexual Assault Center. I tried
unsuccessfully to pry the Diet Coke can from Karen's rigid grip.
  (Flashback as Mom.)
"Mumma? Mumma—"
  (Back to performer in story.)
I gently placed my hand on Karen's back. "It's OK, Karen. It's OK." Just
then two male paramedics came in, and from a completely catatonic
state, Karen went ballistic.
  (Performer enacts the following as if it is happening.)
She bolted upright, slamming both of us against the wall. And when we
came down, she grabbed hold of me pleading, "Don't let them—don't let
them touch me, they're bad! Please, please don't let them touch me!"
And out of this thirty-two-year-old woman's body,
Carrie emerged.
Carrie told me she was six years old
and would not go with the bad men.

I rode in the ambulance with Karen and over the course of the next three
hours, emerging from Karen was six-year-old Carrie, sixteen-year-old
Sara, a German-speaking person, a woman who played piano, and a few
others who weren't around long enough to leave their name. Finally, a
member of Karen's family showed up, and someone drove me to my car.
I drove home,
my head spinning.
I thought, "Wow, from a performance standpoint,
this woman could switch from persona to persona
like nobody's business."
And then I thought . . . and then I thought,
"Wait. Um, *I* can switch from persona to persona . . .
like . . .
nobody's business."

Well,
the fall had already begun.
I spent the next two nights in fitful nightmares
about Karen
and the others
and me.

Carole my therapist kept trying to assure me
   (Flashback to breakdown.)
   (Back to present.)
that what I had witnessed was Multiple Personality Disorder
   (Flashback to breakdown.)
   (Back to present.)
and that I was *worlds* away from that.
But her voice
kept getting farther
and farther away
as I drove around town in circles,
walked around my house in circles,
and ended up in the middle of our family room floor
swaying
and babbling
and falling
in circles.

Two friends found me, called Carole, medicated me, and put me to bed.
I woke up two days later, hazy, alive, and euphoric.
I had fallen, finally fallen;
and I wasn't in a garbage can,
I hadn't turned to salt,
and I was doing multiple personae   only in rehearsal.

A year later a tree of life appeared on my skin with two women dancing,
kicking, and falling. And they are me, and Mom, and Gram and many
many others. The roots flow through us like a corporeal conduit between
the above and below, between stillness and motion,
   (Begin to dance.)
between darkness and light.
And now,
when I move in clarity or chaos,
we women come together.

And on a very good day,
I can hear them singing
and see them dancing.

Notes

1. The Speech Communication Association is now known as the National Communication Association.

Bibliography

Albright, Ann Cooper. "Dancing Bodies and the Stories They Tell." In *Choreographing Difference: The Body and Identity in Contemporary Dance*, 119–49. Hanover, N.H.: University Press of New England, 1997.

Anzaldúa, Gloria, ed. *Making Face, Making Soul: Creative and Critical Perspectives by Feminists of Color.* San Francisco: Aunt Lute Books, 1990.

Behar, Ruth. *The Vulnerable Observer: Anthropology that Breaks Your Heart.* Boston: Beacon Press, 1997.

Behar, Ruth, and Deborah A. Gordon. *Women Writing Culture.* Berkeley: University of California Press, 1995.

Conquergood, Dwight. "Beyond the Text: Toward a Performative Cultural Politics." In *The Future of Performance Studies: Visions and Revisions*, edited by Sheron J. Dailey, 25–36. Annandale, Va.: National Communication Association, 1998.

———. "Performing as a Moral Act: Ethical Dimensions in the Ethnography of Performance." *Literature in Performance* 5, no. 2 (1985): 1–13.

———. "Rethinking Ethnography: Towards a Critical Cultural Politics." *Communication Monographs* 58 (1991): 179–94.

Crawford, Lyall. "Personal Ethnography." *Communication Monographs* 63 (1996): 158–70.

Denzin, Norman K. *Interpretive Ethnography: Ethnographic Practices for the Twenty-first Century.* London: Sage Publications, 1997.

———. "The Many Faces of Emotionality." In *Investigating Subjectivity: Research on Lived Experience*, edited by Carolyn Ellis and Michael G. Flaherty, 17–30. Newbury Park, Calif.: Sage, 1992.

Derrida, Jacques. "The Law of Genre." Translated by Avital Ronell. *Glyph* 7 (1980): 203–4.

Ellis, Carolyn. "Evocative Autoethnography: Writing Emotionally about Our Lives." In *Representation and the Text*, edited by William G. Tierney and Yvonna S. Lincoln, 115–39. Albany: State University of New York Press, 1997.

Ellis, Carolyn, and Arthur P. Bochner, eds. *Composing Ethnography: Alternative Forms of Qualitative Writing.* Walnut Creek, Calif.: Alta Mira Press, 1996.

Ellis, Carolyn, and Michael G. Flaherty, eds. *Investigating Subjectivity: Research on Lived Experience.* Newbury Park, Calif.: Sage, 1997.

Geertz, Clifford. *The Interpretation of Cultures.* New York: Basic Books, 1973.

———. *Works and Lives: The Anthropologist as Author.* Stanford, Calif.: Stanford University Press, 1988.

Gingrich-Philbrook, Craig. "What I 'Know' about the Story (For Those about to Tell Personal Narratives on Stage)." In *The Future of Performance Studies: Visions and Revisions*, edited by Sheron J. Dailey, 298–300. Annandale, Va.: National Communication Association, 1998.

Goodall Jr., H. L. *Living in a Rock and Roll Mystery: Reading Context, Self and Others as Clues.*
    Carbondale: Southern Illinois University Press, 1991.
———. "Notes for the Autoethnography and Autobiography Panel NCA." Paper pre-
    sented at the National Communication Association convention, New York City,
    November 1998.
———. "Turning within the Interpretive Turn: Radical Empiricism and a Case for Post-
    Ethnography. *Text and Performance Quarterly* 11 (1991): 153–57.
Jago, Barbara. "Postcards, Ghosts, and Fathers: Revising Family Stories." *Qualitative In-
    quiry* 2 (1996): 495–516.
Kaplan, Caren. "Resisting Autobiography: Out-Law Genres and Transitional Feminist
    Subjects." In *Women, Autobiography, Theory: A Reader*, edited by Sidonie Smith and Ju-
    lia Watson, 208–16. Madison: University of Wisconsin Press, 1998.
Langellier, Kristin. "Personal Narrative, Performance, Performativity: Two or Three
    Things I Know for Sure." *Text and Performance Quarterly* 19 (1999): 125–44.
———. "Voiceless Bodies, Bodiless Voices: The Future of Personal Narrative Perfor-
    mance." *The Future of Performance Studies: Visions and Revisions*, edited by Sheron J.
    Dailey, 207–13. Annandale, Va.: National Communication Association, 1998.
Madison, D. Soyini. "Performing Theory/Embodied Writing." *Text and Performance Quar-
    terly* 19 (1999): 107–24.
Neuman, Mark. "Collecting Ourselves at the End of the Century." In *Composing Ethnogra-
    phy: Alternative Forms of Qualitative Writing*, edited by Carolyn Ellis and Arthur
    Bochner. Walnut Creek, Calif.: Alta Mira Press, 1996.
Perreault, Jeanne. "Autography/Transformation/Asymmetry." In *Women, Autobiography,
    Theory: A Reader*, edited by Sidonie Smith and Julia Watson, 190–96. Madison: Uni-
    versity of Wisconsin Press, 1998.
Pineau, Elyse Lamm. "*Nursing Mother* and Articulating Absence." *Text and Performance
    Quarterly* 20 (2000): 1–19.
Richardson, L. "The Consequences of Poetic Representation: Writing the Other, Rewrit-
    ing the Self." In *Investigating Subjectivity: Research on Lived Experience*, edited by Car-
    olyn Ellis and Michael G. Flaherty, 125–37. Newbury Park, Calif.: Sage, 1992.
Schechner, Richard. *Performance Theory.* New York: Routledge, 1988.
Smith, Sidonie. "The Bodies of Contemporary Autobiographical Practice." In *Subjectivity,
    Identity, and the Body: Women's Autobiographical Practices in the Twentieth Century*, edited
    by Sidonie Smith, 126–53. Bloomington: Indiana University Press, 1993.
———. "Performativity, Autobiographical Practice, Resistance." *Women, Autobiography,
    Theory: A Reader*, edited by Sidonie Smith and Julia Watson, 108–15. Madison: Uni-
    versity of Wisconsin Press, 1998.
Spry, Tami. "In the Absence of Word and Body: Hegemonic Implications of 'Victim' and
    'Survivor' in Women's Narratives of Sexual Violence." *Women and Language* 18 (1995):
    27–32.
———. "Performative Autobiography: Presence and Privacy." In *The Future of Performance
    Studies: Visions and Revisions*, edited by Sheron J. Dailey, 254–63. Annandale, Va.: Na-
    tional Communication Association, 1998.
———. "Skins: A Daughter's (Re)construction of Cancer." *Text and Performance Quarterly*
    17 (1997): 361–65.

Trinh, Minh-ha. *When the Moon Waxes Red: Representation, Gender, and Cultural Politics.* New York: Routledge, 1991.

————. *Woman, Native, Other: Writing Postcoloniality and Feminism.* Bloomington: Indiana University Press, 1989.

Turner, Victor. *The Anthropology of Performance.* New York: PAJ Publications, 1987.

————. *From Ritual to Theatre: The Human Seriousness of Play.* New York: PAJ Publications, 1982.

10

On Being an
Exemplary Lesbian

✐ My Life as a Role Model

Jacqueline Taylor

This piece has had a curious life, moving back and forth between essay and performance. It began as a serious examination of the complications inherent in the role of lesbian role model and an exploration of the performative dimensions the role imposes on the life and the life imposes on the role. It rather quickly took on a raucous life of its own. By the third draft, the text itself began to exceed the limitations of the page, demanding props, lights, a slide show, music, performance. I have performed this piece in Chicago; Austin, Texas; San Francisco; Saint Paul, Minnesota; and San Diego. The performance includes a basket of props that I unpack at the beginning of the performance and gather up at the end. The basket and its contents function as a metaphor for the process the performance enacts of sorting through and gathering up the experiences of a life. Using the props, I act out the experiences of my overachieving preacher's daughter childhood. I also show slides throughout the performance, including family photographs that span five generations of women — a concrete invocation of a matriarchal lineage of strong women.

Because this piece both interrogates the ways in which a life functions as a performance and serves as a script for an actual performance, the meaning of performance in this essay-script shifts (some might even say, slips). Contemporary performance theory has directed our attention to the continuum of performance that moves from the most highly marked off and formally structured performances, to the impromptu performances of daily life. Judith Butler argues that gender and sexual orientation are always constructed through performative acts. This piece grows, in part, out of these rich discussions of gender as performance. It grows, as well, out of a childhood in which I regularly understood myself to be performing a role for the benefit of my father's church members, a life regularly described by my mother as occurring "in a goldfish bowl." She meant, by this, a life as spectacle, as the constant object of scrutiny. Of course, if one's life is an autobiographical performance, then the meaning of autobiographical performance becomes so capacious that everything is included and nothing is left out. Yet, the project here is to interrogate specifically performative moments in my preacher's daughter childhood and lesbian spokesperson adult life. At the same time that the piece interrogates performance in life, it is also a script of a performance, one clearly marked off by some of the formal markers that signify performance—a specific time and place with an announced performance, a spatial separation of audience and performer, audiovisual equipment, props, lights, a formal beginning and end.

In bringing this piece back to the page, I have added citations that refer the reader to some of the essay's theoretical underpinnings and have included sections that I sometimes cut in performance. The section of the piece that contains dated descriptions of various as-a-lesbian appearances is the one that I sometimes cut, depending on the audience and the length of time available for the performance. Yet the piece is essentially a script —a script that began as an essay exploring performance in life but quickly took to the stage in order to explore life through performance.

ON BEING AN EXEMPLARY LESBIAN

(The stage area contains a table at center-stage, a lectern stage right, and a slide-screen stage left. I enter from the back of the room — behind the audience — carrying a large straw bag over my shoulder. I place the bag on the table and begin carefully unpacking it. White gloves, washcloths, soap, a gilded wooden scepter, a cardboard crown, a Bible, and some shiny fabric are among the objects I arrange on the table. As I near the end of my unpacking, I begin to speak.)

My preacher-father taught me that every message must have a text. His always came from the Bible. My mother taught me that there is a poem for every occasion. I honor both of those lessons tonight, beginning with a Bible verse and ending with a few lines from Denise Levertov's poem "Stepping Westward." First, the scripture: "For we cannot but speak the things which we have seen and heard." Acts 4:20.

(I walk to the lectern, open a notebook I've carried with me from the basket, and, holding it up, announce:)

I'm listed under "Lesbian" in the DePaul University telephone directory. *(Pause while they think about this.)* I know this because of the number of calls I get on the topic.

Of course, there is no such thing as a lesbian listing in the directory of a Catholic university, but at times it seems there must be, because somehow my name circulates on an important grapevine. At first I thought this happened to all gay and lesbian faculty, but as I started to talk with others about it, I discovered this was not true. That naturally set me thinking about how I've acquired this role.

In the past eleven years, I, sometimes with my family, have done interviews for newspapers, radio programs, and books; visited classes; coled a faculty workshop; spoken at extracurricular student meetings; ridden our church's float in the Chicago Gay Pride Parade, and made various other invited appearances as a lesbian. Many of these appearances have been as a lesbian mom. In all of these cases, being a lesbian has not been some incidental or partial aspect of my identity; it has been my reason for being on display.[1]

Of course, I'm a lesbian all the time, whether or not anybody notices. Perhaps in keeping with my Baptist upbringing, I had one of those "road to Damascus" conversion experiences.[2] I was heterosexual, as far as I knew, until I fell in love with a woman when I was thirty-one years old. For a long time I thought we were friends. Then my stomach started to do a little happy flip every time I saw her. Finally one day we kissed each other, and, at that precise moment, as if one door slammed shut and another opened, I became a lesbian.[3] I was astonished and thrilled. Suddenly, love, passion, romance, sex, and a whole lot of other things that I had concluded were overrated creations of Hollywood fantasy mills began to make sense. Although for several months I walked around with a sense of disorientation I can only describe as feeling myself the still, stunned center of a world spinning madly around me, I never faltered in the certain knowledge that I was a lesbian. Instead, I reinterpreted my past, discovering the inevitable lesbian warning signs in my previous heterosexual experience. I know that in actual practice human sexuality does not fit neatly into the rigid categories with which we try to contain it, but, for me, a lesbian identity has never been especially complicated.[4] My conversion didn't come until I had had a number of years to figure out just how unenthusiastic a heterosexual I made. Confronted with a level of intimacy and connection I had only imagined, I knew what I knew.

So I'm always a lesbian. And, for many years now, I have tried to live my life as if that were no more remarkable than the fact that I'm a Kentuckian, or a woman, or a professor of communication, or a mother. What that means is that in the workplace, for instance, I talk about my lesbian life as matter-of-factly as my heterosexual colleagues talk about their lives. This requires an act of translation. I imagine what stories about my family, friends, and experiences I might tell if I were heterosexual, and then I go ahead and tell my own stories as if they were no more loaded than that. *Of course* I'm performing. The world does not feel that safe for lesbians to me. But I'm hoping that if I behave as if what I believe *should* be true *is* true I can contribute to the transformation I believe must come. All this performing is a lot of work in a world that regularly attempts to deny the reality of my life and experience, but, so far, it is the best way I have found to make space for myself and maintain my integrity in the face of all that denial.

But from time to time I am invited to make one of these "as a lesbian" appearances. So invisible are we that there are still plenty of people walking around saying things like, "I've never really known any lesbians." What they mean is, they've never *known* they've *known* a lesbian, even though they go to school with us, work with us, do business with us, and have us in their families. Naturally, it is a lot easier to work up a good generic hatred toward a group of people who have no faces than to hate a real, live human being (though people manage the latter all the time, despite its difficulties). But the hope, anyway, is that as people come into contact with actual lesbians, as opposed to the mythic ones who fuel their nightmares and their hatred, homophobia starts to unravel. Hence, the invitations to appear "as a lesbian," or as one friend so aptly named it, as "an exemplary lesbian."[5]

Mostly we're invisible.[6] When we do appear in the culture, it is often as emblems of corruption and depravity or as avenging furies, determined to overthrow male power and privilege. Lesbians are thought to be everything most dangerous and despicable about women, now raised exponentially to a level of horrid excess. We are depicted as excessively sexual, selfish, loud, large, angry, bitter, evil, ugly, hairy, political, radical, perverse, pushy, abnormal, anarchic, man-hating, feminist, pro-woman, and female. Indeed, it is redundant to say that we are thought to hold these traits in excess since their very presence is often considered excessive.

When I'm invited to be a lesbian exemplar, I'm supposed to counter all that.

(As I say these words I place a single tasteful strand of pearls around my neck and pull on a pair of white gloves of the sort we always wore to church in the fifties and early sixties.)

I'm supposed to be so charming, articulate, well-groomed, and, well, *normal* that all these prejudices melt away and the assembled audience suddenly sees the veil lift from their eyes. I stand revealed as—wonder of wonders—a fellow (sister) human. I'm supposed to look familiar, recognizable, enough like them that they might be lulled into taking me for one of their own.

I know a lot of lesbians, and although I'm not the only one who gets tapped for the role of exemplary lesbian, my family and I get more than our share. In speculating on why that might be, I've come up with several explanations. First of all, I'm a professor—an out professor, on a campus where until very recently that was still much more the exception than the rule. That makes me a visible candidate for some of these invitations. But I think there is more to it than visibility. Embedded in my vocation are issues of education and class. I'm a highly educated middle-class woman in a profession that engenders a certain amount of respect. I'm a professor with tenure. I'm articulate. I'm white. I'm thin. Then there's my style. I'm friendly. I smile a lot. I have a southern accent. However much I might aspire to it, I'm nobody's idea of a butch (well, outside the South, anyway). Instead, I'm pleasantly androgynous in a way that other lesbians recognize but heterosexuals do not find threatening (after all, androgyny has a long tradition among academic women).[7]

Lesbians, in my experience, love to position themselves and others on the butch-femme continuum with various degrees of hilarity or seriousness.[8] I've thought about my position on this continuum within the context of my lineage from a long line of formidable females. There are a number of photos that position my mother as "every inch a lady."

(Throughout this section I show the photographs I describe here.)

And pictures of Grandmama Kerrick and Grandmother Taylor in old age depict them in proper femme (also known as church-going) attire. But I know the iron strength behind these gracious exteriors. And in early portraits from the beginning of this century and the end of the last, two of my great-grandmothers stare back at the camera with a sternly self-possessed composure. In a large family portrait of the Kerrick tribe,

taken a few years before my mother's birth, a solidly planted and un-
blinking Eliza Jane Kerrick anchors the center of the photograph. From
my father, I have inherited a black and white photograph of Malviney
Taylor, a great-grandmother who skewers the photographer with such a
powerful and solemn stare that I'm tempted to jump back each time I
gaze at her picture. Malviney Taylor, I am persuaded, is a woman who
could outbutch Gertrude Stein.[9] She inspires me, but I have to acknowledge that if I peered out at the world with her degree of stern self-
possession, my value as a role model would likely plummet.[10]

When my family is tapped as exemplary, the same sorts of considerations apply.

(A family portrait is now on the screen.)

My partner and I have been in a committed relationship for eighteen
years. Like me, she is middle class, well educated, articulate, thin, and
white. We own the house we have lived in for sixteen years. We adopted
our two daughters, which I think for some people is less threatening than
if we had given birth to them in the context of an intentional lesbian family. Taken all together, we're a photogenic family.[11]

I'm trying to suggest, here, that at least part of the reason my family
and I are invited to serve as exemplars is because we are viewed, for a variety of often repugnant reasons, as exemplary. Maybe the world is not
ready for lesbians in general, the implicit reasoning goes, but perhaps we
can make space for a lesbian as well educated, well behaved, well man-
nered, and nice looking as you. Maybe the run-of-the-mill lesbian is a
dangerous female, but laden as you are with good-girl trappings, maybe,
just maybe, we can make you one of us.

Such thinking occurs not just on the part of heterosexuals but among
lesbians as well. More than half of the invitations to appear as lesbian exemplar have come from other lesbians. I'm the kind of lesbian, my family is the kind of lesbian family, that lesbians and heterosexuals alike believe the heterosexual world might be able to accept.

(Here I step away from the lectern to indicate that I am entering the scene.)

April 1991: WBEZ, the local affiliate of National Public Radio, is doing
a program on single parent adoption. They've heard about our family
and would like us to join the panel as lesbian adoptive parents.

On the day of the program, we're quite an entourage, arriving at the
station with our two-year-old and one-year-old daughters and our care-
giver. We get the opportunity to talk about the discrimination we faced

as lesbians wishing to adopt and to tell some portion of the stories of our adoptions. The social worker reiterates the official adoption worker's position on lesbian and gay adoptive parents, the gist of which is this:

> Adoption is designed to serve the needs of the child. Adopted children have already suffered at least one trauma—the trauma of losing their birth parents. Placing them in a lesbian or gay household exposes them to the risk of further trauma—societal homophobia. In addition, the agencies seek stable families, and a union not bound by marriage is regarded as inherently less stable than one which is.

I talk about the impossible bind lesbian and gay couples are placed in by such reasoning. First, there's the illogic of the argument that the way to protect children from homophobia is to keep them out of gay families. Second, there's the marriage catch-22. You must be heterosexually married to demonstrate a truly committed and stable relationship, we are told. Okay, we say, we'll get married. No, we're told, you can't get married, it's illegal. Meanwhile, children who need families go unadopted.

The conversation is lively and the moderator is superb. One caller expresses horror at the thought of perverts adopting, but other calls are supportive.

Carol and I find that it's a privilege to get to tell this much of our story. It's also an important rite of passage for our family. This coming out experience has given us an even deeper sense of commitment and, in the absence of other defining rituals, it has helped us in the ongoing project of defining ourselves as a family. Back home, the girls seem to catch our ebullient mood. Our two-year-old celebrates by peeing in the potty on her own for the very first time. Her one-year-old sister careens around the house on her new walking legs. We're a family not because anyone agrees to name us so but because we choose to so name ourselves day by day, in an ever-accumulating series of large and small, public and private acts.

November 1991: Along with a gay man on the faculty, I have been asked to offer a workshop on the Gay and Lesbian Community in Chicago for other university teachers. I'm delighted to be asked but it is a delight tinged with apprehension about the additional visibility this assignment confers.

About eighteen faculty members enroll. I know many but not all of them. I'm surprised to see that my co-leader and I are not the only gay people in the room. Is that indicative of gay people's hunger to see ourselves acknowledged and visible within the structures of our institution? One participant, born in and still a citizen of another country, tells us that the silence surrounding this subject in his homeland is so great that it was an act of courage for him to come to the room. He was curious to learn about gay and lesbian people, and yet what if someone saw him at the workshop and concluded that he was gay? For me it is an interesting reminder that David and I are not the only ones who have taken a risk by being in this room tonight. How easy it is for one lesbian and one gay man to contaminate an entire room. What an immense barrier to communication such fear is. I can only guess that this courageous participant speaks for other interested but fearful co-workers who did not enroll.

A colleague from the College of Commerce finds all this material interesting, fascinating, in fact, for he has lived in Chicago all his life perfectly oblivious to the presence of a gay community. But he is at a loss to imagine how knowing this could have any impact on his teaching of accounting. We suggest that even talking to students in such a way as to acknowledge that not everyone in the world is heterosexual can make the classroom more hospitable to gay and lesbian students. We note that an awareness of community resources can be helpful if a student ever wants to talk to him about his or her sexual orientation. Our accounting colleague cannot imagine such an occurrence, and, listening to him, neither can I. This man could not look more conservative and conventional. Most gay students, I suspect, would consider approaching him a poor risk. And he has an air of formality about him that would hardly invite student confidences. Yet, I'm an optimist. I entertain the hope that even this small recognition of gay men and lesbians in the world will exert some subtle influence on the way he talks to students and/or colleagues about human experience.

A lesbian faculty member who makes no secret of her sexuality reports with surprise, after the workshop, her recognition that she has excluded lesbian and gay texts and even the discussion of lesbians and gay men in classes dealing with popular culture. She wonders at her own self-imposed silence on a part of the world she has personally experienced. If she is excluding such material, she speculates, what is the likelihood that heterosexual colleagues cover it?

The presence at our workshop of a faculty member famous on the student grapevine for his sexist remarks surprises me. He asks some good questions and seems intrigued by the notion that lesbian and gay identity functions in some respects like an ethnicity. Does his presence signal a willingness to relinquish some tightly held prejudices? Apparently not. A few months later, he attends a Gulf War panel discussion featuring two of my feisty female department members with decidedly Marxist analyses of the war. Their politics disturb him, and he comments later to one of the men in my department on their leftist critiques. "Lesbians, I presume?" he says with a question mark to my co-worker, who to my horror reports back to us his indignant reply that *one* is a lesbian but *one* is married (to a man, he doesn't add, because it's implied).

I unpack this exchange for weeks. Does my presence as department chair taint the whole department? What a powerful pollutant I am. This is not the only time I've encountered the perception of our department as a lesbian stronghold. Students have reported the rumor that all communication faculty are lesbians to some of our colleagues in other departments (the fact that over half my colleagues are male and a goodly percentage of the others are married to men has not derailed this particular rumor). At a meeting of the National Communication Association, one of my married male colleagues discovered that reports of his homosexuality were circulating on the grapevine. This, despite the fact that he was attending this conference, as he has others, with his wife, another communication academic. There are two of us lesbians (as far as I know) among a full-time faculty of sixteen. This, apparently, is the saturation point (or maybe we're in excess of the saturation point—maybe one was the saturation point).

October 1992: On the basis of a paper I gave, at NCA, on teaching as a lesbian, I have been invited to a commuter college located in the industrial belt at the bottom of Lake Michigan to talk about "Homophobia in the Classroom."[12] The lesbian who recommended me for this talk has described the terror she, as a fairly butch-looking and nontenured lesbian, feels working here. The silence around the topic of homosexuality is deafening. With no small measure of trepidation, I embark on this journey of only fifty minutes, which seems to take me into another world. I joke to Carol that if I am not back by 3 P.M. she should call the police. At least, I hope I'm joking.

The small room where the event is scheduled is packed. Students from a video production class ask for permission to videotape, and, ignoring my sense of anxiety and exposure, I agree. The director of women's studies who has bravely organized this event wants to know if I will do an interview at the local radio station after the talk is over. Again, I say yes. I deliver my prepared remarks and answer questions. The students in the room can only be described as parched for information on this topic. Far from hostile, they seem primarily amazed to see a real live self-described lesbian before them. When our hour together is over, an unbelievably nervous young woman, lacquered in make-up and in danger of hyperventilating, asks if she can interview me for the student newspaper. As we begin, she explains that she has never done an interview before. This, I presume, accounts for at least some of her nervousness. When I carefully explain to her why one of her questions is homophobic, she looks as if she will surely pass out and apologizes profusely. Throughout the interview I find myself assuring her again and again that she is doing fine and that it's okay to ask stupid questions. At last all students are satisfied. The faculty member with whom I have a professional association drives me over to the radio station, thanking me all the while for coming to campus, talking again about how difficult it is to be a lesbian faculty member on this campus. I complete the radio interview and head home, relieved to have emerged intact from my foray into such a homophobic stronghold, and sobered by my recognition of how much easier it is for me to come in as an outsider and address these issues than it is for those who must live and work there.

February 1993: I have agreed to do the same talk for DePaul's Gay and Lesbian Student Association. Somehow, in our mutual haste, the student arrangers and I never communicate about the exact title of my talk. The day before I am to speak I am surprised to learn that my talk is identified on a display wall in the student center as

(Accompanying slide with this same sign.)
"Dr. Jackie Taylor Discusses Being a Lesbian at DePaul." I'm appalled. Although I make no secret of my sexual orientation, I would never choose to plaster an announcement of it on the wall of the student center in letters two feet high. The title I had chosen, "Homophobia in the Classroom," is intentionally abstract and third person—despite the autobiographical nature of my remarks. I am further horrified at the way the title implies that DePaul is a particular site of homophobia and suggests that I am always "being a lesbian" at DePaul in the same sense that I am "being a lesbian" when I make these special appearances.

Maybe I'm being silly, I think. Worrying about a sign that does not really bear the interpretation I am giving it. Deconstruction has taken its toll and my anxiety is a symptom of textual analysis run amok.

I check with several colleagues. The results are not reassuring. I contemplate my options. They are few. I talk with an associate dean and ask him to pass along to the dean my astonishment at having my status as a lesbian announced on the wall of the student center. This grapevine strategy is carefully considered. My dean has been most supportive on this issue, but, so guarded is he on personal matters, I suspect a direct discussion of this situation would cause both of us acute discomfort.

At the student gathering the next night (a tiny gathering, only eight or nine of the faithful), I deliver my prepared remarks. Then, I talk about the sign. We have a conversation about the difficulties inherent in trying to maintain one's integrity in homophobic institutions. I describe my struggle to carve out a position from which I can be heard—avoiding the invisibility of total silence as well as the invisibility of being dismissed as the lunatic fringe. The students, God bless them, are contrite. They know all about homophobia because they live with it. It's just that they had indulged in the fantasy that I somehow manage to live above all these problems. They hurry to remove the sign at meeting's end.

With my class the next morning I joke about my astonishment at being outed on the wall of the student center. Several students have seen the announcement; we fill in those who have not. The tension surrounding the issue is defused. We move on to a discussion of poetry. Two days later one of these students runs into me as I am headed for a workout. She has questions. Do my parents know? How did they handle it? How did I realize I was a lesbian? Don't I have children? Do they know? Are all lesbian couples divided into butch-femme pairs? She has always wanted to talk to someone about this, she says, but didn't know whom to ask. The next day my voice mail contains a message from a newly hired lesbian faculty member who wants to know how she can connect with other lesbian faculty. I phone her with information about a Gay and Lesbian Faculty Reading Group a colleague and I have formed.

I ponder all of this, especially the narrow space within which I feel it is possible, if often uncomfortable, for me to speak as a lesbian. The difficulty of being visible enough to be of use, the risk of being marginalized as excessively lesbian. The aching silences that surround lesbian lives. The hunger for visible lesbians. The exhilaration of speaking, of the inevitable connections such speech produces.

May 1993: A colleague has asked me to visit her class and talk about my experience as a lesbian mom. She is teaching a course called Women Across Cultures. Most of the focus has been on non-Western cultures.

Within U.S. society she has chosen to teach a unit on lesbian culture. She approaches this with what she later describes to me as a great deal of naiveté about just how loaded this topic is. She shows a film called *Choosing Children*, a documentary on lesbian mothers. The class ignites. Many of them are offended by the very notion of lesbian mothers. They read *Odd Girls and Twilight Lovers*, Lillian Faderman's history of lesbians in the twentieth century, but the discussion keeps veering back to the moms. I appear after a couple of weeks of impassioned debate on the topic and am greeted by an extremely polite and restrained group of women. I pass around pictures of my family and briefly describe how we came to be a family, then open the floor for questions. One of the women wants to know how we plan to tell our daughters that we are lesbians. I have heard this question many times and yet it always startles me in its assumption of a sort of closeted home life I cannot imagine. She is visibly surprised to learn that we have no need to tell them since they are growing up with the knowledge. That the moms are lesbians is a taken-for-granted part of our lives together—talked about naturally when it relates to the context. I tell a story to illustrate.

Some years ago, Carol and I were celebrating our ninth anniversary. In honor of the occasion we hired a babysitter and went out to dinner at an elegant restaurant. As I dressed for dinner, I talked to Lucy and Gracie about what we were doing. "Mama-Carol and I are going out on a special date tonight. We're celebrating our relationship. Nine years ago we fell in love and decided to be partners. This is our anniversary and that is why I'm getting all dressed up," I explain as I squirt myself and then each of them with a puff of cologne. Four-year-old Lucy, always eager to make herself a part of any occasion, rummages around in her dresser drawer and returns with two necklaces she created at preschool. She hangs the leather heart suspended from a piece of ribbon around my neck.

(I take the heart-shaped necklace and hang it on top of my pearls.)

"This is for you," she says solemnly. She hands me the other pendant, a red bell jingling on the end of a piece of twine, "and this is for your partner."

When my colleague calls to thank me, she tells me that many of the women in the class were left wishing that Carol and I had been their mothers. Her impression from the subsequent discussion is that the students were entirely surprised to learn that we do not define ourselves as outside the norm and that so much about our family sounds so normal. For many of them, the sense of us versus them got destroyed. One student, the class die-hard, asserted that although she is convinced that I am a wonderful mother, she continues to believe I have no right to *be* a mother. But the majority opinion seems to have gone in another direction.

Months later a woman from the class approaches me at a DePaul function. She reminds me of her presence in the class. She was struck, she tells me, by how much more intentional Carol and I have been in our formation of a family and daily family life than she and her husband have been. Well, yes. Our right to be a family is challenged at every turn. The law of the land and the conventions of society do not support us. To do this at all, we have to do it on purpose, and that purpose must be continually articulated, rearticulated, and insisted upon.

June 1999: The church my family attends in Chicago, Broadway United Methodist, has made national news for its resistance to the denomination's prohibition of services of holy union for gay men and lesbians. Our pastor, Greg Dell, has been suspended for performing such a service for two men in our church. Unrepentant, we are preparing to enter a float in the Chicago Gay Pride Parade. Only at Broadway United Methodist could I sew a piece of white netting to my white terry-cloth sun hat and call it church work. On Saturday night before the parade, Carol, Lucy, Gracie, and I are putting together our outfits—white shorts and T-shirts and, in my case, a wedding veil rigged up on my sun hat— in preparation for our ride on the float. The next afternoon, we're all on board, along with a variety of other couples and individuals from our church. Lucy and Gracie have baskets full of confetti. They wave and toss the confetti to the crowd with a gesture Lucy has been practicing. Flower girls at last, but in what a context!

(Slides of the family on the parade float. I move back to the lectern.)
I was well educated for the role of exemplary lesbian.[13] I grew up as the preacher's daughter in Somerset, a small Kentucky town. The Southern Baptist church my father pastored for twenty-three years was the largest church in our small county seat community. Either live or via radio broadcast, my father preached to a substantial percentage of the local population every week. I think it safe to say that the town had no more public figure than my father, nor no more public family than mine.

We moved into the parsonage when I was seven.

(Slide of the large brick parsonage, with the church looming beside it.)
The parsonage perched literally in the shadow of the church, a position we quickly came to understand was our metaphoric location as well.

(Slide of family in 1958, the year we came to Somerset.)

Early on, members of the church and the community made it clear to my mother that she, my sister, and I were regarded along with my father as public property.

(Slide of my mother, my sister, and me standing outside the parsonage. As I show this slide, I usually point out that I am the only one in the photograph wearing sensible shoes.)

We were examples to the community, a role stressed not only by my teachers and classmates in the public school system, but also by my parents, who embraced the notion that when First Baptist Church hired Eldred Taylor, they hired his family as well.

(Another family portrait, two or three years later, shows the family looking somewhat the worse for wear.)

I took my responsibilities seriously. I had the telephone skills of a receptionist by the age of eight and quickly acquired an amazing capacity to listen politely to all manner of recitations of ills and difficulties, while recording all the essential particulars. By the time I was nine, I was organizing the minister of music's daughters into a Christmas pageant for the staff Christmas party.

(Picture of two other little girls and me costumed as Mary, Joseph, and an angel.)

Was it a harbinger of future directions that I played Joseph, I wonder now? Our performance included Christmas carols, with me accompanying on the violin.

(Slide of this.)

Southern Baptists have their own answer to Girl Scouts in an organization called Girls' Auxiliary, or G.A.s. Instead of learning first aid and camping skills, we learned Bible verses. Our corollary to community service and world awareness was to study the countries and cultures where Southern Baptists had mission work. Our motto was The Great Commission, a centerpiece of evangelical theology: "Go ye therefore and teach all nations, baptizing them in the name of the Father, and of the Son, and of the Holy Ghost: Teaching them to observe all things whatsoever I have commanded you: and, lo, I am with you always, even unto the end of the world." Matthew 28:19–20. We had a song, as well. A hymn, what else?

(I sing this, marching to its military beat.)

"We've a story to tell to the nations, that shall turn their hearts to the right," we sang with typical Baptist enthusiasm and with a perfect innocence regarding the imperialist dimensions of the text. One especially fun project required us to dress up in appropriate ethnic garb and prepare a dinner of the focus country's cuisine. For one such cultural exploration, I puzzled over my G.A. manual, trying to figure out from the black and white diagram just how one was supposed to wrap the yards of fabric that made up an Indian sari.

(As I describe this, I wrap myself in a sari.)

Of course, I'd never seen the vibrant colors of an actual sari; I was trying to construct mine from six yards of pale blue cotton that I would later sew into a dress for my violin recital.

Unlike the Girl Scouts, G.A.s never sold cookies, but we had Christmas in August, an occasion for gathering up soap, washcloths, pencils, erasers, and various other suggested items that none of us could imagine anyone ever wanting to find under her tree.

(While naming these objects, I pick them up from the table and place them in the basket.)

These we dutifully boxed up each August and shipped off to some mission field on a slow boat which would presumably arrive by Christmastime. I'm still trying to sort through the baggage I acquired by receiving my earliest exposures to the notion of cultural diversity through the colonizing lens of Southern Baptist Foreign Mission work.

I was not just the first but also the only one of my age group to move through the various G.A. steps of Maiden, Lady-in-Waiting, Princess, Queen, Queen-with-a-Scepter, all the way up to Queen Regent. For each of these steps you must master a series of challenges structured around knowledge of the Bible and Baptist mission work. Everybody made it through Maiden and Lady-in-Waiting, but the attrition rate mounted with the volume of required memorization.

(Group picture of about thirty girls assembled in the choir loft of the church for a coronation service.)

Queen Regent is sort of like the Eagle Scout award of G.A.s You wear a fancy dress at a special coronation service, along with a gilded cardboard crown, and a green, white, and gold (G.A. colors) satin cape.

(As I enumerate these objects, I pick them up from the table and put them on.)

A gilded wooden scepter is placed in your hand. It's as close as a non-dancing teenager like me was ever going to get to dressing up for the prom.

(Slide of me at my coronation service.)

At the age of eleven, I placed second in the state in a competition called

"Sword Drill." This again involved memorizing Bible verses, recalling and reciting them quickly, and looking up verses in the Bible more rapidly than one's competitors ("And take the helmet of salvation, and the sword of the Spirit, which is the word of God." Ephesians 6:17).

(Picture shows the weekly church bulletin, with me and a couple of sword-drilling buddies in the cover photo.)

We held our special, hardback sword-drill Bibles at our sides and stood in a straight line.

(I pick up my sword-drill Bible from the table and demonstrate as I speak.)

The Bible verse was announced, sometimes by chapter and verse, sometimes by first phrase. The sword-drill conductor called, "Attention!" and we placed our Bibles at our sides in our left hands. "Draw swords!" and the Bibles came to rest in front of us between our flat palms, right hands up, no thumbs allowed over the edge of the hardcover. "Charge!" and we were off, flipping through our Bibles and then stepping forward with right forefinger on the appropriate verse. (Were there different rules for left-handed sword-drillers, I wonder now?) I won the competition in my church (the competition in my church was not keen—most of my friends and my sister would not touch this madness with a ten-foot pole) and my association (this corresponded roughly to the county), and then advanced on to regional and, finally, statewide competition. If I had been first in the state, I would have won a week's visit to Ridgecrest, the North Carolina Baptist Assembly, a prize I keenly coveted, but the boy who won edged me out by a Bible verse.

It is only lately that I have begun to ponder the connection between my education into the role of exemplary preacher's daughter and my current role as lesbian exemplar and proponent of gay and lesbian rights. My moral education never held out the promise of personal gain in this life. "Lay not up for yourselves treasures upon earth, where moth and rust doth corrupt, and where thieves break through and steal: But lay up for yourselves treasures in heaven, where neither moth nor rust doth corrupt, and where thieves do not break through nor steal: For where your treasure is, there shall your heart be also." Matthew 6:19–21. One was called to a higher standard than the pursuit of popularity, material goods, or even happiness. My faith in the importance of working for a world transformed held steadfast even when I cast in my lot with a band of sinners so thoroughly excoriated in my childhood religion that we were not even preached against.

In many ways, my parents sowed the seeds of their own undoing.

Dinnertime involved loud and lively debate about the interpretation of specific scriptures, and action was scrutinized for its correspondence to belief.

(Slide of family and friends seated around the dinner table.)

Belief, in turn, was expected to be grounded in reason, the reasoning based on the interpretation of the scripture that served as the standard. For instance, when my father, during the early sixties, encouraged the church's kindergarten teacher to enroll children of any color in her classes and when he organized a joint worship service with the nearby black Baptist church, there were some members of First Baptist who concluded that he had pastored our church too long already. But he had a Bible verse that justified his action ("For there is no difference between the Jew and the Greek: for the same Lord over all is rich unto all that call upon him." Romans 10:12), and he did not believe they could find one that justified theirs.

As I moved out into what I was finally able to claim as my own life, after years of performing the role of the excruciatingly well-behaved preacher's daughter, I was eager to put as much distance as possible between me and my P.K. (preacher's kid) childhood. I swore I would not marry a preacher if he were the last man on earth (an oath that turned out to be much easier to keep than I had anticipated) and took an extended vacation from church attendance. I enlarged and rearranged my theology to accommodate my lived experience. But my belief in a life of service held as the steadfast center in what sometimes seemed a sea of relativism.

I was thirty years old and fully embarked on an academic career before I stopped to consider the extent to which I had become the preacher I had sworn I would never marry. As an assistant professor at a Catholic university, I spent my days reading and studying texts and preparing lectures, standing before groups of students to profess (that is where we get our name) an interpretation of these texts, attending meetings, talking to students in my office, and doing research.

(During this section, a picture of my father as a young man alternates on the screen with a picture of me. The obvious family resemblance provides an analogue for the text.)

The parallels to my father, who spent each weekday morning in his study preparing his sermons and each afternoon and evening attending meetings and visiting church members, are so obvious that, when I finally recognized them, I had to laugh at the lengths to which my rebellion had not brought me.

The point of all this reminiscence, of course, is that it is not in spite but because of my Southern Baptist upbringing that I find myself once again in the role of exemplar. As I write this, my father inserts himself into the text to remind me that just as surely as he raised me, I raised him, that there was struggle on both sides, and that he continues to be amazed at the uses to which I put the education he and my mother offered. "Train up a child in the way he should go: and when he is old, he will not depart from it," Proverbs 22:6, turns out to be true, but not in the ways any of us expected.

It is always scary and sometimes terrifying to appear as Lesbian Exemplar. Coming out under any circumstances is an uncertain business. No matter who you're coming out to and no matter what you already know about them, there is no way to predict how anyone will respond to this disclosure. All gay men and lesbians live with the knowledge that some people hate us and wish us ill simply because of whom we love. So it is always scary to come out, and it gets scarier when you are coming out to a room full of strangers. At least with friends and acquaintances, I'm coming out to people who have had the chance to get to know me first before this loaded piece of information can begin to overdetermine all their responses to me. When I'm in the role of lesbian exemplar, people know that I'm a lesbian before I ever walk into the room or before they hear my voice. That's why they've come. To see what a lesbian looks and sounds like.

And that is a terrifying part of this equation. I'm invited to stand and speak for all lesbians. I, one particular, specific, no doubt quirky lesbian, represent all lesbians. Since we are so invisible, any time one of us manages to appear, we carry the burden of synecdoche—we are a part that stands for the whole. Now nobody can effectively embody and represent the variety and diversity of a large group of people, let alone a group whose members are often hidden and almost invariably ferociously independent. So, while I know my life to have some things in common with some other lesbian lives, I am burdened by the knowledge that many of those who hear me will take me as representative for my people in ways I cannot be. The shadow of this fear is that I myself will play into this role of speaking, standing for all lesbians. Which, of course, I must do, to some extent, or what is the point? But which, of course, cannot be done.

The other terrifying part of this equation is that it is because of the ways I seem least like the stereotype and most like dominant notions of "regular folks" that I get these opportunities. Accidents of class, ethnicity, appearance, and education have everything to do with my getting the floor. My role in these appearances is to convince audience members that I am just like them, only better. How are we going to develop a politics of inclusion if the only *others* we're willing to include are the ones who are almost like us? And what about this notion of *us*, grounded as it is on an unarticulated assumption of a white, middle-class, heterosexual defining center?

Being exemplary is a lot of work. Outsiders always feel this pressure. Ordinary is not good enough. If we are to establish our right to exist, we must prove ourselves exceptional. Against the stereotype that lesbian teachers will corrupt our students, I find myself at pains to draw the strictest boundaries and out-professional the most professional of my colleagues. Against the stereotype that lesbian relationships are perverted, twisted, grotesque, pathetic, sick, unstable, and short lived, I find myself at pains to demonstrate that my committed relationship to Carol is more stable, loving, healthy, happy, mutually enriching, egalitarian, and generally deluxe than any marriage. Against the stereotype that lesbians are unfit mothers, Carol and I mother with a fury and a passion and an overachieving drive few can match. We ask ourselves each time our children hit a developmental bump whether we have done everything we can possibly do to smooth their paths. We try to protect them as long as we possibly can from the censure or ridicule of others, hoping to instill such a fund of self-respect and pride in family that they can weather the rough times that will inevitably come.

Despite the burdens of this role, it has its rewards as well, or else, why do it? As exemplary lesbian I occupy a rare discursive space in which I am supposed to tell my story as a lesbian. I take pleasure in speaking my truth, in telling a story often omitted, in putting my lesbian life on the record. In the telling, I learn more about who and what I am. In the telling, I participate in a dream that if we all tell our stories to one another, if we can learn to listen to those stories with our hearts, we will learn to live with one another in a community of mutual respect. In the telling, I become part of something larger than myself.

In the end, of course, no one can live up to the burden of exemplariness.

(Here, I begin gathering the remaining objects on the table and placing them in my basket.)

We're each of us only humans, after all, and specific humans at that, incapable of representing the range of experience embodied in any group with which we affiliate. I live in these contradictions. Trying to serve as a model that will make my people—all of them, the gays and lesbians and the Kerricks and Taylors and the Sadtler-Taylors—proud, while insisting on my/our right to be fully and imperfectly human.

> *(The basket, crammed full with relics from my childhood, is on my shoulder.*
> *I quote the closing lines from "Stepping Westward," and exit the room.)*
> If I bear burdens
>
> they begin to be remembered
> as gifts, goods, a basket
>
> of bread that hurts my shoulders but closes me
>
> in fragrance. I can
> eat as I go.[14]

Notes

1. In "Imitation and Gender Insubordination" Judith Butler analyzes some of the complications and contradictions inherent in such public performances of one's lesbian identity. "The professionalization of gayness requires a certain performance and production of a 'self' which is the *constituted effect* of a discourse that nevertheless claims to 'represent' that self as a prior truth. When I spoke at a conference on homosexuality in 1989, I found myself telling my friends beforehand that I was off to Yale to be a lesbian, which of course didn't mean that I wasn't one before, but that somehow then, as I spoke in that context, I *was* one in some more thorough and totalizing way, at least for the time being" (310, Butler's italics).

2. I've learned through performing this piece that this reference is not clear to everyone. Saul, the persecutor of Christians, was converted into the Apostle Paul when God came to him on the road to Damascus in the form of a (literally) blinding light. His conversion was so abrupt and dramatic that he was given a new name. The tension here between the Christian vehicle and lesbian tenor in this metaphor is intentional. Throughout this piece I struggle to occupy what are often seen as mutually exclusive categories—in this case "Southern Baptist" and "lesbian." Because many religions, Christianity well represented among them, have taught that homosexuality is wrong, and because Southern Baptists have a well-earned reputation as hostile to homosexuals ("hate the sin, love the sinner," with absolute certitude about what the sin is and who the sinner is, is as good as it ever gets), people who know that I am a lesbian and learn that my father is a Baptist preacher often gasp. I presume the ones who knew me as a Baptist preacher's daughter and later learned that I was a lesbian gasped as well, but I haven't had to listen to them. In any case, this piece works hard to occupy a space in which one can be both a lesbian and a Southern Baptist

preacher's daughter. Such a move is intended to disrupt the notion of lesbian as a mono-lithic category or totalizing identity. In "Lesbian Identity and Autobiographical Differ-ence[s]," Biddy Martin notes that the very term *lesbian autobiography* "suggests that sexual identity not only modifies but essentially defines a life, providing it with predictable con-tent and an identity possessing continuity and universality" (78). See also Whisman and Hall.

3. My description of myself "becoming a lesbian" at the moment of the kiss flies in the face of narrative conventions regarding gay and lesbian identity. The more common coming out narrative describes the discovery of one's always-already-there and always-fixed sexual orientation. Such a perspective seeps into my performance later in this paragraph when I talk about the reinterpretation of my heterosexual past that followed this awakening. But the awakening, as described here, subverts the heterosexual narrative of Sleeping Beauty awakened back to life by the magic kiss of the prince or the fairy tales that use a kiss to turn a frog into a prince (in either case to undo a spell) by using the kiss to awaken my lesbian self and to turn the heterosexual frog into a lesbian princess. At the same time, the narrative up-ends the lesbian coming-out narratives that portray sexuality as always fixed, although some-times undiscovered, by describing the discovery of lesbian identity as an ontological shift rather than a process of self-discovery. For examples of the narrative genre of lesbian com-ing out stories, see Galana and Cavina, Stanley and Wolfe, and Cruikshank.

4. In "Is There a Lesbian in This Text?" I discuss the difficulties of the category *les-bian* and of determining who is and is not a member of the category.

5. This whole category of the exemplar is, of course, fraught, as this piece tries to show. All groups who face discrimination confront the pressure to prove themselves exem-plary and thus, perhaps, though never fully, "worthy" of assimilation. Throughout this piece I try to trouble this concept, but it's a perilous enterprise and one that is probably never fully successful, since, in many ways, including even in the telling of the well-behaved narratives from which this performance is built, I remain a well-behaved spokesperson in a well-behaved performance.

6. Marilyn Frye's essay "To See and Be Seen" is still one of the best discussions I have found of lesbian invisibility.

7. The notions of positionality with which this passage works draw on two decades of rich work by theorists such as Barbara Smith, Gloria *Anzaldúa*, Cherríe Moraga, Min-nie Bruce Pratt, and others.

8. Many of the lesbians I spend time with do a certain amount of joking about butch-femme roles, while generally believing ourselves to be more or less androgynous. Although much of the lesbian theory and practice that grew out of the feminist movement in the sev-enties and eighties de-emphasized butch-femme dynamics or dismissed them as replicat-ing sexist gender roles, such dynamics have been an important part of lesbian life for many lesbians. Joan Nestle has chronicled some of the history of butch-femme relationships and written eloquently about her own identity as a femme. See also Morgan.

9. After reading Lynn C. Miller's essay in this collection, I have come to question my characterization of both my great-grandmother's stern stare and Stein as quintessentially butch. Yet the reference does serve to confirm existence of the popular perceptions of Stein that Miller's performance resists.

10. This section consciously invokes a matrilineage. Among the various identity is-

sues that gay people have to work out is the question of how one's sexual identity connects to one's family of origin. Here, I construct a line of foremothers who are at least powerful, if not lesbian. This move seeks to authorize me as a spokesperson vitally connected to, rather than estranged from, her clan. Such a positioning resists the notion that gay people have to leave home and family in order to become visible.

11. The reasons for this attitude are troubling. Adopted children are sometimes viewed, I believe, as needing a home so badly that reservations about appropriateness of a lesbian household as a place to raise children are overridden by relief that they have a home (at least for some—as this piece attests, those reservations are alive and flourishing among many legislators, judges, and social workers). Lesbian families with biological children born into the lesbian relationship (as opposed to families with children from a previous heterosexual relationship) are in some ways more of a direct challenge to those who believe gay people should not be raising children. There's another dimension of the symbolic value of our particular family that I do not talk about in this piece. Our daughters are indigenous Peruvians. This only adds, I suspect, to the aura of "exotic otherness" some perceive when they see us. We're another variety of two-for-one, not only a lesbian family but also a multicultural family.

12. This piece appears as "Teacher as Text" in *Queer Words, Queer Images.*

13. I was halfway finished writing this piece when the connections between my current work as spokesperson for lesbians and my childhood responsibilities as preacher's daughter suddenly knocked me off my chair. This section is the most performative of the entire piece. Without it, I suspect the essay would have remained just that.

14. "Stepping Westward," by Denise Levertov, from *Poems: 1960–1967,* 166. Copyright © 1966 by Denise Levertov. Used by permission of New Directions Publishing Corporation.

Works Cited

Bulkin, Elly, Minnie Bruce Pratt, and Barbara Smith. *Yours in Struggle.* Brooklyn, N.Y.: Long Haul Press, 1984.

Butler, Judith. *Gender Trouble: Feminism and the Subversion of Identity.* London: Routledge, 1990.

———. "Imitation and Gender Insubordination." In *The Lesbian and Gay Studies Reader,* edited by Henry Abelove et al., 307–20. New York: Routledge, 1993.

Cruikshank, Margaret, ed. *The Lesbian Path.* San Francisco: Grey Fox Press, 1985.

Frye, Marilyn. "To See and Be Seen: The Politics of Reality." In *The Politics of Reality: Essays in Feminist Theory,* 152–74. Trumansburg, N.Y.: Crossing Press, 1983.

Galana, Laurel, and Gina Cavina, eds. *The New Lesbians.* Berkeley, Calif.: Moon Books, 1977.

Hall, Lisa Kahaleole Chang. "Bitches in Solitude: Identity Politics and Lesbian Community." In *Sisters, Sexperts, Queers: Beyond the Lesbian Nation,* edited by Arlene Stein, 218–29. New York: Plume, 1993.

Levertov, Denise. "Stepping Westward." In *Poems: 1960–1967,* 165–66. New York: New Directions, 1983.

Martin, Biddy. "Lesbian Identity and Autobiographical Difference[s]." In *Lifelines: Theorizing Women's Autobiography*, edited by Bella Brodzki and Celeste Schenck, 77–103. Ithaca, N.Y.: Cornell University Press, 1988.

Moraga, Cherríe, and Gloria Anzaldúa, eds. *This Bridge Called My Back: Writings by Radical Women of Color.* Watertown, Mass.: Persephone Press, 1981.

Morgan, Tracy. "Butch-Femme and the Politics of Identity." In *Sisters, Sexperts, Queers: Beyond the Lesbian Nation*, edited by Arlene Stein, 35–48. New York: Plume, 1993.

Nestle, Joan, ed. *The Persistent Desire: A Femme-Butch Reader.* Boston: Alyson Publications, 1992.

Smith, Barbara. "Toward a Black Feminist Criticism." In *All the Women Are White, All the Blacks Are Men, but Some of Us Are Brave*, edited by Gloria T. Hull et al., 157–75. Old Westbury, N.Y.: Feminist Press, 1982.

Stanley, Julia Penelope, and Susan J. Wolfe, eds. *The Coming Out Stories.* Watertown, Mass.: Persephone Press, 1980.

Taylor, Jacqueline. "Is There a Lesbian in This Text? Sarton, Performance and Multicultural Pedagogy." *Text and Performance Quarterly* 15 (October 1995): 282–300.

———. "Teacher as Text." In *Queer Words, Queer Images: Communication and the Construction of Homosexuality*, edited by R. Jeffrey Ringer, 289–95. New York: New York University Press, 1994.

Whisman, Vera. "Identity Crises: Who Is a Lesbian, Anyway?" In *Sisters, Sexperts, Queers: Beyond the Lesbian Nation*, edited by Arlene Stein, 47–60. New York: Plume, 1993.

A Clean Breast of It

e_⊘

Linⱥa Park-Fuller

"A Clean Breast of It" is a one-person, autobiographical performance piece (or one-act play), which recounts experiences surrounding my diagnosis and treatment of breast cancer. In addition to my story, the play includes excerpts of a song and a poem (borrowed from other composers), a smattering of statistical information, and some digressions into the politics of breast cancer research and treatment. I composed the piece in 1993—four years after the events. At this writing, I have performed it more than fifty times in diverse venues, such as hospital auditoriums, university lecture halls and classrooms, community centers, manufacturing plant resource rooms, libraries, church sanctuaries, and hotel conference rooms, as well as in theatre auditoriums. I continue to perform it whenever my schedule permits.

Three dynamics operated in the formation of this piece: an educational impulse, a sociopolitical impulse, and a performative impulse.[1] I composed it as an intervention against the silence surrounding the disease. I also composed it as an intervention against the dominant medical discourse that privileges abstract knowledge over individual stories about cancer. And I composed it as an intervention against the power of the disease (or of cultural mythologies about the disease) to *desubjectify* my experiential identity—to force me into a passive life-role of "cancer victim." In the telling of my tale, I attempt to break out of the prescribed, marginalized role of "patient-victim" and exercise sociopolitical agency in the world. That exercise of agency, in turn, circles back to transform and constitute me as actor-agent—as *survivor.* In that way, the piece functions performatively to recompose my subjective identity and to influence society.[2] Since I have written about these impulses elsewhere, I will not replicate those discussions and arguments here.[3] Rather, I will sketch some of the background of the piece, describe the composition process, explain some salient strategies, and consider its efficacy.

BACKGROUND AND COMPOSITION

In the late 1980s I became interested in performance composition as a form of artistic expression and as a subject worthy of academic study. Influenced by artists such as Terry Galloway, Spalding Gray, Whoopi Goldberg, and Anna Deavere Smith, I encouraged my students to perform their own personal narratives, fictive monologues, and replicated interviews. In March of 1993, my students and I were invited, along with representatives from approximately twenty other universities, to take performances to a conference at Arizona State University on HIV Education and the Performance of Personal Narratives.[4] The many and varied presentations at that conference affected me profoundly. I saw the rich potential of using personal narratives to educate people, not only about HIV/AIDS but about other diseases and issues as well. That fall I was invited as a guest artist to present a solo performance at the Petit Jean Performance Festival, an intercollegiate conference in Arkansas. Having been so persuaded of the power of personal narrative that spring, and having encouraged my students to use performance forms that *I* had never attempted, I decided to take that opportunity to see if my own story of breast cancer might have some value for others. The first question was where to start.

Trained as a performing artist–scholar who specializes in the performance of lyric and narrative genres, I did not consider myself a "writer" but rather an appreciative critic and a "page to stage" translator of writers' words and the worlds they evoked. I had adapted a number of works for the stage, but I did not have much confidence in my ability to "make up" a story, even if the story was made from my actual experience. I also feared "dredging up" the emotional trauma I had experienced during the time of the cancer diagnosis. The very thought of trying to write at a computer terminal made me panicky—as did the thought of working in a studio, for that matter. I needed distraction from the fear of writing about myself, the fear of performing my own work, and the fear of cancer memories. So I took my heels and started walking and talking aloud to my dog, Buster, who accompanied me. I decided I could safely tell *him* my story.

We lived in the country, so no one but Buster had to listen to me ramble on as we rambled over those country roads. He wasn't put off by my overindulgent "first drafts," nor did he become upset at my tears. I knew that I would have to work through those emotions *alone* before I could get to the point of telling the story *to* someone, so I appreciated Buster's courteous disregard. This "writing" strategy worked well for me. Reciting while walking was a technique I used frequently as an actor when memorizing lines, so it was familiar and comfortable. The physical exertion of the walk allowed me to work off the stress of the memories and of the composing process. And, when I could no longer go on composing, I would simply stop talking and be transported from that frightening fictive world into the pleasant natural setting surrounding me.

Eventually, my emotions settled down and my critical impulses began to take over. I began to enjoy the process of selecting and arranging incidents and ideas, adding dialogue sequences, choosing important words and phrases. On these walks, I also realized that I liked conceiving of the text as an *oral-performance* text—as an outlined work—rather than a precisely wrought literary text. As I have discussed elsewhere ("Narration"), the improvisational nature of the piece reflects my philosophy of "life after cancer," an important theme in the work and a part of its constitutive power. All life is improvisational. Nothing is "fixed." Everything is subject to interruption and revision. Anything (and everything) is possible.

STRATEGIES

Beyond Buster, the "anticipated audience" of the first scheduled performance influenced the work's composition. I knew that I would be speaking to a group made up largely of undergraduate students and their scholar-artist teachers. My first challenge was to make relevant to teenagers a story about what some might call "an old woman's disease." My second challenge was to problematize and politicize a common story of crisis and survival. The strategy I adopted to meet these challenges was the question-answer frame that interrupts the narrative to stimulate the listener's own involvement in the story. At one point, for example, I ask, "How do you make love to a woman with one breast?" Though that question has relevance for both men and women and for adults of all ages, I especially intend for those people who might consider themselves safe from the disease to recognize that this disease can affect them in significant ways and at any time. Similarly, when I question the cost of cancer drugs or mention the unavailability of insurance to many women, I intend to politicize the events—to stimulate the audience to look at but also beyond the specific breast cancer experience of my story, to the broader social and economic issues surrounding the disease.[5]

Other strategies of the performance arose for different reasons. The excerpts from the song were used for aesthetic purposes. They function rhythmically to break up the narrative; their lyrics establish and reinforce the theme of improvisation; and their repetition provides unity to the piece. The quoted poem encapsulates the theme and provides a new form to balance those of story, song, and public address. The dedication, which was added later, serves two functions. First, it provides an opportunity to establish a stage relationship with the audience that is not as formal as a "fourth wall" theatrical aesthetic but not as informal as a discussion. With the dedication, I can, in the first few moments of the performance, negotiate the dual role of speaker and actor that this play demands and signal that this negotiation is part of the performance aesthetic. Second, the dedication allows me to offer a disclaimer. While the wording of the dedication may change with specific audiences, I make it a point to indicate that my story is not meant to "stand in" for stories of other cancer survivors.

My responsibility of speaking as a representative of people who have suffered breast cancer is more complex than I can fully address here.[6] However, I want to comment briefly on the evolution of one device used in relation to that responsibility, specifically, the electronic timer. The timer was not part of the original performance. Instead, I used a chime to "announce" and punctuate the question-answer sequences that referenced larger issues and hinted at broad aspects of the disease. Later, in playing with the potentials of the chime sound and of the question-answer sequences, I wondered if I could reference others' experience by using a timer.

In performance, I set the timer to go off every thirteen minutes, symbolizing the death rate of breast cancer in the United States. In retrospect, I can now say that it serves three purposes. First, as a social-medical critique, it sharpens our comprehension of how many people die from the disease and how little progress has been made against it. Second, aesthetically, it symbolizes the themes of life's interruptions and improvisation, since I, as performer, cannot predict exactly when the timer will go off. Like the cancer that occurred so unexpectedly, forcing me to stop, reevaluate and revise my life, so the sounding of the timer forces me to stop and revise my performance. And, third, ethically, the timer evokes awareness of others whose stories do not end as fortunately as mine. Over the course of the play, it comes to represent them. By interrupting my narrative (the *survivor's* narrative), it symbolically gives the power to contradict my story to those who cannot tell their own. Their stories are not heard within the frame of my performance, but drawing attention to their absence reminds audiences that *someone had a different story that will never be told.* In this way, the piece attempts to transcend the "merely personal" in personal narrative—*to stand with*, not to *stand in for*, others' stories.

QUESTIONS OF EFFICACY

The piece was designed to educate the general public about the experience of breast cancer. It grew out of the anguish and isolation I felt when I was diagnosed. I knew nothing about the disease or how to live with it, and I did not find much guidance from medical personnel. I wanted those "just-diagnosed" patients to know that many people survive it; I wanted them (and their friends and families) to know something of what it is like to go through it and I wanted them to have access to some possible coping strategies; I wanted people to realize that they have a right to speak up (or in bell hooks's words, to "talk back") to representatives of the medical community about their experiences; I wanted everyone to know the importance of fighting the disease (personally and politically). However, I have not attempted to assess, in any systematic critical fashion, the show's success in achieving those ends. I will, at least, raise some questions about it here.

Whenever written audience evaluations are collected within the context surrounding the performance, the responses are usually highly positive, indicating that audience members were moved, informed, persuaded. On the other hand, some viewers may not complete and return evaluation forms, so the written responses do not constitute a completely reliable measure. Verbal comments after the show are usually positive, but people may choose not to share their comments if they disliked it or resisted it. Many cancer survivors and survivors' family members and friends claim that the play serves a therapeutic (validating) function for their experiences. If it offends or negates others' experiences, I have not heard. One hospital rejected it because the staff thought it might paint an unfavorable picture of physicians. Nevertheless, with the exception of university-sponsored shows, the performance has not yet appeared in any not-for-profit or commercial theatre—though it has been offered to a few. My performances have been reported on, but never formally reviewed. Sometimes house numbers are large, but other times they are small. The social stigma of a taboo subject or the anticipation of a "depressing" show may account for the lack of critical attention.[7] But it would be naive not to consider that other factors as well might be operative.

Unfortunately, that consideration is beyond the scope of this essay. However, it might be useful to point out that audience involvement has always been an essential element of the performance context of this show. Because of its educational importance, I provide a bibliography, encourage the presence of someone with a background in health care, and recommend that the performance be followed by a discussion. The discussion allows people to ask questions, to share their own comments, insights, and experiences, and to learn from one another. Sometimes these discussions involve medical experts and sometimes they do not. Sometimes they involve other survivors. If medical experts (particularly physicians) are very prominently featured, discussion centers on medical questions, rather than on audience members' experiences, so, in some ways the educational potential is expanded, and in some ways it is diminished. Audience members have the opportunity to gain more scientific knowledge about the disease. On the other hand, the presence of the experts functions to stifle the sharing of stories and thus acts to "recuperate" subversive personal experience stories back into the authorized and dominant impersonal discourse of the medical field. In these instances, ironically, the discussion may be counterproductive to the show's intents.[8]

When it is possible, a workshop is offered in addition to the performance, where, if they choose, audience members are empowered to share their stories of cancer—as it has affected them or their family members or friends. This audience involvement extends the show's attempts to transcend the personal—to move toward community efforts to break the silence of the disease. In 1995, the show helped to generate and excerpts were included in a distance-learning video conference sponsored by the Northern Appalachian Leadership Initiative on Cancer (NALIC) which is, in turn, sponsored by the National Cancer Institute. The conference was downlinked to groups of breast cancer survivors throughout the consortium's rural counties, and their questions and comments were uplinked back to the presenters, many of whom were also survivors. The project, entitled "Women Alive!" encouraged interested women who had had the disease to share their stories with other women in their communities as an educational strategy. To assist women in making an informed choice about telling their stories, and in learning various storytelling methods and techniques, NALIC developed storytelling workshops that were pre-

sented at various sites. One of the criteria we insisted on in these workshops was to allow women to tell the story of their own experience in their
own way—giving them access to accurate and up-to-date information,
but without scripting or coaching them in the official educational discourse of the medical community (for example, the National Cancer Institute or the American Cancer Society). Data on the effectiveness of this
strategy are not yet available, and the project itself deserves closer
scrutiny, but projects like these evidence the potentials of personal narrative performance in the civic community, and the NALIC organization
deserves credit for exploring this survivor-centered approach to health
education.[9]

I close with a consideration of the future of "A Clean Breast of It." I
continue to look for ways in which it can serve to educate. I am fascinated
by methods used by artists like Robbie McCauley and Joni L. Jones to
bring audience members' voices into the performance, and I have considered experimenting with similar methods.[10] So the text may continue to
expand. Or perhaps it will not. I prefer to leave it open-ended. Similarly,
the show continues to provide a ground from which I can study personal
narrative—its potentials and problems. I hope to continue that exploration through more studies and stories.

One thing is certain. I look forward to the day when I will cease to
perform this show simply because it is obsolete. When we live in a
cancer-free world, there will be no need for this performance, except as a
historical piece. It will be simply a testimony to an unfortunate time in
history. I so look forward to that day.

SCRIPT

The presentation space has three areas. Down right is a bench or straight-
back chair that serves as the doctor's office, recovery room, and hospital
bed. It is attractive but institutional. Upstage center is a small decorator
table with tablecloth, flower arrangement, glass of water, and a small electronic timer. To the left of the table is an armless, straight-back chair. Left
of the chair is a guitar on a guitar stand. A down left area serves as the surgeon's office, among other things.

The text is a "story"—told somewhat differently each time—with
different emphases for different audiences, and with up-to-date information, examples, and statistics. The performance style is very conversational. The electronic timer is set to go off every thirteen minutes. Since

the "telling time" varies, the performer doesn't know (any more than the audience knows) *when* the timer will sound—it can happen at an opportune or inopportune time. Whenever it goes off, the narrative is interrupted. I stop, turn it off, and reset it—allowing time for the significance to set in—and then try to pick up the narrative, but without attempting to precisely resume and skipping entire parts, if necessary. Also, the question-answer sequences are prefaced and followed by a chimelike sound made by plucking a guitar string, as if sounding a bell for attention.

> *(At curtain, the house lights go out. She [narrator-performer] walks to down center and introduces the performance.)*

SHE: I am delighted and honored to be here and I want to thank you all for coming out this evening/afternoon. This performance is for all those who have struggled with breast cancer—those who have survived and those who have not. They all have their own unique stories, and I do not claim to speak for them. But I dedicate this performance to them.

> *(Crosses to chair, sits, picks up guitar, and sings the first chorus of "It'll Come To Me.")*[11]

>> It'll come to me just like a song
>> I'll make it up as I go along
>> The push and pull, the give and take
>> Will even out, for goodness sake.

>> The sun might shine or the wind might blow
>> I can't say, 'cause I don't know
>> Whatever it is that's meant to be
>> Sooner or later, it'll come to me.

> *(Hesitantly speaks as though calling to someone in a light booth.)*

Could we have some light on the house please?

> *(House lights come up.)*

Thanks.

> *(To audience.)*

Sorry, I like to see who I'm talking to, see if I'm putting anybody to sleep, see if anyone is paying attention.

> *(Playfully.)*

Is anyone paying attention? Let's see: Question:

> *(Plucks string.)*

How many people in the United States will be diagnosed with breast cancer this year? Answer:

(Plucks string.)

One hundred eighty-five thousand. Most of them, women. Question:

(Plucks string.)

How many people in the United States will die of breast cancer this year?
Answer:

(Plucks string.)

Forty-four thousand.

(Setting electronic timer.)

This means that every three minutes someone is diagnosed with breast cancer and every thirteen minutes, someone dies of the disease. Is anybody paying attention?

(Putting down guitar.)

Before I was diagnosed with breast cancer, I guess I was one of those who wasn't paying much attention. I didn't know very much about cancer. Funny isn't it? Considering that one in four people will be diagnosed with cancer during their lives, and considering how much information is available in magazines and newspapers, it's funny that I didn't know much about cancer. Oh, I knew that it's a dreadful disease, and that it kills people, and sometimes without much warning. I knew that scientists don't understand what causes it and doctors don't know how to cure it, and I suppose, knowing that much, I didn't want to know any more. If you can't do anything about it, why depress yourself by thinking about it?

So, when I first felt the lump in my breast that morning in the shower, getting ready to go to work, I hadn't been doing regular breast exams. And so, I wasn't sure if what I felt had just appeared or had been there for some time. I knew enough about doing breast exams to know what you were supposed to look for—a lump or a swelling—something round, I thought they said, like a coin or a pea or a seed. And this wasn't like that. This was like a line or a bumpy "ridge" just above my left nipple. So I thought, "That can't be cancer."

When I first felt the lump in my breast, that cold January morning in the shower getting ready to go to work, my life was going along pretty well—at least on the surface—and I didn't need any more excitement. I had a good marriage and a good job. I enjoyed teaching and had just been elected to an administrative office at the university, which was exciting and challenging. I was living a fairly "successful" life, I guess. But under the surface, there was a lot of stress and fear. I had become obsessed with the details of everything I did and had lost sight of the larger view. I was afraid that I might not always be able to keep all the balls in the air—

afraid that I might not do something well *enough*, or *on time*, you know?
So I had become something of a perfectionist—you know, one of those
people you just hate, who has to have everything right the first time, and
expects everyone else to have it right also. I was not, at that time, someone who would just let life "come to me."

I called my doctor that morning when I felt the lump in my breast
because I'm not the type of person who worries about vague possibilities.
If I'm going to worry, I want to *know* what I'm worried about.

(On phone.)

"Hello. This is Linda Park-Fuller calling. My doctor is Dr. Taylor.

(Pause.)

"Yes, well, I was calling about . . . I was wondering if . . . I think I've found
a lump in my breast and I . . .

(Pause.)

"Oh. Well, yes, I have a break between classes this morning and could
come in around eleven o'clock? Okay. Yes. Thanks."

Well! What a surprise. "Come in any time," they said. I didn't even
have to wait for an appointment. I didn't know if that was a good sign or
a bad sign.

(Crosses to down right area.)

When I got to the doctor's office, he examined my breast and the lump,
and then he said he was going to aspirate it, that is, he was going to insert
a needle into the tumor to see if he could draw fluid off of it, because, he
said, if he could draw fluid off it, then it probably wasn't malignant. And
I don't remember very much about that test. I just remember how I felt
when he said that he could not draw any fluid off it. I think that was the
first time I felt what another cancer survivor has called "the temperature
of fear." Cold. Ice cold.

My doctor suggested that I talk to a surgeon, a colleague of his, to see
if he thought that the lump should be surgically biopsied.

(Rises.)

And so I did.

(Crossing.)

You know, they say, "First you cry." Do you remember? That was the first
book written about breast cancer from a survivor's point of view, the first
movie made: *First, You Cry* by Betty Rollins (the news correspondent).
But I don't think that's the first thing that you do. I think the first thing
you do is pray, or curse, or some combination.

(To self.)

"Oh God, not cancer. Not me. Not *now*."

(Crosses to stage left area.)

The surgeon examined the lump, and said that yes, it should be surgically biopsied, and if it was convenient, he had an opening that afternoon. Oh, *that* was when the tears started! I wasn't hysterical or anything, I just couldn't stop the tears, because it seemed so real! And I felt so alone! You see, my husband had just left on a trip, and I wouldn't be able to get in touch with him for two days! So on the one hand, I thought, "No, I think I'll wait until he gets home, so we can go through this together." And, on the other hand, I thought, "But if the surgeon wants to do it today, maybe that means that every second counts!"

(To self.)

I'm sure I won't sleep until I know if it's malignant or not. And anyway, it's probably benign. My mother had a lump biopsied once, and it was benign.

(Crossing; to audience.)

And this way, I won't have to worry my husband. When he calls, I can say, "We had a little scare here, but it's all right, I had it checked out, and I'm okay, I'm fine." And so we scheduled the surgery for that afternoon.

(Crosses back to stage right, sits.)

When I came out from under the anesthetic, the surgeon was in the room with me. He came right over. He didn't mince words.

SURGEON: "Well, it's malignant. We'll have to do a modified radical mastectomy."

SHE: "Oh,"

(Aside to audience.)

I was a little groggy.

(To surgeon.)

"What's that?"

SURGEON: "We remove the breast and some of the lymph nodes from under the arm. We leave some tissue on the chest wall, however, so that you can have reconstruction surgery later if you like."

SHE: "Oh. You mean, like an implant?"

SURGEON: "Yes. The other option is a lumpectomy where we remove the tumor but leave the breast. But, well, it's really not an option in your case, because the tumor is so large and your breasts are so small."

(To audience.)

SHE: Huh! "Insult to injury" wouldn't you say?

(Stands, crosses.)

As I left the hospital that afternoon with some friends—one who said she'd stay overnight with me to make sure I didn't suffer any ill effects from the anesthesia, and another who said he'd take my car home—as we stepped out into that cold January evening, the first thing I did, the very first thing I did, was to light up a cigarette! Oh, man, I don't know when I've needed a cigarette so badly in all my life! And my friend said (rather cheerfully, I thought, given the circumstances), "Well I suppose you'll be giving those up." And I, who didn't think that there was any connection between breast cancer and smoking; and I, who had smoked for over twenty years, and had *tried* to give it up, and *had* given it up, and had *taken* it up again, and had *given up* on giving it up, I thought to myself, "If it can extend my life one day? One hour? Oh. You bet. You bet I'll give it up."

(Cross to center chair, sit.)

The next few days were harried and busy as we got ready for the surgery. My husband came home right away, of course. My mother came to stay with me during the surgery and recovery. I had so much support from my friends and colleagues, my husband, family, my students, even people I didn't know! A woman from Yale called me—she was the mother of a teacher in our art department who knew I was having surgery. This mother of my colleague called long distance and talked for forty-five minutes, just to let me know that she, too, was a member of what she called "that rapidly growing sorority," and yes, we could survive it.

But in spite of all that reassurance and support, there were times of great fear.

(To self.)

Will I live? Oh, God, I don't even know how to live. I don't really know why I'm living. I think there are some things I ought to be learning here, but I might not be paying attention to the right things.

(The timer sounds sometime during these speeches. She attends to the timer — turning it on, resetting it. She repeats: "And every thirteen minutes, someone dies.")

And there are so many things I want to do.

(Thinking.)

I want to learn to clog! I want to learn to play the guitar.

(Picking up guitar.)

I want to learn to love, myself and others, unconditionally. I want to learn to forgive.

(Singing.)

I've spent so many yesterdays worrying about forever
But no amount of worry makes the day go any better
And no amount of planning makes the difference worth a dime
Whatever's gonna happen, it's gonna take its own sweet time.
And it'll come to me just like a song,
I'll make it up as I go along.
The push and pull, the give and take
Will even out for goodness sake.
The sun might shine or the wind might blow
I can't say because I don't know.
Whatever it is that's meant to be
Sooner or later it'll come to me.
Question:
(Plucks string.)
How do you make love to a woman with one breast? With no breasts?
Answer:
(Plucks string.)
Well, you might tell her that with all her other charms, she doesn't need breasts. You might tell her how strong and courageous she must be, and how glad you are that she survived. And then, you might show her just how competent you are in locating all her other erogenous zones!
(Resuming narrative.)
The surgery was successful. At least the surgeon thought that he had gotten all of the tumor. Of course, it would be a few days before we got the pathologist's report to learn whether or not any of the cells had "metastasized," or broken off from the tumor, and gone into other parts of the body, like the lymphatic system, or the blood cells, or the bone marrow. And so I had some time to think. And I thought a lot about cancer.
(Stands, crosses downstage left.)
Because cancer is such a weird disease! It's not like a bacteria or a virus that attacks the body from the outside—that you come in contact with through food or the air or other people. It's your own body turning against you! I've read a lot about cancer since I was diagnosed, and I still don't understand all of it—the estrogen receptors, the neurotransmitters, the peptides and all. But I did have it explained to me this way once, and it made a lot of sense.

You see, a cancer cell is a low-frequency, low-amplitude vibrating cell, an embryonic cell. It's a weak cell, a dazed and confused cell. So it doesn't take direction from the control centers of the body, the DNA, and such, and it starts multiplying itself in a chaotic manner with no stops to it! Replicating and reproducing more sick cells that make more sick cells, et cetera. And, not only does it not *take* directions from the body, it also *sends* confusing messages. So that sometimes the body recognizes that this is a renegade cell run amok, and sends in the white blood cells to kill it. But sometimes, because it's an embryonic cell, sometimes the body thinks it's making a baby! Sometimes the body thinks that this is good re-generation. And so rather than sending in the white blood cells to kill the tumor, it sends in the red blood cells to nourish it. And it diverts nutrients from other vital organs, and the tumor grows and grows, and eventually crowds out the other organs. The body dies, and the tumor dies with it. It's like a suicide you didn't agree to participate in!

But what fascinates me most is that cancer is all about communication—intercellular communication, about how the cells communicate (or fail to communicate) with one another. When you think about it, cancer is just one big misunderstanding!

(Crossing stage.)

And so I thought, why are my (otherwise intelligent) cells failing to communicate with one another. Was it something that I've done? Was it the tobacco? Did I set up some kind of smoke screen that didn't allow them to communicate? Was it alcohol? Was it the cocktails I would have in the evening to handle the stress? Were my cells drunk that they couldn't communicate? Or was it the stress itself? Was I saying, on some subconscious level, "Stop the world, I want to get off!" And my cells took it to heart, and started to shut down? Was it lack of exercise? or a high-fat diet? or pesticides? or preservatives?

Oh, I know this all sounds dangerously close to "blaming the victim." And I don't want to do that. It's bad enough to get cancer; you don't want to think that you caused it. And I know how dangerous that kind of thinking is because if we make everyone personally responsible for all their problems then it lets us—as a society—off the hook! And we can ignore others' problems as "their" problems, not "ours." We stop asking the tough questions, like, for example, why did the FDA approve a "bovine growth hormone" to be given to cattle to increase milk production, when there was evidence of links between milk that came from those treated cattle and breast cancer in humans? Why would the FDA take such a risk? Particularly when we already have a surplus of milk in this country! And as new evidence gives support to the link, why haven't they banned

its use? And why can't we go to a grocery store and read on the milk car-
ton labels information to see if that milk has come from cattle given the
growth hormone, or not? These are tough questions. Who will ask them
if we don't? Not the people with cancer. They're too busy trying to heal.

So I know how important it is to ask the tough questions on a social
level. But on the other hand, when you're facing the possibility of recurrence or death, you tend to take things personally. And I needed to do
something to help myself *now*. Social activism produced results too
slowly. I couldn't just "wait patiently" for the FDA or the government or
chemical companies to find what caused this or how to cure it. I couldn't
just lie down and become the battleground on which the "authorities" or
the scientists or doctors fight the Great Cancer Antagonist, over my
(quite possibly) *dead body*. I couldn't live like that. That to me would be
pure victimization.

(Cross right.)

So I resolved to make some lifestyle changes that might help me survive.
No more tobacco, no more alcohol. Spend more time in daily meditation
and prayer and exercise to help handle the stress, and watch what I put in
my mouth. And learn a little more about living, just living life. And be
kinder to myself. Because I discovered that I really love my body. Oh, not
in the vain sense, I don't mean it that way, I mean I love it like a friend. It
takes me places, allows me to see things, to dance, et cetera. Anyway, I've
had it ever since I was a little girl. It was a gift from my parents.

(Sitting.)

So I resolved, too, that I would start telling my body that I loved it,
instead of "bad-mouthing" it all the time (oh, my thighs are too big, my
eyes are getting weak). No,

(Patting shoulder.)

good job, muscles. Ah, you're feeling clear and bright today, cells. Looking good, bones! It may sound silly, but you see, as a teacher, I believe that
all living things respond positively to praise.

DOCTOR: "The test results are in. There's no discernible cancer in the lymphatic system, no discernible cancer in the blood cells or the bone marrow."

SHE *(To self.)*: "Oh, God, thank you. Reprieved. Reprieved?"

(Resuming narrative after a pause.)

So, I was making all of these resolutions to eat right, yes? And at the time,
I was eating hospital food! Which, as you may know, doesn't taste that
great, but I don't think it's particularly good for you, either. I mean, they

were serving me fried bacon and eggs for breakfast, and even I knew that wasn't exactly health food! But the funniest thing occurred at lunch one day, when they served me a six-ounce can of diet Shasta soda pop. As I was pouring it into the glass, I noticed some printing on the side of the can. It said: "Warning: This product contains saccharine, which has been known to cause cancer in laboratory animals." Hah! Doesn't anyone talk to anyone else in this hospital? I mean, what am I in here for?

(Stands.)

So, that's when I realized that if I thought behavioral changes were going to make a difference in preventing recurrence, then I would have to—

(Timer sounds. She responds as before but no words are necessary. Picking up the threads.)

If I thought I should make changes then I would have to initiate them myself, because, at that time anyway, doctors, the medical establishment, weren't talking about diet or meditation or exercise. They didn't tell me how to help myself. They were going to treat my cancer in just two ways: surgery and drugs. Drugs.

(Crossing.)

Although I didn't have any discernible cancer in my body, my oncologist, or cancer doctor, told me that, because of something about my estrogen receptors, I should have six months of adjuvant chemotherapy—"adjuvant" meaning "just in case" chemotherapy—"just in case" some minuscule cell had gotten away, and was setting up a colony somewhere in my body. And so I agreed.

Oh, boy, if I didn't know anything about cancer, I sure didn't know anything about chemotherapy. Oh, I'd heard the word, of course, and knew it was connected to cancer, but I don't think I'd even seen it written. I thought it was spelled with a "k." But, as I soon found out, and no doubt you know, "chemo" is short for chemical—chemical therapy, drugs . . . drugs. And these drugs are toxic; they're poison. And you take them orally, or through drip IV, or they're injected into your veins. The idea is that most of the poison will be absorbed by any rapidly dividing cell masses, so that the tumor will die before you do—of either the cancer or the chemotherapy.

But of course you can't put poison into your body without having some ill effects, and not all "rapidly dividing cell masses" in your body are harmful ones. So, although I was fortunate, and didn't have extreme nausea and such, and was able to continue teaching through it all, still, I just felt lousy all the time, you know? It was like a low-grade fever, and I often had an ugly taste in my mouth, and stomach problems, and then, worst of all, I started losing my hair. I had long hair at the time, and I suppose I was kind of vain about it. That was probably the most debilitating part of the whole process for me. I don't know what it is about our hair—men or women—we don't like to lose our hair. I guess because it represents to us something about our attractiveness, our youth, our sexual identity.

Oh, I know that sounds odd. Here I've just lost a breast, and I'm worried about the loss of my *hair* affecting my sexual identity? Yeah. Don't get me wrong. It was *hard* to lose my breast; I don't mean to minimize that. I mean, even if it was small, I was sort of attached to it, you know? But my husband and I were able to talk, early on, about how this might affect our sexual relationship, and how we were going to meet the challenge, so I wasn't worried about that aspect. I felt that I was sacrificing my breast for my life, and there was no question that was more important. And then, too, I knew I could wear a prosthesis or have reconstruction surgery done so not everyone had to know about that part of my "altered body." But it's hard to hide a bald head. And I suppose the loss of hair hit me harder because the devastating effects of the whole process were cumulative. I mean, I had lost the breast, and now my reproductive system was being destroyed by the chemo, and I was too young for that. I was gaining weight from the drugs, and I had all these muscle pains, and I just felt so old and ugly. And then my hair kept falling out. I would take showers and wash my hair, and when I pulled my hands back, I'd have fists full, just *full* of hair that would go right down the drain, and there was nothing I could do about it.

And I was so angry! I was angry because I had cancer in the first place, and I was angry because I had to take this stupid chemotherapy when we didn't *really* know if there was any more cancer in my body. And it was making an old woman of me! And I was angry because I was spending so much of my time in doctors' offices and waiting rooms when I could have been doing something productive with whatever time I had left! One time I had to wait longer than usual for my chemotherapy treatment (which I wasn't looking forward to), and as I sat there, I got more and more impatient, and when I finally got in there, I just *vented*, you know? And the chemotherapy nurses were so kind, and so supportive, and so sympathetic. I thought, "How do they do that? How many people do they see every day who are just like me—angry, and frightened, and hurting? How do they keep their patience?" So I felt pretty embarrassed. But not as embarrassed as I felt later, when they brought in a little boy—

about four or five years old—for his chemotherapy in the booth across from mine. And he didn't complain.

(Stands, crossing center.)

Question: Why is it that in Canada and other countries sixty tablets of the cancer drug, tamoxifen, sell for $12.80, whereas in the United States, those same sixty tablets of the same tamoxifen drug sell for $156.42? Answer: I don't know, but it's a good question!

(Cross up to chair, table.)

About four months after the surgery, I was making progress, and learning to live with the chemotherapy. I was still doing my "crawling the wall" exercises. You see, during the surgery, so many muscles had been cut that I couldn't raise my arm any higher than that.

(Demonstrates.)

So the American Cancer Society gives you these physical therapy exercises that you're supposed to do to get back your range of motion. And I hated them. I called them my "crawling the wall" exercises.

(Miming, as if struggling with the exercise.)

They were tedious and painful and time-consuming. But,

(Stretching arm.)

they work. They work.

Things were getting better, and spring was coming on, and I was getting accustomed to the effects of the chemo—no more big surprises. It was the week before finals and you know what that's like on a college campus. I was grading papers, and meeting with students who had questions, and making out exams, and writing recommendations for graduating seniors, and generally looking forward to a summer that I would spend just trying to heal. That afternoon I had just come back from class, and the telephone rang. It was my husband. He said our house had burned down.

(To phone.)

"Our house? Our house has burned down?"

(Sitting, to self.)

"Oh God, what's going on? I've lost my breast, I'm losing other parts of my body, I could be losing my life, and now our house? All our stuff?"

(Pause, picking up guitar, then, dryly, to audience.)

It was the year from hell.

(Singing.)

Now some folks say the end is near, and others say it's far.

(Timer sounds.)
And some folks say it's written in the stars or in the cards.
Well, who am I to disagree, who knows what's right or wrong?
As long as I'm alive I'm leaving well enough alone.
'Cause it'll come to me just like a song;
I'll make it up as I go along.
The push and pull the give and take
Will even out for goodness sake.
The sun might shine or the wind might blow
I can't say, 'cause I don't know.
Whatever it is that's meant to be
Sooner or later, it'll come to me.

I don't know how I happened to be so lucky that year. And I was lucky. I didn't know it at the time, but I was. I was lucky because I found the lump in time, and so many people don't. I was lucky because I had a good medical team and good insurance, and there are millions of women, even in this country, that don't have that luxury. And I had good support from my husband, my family, and friends—who let me talk through the experience until I could make sense of it all, who put up with my rages, my "post-traumatic stress," until I could get my feet back on the ground. And I was lucky because it happened at a time in my life when I was young and strong enough to withstand the chemo and to make the lifestyle changes that I felt I had to make—if only for my own peace of mind. I've made some lasting changes, but I have a long way to go. I'm still struggling with perfectionism, but, as you might tell from my musical display, I'm making some progress against it!

And I was lucky because we found another house, one that we liked better, in a peaceful valley with lots of trees and animals and flowers. It didn't take long to fill it with "stuff." And, I was lucky because last January marked the thirteenth anniversary of my diagnosis, with no recurrences, and, for some doctors at least, five years is pretty close to a cure. But we all know people who have met their "cure date" and been rediagnosed. So you take it one day at a time.

(Singing.)
So swing your partner and do-si-do
The future is not ours to know.
Hold him tight and promenade
Tomorrow is another day.

A week after the fire, when we were living in a motel, and trying to sort things out and put our lives and emotions back together again, I received a spiritual magazine that had a poem in it. The poet's name wasn't given, but I've since found out that it was written by Patrick Overton. The title of the poem is "Faith," and it goes like this:

> When you walk to the edge of all the light that you have
> And take that first step into the darkness of the unknown,
> You must believe one of two things will happen:
>
> There will be something solid for you to stand upon
> Or we will be taught how to fly.[12]

(Singing.)

> And it'll come to me just like a song
> I'll make it up as I go along.
> The push and pull, the give and take
> Will even out for goodness sake.
>
> The sun might shine or the wind might blow
> I can't say 'cause I don't know.
> Whatever it is that's meant to be
> Sooner or later, it'll come to me.

Question:

> *(Plucks string.)*

How many women in the United States have died of breast cancer in this century? Answer:

> *(Plucks string.)*

More than all the U.S. citizens killed in the combined conflicts of World War One and World War Two and Korea and Vietnam and the Persian Gulf War. Question:

> *(Plucks string.)*

How many women will be diagnosed with breast cancer sometime during their lifetimes? Answer:

> *(Plucks string.)*

When I was diagnosed it was one in ten, and now it's one in eight.

> *(Pause.)*

Is anybody paying attention?

> *(Lights fade out.)*

Notes

1. For a discussion of how the political and the performative relate in the area of personal narrative, see, for example, Langellier. For a discussion of the political and performative in women's autobiography, see, for example, Perreault.

2. Like D. Soyini Madison, "I do not mean to imply that one performance can rain down a revolution, but one performance can be revolutionary in enlightening citizens to the possibilities that grate against injustice" (280).

3. See Park-Fuller, "Narration" and "Performing Absence."

4. See Corey.

5. Robbie McCauley discusses the kind of audience participation I describe here. She states: "I invite them to participate and the ritual happens differently each time. Your part in it may be to listen, but that is certainly a participatory listening that I'm asking you to do because you're in it" (Patraka 36).

6. As Linda Alcoff has demonstrated, it is neither possible nor always desirable to speak for others or to avoid speaking for others. Instead, following Gayatri Chakravorty Spivak, she advocates a position of speaking to and with others. For similar positions from a performance point of view, see Pelias and Dwight Conquergood.

7. The controversy surrounding critic Arlene Croce's refusal to review Bill T. Jones's dance concert *Still/Here* is relevant here. Though she did not see the show, Croce felt that the piece could not be fairly reviewed because, as "victim art," it played on audiences' sympathies and was "beyond the reach of criticism." For an excellent response to that argument, see Bordwell.

8. This effect confirms the insights of Alcoff and Gray in their discussion of the expert mediator in stories relating to sexual assault survivors: "To alter the power relations between the discursive participants we need to reconfigure or eliminate this [expert] role" (282).

9. The scope of the project expanded as NALIC project manager Ann Ward and I presented a workshop on personal narrative performance at the World Breast Cancer Conference in Ottawa, Canada, July 1999. More information on "Women Alive!" is available from Ann Ward, the Northern Appalachian Leadership Initiative on Cancer, 111 Borland Lab, University Park, PA 16802.

10. See McCauley in Patraka and see also Jones.

11. "It'll Come To Me," Don Schlitz and Beth Neilsen Chapman, Nashville: Copyright Management, Inc., and Los Angeles: Warner/Chappell Music, Inc., 1990.

12. Patrick Overton, 129. Reprinted by author's permission.

Works Cited

Alcoff, Linda. "The Problem of Speaking for Others." *Cultural Critique* (winter 1991): 5–32.

Alcoff, Linda, and Laura Gray. "Survivor Discourse: Transgression or Recuperation?" *Signs* 18 (winter 1993): 260–90.

Bordwell, Marilyn. "Dancing with Death: Performativity and 'Undiscussable' Bodies in *Still/Here.*" *Text and Performance Quarterly* 18 (1998): 369–79.

Conquergood, Dwight. "Performance as a Moral Act: Ethical Dimensions of the Ethnography of Performance." *Literature in Performance* 5 (April 1985): 1–13.

Corey, Frederick C., ed. *HIV Education: Performing Personal Narratives.* Tempe: Arizona State University Press, 1993.

Croce, Arlene. "Discussing the Undiscussible." *New Yorker,* 26 December 1994/2 January 1995, 54–60.

hooks, bell. *Talking Back: Thinking Feminist, Thinking Black.* Boston: South End Press, 1989.

Jones, Joni Lee. "sista docta: Performance as Critique of the Academy." *Drama Review* 41 (summer 1997): 51–67.

Langellier, Kristin M. "Personal Narrative, Performance, Performativity: Two or Three Things I Know for Sure." *Text and Performance Quarterly* 19 (1999): 125–44.

Madison, D. Soyini. "Performance, Personal Narratives, and the Politics of Possibility." In *The Future of Performance Studies: Visions and Revisions,* edited by Sheron J. Dailey, 276–86. Annandale, Va.: National Communication Association, 1998.

Overton, Patrick. *Rebuilding the Front Porch of America: Essays on the Art of Community Making.* Columbia, Mo.: Front Porch Institute, 1997.

Park-Fuller, Linda M. "Narration and Narratization of a Cancer Story: Composing and Performing *A Clean Breast of It.*" *Text and Performance Quarterly* 15 (1995): 60–67.

———."Performing Absence: The Staged Personal Narrative as Testimony." *Text and Performance Quarterly* 20 (2000): 20–42.

Patraka, Vicki. "Robbie McCauley Obsessing in Public: An Interview by Vicki Patraka." *Drama Review* 37 (summer 1993): 25–55.

Pelias, Ronald J. "Empathy and the Ethics of Entitlement." *Theatre Research International* 16 (summer 1991): 142–52.

Perreault, Jeanne. *Writing Selves: Contemporary Feminist Autography.* Minneapolis: University of Minnesota Press, 1995.

sista docta

ℎ

Joni L. Jones

conceived and performed by Joni L. Jones
choreographed by Llory Wilson
drummed by Alli Aweusi

"sista docta" is a one-woman show with drum accompaniment that examines the complexities of being an African American woman professor in predominantly European American institutions. This sixty-minute participatory performance combines poetry, improvisation, and dance. Audience members are active participants as they freely move in and out of the performance space, assisting in the exploration of academic identities. The drum provides a continuous earth rhythm, encouraging all present to examine their own identities and to contribute their experiences to the performance. "sista docta" is designed to share the specifics of an African American woman's reality and to initiate dialogue about issues of race and gender in the academy.[1]

SISTA DOCTA

(The performance opens with Aweusi drumming while Jones greets people and hands out numbered cards that will be used in "the faculty party." Aweusi drums while walking through the audience to the performance space. He finishes this drum solo and takes his seat upstage left where he remains throughout the performance. Though not always specifically noted in this text, Jones dances throughout the entire performance. Aweusi resumes drumming while Jones asks, "How many sista doctas are in the house?" After noting the number of hands raised, she continues, "I'd like to dedicate this evening's performance to all sista doctas, and to one sista docta in par-

ticular." Here, she names an African American woman who recently completed her doctorate, and concludes this introduction with "This one is for you!" The titles for each section are provided in the program but are not spoken during the performance.)

"arrival"

(This poem is an adaptation of Mari Evan's "Status Symbol." Jones's additions are noted in bold.)

> i
> Have Arrived
> **M.A.—NU**
> *(Aweusi strikes the drum.)*
> **Ph.D—NYU**
> *(Aweusi strikes the drum.)*
> **Tenure at UT!**
> *(Aweusi strikes the drum.)*
> i
> am the
> New Negro
> **cowries and silk**
> **kente and linen**
> **Christmas and Kwanzaa**
> i
> am the result of
> **MTV, BET, PC, AME**
> President Lincoln
> World War I
> and Paris
> the
> Red Ball Express
> white drinking fountains
> **white guilt**
> **Affirmative Action**
> **Target of Opportunity Money**
> sitdowns and
> sit-ins
> Federal Troops
> Marches on Washington

Brown vs. The Board of Education
Central High
bussing
and prayer meetings
today
They hired me

it
is a status
job . . .
grants, conferences, receptions
meetings
office computer and voice mail
meetings
medical plan, dental plan, retirement plan
meetings
along
With my papers
(Aweusi accentuates this pause with three strikes on the drum.)
They
gave me my
Status Symbol

the
key
to the
White . . . Locked . . .
John
(Aweusi gives a strike on the drum which marks the end of the poem.
Aweusi begins a vigorous drumbeat. Jones dances upstage, removes her loose
comfortable jacket, and hangs it on the back of Aweusi's chair. Jones then
begins a dance with movements that will appear at different moments
throughout the performance.)

"family talk"

(The following dialogue is a transcript of a taped conversation about the
work that Jones does as a university professor. Participants are Jones's sis-
ters, Regina, LaVerne, and Willetta; her niece, Melanie; and daughter,
Leigh. At the time of the recording, Leigh was nine years old. Throughout

this section Jones employs Everyday Life Performance, or ELP, techniques
for the vocal representations of family members while dancing through the
lines of dialogue.)

WILLETTA: Why are we here, Joni?

REGINA: The sound on the tape—

WILLETTA: So you're doing a performance and you want us to talk about your work and you're going to use that in the performance? Is that it?

LAVERNE: What I like about what Joni does is that she is probably the only person that I know right now intimately who finds joy in her work.

REGINA: I find joy in my work. I just don't enjoy the people.

LAVERNE: Then it seems to me you don't find joy.

LEIGH: I like that Moma and I get to go to plays, and sometimes I go to her classes and I get to help her direct. What I don't like is that Moma travels a lot and I have to stay with babysitters and one time she was at a conference and she couldn't make my costume for Halloween.

REGINA: If we get into the don't like, I don't like the uh, the uh—

MELANIE: Bureaucracy.

REGINA: —bureaucracy, the white establishment mentality which I hate—

LAVERNE: Well, I'm going to say something into this tape that everybody here already knows and that is that white folks are toxic and oppressive. They can't help it. It's in their genetic coding.

WILLETTA: But Joni works with white folks.

LAVERNE: I wouldn't be going to none of their parties and putting on pantyhose. I wouldn't be doing none of it.

WILLETTA: But Joni can hang with white folks.

LAVERNE: You can hang with white folks?

"what I like about my work is . . ."
(Jones walks in a circle as she improvises a soliloquy about what she enjoys
in her work. The pace and spirit are private and gentle. This section was
added to the production after a presentation at the University of Texas
where a student asked Jones, "If it's so hard, why do you stay?" This im-
provisation concludes, "I believe that the work can be transformative.")

"the faculty party"
(Aweusi begins a vigorous rhythm while Jones repeats some of the earlier
dance movements. Jones then says, while dancing throughout, "We are now
at the faculty party! Several of you agreed to help me out before the show. If

you did, you are holding white cards. Those of you with white cards, please stand up! You are white faculty members at the faculty party! Now, one thing we have to remember about the faculty party — no music!" At this point, Aweusi abruptly stops drumming. While still dancing, Jones continues, "Each of you has your lines on your card, and the cards are numbered one through eight. If you are number three, you must wait for number one to go, then number two to go, then it is your turn! Speak loudly and give it plenty of personality! When you have finished speaking, you may be seated. I will be moving throughout the space, but don't let that distract you. Our signal to start will be when I say 'begin.' Are there any questions? Then, begin!" Audience members then deliver the following lines while Jones runs from one to another, first as if sipping wine at a party and eventually in very weighted dance movements.)

"I really liked your presentation last night a great deal!"

"After last night, I just wanted to say I continue to be impressed with your performances. I am glad to have you as a colleague."

"As I've said to you before, your teaching is solid and your service seems right on target."

"Now, you went to well-respected schools, you've taught at recognized institutions—why do you think you're different than us?"

"I just wanted to tell you, I think you should be careful of how white women might be using you."

"That's great! You say you'll be doing a book chapter on Lorraine Hansberry. That's really great—now, who is Lorraine Hansberry?"

"You know we're moving. Well, it will be good to be in a city where the only people who stay home during the day aren't on welfare."

"Yeah, I think the move will be good for us. We just found a great house. It looks just like a plantation!"

(The "faculty party" ends with Jones delivering three strong stomps on the floor that conclude in a crouched position.)

"HBCU"

(An HBCU is a Historically Black College or University. Aweusi says, "And now, for the Sophisticated Dahomeans!" Jones strikes a move characteristic of Black Greek step routines. Aweusi shouts, "The Sexy Divas!" Jones gives another pose. Aweusi concludes, "The Sista Doctas!" Aweusi begins a new drum rhythm while Jones gives stomping movements found in Black Greek step shows. She delivers the following lines while continuing with the step routine.)

We are the sista doctas
From the HBCUs
But when we talk about our differences
Blacks give us the blues!
At black colleges they preach unity
But forget feminism and sexuality!
(In silence, Joni offers a brief step routine.)
When a sista docta says
What about women's rights
They tell her she's been hanging out
With too many whites!
When her analysis includes sexuality
They say, "Hey, that sista docta sho'nuf must be gay!"
*(Jones repeats the same brief step routine, then takes three long strides away
from the audience and flings her arms up into the air just as Aweusi gives
one strong beat on the drum.)*

"never tell a woman to wear lipstick"
*(The following poem, by Joni L. Jones, is delivered without drum accom-
paniment. The first lines grow immediately out of the uplifted movement
from "HBCU.")*
and she sprang forth
fully formed
limbs lean
torso taut
feet sturdy nimble
a mind like quick silver
darting at the speed of light
a heart open yielding
a soul (her best feature)
large like the Sahara
dense like the Amazon
ancient like the Nok terra cottas in all the Western museums
a natural work of art

her self-package was not K-mart
but kente and asoke
courageous conscious marketing

counter hegemonic moves at every turn
crafted by the master carver
whose medium is always spirit, not flesh

if paint adorned her face
it would chart the course of the moon and the stars
in copper kohl across her brow
trace the lotus of her cheek and the yoni of her lips
in indigo cream
map the shadow of the goddess lurking on her lids
her face a canvas on which to play

for her mirror conjures Alice, not Diana

no ruby mouth and apple cheeks
for a righteous sista
no synthetic locks or press-on nails
for a soul-seeking soul
no magazine poses and visionless visions
for a for real kinda woman

so when you tell her
out of "friendship"
that she could really use a little lipstick
know what vast beauty
you seek to erase

(Aweusi begins a Yoruba-inspired rhythm while Jones dances a Yoruba-inspired movement that will serve as the transition between many of the following sections. This transition concludes as Aweusi offers a closing rhythm and Jones finishes the movement in front of a rolling chair.)

"girl talk"

(Throughout "girl talk," Jones offers the same dance as in "family talk," but this time she performs the dance in the rolling chair, spinning and gliding as much as possible across the performance space. After each quotation, Jones extends whatever movement she is offering so that the naming of the speaker is given special visual attention.)

"If I know my name, I know that in the academy, like in America, the sister is caught between the rock of racism and the hard place of sexism."
Johnetta B. Cole

"It made me feel alienated, as a black *woman* in *white* universities, teaching *every white boy* to be Biff and Happy! Is *that* pedagogically sound, in this time?"
Anna Deavere Smith

"being an afro-american writer is something to be self-conscious about"
Ntozake Shange

"Black women intellectuals . . . must recognize the call to speak openly about . . . our work as a form of activism."
bell hooks

"I've realized people in academic circles aren't really talking to me. They're trying to figure out if I'm smart or not."
Anna Deavere Smith

"While courageous individuals have organized and fought to make the walls of academia less impenetrable, these very victories have spawned new problems . . ."
Angela Davis

"The absence of race and culture in much of our communication theory and research, in fact, has impoverished that same theory and research."
Navita James

"How often do we truly love our work?
Audre Lorde

"Every black writer knows the very people you may want most to hear your words may never read them . . ."
bell hooks

"How do we convert a racist house into a nonracist home? The answer could save our lives."
Toni Morrison[2]
(Jones ends by pushing backward in the chair with arms and legs spread to form a large X.)

"the machine"
(Just as Jones forms the X from "girl talk," a recording of her answering machine begins to play. Between each message, there is the "beep" from the machine. With each message, Jones performs an energetic dance that begins with jogging in place, moves to spins and loud exhalations of air on the floor,

and finishes by returning to the jogging position. The jogging is maintained until Jones recognizes the voice of the caller, then she begins the sequence from floor back to jogging. The eventual sweat and exhaustion are an important commentary on being a sista docta.)

(Beep.)

"Dr. Jones—I know you're busy, but I would like for you to be on the board of First Stage productions. Girl, you know we could use someone on our board like you."

(Beep.)

"Dr. Jones—I'm calling for Texas Folklife Resources and we were wondering if you would emcee for us again—you were so good with that dance series—so we thought you might emcee this celebration we are having for this local blues singer. Give me a call if you can do it."

(Beep.)

"Dr. Jones—I wanted to remind you that Black Arts Alliance is having a board meeting tomorrow at six. You said you teach until six so we know you'll be late."

(Beep.)

"Dr. Jones—I'm sorry to bother you at home, but—well—I just don't know how to play Sula—I mean—what's black about her? Do you know what I mean? I'll try you at your office."

(Beep.)

"Hey Joni—I'm doing that Langston Hughes program again and I was hoping that you would read in it again this year. I know you are busy, but I would love to have you. We would begin rehearsals right away."

(Beep.)

"Dr. Jones—My rehearsals have changed and I need to give you the revisions. Drop by any time you get a minute. Oh—and do you have time for advising tomorrow? I have to turn in that form with your signature by Friday. Well I'll see you tomorrow."

(Beep.)

"Joni—I have a favor to ask. Will you write the introduction to my book on African American holidays? And can you proofread my book on the Black Panthers? They're both almost done—I just can't seem to find the time to write. I know you can relate. Check you later."

(Beep.)

"Joni—just a reminder. There's a budget council meeting at two. Usual place. See you there."

(Beep.)

"Joni? Is this Joni Jones? Or Dr. Jones? Look, I'm the woman who ran the meeting tonight, and well, I'm sorry. I really didn't mean to offend you. I mean, it's just that . . . well, you know. Some of us, when we start getting those degrees and things . . . you know, we start acting all uppity! You know how black folks are . . . and I know you're not like that but some of us start getting those doctorates and well, look, I should be saying this in person, I mean—"

(During the last message, Jones continues the jogging movement eventually running in a circle that spirals out of control with the last elongated sound from the answering machine.)

(Beeeeeeeep. The machine shuts off. Jones slowly walks upstage, wiping her brow and obviously catching her breath.)

"the stats"

(Throughout "the stats," Jones uses movement from "the faculty party" to accentuate the statistics.)

In 1996, the percentage of doctorates awarded to African American men and women was—

(Jones pauses, poised on her toes.)

three-point-seven percent.

(Jones stomps three times while Aweusi simultaneously strikes the drum three times.)

In 1992, the percentage of tenured faculty who were African American women was—

(Jones pauses on toes.)

two-point-five percent.

(Jones stomps; Aweusi beats.)

In 1985, the percentage of full professors who were African American women was—

(Jones pauses on toes.)

zero-point-six percent.

(Jones stomps; Aweusi beats.)

In 1997, out of 2,517 UT faculty, how many were African American?

(Jones pauses on toes then asks the audience to offer guesses.)

Seventy-six.

(Jones stomps; Aweusi beats.)

Of that seventy-six how many were African American women?
(Jones pauses on toes and asks for guesses.)
Twenty-nine.
(Jones stomps; Aweusi beats.)

Who was the first African American woman to be hired by the Depart-
ment of Communication Studies at the University of Texas at Austin?
(Jones pauses on toes.)
Me!
(Jones stomps; Aweusi beats.)

"imperfection"

*(The following narrative is a recording of Jones speaking. Throughout this
section, slides are shown from Jones's childhood — high school band photos,
newspaper clippings about success on the speech team, photos with her family, scholastic awards. The house is darkened so the slides can be seen, and
Jones dances in the darkness. Frequently her movements comment on the
slides and the following narrative. About a quarter into the narrative, Jones
sits on a bench, faces upstage with her back to the audience. She slowly un-
dresses from the waist up. She washes her breasts and face from a small bowl
of water. She dries herself, and completes dressing just as the narrative comes
to a close.)*

When I was little, I used to bring my report card home to my father for
approval. He respected education. It was a sign of status, of class—and I
so wanted him to be proud of me. He had said how beautiful my oldest
sister was, and he seemed to really have a special fondness for my second
oldest sister—and I also wanted a place in his heart.

For my mother—I cleaned the kitchen. I went down on my knees
with an old rag and Comet cleanser and scrubbed all the wax off of the
yellow tile kitchen floor. Wiped up all the gritty cleanser, then put down
a new thin layer of Johnson's wax. I cleaned the greasy film from the top
of the refrigerator, I neatly arranged the salt and pepper shakers, the nap-
kin holder, the toothpick holder, and the odd knickknacks on the yellow
formica kitchen table. I made the kitchen really shine. This I did for my
mother—I knew she would love it, and gasp at how clean it was, "Ooo
Joni, you have done such a good job! You are the one I don't have to worry
about"—and I knew that the more my knees ached from the scrubbing
the more she would be pleased, the more painful it was for me the more
love I would get from her. That's the love formula.

But the report cards were for my father. The camera of my memory sees me walking from the kitchen into the living room where my father sat waiting to see my grades. The camera is right over my right shoulder so that the audience—me—can see my hands holding the folded thick paper stretched toward my father seated on the couch like a judge or a king or both. I walk slowly toward him, past the piano that my oldest sister played, and past the carpeted staircase that led to the bedrooms, and past the wooden mural my father had made for the wall.

On one occasion, Daddy was sitting in the living room after having been in a car accident. He had broken some ribs and was sitting stiffly in the center of the couch with the glow of the picture window behind him. Or maybe this didn't happen at all and I just want this movie to be true—Daddy there—the man who could bestow upon me my worth, sitting in judgment, doling out approval or condemnation. Smiling that almost menacing smile, and I float toward him like in a Spike Lee film—the grades were my offering, my veiled dance, my tap dance and coon song, surely this would be enough, surely he would love me unquestioningly then, surely I could rest now.

Then there was high school and hours of overachieving—the band, the speech team, the precision dance team, the honor societies, national merit scholar, valedictorian, the graduation address—the sleepless push for perfection. Surely Daddy could see, surely I was as beautiful as Regina and as sensuous as LaVerne. Smarter than Moma, more entertaining than Willetta. Surely I could rest now.

I float toward him with my sacrifice in my hand, a moment of perfect pain, of delicious horror—my worth scribbled in blue ink by teachers who always commended me for being nice—a nice colored girl—and one teacher, Mister Finnegan, who had gone to Vietnam or was at least drafted and sent a letter to our class with instructions for me to read it—me!—and I stood before the class with the sheets of white paper outstretched before me, confirmation of my worth, of my superiority.

And in the memory movie, I am always walking toward Daddy and I never quite get the report card to him—my king, my god to whom I bowed in submission and devotion. Always outstretched but never arriving. Never there.

And I prepared my credentials, the sum of my worth—these essays, these book reviews (of much lesser value), these productions (of almost no value at all). And I bound them neatly, beautifully in folders—clearly marked so my worth would not be missed, beautifully packaged so I would shine above the rest.

And there I sat on a shelf waiting for Daddy to review me, to confirm me, to say, "It's okay. You will never be as good as me, but I can see that you work hard. Hard work is not as good as intelligence but it is something. Such good work for a Negro." There I sat on the shelf waiting, still, quiet, terrified. The sum of me typed on sheets, gashed with three-ring holes and strapped to folders.

And I hated myself as I gave away my power. And I hated the floating walk, my faceless self. I hated the men who smiled almost menacing smiles—"it must be nice to be a performer," "how about a little sugar," "I just want what's best for you." And Leigh just said "fuck 'em" and Reggie said "why do you choose pain" and Laurie said "they don't have to like you." But I stretched my hand out to my daddy and I never quite arrived.

"explore/improv"

(Here, Jones begins the performance of one or two improvised scenes based on experiences African American women professors have shared about their work at their institutions. Jones typically uses scenarios she has gathered from the women present in the audience. Jones dances throughout the instructions and improvisations. Much of this work is based on Theatre of the Oppressed techniques in which the audience joins Jones in exploring the given scenario. Different T.O. exercises are employed depending upon how responsive the audience is to the act of improvising. Jones says to the audience, "And now, you get to help me with a part of the performance! Before the show, I spoke with some sista doctas about their work here at [she names the university where she is performing]. This is the story one of them told me." Jones tells the story, then solicits support from the audience. "I'd like for us to play around this story for a bit. It doesn't require any acting skill, just a willingness to explore. This is also an opportunity to play someone different from yourself. We can cross race or gender or sexuality! A white man might want to play the sista docta in our story! And don't think there are easy heroines or villains. The idea is to explore the humanity of each of the people involved. So, who would like to be the sista docta in the story?" Jones continues to encourage the participation until she has cast both "characters" in the scene, and has invited them to join her in the performance space. She continues with the instructions. "Now, the rest of you sitting out there are not off the hook! Pay close attention. If you see something you want to

change, raise your hand. Maybe you have another idea about how the scene should go, or maybe you want to replace one of these performers, or maybe you want to be a new character in the scene. I will stop the scene then ask you to reshape it. The drum will continue as an earth rhythm providing support to the performers and if they are ready, we will begin." The audience volunteers now improvise the scene they were given, while Jones continues to dance upstage near Aweusi. Jones might pause the scene and ask someone to suggest what one of the "characters" might be thinking but not saying. Jones might ask the audience for ways to move toward a mutually satisfying solution. New audience members might join the scene. When there seems to be a natural cessation of energy, Jones ends the scene. The drum continues, Jones invites all persons who contributed to the scene with suggestions or additional performance to come into the performance space. She will also invite the woman who shared the original experience into the space if the woman had already agreed to be identified. All persons on stage now huddle in a circle as they embrace and Jones tells them, "Thank you for exploring this idea with me. Let's release this energy and return to ourselves knowing that we need not own any of what we said—unless of course we want to!" The drum continues, the audience members return to their seat and if everyone seems willing, Jones tells another story told to her by a sista docta in the audience. If it seems time to move on to the next part of the performance, Jones says, "I want to thank everybody for contributing to that story. This work in this setting can't come to a solution, but it can help us to explore the possibilities for resolutions. So, for now, no solution, just exploration." Aweusi gives a strong accent on the drum as Jones says the final word for this segment.)

"leigh's version"

(This poem was written by Leigh Gaymon-Jones in response to Jones asking her what it's like to be the daughter of a single-parent professor. In performance, Gaymon-Jones is speaking the poem through a recording. "You'll Find a Way," by Dead Prez from the Let's Get Free *CD is playing under the poem. While the recordings are played, Jones performs a hip-hop–inspired dance.)*

"concentration
ishi-oshi-ation
thinking of (clap clap)
heroes (clap clap)
starting with. . ."

Moma
she *is* superwoman
and there is no kryptonite
soaring over private schools to save me
diving into fires, says prayers for me
knocking out ignorant boys who act crazy
And this is how my Moma raised me
All praise to thee

class/rehearsal/out-of-town/meeting
rehearsal/*ile*/work/office/performance/
out of town
wait, what day is it?
oh, right
meeting/dinner/performance/class/meeting
is it Thursday?
oh yah, out of town . . ."Don't forget to take out the trash"
rehearsal/class/performance/office
me . . . me . . . me
but you're late . . .
let's eat out . . . rent a movie

never neglected
opinion always respected
forever protected
        Moms
never alone
always felt at home
even when I thought I was grown
        Moma
stressed, always
busy, maybe
careless, never
        Mommy

rock, rock
nonstop
in her arms wrapped up
always big hugs

kisses on eyelids
like eskimo love

you think I'm pretty?
i know, my mother shines through well
my spirit's beautiful?
it's an inherent gene passed through her cells

"am I doing this right?
is this what a mom is supposed to be?"
yes, you lift me to infinite heights
and teach my light how to flow free

class/rehearsal/meeting/class/performance/out of town . . .
superwoman
soaring
forever protected
infinite heights
eskimo love
rock, rock
even when i thought i was grown
and this is how my Moma raised me
(The recordings end. Jones concludes the dance.)

"self-defense"

(Aweusi begins a new rhythm while Jones assumes a traditional self-defense posture. She then addresses the audience. "How many times have you wished you had taken self-defense? Some of you may have had classes to ward off a physical attacker, but what about verbal attacks? How do we protect ourselves against those? You know, those stupid statements about race that people say all the time! We get home that evening and think, 'I wish I had said . . .' But by then it's too late. Your verbal attacker is long gone. So today, we are going to practice a little verbal self-defense against those daily stupid statements. I will offer five Stupid Statements, and after each you will say, 'Be careful, your misunderstandings are dangerous!' [Aweusi punctuates the audience's chant with drumbeats.] This will be your signal to start speaking." At this point, Jones shows the audience a self-defense move that will serve as the signal for them to speak, then they loudly practice saying their line. Jones then begins with "Stupid Statement Number One . . .")

Uh, excuse me, Dr. Jones, are you busy? I really like the class a lot. I mean, I never thought about doing performance before, but I really like it, yeah, you know. Dr. Jones, you know in class you were talking about participating in the march about affirmative action, yeah, I mean, I know it's a good thing and all, but I can't be joining no march. I mean, Dr. Jones, they already think I'm stupid, you know, that I'm just here to play ball— so if I join the march, that will just be the proof that they need. You understand, if I march, they'll think it's just because I didn't earn my way in here. If I support affirmative action people will think that it's because I'm not smart and that I don't want to work for what I get. If I join the march it will just prove that I'm stupid.

(Jones gives the signal and the audience chants, "Be careful, your mis-understandings are dangerous." Aweusi punctuates with drumbeats. Jones then says, "Stupid Statement Number Two . . .")

Hey Dr. Jones! I really like your outfit! That's nice! You know I haven't been performing since I was in grade school, and I love it! Yeah! Dr. Jones, I wanted to ask you about something. In class we were talking about affirmative action, right? Well, my mother's an attorney and my father's a pediatrician, and they didn't use affirmative action. And look at you! A professor! You are living proof that we really don't need affirmative action!

(Jones gives the signal and the audience chants, "Be careful, your mis-understandings are dangerous." Aweusi punctuates with drumbeats. Jones then goes on to "Stupid Statement Number Three . . .")

Excuse me, Dr. Jones, but I was really upset in class today. I mean, I understand that there's racism—really, I do. But that doesn't give some students the right to get into school ahead of other students! My parents didn't go to college and they are really struggling to put me and my brother through school. It's just not fair for Black students to bump out white students. Affirmative action is just reverse discrimination!

(Jones gives the signal and the audience chants, "Be careful, your mis-understandings are dangerous." Aweusi punctuates with drumbeats. Jones then goes on to "Stupid Statement Number Four . . .")

Joni, you were great in the meeting! You always speak your mind! Yes! There's something I wanted to talk to you about from the meeting. I know that ETS has admitted to bias in its standardized tests, but what are we going to do? We can't admit all the applicants, so GRE scores give us something to work with. If we toss out the GRE, we won't have any clear way of evaluating the students!

(Jones gives the signal and the audience chants, "Be careful, your mis-understandings are dangerous." Aweusi punctuates with drumbeats. Jones then says, "Stupid Statement Number Five . . .")

Um, Joni, you really help to keep the meetings lively! May I shut the door? I just wanted to tell you this, and maybe I shouldn't, but oh well . . . it's this—I really think the work you are doing on campus is important. Universities have to allow for freedom of expression, and the protests you participate in are an important part of that freedom of expression. But not all of our colleagues are as open-minded as I am. And I just wanted to tell you that your activism might work against you when it comes time for promotion. Some people are keeping track of such things, and I advise you to hold off on the activism until after your promotion. Get your promotion first, then go back to your protests.

(Jones gives the signal and the audience chants, "Be careful, your mis-understandings are dangerous." Aweusi punctuates with drumbeats. Jones continues, "Very good! Now you have a little verbal ammunition the next time someone hurls a Stupid Statement at you! I hope you remember to use it!")

"arrival?"

(Aweusi begins the Yoruba rhythm while Jones performs the Yoruba dance as she travels to the rolling chair. She picks up a conservative jacket from the back of the chair. Aweusi gives a signal on the drum, and Jones stops dancing with the jacket outstretched before her. Jones then puts on the jacket which is obviously too small. Jones delivers "arrival?" while trying to dance as she did to the earlier "arrival," but she is constrained by the tight jacket.)

i

Have Arrived?

i

am the
New Negro

i

am the result of
President Lincoln
World War I
and Paris
the
Red Ball Express

white drinking fountains
sitdowns and
sit-ins
Federal Troops
Marches on Washington
And
prayer meetings
today
They hired me

it
is a status
job . . .
along
with my papers
They
gave me my
Status Symbol

the
key
to the
White . . . Locked . . .
John

(Jones slowly takes off the jacket and lets it drop to the floor.)

"what i like about my work. . .part ii"
(Jones again improvises a conversation with herself about the joys of her do-
ing her work. She walks slowly in a circle during this improvisation, which
once again concludes with "I believe the work can be transformative.")

"to the ed."
(The following poem is by Joni L. Jones and is delivered standing very still
while facing the audience.)
she said she was my sister
but
sisterhood
is being redefined
without my consent

she pressed my hair
and she wasn't even my moma
no comfort of familial straightening
no warm momahands on Saturday night
before Sunday school gotta look good

she pressed out kinks of me-ness
of slash marks and nouns into verbs
and umph umph umph

she thused and therefored my hair to a
stiff straight flatness
a spit polish shine
Dixie Peach
the overpressed awkwardness
apparent in every word

did she know how hard it was to find this nappy freedom
to close away that straightening comb in the kitchen drawer

after all
there was the thousand years of silence
after all
there was my daily institutionalization
after all
there was the ph.d. where i was dissed to death

i hope my edges go back real soon
go back from sweat and living

she said she was my sister
but
sisterhood
is being redefined
without my consent

"return"

(*Jones slowly walks over to the conservative jacket left on the floor, then picks it up. She then walks over to Aweusi and takes the comfortable jacket from the back of his chair. Jones holds the jackets together, then folds them over her arm. Aweusi begins a vigorous drum rhythm while Jones delivers the final lines of the performance, which are modeled after the closing of Ntozake*

Shange's "for colored girls who have considered suicide/when the rainbow is enuf.")

And this is for *sista doctas*!
Who are making our own arrivals!

(Jones bows. Aweusi increases the volume, while Jones dances out of the space through the audience.)

Notes

1. An abbreviated production history: Speech Communication Association National Conference, New Orleans, Louisiana, 1994; University of Rhode Island, Kingston, Rhode Island, 1995; Amherst College, Amherst, Massachusetts, 1995; Second Annual Conference on Performance Studies, Northwestern University, Evanston, Illinois, 1996; Texas Speech Communication Association, Dallas, Texas, 1999; Black Women in the Academy II, Washington, D.C., 1999; Miami University, Oxford, Ohio, 2001; Pedagogy and Theatre of the Oppressed Conference, Omaha, Nebraska, 2001.

2. Johnetta B. Cole, "Black Women Academics Meet, Send Message to Clinton," *Black Issues*, 10 February 1994, 16; Anna Deavere Smith, "Anna Deavere Smith on 'Fires in the Mirror,'" *Text and Performance Quarterly* 14 (1): 71; Ntozake Shange, *Three Pieces* (New York: St. Martin's Press, 1992), xii; bell hooks, *Breaking Bread* (Boston: South End Press, 1991), 164; Anna Deavere Smith, quoted in Carol Martin, "The Word Becomes You," *Drama Review* 37 (winter 1993): 49; Angela Davis, "Black Women Academics Meet, Send Message to Clinton," *Black Issues*, 10 February 1994, 19; Navita James, "Memories of a Communication Sojourner," *Connections* 13, no. 3: 11; Audre Lorde, "Uses of the Erotic: The Erotic as Power," in *Wild Women Don't Wear No Blues: Black Women Writers on Love, Men, and Sex*, ed. Marita Golden (New York: Doubleday, 1993), 51; bell hooks, *Yearning: Race, Gender, and Cultural Politics* (Boston: South End Press, 1990), 11; Toni Morrison, *Black Issues*, 19 May 1994, 13.

13

The Performance of Drowning

ᥱᥣ᧐

Terry Galloway

When I was twelve I tried to drown myself during a swimming competition at the Lions Camp for Crippled Children. I was racing a blind girl
and a one-legged girl for an ugly, plastic two-handled cup with the word
Best lettered across its middle. The race for Best Swimmer was confined
to just the three of us because we were the only children among the many
dozens at that camp for cripples who were allowed to swim in the deep end
of the pool.

We were allowed to swim there, compete among ourselves, because
we'd lucked out. We had the muscle to lift up our heads, the coordination
to get a fork full of food to our mouths, the sensation to know when we
had to shit or pee, and enough physical control to hold it until we could.
These skills marked us as separate from our peers. For our mastery of
these skills we were granted the boon of racing a half-hour each day from
one end of the deep pool to the other, using a variety of strokes taught to
us by the Deep End Instructor.

There was just one Deep End Instructor. She was tall, tan, accomplished, and wholly ours. After our half-hour sessions she'd treat us to one
of her own perfect splashless dives. We loved her for her body alone. The
beauty of it as it knifed through the water. So unremarkable, so unmem-
orable, so very normal, with nothing to distinguish it but the grace with
which it moved. Our hearts throbbed with her every stroke.

I don't remember my heart throbbing for any of the shallow end in-
structors. I suppose they were too busy to display their accomplishments
or even to have any. They spent their time looking out for the other kids
in the camp. The kids, who couldn't feed themselves, couldn't hold it,
couldn't turn their heads or lift a finger.

Those women always worked in pairs floating their charges in large lazy circles at the shallow end. They talked incessantly, telling those children, who were always made anxious in the water, to relax, to expand their lungs just a little more, just enough to pull in an extra bit of air.

I would watch those other little girls from the floating line that separated deep from shallow, us from them. I was fascinated when one of them would take in a breath, turn her face into the water, and with that extra push of air create a ripple across the surface.

Watching that effort made me uneasy. It frightened me to see those children struggle so. And for what? That was always the question—about them, about crippled children generally, and about the three of us, of course. Even though we would have scoffed at the idea. We were, after all, the favored.

Competition among the favored was fierce. And at the deep end of the pool competition was scored not just by effort but results. And what determined those results were the daily races.

My compatriots and I were already unquestioning little capitalists. We grasped the basic math. Accumulate the most daily races, win the ugly plastic cup. But we were most anxious to claim the unspoken dividend of winning that ugly cup—the attention of the Deep End Instructor herself.

At the gala end of the summer awards ceremony it would be she who would bend her pale-eyed gaze on the most deserving one of us; she who would pass that cup like a torch, proof that here was one little girl, crippled though she might be, who was unarguably worth the effort it might take to keep her alive.

I simply had to win that thing.

For years I thought it was the depth of my desire that had propelled me past the competition. Because I usually did win those races. Only recently has it occurred to me that maybe the one-legged girl still hadn't quite figured out how to get the necessary ballast to push her lopsided weight through the pool and perhaps that was why she'd end up swimming in circles; or that the blind girl, newly blind, might have been freaked out by the clueless texture of the water, and maybe that was why she'd bonk her head against the side of the pool.

But I was a kid. I didn't care about complexities. I just cared about winning. And truthfully I felt entitled to win, because, of all the bodies in that camp, my own body looked the closest to normal.

And so long as I won and kept on winning, the tactics I employed to win remained entirely honorable. But then fate took a downturn. And when it did, my winning tactic became to drown.

There were a couple of extenuating circumstances. Usually, at the start of the race the Deep End Instructor would stand at the opposite end of the pool in that vivid red bathing suit of hers which always got and held my attention.

Then, after a suspenseful pause, she'd chop her arm down like an ax while screeching "Go!" The chop was for my benefit; the screech for the blind girl. But this day we had begged for the privilege of doing the ready-set-going among ourselves.

First dibs had gone to the one-legged girl, who in addition to having just one leg also had a mild speech impediment (which, as an aside, was in no way connected to the accident that had deprived her of her leg).

But even if she had had the necessary crispness of enunciation, the fullness of volume, the perfectly modulated emphasis that would have left no doubt that "gloah" did indeed signify "go," it wouldn't have mattered. It was still too subtle for me to get. I was expecting an unmistakable sweeping chop of air, and all I was getting was a slurring blur of lips.

And even though I knew that somewhere within that blur, all that was being said was "ready set go" I just couldn't bring myself to trust my own crude perception; even though I knew, crude as it was, it could still steer me right, get me out of the chute in time.

And I would have deserved to die on the spot because my mind wasn't being befuddled really—it was being snotty. It wasn't going to accept any information given to it by a moving blur. And in that instant of hesitation when my mind chose to be a stickler in its stubborn insistence on perfection of form over a shrugging, ragged, intuitive leap, the race was lost.

Now I'd lost races before. And this wasn't going to be a particularly humiliating one. Not with those guys swimming in circles and bonking their heads.

But it had been a long day. And I'd been berating myself for even being at this sorry excuse of a camp. Camp was supposed to be the place where I'd finally come into my own, shed this fleshy misinterpretation of my soul and suddenly be transformed into the beauty I knew I was meant to be.

And instead, there I was, my own tubby, ill-favored little self, in messy competition with two other cripples who were going to beat me in a pathetic water race for a plastic two-handled cup.

In that chill moment I realized "life was ruthless." Just as ruthless as the one-legged girl or the blind girl would be if I suddenly stopped swimming, called back the race by claiming the truth—that I didn't hear the word "go" and that's why I wasn't going to win.

I knew how those two would react to that. The same way I would have. The blind girl wouldn't even bother, maybe wouldn't know how, to hide her visible contempt. And the one-legged girl would swirl her stump around in the water and flick a look at the shallow end of the pool—it, like her stump, a reminder that far greater, far more visible tragedies than mine existed.

And that is when I slipped into my dark watery epiphany. No matter what excuse I offered, there was no excuse. The rest of the world was going to look on me the way I looked on the shallow enders. In the context of a good hard race they were a joke. So what if they were working just as hard, no harder, than I would ever work in my life, for the dubious pleasure of blowing a few fucking bubbles in the water. No one would ever call that winning would they? Not in this world, this larger context where the push was always toward beautiful completion, flawless efficiency, perfection of form, or, at the very least, some kind of solid utilitarian usefulness. All those words words words we cripples could never hope to embody. Words that we knew, even then, young as we were, would determine who lived well and who didn't; or even who simply lived.

The lives of all those children in the pool really were destined for the ash heap of history.

And I? Oh, why bother with first person singular in a place where even the deep end of the pool signifies nothing.

Of course I didn't think it like that then, articulate it like that then. I was just a kid. I just felt it. A whirling, terrible loss of heart. So I took the only action I could against that sea of troubles. I drowned.

That is not as easy a thing to do as you might think. Forcing yourself to drown, willing yourself to sink. But I did it. I sank. I dropped an inch under the water and then my natural buoyancy bobbed me right back up.

The Deep End Instructor had already seen me go under. I could feel her eyes on me the moment I decided to let go. By the time I bobbed back up, the pretense (if it was a pretense) was already long out of hand.

We were a camp for Crippled Kids. Everything that surrounded us was viewed as a potential danger. Many of those kids needed the simplest things just to keep them alive, keep them breathing.

In a camp like that, pretense could never be just a pretense. It was always a harbinger, a reminder of the possibility of the real tragedies that always could exist because they did exist. As far as those counselors were concerned, a cry for help was always and only the real thing.

I had no choice. I had to choke and flail and keep on drowning. It seemed infinitely preferable to drown rather than admit I was faking a crisis because I couldn't see the real victory through. And I didn't have the skill, the power, the language to explain that I had suddenly (some might say opportunely) found it impossible to believe that such a thing as a "real victory" actually existed.

I had to carry out my performance of drowning to the bloody, chest-compressed end. And it was an excellent, convincing performance, if I do say so myself.

I knew the mechanics for drowning from TV. How the body is snatched down, then shoots up again spluttering. Three times they say but I knew, again from TV, that it wasn't quite that clean, that clear.

The real act of drowning was all about the deprivation of air. I knew that from watching the kids at the shallow end. I had learned from them how to make my fight for breath seem desperate and real, how to make myself actually fear that my last suck, my last gasp, was the one I had already taken the breath before.

And I knew from my own overwhelming moment of existential despair how to give up, give in, be perfectly drawn down.

And I knew, I'm not sure how, that on my way up I ought to pull in great gulps of liquid, as if the pathetic victim I was making of myself had tragically mistaken the killing element of water for the saving grace of air.

I came as close to drowning as I possibly could to make my act ring true, look real, be worthy of rescue. I was so perfectly convincing that my audience was taken in—blind girl, one-legged girl, shallow enders all—the actions of their lives were brought to a halt by my performance of drowning.

And they were completely enthralled when, with perfect verisimilitude, the Deep End Instructor joined me in my act, dived in to play out her own role of savior. She cut through the churning water, reaching down, lifted my head up to face again the flat blue sky that was above us; and then, with perfect strokes, exactly as she had rehearsed, she pulled me away from that beckoning deep and hauled my ass out of the water.

On the hot concrete where she laid me, we made an elegant duo. She would push my chest and I would let the watery froth come rolling out of my mouth as if it had been lodged in my lungs, not merely held near the back of my throat. And when finally I thought the timing right, I gagged, spluttered, opened my eyes. And she, looking into that perfectly mim-icked dazed, unknowing/all-knowing gaze of someone who had eyeballed death in the water (as, ah yes, I had)—she pulled me to her and held me tight against the wet, panting, perfect body that I loved.

So I was saved. It was such a sincere, driven act of rescue. And with that excruciatingly sexual culmination tacked on how could I bear the shame of revealing I'd only been acting? Even if I had been acting out of real despair. Even if what I had been performing was the invisible damage of a damaged body.

No. I had to take my punishment: Awards Night.

I'm not sure what I expected from Awards Night, but early on I began to realize that there were awards for both real and, shall we say, fictive ac-complishments. By the time the little girl with MS (whom the rest of us knew to be a fatuous brown noser) was given Most Cheerful, the jig was definitely up.

So when the girl in the wheelchair next to me grabbed the box speaker of my hearing aid and shouted "You won!" I couldn't help but roll my eyes. Was this the Almost Drowned sympathy vote? Had I really perfected the art of swimming or had I just beaten the other cripples out? And who cared anyway?

I no longer needed some chintzy bit of plastic to forge a bond of kin-ship with the Deep End Instructor. I'd already been intimate with the woman for god's sakes. And art, not athleticism, had got me that em-brace—a single dramatic performance of mine got me miles beyond what any dinky old swimming award could.

Late that night, the last night of camp, I stayed awake on my cot brooding over my ill-gotten knowledge. All I needed to complete the scene was a cigarette dangling from my lips.

Once when I was five and on my way home from school, I had fixed my white cotton sweater to look like a sling and told the bus driver that I'd broken my arm. He'd known I was lying. His sorrowful eyes had both-ered me for years. And this was a much more serious breach.

I knew that I could probably get up from that cot and go down the hall to the Deep End Instructor's room and even if I just stood there and looked beseeching, she no longer had the option of turning me away. She might even let me under the covers and maybe even stroke my back until I slept or just passed out from the sexual tension. But I didn't dare.

Because I had a secret: none of what had so intimately passed between us before was remotely real. The award she had so innocently presented to me was not for Best Swimmer but Best Actress. And that was a secret we could never share.

Long before I came unto Shakespeare, I knew what he was about. All the world's a stage. And my guilt and exhilaration in using it as such would throw me straight into the arms of theatre.

14

Death in the Art and Life
of Linda M. Montano

e✿🄰

Linda M. Montano

GENESIS OF THE SCRIPT

I wrote this piece for three reasons:

1. I had entered academia at forty-nine and caught the critical theory, publish-or-perish bug, which isn't such a bad thing since it encouraged me to do more writing, one of my deepest loves.

2. I had entered postmenopause at forty-nine and as my legs changed, my supposed spirituality was unmasked because losing my looks really, really mattered. Death, cellulite, aging became hot inner dialogue topics for me.

3. Seeing my work architected and templated by death made great sense and allowed for cultural, symbolic, and personal connections, allusions, and references that elevated my work to a new level of discourse.

Time, Place, Theatricality of It

This piece, although meant as a performance slide lecture, is quite adaptable. In the early 1990s, I performed it at Diverse Works in Houston. The structure was:

Part 1. I was locked in their bathroom for three days, repeating a mantra my friend Dr. A. L. Mehta had given me; one that dissipated the fear of death. Eating only fruit, I was in phone communication with Dr. Mehta and his wife Dr. Aruna Mehta.

Part 2. They came to the space after three days, opened the door, and I came out and read this paper, "Death in the Art and Life of Linda M. Montano," to the gathered audience at Diverse Works.

Part 3. The Mehtas performed a Hindu fire ceremony outside, on the cement porch of Diverse Works. The purpose was to assist all participants to give up their fear of death.

Since then, as I have changed, the piece changes. It has become wildly interactive, with co-performers giving massages to audience members during the lecture; audience members dictating letters to death (to a co-performer); co-performers making themselves available as "talkers" so audience members can break through the proscenium, that is, come up front, stand up, interrupt, shout out, and talk to the seven other co-performers about sex and death, money and death, courage and death, et cetera. In fact, when I did this piece in San Francisco, it turned into a performance "slam," quite a nice invitation to chaos and layering.

"Death in the Art and Life of Linda M. Montano" was also a fitting good-bye event for my stay in the art department at the University of Texas–Austin. Fifteen students dressed as nuns massaged (nurtured) audience members, one "signed" the lecture while cross-dressed in red, and all participated in helping me bring closure to my seven years at Texas while co-addressing death, the Final Closure.

How Time Dramatically Changed This Paper

The summer of 1997, I went to Benares, India, a city dedicated to not hiding death. There I watched cremation after cremation after cremation. And on a hot August afternoon, five feet from ten burning bodies, three Benares teenage boys teased a passing goat to erection by making a mating sound. Somehow sex dislodged death for me! I watched an excited, out-of-control goat run around, erect and confused, and I laughed. Laughed with/at sex, laughed with/at death, laughed with/at my seriousness and fear.

Post 9/11 Update

Silence.

How to Read This Paper

1. Make a workshop out of it. Invite friends over and read the text performatively on a foggy winter night.

2. Use the text as an invitation to do research on the topic in your own way.

3. Your comment:

Conclusion

I thank Lynn Miller, performance friend, for giving me this opportunity to share with you. And I end with words my seventy-five-year-old mentor, best friend, and spiritual guide, Dr. Aruna Mehta, said to me this morning: "Love! Nobody knows what will happen the next day."

DEATH IN THE ART AND LIFE OF LINDA M. MONTANO

(Slide 1: Dr. A. L. Mehta and Dr. Aruna Mehta.)

It is with great happiness and good fortune that my friends, Doctors Aruna and A. L. Mehta, are here today. Both are ayurvedic doctors from India, now living in the U.S. Mrs. Mehta has delivered over two thousand babies and she continues to protect, inspire, and nurture her family, friends, and all who know her. Dr. A. L. Mehta, her husband, was the principal director of an ayurvedic university and still performs amazing and magical cures for innumerable and lucky patients. His knowledge is vast and his techniques unique.

Although this slide presentation is about death, the Mehtas have become my teachers of life, of energy, of relationship. They have almost adopted me into their family, and their compassionate wisdom has greatly influenced my life and work.

After this lecture, there will be an efficacious and powerful fire ceremony, which they will perform. The intention of the ritual will be to help everyone present understand death in their own unique way.

(Slide 2: Linda as eighteen-month-old adorable infant.)

Death in the Art and Life of Linda M. Montano.

This lecture is interactive: if you so choose, follow the suggestions so that you can perform along with me, but do so only if you are comfortable with the imagination process.

It is a great honor to be presenting this paper. But I want it to be more than a paper. My vision includes the reader and listener, so all of us can address the most challenging life event that we all face: the death of the physical body. Let's begin with this image.

(Pause.)

Choose to remember when you first:

Saw a death

Heard about death

How old were you? How did you feel? Fascinated? Detached? Curious? Frightened? Mystified? Anxious? Indifferent? Sit with that young self. Hold his or her hand. Dialogue with that aspect of yourself. Talk about life. Talk about death. If necessary, adjust your current belief system about death.
(Slide 3: Linda at seven. Lost front tooth.)

Part I: The Therapy of Seeing

I was born in a small village, upstate New York, into a strict, conservative, Roman Catholic family. Interviews I did with my mother revealed that I was outgoing, always giving flowers. Surviving milk allergies and childhood diseases, I lived, even though approximately two hundred thousand people die every day.
(Slide 4: A European cemetery.)
My childhood was immersed in Catholic ritual, prayers, and parochial school. At recess, the girls would walk around the cemetery next to the school, telling stories about death, premature burials, stories about unearthed coffins that were found filled with fingernails stuck in the gorged satin lids.
(Slide 5: Open coffins.)
All of us have watched TV shows like *Hard Copy, 20/20*, et cetera, and have our own stories of death. For example, we have heard of coffins designed with windows so the deceased can see outside, or with bells to inform the living of the mistake that was made, or of videos included both above and below ground, leaving messages for the living, and TV in the grave for the dead who might still want to watch the nightly news.
(Slide 6: Jesus on crucifix, muscles anatomically rendered.)
Death was always a fascination for me, but one that felt taboo in its mystery. At seven, I was taught by the nuns that if I sinned, the Devil would send me to hell when I died, where I would burn forever, but that Jesus died for our sins and offered an opportunity for salvation. None of it seemed very happy. It was about piercings and crucifixion—a sacred, somber event. Often I would faint in church—everything was so ponderous and unspeakably, devastatingly ecstatic.
(Slide 7: Junk sculpture by Montano of crucifixion.)
At twenty, I appropriated my greatest fear, death/suffering, by making a crucifix. This junk sculpture magically related me to Jesus, allowed me to speak the same language, and to be Christ the only way I knew how—by depicting suffering myself.
(Slide 8: Fiberglass sculpture by Montano of skeleton.)

A later fiberglass sculpture (1967) entitled "Death" was another attempt to explore my feelings about the subject, to look at a taboo by making art about it. Art became a safe space, often the only place where I could explore my fears and fascination.

(Pause.)

How would you make art about death? What would it look like? Be like?

(Slide 9: A tomb in Naples.)

Death elicits emotions of terror, sadness, and anxiety, but I continued to study it and look at it, hoping the denial would diminish.

(Slide 10: Catacombs in Italy.)

(Slide 11: My Guru, Dr. Ramamurti S. Mishra, at forty years old, smiling.)

Part II: The Therapy of Knowing

An incredibly influential spiritual friend and teacher in this process has been Dr. R. S. Mishra (Brahmananda Saraswati), my guru and patient guide. Since 1971, he has said, over and over, "Linda, you were not born, you cannot die. You are not the body and mind. Unless you understand your own death, you will have dis-ease."

His teachings are simple yet complex, Eastern yet Western. Once I began meditating under his direction, my Roman Catholic fears of death and the Devil were no longer the dreaded enemy but eventually became words and issues that I could experience and examine from another cultural and mythological perspective. Yoga literally saved my life and my soul, and I would like to thank all of the Eastern teachers—Jain, Hindu, Tibetan, Zen, Sufi—and the Latins for opening my psyche to their spiritual technology.

(Slide 12: Mexican skeletons playing musical instruments.)

(Pause.)

Who is your death teacher? What do they tell you about death? How does your death teacher prepare you for your death? These two stories I will read of death experiences are totally different but equally inspiring.

First:

Some masters pass away in sitting meditation with the body supporting itself. Kalu Rimpoche, one of my teachers, died in 1989 in the Himalayas with a number of masters and a doctor and nurse present. His closest disciple wrote:

"Rimpoche tried to sit up, had difficulty. One of the lamas felt it would be good to support his back so he could sit. He wanted to sit absolutely straight, indicating with a hand gesture and saying so. The doctor and nurse were upset by

this, so Rimpoche relaxed his posture slightly. He nevertheless assumed a medi-
tation posture, placed his hands in meditation mudra, opened his eyes in medi-
tation gaze, and his lips moved in mantra. A profound feeling of peace and hap-
piness settled on us all and spread through our minds. All of us present felt that
the indescribable happiness that was filling us was the faintest reflection of what
was pervading Rimpoche's mind . . . slowly Rimpoche's gaze and his eyelids low-
ered and the breath stopped."[1]

Second:

In a March 1996 National Enquirer, *Katharine Hepburn is quoted as*
saying, "If I'm going to die, I'll be damned if it is here in a hospital surrounded
by strangers. I'm going to die in my own bed with my family at my bedside."
After she signed herself out of a New York hospital where she had been admitted
with pneumonia, she told a relative, "Dry your tears and don't be sad, because
I'm going to join Spencer now. I've waited almost thirty years for this moment.
I want to take him into my arms again."

Neither of these great beings feared death. How does your death teacher help
you not fear death?

(Slide 13: Montano blindfolded for a week.)

To prepare myself for my death, I continue to study meditation and after
experiencing the exhilaration of meditation training, I began going inside publicly *as art,* doing sensory experiments (often blindfolded for a
week) to explore dying to one of my senses. Ramana Maharshi, an eloquent death teacher, suggests we die daily. He overcame death anxiety
after years of meditative experiences.

(Slide 14: Montano, lying as if dead.)

In 1970, I began a series of death simulations. Lying as if dead, having
seen my embalmed grandparents in coffins, as if asleep.

(Slide 15: Lying as if dead, hypnotized to sleep, dream, and sing the dream
'73, Berkeley Museum.)

In placing the template of death over my work, I contend that everything
that I have *ever* done has been an art of death or manifestation of grief.
Basically, my art has been appeasing my own death anxiety by allowing
me to die over and over and grieve, as art. I use these slides from other
cultures and their death rituals to expand and illustrate the thesis that we
all deal with death uniquely and culturally.

(Slide 16: Israeli funeral procession.)

In Israel, the body is not taboo. It is tenderly washed, not embalmed. It
is shrouded and buried. If the death has occurred in the Holy Land, it is
not coffined.

(Slide 17: Gypsy King's body surrounded by Gypsy mourners.)
Gypsy tribal kings head extended families, including several hundred members who must attend their funerals. The wake continues three days, all camp in and around the funeral home. The open casket contains a change of clothes because the dead are thought to return. Gold coins are placed in the casket on the eyes. Emotions include loud weeping. They kiss the forehead and knuckles and a funeral feast is eaten in the same room where the body lies. The funeral procession is a spectacle with music, violins, flowers. At the grave, the casket is opened again and all cry out in Romany their sorrows. The women fall on their knees and hit their heads against tombstones, knocking themselves out. More coins are thrown in the casket, wine poured in, and wailing continues. A cloth is then spread on the ground next to the grave and a feast is eaten.

(Slide 18: Montano sitting in a chair, white gauze as a garment, white face.)

(Slide 19: Dead African chief sitting.)
A dead Nigerian chief sits, swaddled, after having been washed and rubbed with aromatic herbs. Chiefs are buried in a sitting position, symbolic of his reigning in life from a throne or royal stool. The chief is lowered into the ground and a ceramic pot with a small hole is placed over the tomb. The hole allows the chief's soul to pass through it.

(Slide 20: Montano sitting as Chicken Woman, 1971.)

(Slide 21: Ibo medicine man.)
An Ibo (Niger) medicine man is painted white to keep away the spirits of death. At death, his tools were gathered, sacrificial blood spilled on them to keep death away; the closest kin were painted white; the women danced a dance of sorrow. Then the dead person was taken from his hut, seated on a chair to be viewed and buried in their own backyard. A small leaf roof marked the grave.

(Pause.)

Are you the descendant of an ethnic group? How does your group address death and death rituals? If you have no death traditions, how would you personally design a ritual? See it, feel it, hear it, practice it?

(Slide 22: Gilded skeleton.)
At certain times in our history, death has been glorified, romanticized, gilded, sentimentalized, but the nineties have changed the climate of death.

(Slide 23: Marble tomb of European king and queen.)
Anyone who has seen a person die of AIDS or advanced cancer knows that disease is not romantic. (Gurugi says TV has made Buddhas of us all,

referring to the fact that we see images of suffering as did the Buddha when he left his father's palace and saw a corpse for the first time.) AIDS deaths can include tubes, respirators, sores, lesions, inflated and cooled mattresses, balding, infections; men and women reduced to skeletons.

AIDS and the media have politicized death. It can no longer be avoided or sentimentalized. (Our next challenge is to keep it from being commodified.)

Part III: Movement and Death

(Slide 24: Montano dances on the Golden Gate Bridge in a blue prom gown.)

This dance was a memorial for all those who have committed suicide on the bridge.

(Slide 25: British funeral procession.)

In all cultures, the therapy of movement is included in the death ritual. In America, cars move funereally, with police escort, lights on, stopping traffic and the oncoming/outgoing breath of the onlookers.

Movements in other countries may include contortions of the limbs, jumping, running, rolling the eyes, injury to the self-using weapons. The commonality is that actions continue until the mourner is exhausted and clear of emotion.

(Slide 26: Korean funeral procession.)

In Korea, a canopy-covered *sanyu* holds the dead.

In New Orleans, brothers and sisters dance in defiance of death. A marshal and band precede the hearse, and an explosive shout erupts from the crowd under the hot New Orleans sun:

> Are you still alive?
> Yeah
> Do we like to dance?
> Yeah
> Do you want to dance?
> Yeah
> Well damn it, let's go.

(Slide 27: Montano walking uphill on a treadmill telling her life story, wearing a smile device.)

(Slide 28: Aboriginal funeral pole.)

Making funeral poles are a major emotional outlet for Australian aborigines. Cut from blood-wood trees, twenty feet high, three feet in diameter, they are smoked over a fire after carving. Each man makes one. It is not a profession but a social duty. Songs and dances are held around the poles. Relatives dance as if something is wrong with them—with their legs, arms. Women hold their breasts as if injured. At the grave, they slash their scalps with knives, beat their bodies with clubs, and perform other ritual expressions of grief. The poles are left on the burial site to weather.

(Slide 29: A marble sculpture funeral pole Montano made in Italy.)

Part IV: The Therapy of Mourning and Burial Customs

(Slide 30: Hungarian woman in white mourning clothes. A hand-embroidered death cloth hangs by her side.)

(Slide 31: African son of the deceased, painted white to keep away the spirits of death, views the dances with a profound look.)

(Slide 32: Montano with acupuncture needles in her face.)

After my ex-husband Mitchell Payne's tragic death in 1977, I mourned on video, in performance, and by writing. After two years, I was able to join the world again. In other cultures, inner pressures resulting from loss include making inarticulate sounds such as moaning, sobbing, screaming, keening, shouting, and ululating.

(Pause.)

Listen to your heart. What does it say about death? Listen to each room of the heart: room one, room two, room three, room four. Give your heart attention.

(Slide 33: Montano and friends dressed as nuns/priests, telling guilts.)

I mourned by listening and by telling guilts from the San Francisco Museum of Modern Art balcony.

(Slide 34: Temple of Silence, Persia.)

Persians bury their dead in the temple of silence. First the dead body is laid on a stone slab. With a nail, three circles are drawn around it and no one but funeral bearers can enter the circle. Sandalwood incense keeps away demons, disguised as flies. A dog leads the funeral procession, and tradition says a dog would howl in terror if the body were not really dead. The body is placed on iron, not wood, because the body is taboo, restricted, and would defile the elements. Therefore, it is not cremated because it would contaminate the fire. So the body is placed on a ledge inside the hollow temple of silence. Vultures strip the body in a few hours, then the bones are gathered from the ledge and thrown into the deep pit in the center of the temple of silence.

(Slide 35: Benares, India, cremation ghats.)

A Hindu, on the other hand, can be cremated. At death, the body is garlanded, the navel is oiled, nostrils plugged, big toes tied together; relatives are informed; women lament; mortuary specialists perform the ceremony since death is defiling. The banks of the Ganges and especially the city of Benares are the most auspicious places for cremations. There, the waterfront is given over to burning ghats—a place where funeral pyres are built. When the body reaches the site, it is immersed in Ganges water then placed on the pyre and smeared with *ghee* (butter). The son lights the firetorch—at the head for a man, at the feet for a woman. Mourners march around the fire, and although they are forbidden to look into the flames, they must notice if the skull bursts. If not, the son hits it with an implement, since Hindus believe that at death the soul is trapped in the skull and breaking it releases the soul. Then the mourners bathe in the river and recite:

"Vain is he who seeks to find the changeless in the human form. Life must terminate in death."

Part V: Therapy for Mourners
The following is a list of purification rites collected from different cultural traditions. They include restrictions which help "avenge the death" and appease ancestors, ghosts, et cetera.

Shave head
Pull out hair
Not wash hair
Not comb hair
No butter in hair for year
Mimic battle
Sift sand on body
Wear a band on wrist
Sacrifice a herd of oxen
Neglect gardens and fields
No jewelry worn
Paint body
Wear copper ring
Go into seclusion
Cutting the thumb
No touching cooking pots
Erect memorial stones
Burn down the hut
Carve poles

Fasting
Girls deliver water to all homes
Go bareheaded
Wear black
Wear white
Leave hair unbraided
Plant tree on grave
Say novenas
(Pause.)
If you had complete permission to mourn any way you would like, what would you do or not do?
    In my own experience, guilt and unfinished business with the death of friends have been my biggest obstacles with this subject of death. I invite only those who feel most comfortable to join me in the following visualization in saying good-bye to a dead loved one. The visualization is taken from the book The Tibetan Way of Living and Dying *by Sogyal Rinpoche.*

Can you imagine the face of a dead loved one? Keep your heart open. With your whole heart and mind, visualize that this loved one is looking at you with a greater love and understanding than he or she ever had while alive. Know the dead person wants you to understand that he or she loves you and forgives you and wants to ask for your forgiveness, then truly say farewell and really let go of the person.

    (Slide 36: Montano handcuffed to Tom Marioni.)
In '73, I was handcuffed to Tom Marioni for three days.
    Was it a mourning ritual?
    Is danger a way to avenge death?
    Is this kind of mourning a premature deathlike action which homeopathically keeps death away—tricking death by acting as if it already happened?
    (Slide 37: Montano tied to Tehching Hsieh.)
Was being tied by a six-foot rope a ritual of penance and alteration of consciousness?
    Tehching Hsieh, master of endurance, was looking for someone to be tied to for a year, while not touching and remaining always in the same room. By staying tied to Tehching Hsieh in his One Year Performance, I died a little every day, learning humility and collaboration.

(Slide 38: Mildred Montano as a young woman.)
When my mother died, I had a chance to redefine my beliefs. It was ten years after my ex-husband's death in 1977, and, with my mother's death in 1988, I was ready for some new information about death.
(Slide 39: Balinese effigy burning.)
A Balinese effigy is burned at funerals in that country.

In my life, it seemed as if each of *my* selves was an effigy dying, as my mother died slowly of colon cancer. After five years, she died painfully in the hospital—drugged, prodded, poked, and in excruciating pain.
(Slide 40: Seven slides of Montano in seven different colors corresponding to the seven chakras.)
Each year of *Seven Years of Living Art* and *Another Seven Years of Living Art*, I changed accent, personas, color, sound. It was my way of dying to myself—I was losing my mother, my friend, and myself. And I gained an expansive spaciousness and feel of the void that is ever-present.

Steven and Andrea Levine write:

The death of the body is accompanied by less agony than the death of an ego. The death of ego is a tearing away of everything we imagine to be solid, a crumbling of the walls we have built to hide behind. Letting go of self-protection, there may arise dizziness and nausea. When all we imagine our self to be dies, everything is seen in its essentially empty, impermanent nature.

(Pause.)
Who have you lost? What does your spaciousness feel like?

Part VI: Current Preparation
We baby boomers are aging and as we age, we transform and observe the body's decay—the change in metabolism, graying at the temples, middle-age stomach, lowering of energy levels, lessening of muscle tone, loss of hair. How, without silicone implants, cosmetic surgeries, collagen injections, vitamins, and liposuctions, can we deny the temporariness of the body? We cannot disregard death.
(Slide 41: Montano as half male, half female.)
(Pause.)
Meet yourself as a 108-year-old. What is the message your elder self gives to you?

Part VII: Therapy of Study

As death comes further and further out of the closet, blushing with shame and the innocence of newness, we continue our research. How to do that? Here are some suggestions:

(*Slide 42: Henry Montano as a young man.*)

1. Talking with our elders: my eighty-year-old father said, when I was complaining about car insurance and my house, "What's all of that in the face of eternity?"

2. Writing our wills, our living wills, making provisions to donate organs. In China, coffins are made and then placed in the home as furniture.

(*Slide 43: Montano as a priest-nun.*)

3. Choose the officiant for our funerals now. Will it be Father Amara or Sister Rose?

4. We can decide ecological ways to dispose of the body.

(*Slide 44: Tree burial.*)

A. Plains Indians scaffold burial.

(*Slide 45: Balinese cremation.*)

B. Balinese effigies are burned with the body.

(*Slide 46: Tibetan monk blows femur horn.*)

C. Himalayan priests summon flesh-eating birds with a horn made from a human femur so the birds can eat the dead body.

(*Slide 47: Tree burial.*)

D. Sioux Indians bury their dead in trees.

E. Will we decide to take up space and be buried on this shrinking planet?

(*Slide 48: My Guru in his sixties.*)

5. We can take charge of our death by defining and experiencing consciousness while we are alive. Brahmananda Saraswati's teachings direct me in this area.

(*Slide 49: Mexican candy skull.*)

6. We can face death by living life fully and laughing *with it* and *at it.*

7. We can face death by letting go of those who have already died.

8. We can re-see and re-join our spiritual roots for comfort and protection.

(*Pause.*)

How do you envision a ceremony for your death? Who will be there? What will be said or done?

As we complete this process together, let's take one last look at the subject from seven different aspects of ourselves.

(Pause.)
(Slide 50: Montano in red, hands on first chakra.)
Can you imagine the earthy you addressing death? How would that aspect of yourself relate? What would be said or done?
(Slide 51: Montano in orange, hands on second chakra.)
Can you imagine the earthbound you addressing death? What would you say to death about your possessions?
(Slide 52: Montano in yellow, hands on third chakra.)
Can you imagine the courageous and gutsy you addressing death?
(Slide 53: Montano in green, hands on fourth chakra.)
Can you imagine the compassionate and loving you addressing death?
(Slide 54: Montano in blue, hands on fifth chakra.)
Can you imagine the clear communicator aspect of yourself addressing death?
(Slide 55: Montano in purple, hands on sixth chakra.)
Can you imagine your intuitive self addressing death?
(Slide 56: Montano in white, hands on seventh chakra.)
Can you imagine your bliss-filled self addressing death?

I end this lecture with the reading of the main verses of the six bardos, a Tibetan Buddhist teaching.

The Main Verses of the Six Bardos
(Slide 57: Death/Life mask of Linda M. Montano.)
Now when the bardo of birth is dawning upon me,
I will abandon laziness for which life has no time,
Enter the undistracted path of study, reflection, and meditation,
Making projections and mind the path, and realize the three kayas;
Now that I have once attained a human body,
There is no time on the path for the mind to wander.

Now when the bardo of dreams is dawning upon me,
I will abandon the corpselike sleep of careless ignorance,
And let my thoughts enter their natural state without distraction;
Controlling and transforming dreams in luminosity,
I will not sleep like an animal
But unify completely sleep and practice.

Now when the bardo of samadhi-meditation dawns upon me,
I will abandon the crowd of distractions and confusions,

And rest in the boundless state without grasping or disturbance;
Firm in the two practices: visualization and complete;
At this time meditation, one-pointed, free from activity,
I will not fall into the power of confused emotions.

Now when the bardo of the moment before death dawns upon me,
I will abandon all grasping, yearning, and attachment,
Enter undistracted into clear awareness of the teaching,
And eject my consciousness into the space of unborn mind;
As I leave this compound body of flesh and blood
I will know it to be a transitory illusion.

Now when the bardo of dharmata dawns upon me,
I will abandon all thoughts of fear and terror,
I will recognize whatever appears as my projection
And know it to be a vision of the bardo;
Now that I have reached this crucial point,
I will not fear the peaceful and wrathful ones, my own projections.

Now when the bardo of becoming dawns upon me,
I will concentrate my mind one-pointedly,
And strive to prolong the results of good karma,
Close the womb-entrance and think of resistance;
This is the time when perseverance and pure thought are needed,
Abandon jealousy, and meditate on the guru with his consort.

With mind far off, not thinking of death's coming,
Performing these meaningless activities,
Returning empty-handed now would be complete confusion;
The need is recognition, holy dharma,
So why not practice dharma at this very moment?
From the mouths of siddhas come these words:
If you do not keep your guru's teaching in your heart
Will you not become your own deceiver?

Thank you for attending this "performance" and remember, "Love! Nobody knows what will happen the next day"—Dr. Aruna Mehta.
    Sincerely,
    Linda

DEATH NOTES

Death Notes is included in this article for those wanting grief counseling.

In 1988 my mother died. It was a five-week hospital death. Colon cancer. I was with her much of that time. These are some of the things I learned.

1. *Ask* the dying person questions and *wait* for verbal/nonverbal responses. For example: "Should we stop this medicine?" "What do you need?" et cetera. (I didn't always ask my mother's opinion and now I wish I had.)

2. *Listen, listen, listen.*

3. See if they have unfinished business they want to work with, such as unexpressed thoughts, feelings, wishes. (My mother said, "I always wished I had written a book," knowing that I would hear her and do it for her. I have.)

4. If they prefer, let them leave consciously, alertly, with awareness. (Because one medicine was stopped, she became comatose. I didn't know that would happen and I missed saying good-bye because of that.)

5. If they agree, play nature tapes in the hospital room. It creates a no-panic atmosphere. (I played one and nurses used to come in the room because it felt "good in here.")

6. Help the way they need to be helped, not the way you need. (Once I was chanting, praying, laying my hands on her abdomen, teaching her to breathe. My mother, always the comedienne, opened her dying eyes, looked at me with an Imogene Coco–look, and said, "Linda, *please!*")

7. Confess by their bedside. (Clear your heart but do it telepathically. Tell everything you need to tell. Do unfinished business without their hearing. Sotto voce.)

8. If the person is on heavy painkillers, they might change their behavior toward you, positively or negatively. Be ready! (My mother became a hippie on morphine. She pulled me close to her, tried to show me her aura, touched the peach fuzz on my cheeks. We re-bonded.)

9. Get counseling for yourself from friends, twenty-four-hour telephone hotlines, hospice volunteers, et cetera. (I talked with a hospice volunteer for four years on the phone while my mother was sick and dying. Hurrah for hospice!)

10. Know what "patient's rights" means and use the information appropriately. (I asked one nurse, "If this were your mother would you allow a nurse to take blood and do 'vitals' while your mother was comatose and had only a

little time left?" The nurse said, "No." I said, "Then please do not take blood and stop all orders at the desk.")

11. Be prepared for each family member and close friend of the dying person to have a completely different response to everything. Emotions are close to the surface; everyone's death anxiety button is being pushed.

12. Use TV and VCRs as teaching tools. (When my mother wanted TV on I turned to cartoons. The flying horse image from *My Little Pony* did wonders for her attitude and actually kept her pain-free.)

13. Inconspicuously breathe together (match your breathing pattern to theirs), and gently sound the exhalation. (Steve Levine teaches this technique. It's Tibetan and comforting for both patient and caretaker.)

14. Whisper messages near an ear. Keep messages positive and in words they need to hear. (When I said, "Relax, Ma, Mitchell and Karl will take very good care of you," she responded positively. These were friends who were dead and whose company she loved.)

15. Go as far as you can go with the process at the end. (Those last fifteen hours when she was comatose, I felt a need to meditate, give her space, not touch her as much. Check out your own situation; it will be different.)

16. After the death, participate in the process as much as you can given place and circumstances. Help wash the body, close the eyes. (I didn't see the spirit or soul leave. Some people do.)

17. Never, ever judge how you or anyone else mourns or deals with a death. (I demolished and rebuilt an abandoned building for two years after she died. I rarely cried, but my body sweated.)

18. Be watchful for messages, dreams, symbolic visits. (She comes as a butterfly or sometimes a wave of feeling. I continue a dialogue with her.)

19. Daily: Prepare for your death in your own way.

20. Your comments:

Notes

1. Sogyal Rimpoche, *The Tibetan Book of Living and Dying* (San Francisco: Harper), 317.

This is the end.

15

Shaping the World
with Our Hands

෴

Laila Farah

As a borderland person embarking on a journey into Lebanese women's lives, I find myself "crossing over/under" numerous borders, none of which are safe, being forced to present my "certifying papers" to everyone to signify my status. It leads me to reflect on the nature of my position-in-the-world. In listening to and reading stories of decolonization, narratives of legitimacy, and the narratives of the inheritance of culture in this project, I begin to feel the resonances of my own hybrid narrative emerge and intersect with women living within similar bodies of knowledge: American women of color, "third world" women, Lebanese and Palestinian women, *mestiza* women, lesbian and queer women.

As postcolonial theory notes, women's voices or lived-experiences have not been present in the narratives of nation-states, particularly women of the third world. The privilege of my position as a dual-national academic offers me an opportunity to articulate various bodies of knowledge, including my own, and to present what we might learn from these glaringly absent narratives of women's lives. It is precisely this multivocal juncture between Lebanese and American which reveals my balancing act on the hyphen (Rodriguez 159) which I am laying claim to by birth, by choice, by necessity, by theory, by ethical need, by global demand. This juncture is not explored merely to share women's stories and experiences, but rather to open up what is learned from them and what is learned from the sharing process itself through the voices themselves, and through the performance of these same voices.

Tareekhi, my story, weaves the voices of Lebanese and Palestinian women, filling the gaps, bridging the gulfs between Arab and American, between third and first worlds, between the colonial and postcolonial, between the Atlantic and the Mediterranean. It is my intention that my agenda never be absent, for what Gloria Anzaldúa calls my *mestiza* status is what it is—a standing at the border, waiting for my "papers" to be examined, between one end of the hyphen and the other, one culture and the next, one identity and the next.

In theorizing my life-world, I found myself struggling to find a language that would speak to my experiences. I wonder how much of my tongue I have had to cut out to include everything that must be and simultaneously cannot be in this narrative. I wonder at the separation-alienation-distantiation that has occurred within me from Lebanese culture by the very act of completing this document. My feelings of "selling out" are with me. I wonder what is mine in these politics of location. As Behar asks, "How many masks [can] I wear without my face starting to stretch?"

These sensibilities, coupled with an emerging sense of my *mestiza* status, enabled me to recognize the power that resides on a border, the natural subversiveness, an openness of terrain most of my colleagues and friends do not possess by birthright. Previously, the margin was a painful place of disempowered confusion. As Anzaldúa aptly puts it, I am at "los intersticios, the spaces between the different worlds [I] inhabit" (xv–xvi). She follows the development of the identity of the *mestiza* in *Borderlands/ La Frontera* into what she terms the *mestizaje*, or a hybrid peoples born of three and four racial lines and cultures as a means to help understand how the Chicana/o identity came to be. This notion of hybridity is precisely where I locate myself along the lines of blood and culture.

It is not so simple as to conflate these understandings of self into a politics of location, where my being is located. It is not *merely* a question of racial or ethnic identity or sexuality or national origin either. Rather it is a question of shadow and light and the play between the two. As Torrecilha says, "I have become my own creation. I am the product of different cultures, but I resemble none in its entirety. I experience life differently according to the cultures that define who I am" (272).

The path to this place of empowered comfort has not been without pain and debilitating confusion. How do you learn to harness your voice and unleash it out into the world when you have been taught from infancy that to do so is an affront and an *aiyb*, a shame? hooks reminds us of how young women were expected not to "talk back" to anyone. And so it is the transformation of voice that leads to a transforming of space and a shift in

approaches and methods which third world feminists and postcolonial
theorists have been espousing for some time: there is much to learn from
the discourses of the unheard, the unsung, the unrecorded, the unnoticed,
the "uneducated," the un-American, un-Anglo Saxon, uncanonical lexi-
cons. Chandra Mohanty provides an insightful discussion that helps one
to understand that the constraining constructions of third world women
circumvent the possibility of understanding anything about their worlds,
as they are always already, in the eyes of the West, in a substandard position. Hence, Mohanty explains, any research conducted about these
women offers a skewed understanding of how millions of women really
exist in their daily lives (4).[1]

The focus of the research for this project metamorphosed as time
passed and readings continued, interviews were conducted and tran-
scribed, and finally pared down into a manageable size to be performed in
a one-woman production entitled, "Shaping the World with Our Hands."
The four narratives represent women from various ages, educational
backgrounds, professional orientations, religious affiliations, cultural upbringing, and geographical locations within Lebanese society. The narrative form of the script follows my encounters with these women in the
field, and my autoethnographic journey ties the narratives together. The interpretive links between the intersubjectivities of my narrative, the women's
individual narratives with my own, and the audience's narratives with all
of ours require live performance to deepen our understanding of how
storying our lives can transform knowledge bases into nonhegemonic
forms. The theoretical questions I am currently problematizing in this
document are included in my narrative as a means of situating the audience both to these women's lives and to the dilemmas of encountering another culture through fieldwork and performance. Françoise Lionnet
maintains that autoethnography is "the defining of one's subjective ethnicity as mediated through language, history, and ethnographic analysis"
(99). It would seem then, in the spirit of reflexivity, that through autoethnography, the researcher might create a system of checks and balances of one's own practices in the field in order to determine degrees of
distantiation, myopia, or exploitation.

I returned to Lebanon to conduct my fieldwork in 1994, and made a
number of contacts who were representative of the diversity of the population of Lebanon in terms of religion, cultural background, economic
status, family status, educational background, regional location, and age.

My initial intent was to gather a random sampling, not to quantitatively represent a certain number of women from each co-cultural group. As the focus of this project is to foreground women's lived experience in order to provide an alternative perspective of how certain women live their daily lives in Lebanon, I did not believe that a large number of women's narratives were needed. As each woman offers her oral history, stories emerge that differ from those traditionally reported from Lebanon: war narratives of horror and mass destruction, political narratives from religious and political leaders, journalistic reportage, and demographic studies within specific communities. I am interested in understanding better the dailiness of women's lives and the counternarratives our stories provide. As the Personal Narratives Group asserts, it is important to understand these women's "[t]ruths, a decidedly plural concept meant to encompass the multiplicity of ways in which a woman's life story reveals and reflects important features of her conscious experience and social landscape, creating from both her essential reality" (14).

The autoethnography in travelogue format seemed to be the most effective vehicle for connecting the individual narratives, as well as a link for the audience to engage these narratives of women so distant from their own life-worlds. This perspective offers a close examination of spurious assumptions that have been made about postcolonial and neocolonial peoples by focusing on the configurations of Western hegemonic knowledge production. As peoples of the postcolonial world enter "first world" arenas, due in no small part to the establishment of global economies, the necessity for cross-cultural and cross-national analysis from *within* these same communities of peoples is undeniable. Furthermore, this perspective challenges racial, ethnic, national, economic, and sexual structures as constructed by Western intellectual communities. Foremost in this activity is the laying bare of one's own positionality and praxis. I join the ranks of Lila Abu-Lughod's "native quarter," drawing upon her discussion of Viswsewaran's notion of the "hafie," whose "agony is not how to communicate across a divide but how to theorize the experience that moving back and forth between the many worlds [I] inhabit as a movement within one complex and historically and politically determined world" (26). I turn to Bhabha here: "[T]he postcolonial prerogative seeks to affirm and extend a new collaborative dimension, both within the margins of the nation-space and across boundaries between nations and peoples" (175). The exposure of colonized, neocolonized, and decolonized economic and political structures is integral to understanding how agency in these countries and nation-states can and must be viewed as nonvictimage, and that one must begin the search for understanding embedded in daily lives.

The interdisciplinary hybridity of the project in its current form pushes through the boundaries of "traditional" modes of inquiry as well as the boundaries of my own training, challenging them through postcolonial notions by using narratives of violence, recognizing the multiple identities of women's lives, deconstructing colonial images of third world women, and revealing their narratives as sites of contestation.[2] I contend that it is precisely the breaking of the "privatism" of third world women's lives that renders these voices more politically and culturally useful, particularly at a time when the reconceptualization of global and local space is in such flux. The charge I set for myself in this endeavor is representing these women's narratives, as well as my own, without the pitfalls of hegemonic theory production. The women I interviewed indicated time and again that they wanted their stories to be heard in "*Amerca*" as "real women's" stories, stories that come from "flesh and blood." It is in response to their charge then that I create a space, a "house of performance where thought is felt and feelings are thought," in which to take on the role of cultural critic in the name of social justice, of cultural, social, and political awareness, to present a community of women who wish to celebrate their tactics of survival, resistance, and cultural membership.[3]

SHAPING THE WORLD WITH OUR HANDS

(The stage is set with four separate areas, each lit separately with different light tones. The fifth area is in the center of the circle, formed by the chairs and side tables in each area, lit with a warm amber light. Arabic music plays as the audience comes in. Each chair is adorned with costume changes and each coffee table has different props. The blocking for the entire show is circular in style, with light shifts from area to area, signaling a new persona's introduction. The center space is always used for the autoethnographic segments.

The house lights dim and the center spot becomes brighter as I enter the stage from the wings and wind my way around the circle, moving in and out of the circle during the following narrative, ending in the center area.)
In all the time I spent growing up in Beirut, I never believed that fear was something I could embody. The only thing I could embody was fight. During the Israeli invasion of Beirut, I learned whole new meanings of

the word resistance. We had a word we used for those of us who would rather die than leave, *samidoon*, which means those who will save, meaning save the city—no matter what was done to us, no matter how little water we had, no matter how long the bread line or how full of bugs the flour was, or how little gasoline there was, or how sporadic the electricity schedules, no matter how close the bombs were, no matter how many times the planes would fly over, or how many times we had to drag our mattresses into the hallway or run down flights of stairs for "safety," or how many loved ones and friends and friends of friends we knew were killed, or whether the roads were open, or whether I would see the next hour—never mind the next day. It was precisely during this time in the summer of 1982 that I learned how resistance had nothing to do with revolution; it had everything to do with living.

The narrative of resistance is a narrative born in the dailiness of women's lives, in the way we think, in the way we work, in the way we dream. And as I dream of these women with unmeasurable resilience, my work begins—as a recorder of women's lives, as a performer of women's lives, as an advocate for women's lives. My resistance comes in many forms: I resist the loss of Lebanese culture to the insidious infusion of McDonald's capitalism, the hamburger for the shawarma, the hotdog for the kabob, the pizza for priceless recipes and traditions. And since women are the preservers of culture, and their nonwaged labor isn't valued, it is precisely at this moment that the "preserves" must be made. I began to think about the ways in which culture and tradition had been handed down to me and I began to dream the women in my own history . . .

Another way in which I perform resistance in my dailiness is by refuting the ways in which gender is represented in the Middle East, especially outside of the Middle East. You know what I am talking about. The veiled hysteric beating her breast in the street, the uneducated peasant in the field, the subjugated and oppressed victim constructed by media stereotyping and even by Western feminists. And yet I understand the value of cultural critique without romanticization . . . and I began to see that as I dreamed these women, their images and words needed to be heard, in some cases, because they could not be heard in their "home space." And so I struggle with visas and ethics in these border crossings, and in the end, I say better to have the voices heard than to remain epitomized the way they always already are . . . and who better than this border crosser . . .

(The center area is fully lit during the following segment; all other area lights go to black. Music fades out simultaneously.)

Oeuvre

Adouma, my grandfather's sister, made hommos nice and tart. She used a lot of lemon. My auntie Khowla, my father's sister, makes it the same way, and they taught my mother to make it that way too. For years, I would sit in these women's kitchens and watch the making of hommos: the beating of garlic in the mortar and pestle with salt, the squeezing of lemons until the fresh acid citrus smell filled the room, the heavy scent of cooking chick peas filling the air, earthy and sweet all at once. I can still see them shaking the tahini container vigorously, trying to reintegrate the sesame oil and the solids back together to add to the peas, watching each woman grind the peas differently, using minutely varied amounts of cooking liquid from the peas, but never straying far from each other in measure. How each woman's soft upper arm swayed with the rhythm of her beating the ingredients together in the bowl, odors mingling and meshing in my nose as they became creamier under these insistent arms. How each woman would ask me to taste the mixture by dipping my pinky into the thick paste on the spoon, and then being invited for an obligatory second taste, just to be sure. And how I would inevitably nod and say it was perfect (as it always was), and how they tasted from the same spoon, for the final pronouncement of perfection. How they would spoon the paste into the traditional shallow glazed pottery dishes hommos is always served in. How their adept hands would unconsciously smooth the paste up-up-up the sides of the bowls, leaving a small mound in the middle forming a moat to pour the olive oil into. Hommos can never be served plain! How they each taught me different ways of decorating: Adouma with paprika sprinkled in the sign of the cross, Aamto Khowla with a small bunch of reserved cooked peas for the mound in the middle, and Mother, who put pickles at the four directions. Each with a precision, born of years of doing, of knowing, of body rhythms not noticed by anyone, until now, perhaps. So this is cultural preservation, an active state born of an ache to see and smell and taste again, born of the need for the comforts that used to reside in those kitchens, which now reside in mine. My arm moves in the same rhythm, soft flesh swaying, imprinted in patterns of a mosaic of tradition. Hommos is a traditional Lebanese dish. It is served at virtually every table of every Lebanese household and made by women in numbers that are staggering. It has always been so, and it is the doing which preserves the knowing and the rhythms that beat the hommos into a smooth paste.

(During this closing segment, I am motioning a beating of the hommos in a broad gesture.)

In the absence of any offspring or kinswomen around me, I pass these rhythms on to newfound clan sisters: Janet, Tami, Chris, Elana, Patricia.

(Freeze. A general lighting wash lights the whole stage, which is added on top of the center spot. Underscoring music fades up. A cross-fade of spots occurs as I move to the first chair downstage right. During the following fugue, I tie my hair to the side and don a scarf.)

Fugue 1

I arranged to meet my old friend Nowal at her sister Amal's place in Beirut. I hadn't seen Nowal in a while. She and I evacuated with marines thirteen and a half years ago. I had met Amal once, but didn't remember her. Amal opened the door with all the graciousness of a Lebanese hostess. We had cold juice, Arabic coffee, and lots of cigarettes. I fought off the luncheon invitations vehemently.

The meeting with Amal made me realize I had the ability to sink into a comfortable remembering of "how-to's" . . .

(Begin series of improvised Arabic call/response inserts during the following.)

I know how many times to refuse that fourth cup of coffee so they will finally accept that I really don't want it and that I'm not just being polite. I know how to respond to all the phrases of greeting, food praises, inquiries of family members' health, and leave taking. I know what subjects I can and cannot ask them in front of their menfolk. I know what personal subjects are taboos. I know how to dress for each interview and who I may shake the hand of and who I may not and who I have to pay special respect to. It feels like no time and all the time in the world has passed.

As I return for the interview, I can't help wonder how I'll negotiate all the changes in me as I get deeper and deeper into this project. I feel in-between, balancing on the hyphen.

(Music fades out, as does the general wash and center spot, leaving only the full lighting of the downstage right chair. This coffee table has a plate of fruit that I cut, offer, and eat during the narrative.)

Amal Moawad

On a day like today, when the water comes . . . the first thing I do, I make my coffee. I don't do anything before that. I get up at five. I like to get up alone, without my husband even. Then, if the water is coming, I begin. What do I have that's empty? The washer has to be filled, the containers have to be filled, the water tank in the attic has to get filled, all the bottles have to get filled, the plants have to be watered.

But that depends if the water is coming strongly or not. Sometimes it comes strongly like now, because we haven't had water in a long time. But if it has come recently, it's a thin [draws this out] thread, so each bucket needs a quarter of an hour, to get full to the brim. Then you have to empty that into other things and then fill it again and empty and fill. It takes me half a day, because it will be one or two before the water is done coming up.

Aah. In the meantime, I would have put the bucket under the faucet. Whatever else I have to do that needs finishing, I do. I have to work on the brass, I have housework to do, I have to cook, everything that I have to do, I do entretemps, between bucket and bucket. And then I am running and carrying and toting and going back and carrying more to get the bottles filled.

All these things I do in the house that I work at during the day, why would I pass these things on to my children?

Oh, some of these things are not a *problème* for me. I will pass on to Lama how to be a lady of the house. Is it a shame that she would be a lady of the house? Is it a shame to cook? To take care of her house if she likes that? Is it a shame for her to take care of her possessions? These are her things. Maybe she will have a servant. My mom didn't have one, there is nothing wrong for her to do the work in her own house and her husband to work in the house. It's for the two of them. I don't work in my house because I am forced to. I know people who hate to do it. I love it. You understand loving it? OK, I don't love to do things with water and scrubbing, but my daughter should learn to take care of her house.

Now what I know of our traditions—I know them—but they don't mean too much to me. I cook certain dishes, but I don't do anything I don't like. I don't make them because they are Lebanese, or that this is traditional, so you should learn it, no. For example, I don't learn something the way they do it in Baalbek because my people are from there, or from Jebeil or . . . this is the last of my concerns, Jebeil and Baalbek. The last thing I want to do is sit for eight hours in a car to go up to Baalbek to see the pillars standing. I mean, I will talk to the children about this, but *c'est tout.* It's in the passing of the road—there was that—finish.

But what is important to me is family—*yani,* not only my family—

my husband's family. I always sit with my mother-in-law and say, "What did Elias's father do? Tell me what Elias's grandfather used to do." My husband is fifty years old, so imagine how much I am going back. Right now, I tell my son, your father is Elias, his father was Elias, his grandfather was Najeeb, and Elias's father's grandfather's name was Nasrallah. This is important, where we come from, that we have lived, not things like cooking, but our traditions and our history. These other things don't do anything for me inside.

(Freeze. Each woman's narrative is punctuated by a five-second freeze. Underscoring music fades up along with the general lighting wash. I remove the costume changes in the area before moving. As I cross to the upstage left area, the spots of each area are cross-faded. During the following fugue, I put on a blazer and tie my hair back in the upstage left area.)

Fugue 2

I feel myself asking the same question over and over again. . . . What am I looking for? What if I can only find what I set out to find? You know it's entirely possible for me not to be able to see these women in any way that varies from the image in my mind. OK, OK, not to worry. Identify what I am bringing into this project. All that baggage about coming back into Lebanese-Arab culture and not wanting to embrace it. In fact it feels so restrictive and oppressive I want to be as far away from it as possible. But if I am so distant, how will I be able to see the obvious?

As I drive into Saida in Mom's old Buick, hoping I haven't gotten lost, I feel nervous about meeting these women who have been in the trenches for so long. I expect hardened, resilient women who won't have any patience for an academic asking questions about the obvious. I am now completely lost and sweating like hell and wondering how traditional these women can be, if they are heads of educational foundations and headmistresses of schools.

(Music fades out along with the general wash lighting. This area has an Arabic coffee pot with Arab cups on the table. I pour and drink this during the narrative.)

Im Nizar

My parents came from Palestine in '42 and they lived in Nabatiyeh, the Palestinian refugee camp. My mother gave birth to ten children here in Lebanon. I was born and grew up in Nabatiyeh. My father was a communist, from the very staunch communists. He believed that since such a large Palestinian population was together, we should work from the inside and keep the struggle to return to Palestine. We lived in the house with this upbringing. Then, in all our actions, we reflected this. I looked back at our childhood and can't remember one day where there was happiness and smiles. Not one day.

The intelligence bureau were constantly in our house. They always used to break our door in at night with their feet and come in on us when we were little and interrogate us. They would beat us, and many times they would beat Father in front of us and put him in the Land Rover and take him away and question him. So we lived in that environment.

Then I got married and my husband was also a member of the Palestinian communist faction and he was also very, very active in the party. I tell my children these stories all the time. Even my husband, who was in Nahr el Bared . . . You know that camp? . . . He was very persecuted also, either beaten, or harassed in some way. So during this environment of him going through so much, I was never far from the action. I was living in one camp and then I came to Ain el Helwe camp. *Yani*, our daily bread is carrying our history and struggle with us.

So this is what I think is giving me the *jasad* (materiality), that these children, out of all the children of the world who are living happily, the Palestinians are living in difficulty, and the feelings of being vanquished and the feelings of oppression all builds on itself. So, that gives encouragement, and day after day, my resolve is strengthened for my need to help children. So, you see, I have a strong conviction in their future, in the future of all Palestinians. That's why I forget the fatigue, and I feel at peace with myself because I am doing something I want at the school.

My children at home, honestly, what do you say? They have taken these things with their breast milk. I fed them this resistance from the time they were small babies. In our house, all the time my children hear the popular songs of the Palestinian resistance. They know our culture. They know the story of the Palestinians. If they want to give a gift to their friends, or get their friends something, they get something Palestinian. They like national dishes, like *moughrabiyeh* (grain dish with lamb), *msakhan* (vegetable stew). Also, our customs. For example, we had a wedding in Tripoli, one of my husband's relatives in Nahr el Bared. They made a lunch that would feed the whole camp; the whole camp was at the wedding. How they got the rice to be grain for grain and how each sheep's head is cut in the butchering, how the groom is bathed and how they washed his hair and sang all the Palestinian songs to him and how they dressed the bride, dancing Palestinian dances. My daughter was twelve years old and knew all the customs. They like it. When they put music on, they dance the traditional dances. I love this in my children.

And then, my in-laws, my children are very close to them. When I was working all the time, I used to take them there. Also my in-laws are very knowledgeable in all things Palestinian. My father-in-law still wears the *ghalabiyeh* (traditional long gown) and the headdress. And my parents are also very involved in the culture and keeping it alive.

There is not one thing that I think, or feel, or believe, that I don't talk to them about. Some children may not know where their home is in Palestine. My children know every detail about Palestine: the name of the town, which area, what is there, who is there, what they do for a living. I insisted they know all these things since they were five years old. Sometimes my daughter asks me, "There is the camp—why are we living like this? Some other children don't live like this." At school, a lot of times their friends have very wrong ideas about Palestinians and then my kids pass the correct ideas around.

In respect to the school, you see, the foundation's philosophy is we must give the children a full educational background and then we give them a nationalistic education. For example, in the kindergarten, a child must know his roots, his camp, he must know his customs, the traditional foods of ours. They need to know the flag and their national anthem and the special days and occasions. We sing them Palestinian songs, and dance *dabket* (folk dances) and make things that are Palestinian and we bring Palestinian groups to perform. So the children learn that they are in the camps, but that they are not Lebanese. We pay special attention to these things because if no one does, slowly, slowly, slowly, they will lose their Palestinian heritage and they will be lost.

And do you know, Laila, these children have nothing: they have no land, they have no home, they have no garden. They need to know why we are living like this. They need to know their circumstances, love their country, identify with their country. Look, they have taken this in with their breast milk. Why else would you see a three-year-old duck when a plane flies over? They know this in the camp.

Now there is the problem of people leaving and immigrating outside. A lot of the young men are immigrating out to Denmark, to Sweden, to Italy. It's an exodus of massive proportion. I think that this is normal, when a man cannot work, cannot provide for his family, cannot feed his children. And so when a country opens a door for immigration, he

will continue going and that is what should happen so the people can survive.

That is also why a person must carry all their heritage with them.
This is how the Palestinian people will endure anything.

*(Freeze. Music fades up along with the general lighting wash. The spot
from upstage left is cross-faded with the upstage right area spot by the end
of the fugue. I remove the costume changes in place before moving out of the
area. As I move to the upstage right area, I let my hair loose and put on a
long vest.)*

Fugue 3

I can't resist the comparative move in my head—how different this notion of liberation? Especially in comparison to what women have
achieved in the U.S. and in Europe. Shit. I can't believe that I just did that,
with all my feminist theory of taking each woman's context into consideration and blah blah blah. I could be too resistant to their words, their
experiences, their perceptions. On the other hand, I could be too em-
bracing and turn them into the noblest of savages.

So women like Ellissar, whose ideas seem closest to my own, are
threatening the survival of the customs I value so much or at least am
holding in a mythical childhood stasis. Or maybe those customs are exactly what are holding women back and oppressing them. I sign in at the
TV station and wait to get my bag checked. I think about getting hassled
because of the recording equipment. Actually, I am more concerned with
the madness of this place and the hell I may have to go through just to get
a decent interview. It's so chaotic here.

*(General wash lighting and upstage left spot fade out with music. This area
is set with an ashtray, cigarettes, a lighter, and a glass of water.)*

Ellissar

1. Going back home and having parents tell you where were you?
2. Going back home alone.
3. Not being able to talk on the phone from my own house.
4. Not being able to receive phone calls.
5. Not being able to receive people.
6. Being restricted by society.
7. Leading a fake life.

I'm resisting now by ignoring these things and doing what I want and
what brings me happiness, whether it's going to shock people or not. I

don't care now. I feel like I'm wasting time, precious time. I spend most of my time with my friends and feel that I get love and I get emotions and I get intensity and I get everything that I really need to live. We just run away and find our own place and spend time with each other.

(I light a cigarette.)

That was a major step that I took. That was something out of the blue, to live on my own or try to make an attempt at doing so. The family tried to stop it at first but then it became an OK thing to do. My mom started accepting it indirectly; she hasn't said anything, but she asks, "Are you coming home tonight or are you sleeping out?" So there is a change in her tone.

Oh, that is *so* resistant because of my other secretive life, which will remain secret for a very long time in this land. Because to my mom, sleeping out means sleeping with other women and there's always a problem—if it's not women it's men. Marriage is very important in my home. I keep hearing the question, "When are you getting married? When are you getting married?" Even though my mom was working on being financially independent and said this was the most important thing I should aim for in my life. When I became financially independent, she said, "I don't want that. You have to get married." You can't, you can't, you can't. The contradictions in the homes, on the streets in Lebanon are too much. But it's fun sometimes—the contradictions—just going crazy in front of people who are so concerned to see what you are doing. I really want to enjoy these few energetic years I still have.

I want to do this by changing the fact that parents have to live your life for you until you are married and changing the fact that they have to pick your future for you and changing the fact that you can't work because you are a woman and changing the fact that, uh, you can't stay out late because you are a woman. The comment I hear is, "What are you, like the guys that you stay on the streets until the end of the night?" So all those chains that they put on you, I can't take them anymore. And a lot of other friends—women friends—are starting to do this.

(I put out cigarette.)

It's not just involving my sexuality; it's just that it's this whole idea of a woman remaining a virgin until she's married and things like that. You don't have to be gay, or heterosexual, or whatever. But everything that has to do with sex, the sexual side of the woman is very sacred. And kissing on the street, feeling free on the street, not walking miles apart—and they are not really walking miles apart—and you know that they know and they know that you know—but you can't do it anyway. So it's a whole vicious circle that we are trying to get out of.

I have future plans to leave the country because I've given up. It's unfortunate, but I don't feel I belong here and I don't feel that I belong abroad and I don't know where I belong. You know what I mean? Of course *you* do. Now you made me have tears in my eyes because that is a feeling that I have all the time here. I cry a lot. It's good, no? It washes the eyes and the nose.

(Freeze. Music fades up along with general wash, as I remove the vest. The downstage left spot cross-fades up as the upstage right spot fades out during the cross downstage. During the following fugue, I put on a cardigan and put my hair up in a bun. This area is set with a plate with a huge mound of grapes on it.)

Fugue 4

I want to know that my—oof, I just owned it—my culture will be preserved by capable, strong women. Every recipe, every story told, every heirloom passed on. I feel like I am being pulled in so many different directions. I resist the customs and at the same time crave the comforts and the richness of them. My exodus narrative bleeds all over everything. I am the prodigal daughter, a deserter, an insider-outsider. So my auntie puts on a dress and heels and has the housekeeper bring the coffee and fruit, et cetera. She usually wears a housecoat and slippers and props her varicose-veined legs up when I come to take coffee. She's definitely more formal than usual and I feel even more like an outsider. And I know it's not just the tape recorder . . .

(Music fades out along with the general wash, leaving only the downstage left area lit.)

Khowla Chahine

Do you want a biscuit? Red grapes? Have some more grapes. They are here, hmmm? OK. My grandmother used to teach me a lot of things. Do this, take that, and put that. Back in those days she would do it in front of me and I would do it with her. She was very neat and fastidious, but slow, my grandmother. She was very clean, scour that pot and scour and rub and rub and rub and she would kill me with rubbing!

(Laughs.)

The first time I made *mahshee koosa* (zucchini stuffed with rice and meat), I told her that I want to core the zucchini. She said, you don't know how.

I used to be very curious. From the first *koosayeh*, it went into two pieces. I threw it off the north balcony. The second one, I threw away. I threw away about six *koosayet* (zucchinis) and then I started to core well and that was it. I learned. I didn't want her to see them because she would shout at me! I was maybe fourteen, thirteen years old.

The first time I did the olives on the floor and took them to the press was in '56. I was pregnant with Wassim. Then I learned what the olives were! The women used to come from Hsaraat and sleep downstairs. And in the evening, the women would peel quinces and apples and we would make jam the next day. There were ten of them; we had a lot of olives and we would sort and work.

There is the green *zeitoon* (olives) that you have to make; they press and pickle it immediately. Not me, I press them a bit and then let them stay in the brine a bit to sweeten them. Every day, I change the water, then I put sea salt. Later, you put peppers and leaves of *Abu sfeir* (local herb) and pieces of lemon and then you put the water and you leave it, a bit of oil on the top if you like. I used to make *msharah* (cut olives with lemon). With *msharah*, you bring the knife and you begin to slice it, one-two-three, one-two-three. I even taught the kids. I would give them small knives, but you have to cut them and immediately put them in the brine so they don't get black. There were women from Dhour al Shwer and they used to teach me this method. There is a way to sweeten it, how we do it now. It takes a long time, and you feed the men and then one gets fat and then you get picked on and asked how come *you* are gaining weight.

I used to ask, this one and that one how she would do it and how much sugar they would put to the fruit. I make fig and quince and apricot jam. My grandmother used to make apricot, but she would not put too much sugar, and she would put it in the sun to sweeten! But apricot jam needs a lot of sugar so that it isn't too tart. But she was very tight! Now I make it my way and sweeten it. When I do figs, I cook five kilos at a time. One pot, five kilos. I get my figs and we pick them and split them and we put them on trays and put them aside until I want to cook them. I put one bottle of water in the pot, and rose geranium, a few sprigs, and then for each five kilos of figs, I put three kilos of sugar. And this way they come out properly. I put half a sour orange and a bit of lemon. I put them all together and leave them for a day. When they come to a hard boil, I take off the foam from the top and take out the geranium. Then I leave them to boil until they are like loose syrup. Then I would already have the sesame seeds toasted and have the Damascus gum pounded and put on the side. I wash the anise seed. All this is prepared in advance, before I start with the cooking of the figs. Then I pull the figs apart and turn them in—you turn it—*yalla, yalla, yalla* and then you stick the spoon in and make sure they are thickened, then you put the anise seed and the almonds. You break them a bit and put them in and you turn it, just when they are almost cooked, I turn the flame down. Then I add sesame and turn it and add sesame and turn it, but not too much, because then the flavor will overpower the figs. Then you put a touch of vanilla and the Damascus gum: sometimes we don't put the vanilla because they say that the vanilla is *"Frangie"* (French) and the figs are Arab. You put what you want! You turn them once or twice on a low flame, and then I fill the jars when it's still a bit hot, so that it takes the form of the jar. I leave them at first without a cover, ten hours, but I put a piece of cloth on them so flies don't land on them. Once they are properly cooled, you close them and that's it.

Food dishes, we learned them as we learned. I make *sayyadiyeh* (fish with rice and nuts), *warak aanab* (stuffed grape leaves), and stuffed tripe and *kibee* (ground lamb with burghul) and these things. I still make *Maamoul* (Easter cookies stuffed with either dates or nuts) and they come out top. My daughter Boushra knows and your cousin Rima knows. They ask and they learn how one does. They see how their mothers are doing it. Cooking is not difficult if one has patience for cooking. One time, the mother of Imad Abi Fares said to me that food is not intelligence—food is the waiting. I liked those words. Sometimes you make your dish and you put it and then you turn your back and it burns the dish without you noticing.

Here in the village everybody does grape leaves and these difficult dishes. But they don't eat. Today they won't let me use *ghee* (clarified butter). We are now cooking with corn oil, everything in Mazola. You don't feel that things have that nice heavy flavor anymore. Today my son says to me, "You are going to give me clogged veins." Today people don't work on things by hand that are difficult and they don't sweat.

But look, there is nothing to me that is still called tradition. Most of them do very little. Nobody is going to get a kilo of lentils and if we find it's good, then we would get seven or eight kilos, and we would wash them and salt them and them spread them out and they would last until next year. Now, you get it by the kilo from the supermarket, and when the kilo is finished, then you get more.

You still have some people who do things the traditional way. Here among us, it's gone. We are going along with the new *aasr* (generation), just like the old days. No one is free, Laila. There are no more visits. When you want to go somewhere, you have to call first, even. Welcome and come in, we don't have that anymore. I keep the door closed all the time and now strangers have come. It's the war, on the one hand, and then the people are like in the States. We are getting tired, Laila. You see, *en generale*, life is hard.

Don't you want to taste these grapes off our vine? Taste these grapes. Eat, eat one. They are delicious. *Yalla!*

(Freeze. Music fades up along with general wash lighting and the center spot. I remove the cardigan and replace the grapes before moving out of the area. The downstage left spot cross-fades out, and the center spot is all the lighting that remains during the first half of this fugue.)

Fugue 5

I realize that the main task of my day is an interruption in theirs. Just who is uncomfortable in this process? These women are empowering, but at the same time I feel small, examined, and judged. I can only wonder what they feel when they encounter me. But I can't help look at their survival tactics as my own. This *is* my dissertation research after all. So many echoes of struggles: basic services, checkpoints, getting my papers scrutinized, not being able to go where I want because the Israelis decided to bomb this week.

(During the following, the spot begins to fade as I repeat the beating of the hommos gesture from the opening narrative. The lighting fades as I continue this in silence for some beats until the stage is black.)

My narrative runs into theirs and their work becomes my work, and the rhythms that beat the hommos into a smooth paste resonate through our bodies much too loudly for comfort.

(The five areas come up to full, as I remain in the center spot for curtain call. Immediately after, the house lights are raised to full, as I begin the discussion talk-back. The performance is always followed by a discussion session with the audience. There is no break in between.)

Notes

1. For an excellent problematizing of the term "third world women," see Chandra Mohanty's discussion in *Third World Women and the Politics of Feminism.*

2. Darlene Hantzis discussed this concept in her presentation on Sri Lankan resistance at the Otis J. Aggert Performance Festival, Terre Haute, Indiana, February 1997.

3. I borrow the phrase from Robert Branham's presentation, "Keynotes in a New Key: Sweet Freedom's Song," Central States Communication Association, Saint Louis, April 1997.

Works Cited

Abu-Lughod, Lila. "Can There Be a Feminist Ethnography?" *Women in Performance* 5 (1990): 7–27.

Anzaldúa, Gloria. *Borderlands/La Frontera: The New Mestiza.* San Francisco: Aunt Lute Books, 1987.

Behar, Ruth. *Translated Woman.* Boston: Beacon Press, 1993.

Bhabha, Homi. *Nation and Narration.* New York: Routledge, 1990.

hooks, bell. *Talking Back: Thinking Feminist, Thinking Black.* Boston: South End Press, 1989.

Lionnet, Françoise. *Autobiographical Voices: Race, Gender, Self-Portraiture.* Ithaca, N.Y.: Cornell University Press, 1989.

Mohanty, Chandra, Ann Russo, and Lourdes Torres, eds. *Third World Women and the Politics of Feminism.* Bloomington: Indiana University Press, 1991.

Personal Narratives Group, ed. *Interpreting Women's Lives: Feminist Theory and Personal Narratives.* Bloomington: Indiana University Press, 1989.

Rodriguez, Richard. *Days of Obligation: An Argument with My Mexican Father.* New York: Penguin Books, 1992.

Torrecilha, Ramon S. "Wandering between Two Worlds, One Dead, the Other Powerless to Be Born." In *Names We Call Home: Autobiography on Racial Identity,* edited by Becky Thompson and Sangeeta Tyagi, 264–73. New York: Routledge, 1996.

16

"Orchids in the Arctic"

ᥱᥩᥩ Women's Autobiographical Performances as Mentoring

Elizabeth Bell

Often, when I'm in the throes of writing at my computer, the obnoxiously loud buzzer on the clothes dryer screams out. Instead of resenting the interruption, I welcome it. I enjoy the break that leads me into the laundry room, and I lift the hot clothes into the laundry basket. My mind continues to tread over the last sentence, paragraph, or idea, while I mindlessly and automatically fold and stack the clothes. I then walk down the hallway to the bedrooms, putting clothes into the appropriate drawers. I return to the keyboard knowing that I've accomplished at least one thing today—my children will have clean socks and underwear in the morning—and that closure, amid the open-endedness and uncertain evaluation of much academic labor, feels good.

I've often wondered how different my curriculum vitae would look if loaded not with academic labor but with the minute accomplishments of daily life: laundry washed, meals cooked, flowerbeds planted, carpools driven, Monopoly played, bikes ridden. The numbers would be staggering. And, how differently a vita would sound if not self-centered, but other-directed. Many of the authors in this book would show up on my "other" vita, acknowledging the multiple ways that their writings, performances, and stories have served as lessons for me in the academy and in my life. My other vita would acknowledge these women as friends, teachers, colleagues, intellectual guides, and most importantly for this essay, as mentors. Carolyn Heilbrun writes poignantly of women's lives portrayed in eighteenth-century autobiography: "These women had no models on which to form their lives, nor could they themselves become mentors since they did not tell the truth about their lives" (25). All of the essays and scripts in this book tell the truth about individual women's lives, and they perform the work of mentoring women in the academy.

FEMINIST PERFORMANCE WORK IN HOSTILE TERRITORY

The academy is often a hostile place for women, a hostile place for performance work, and a hostile place for feminism. Put these all together and they spell disaster. The litany of ways the academy creates an "environment in which research, scholarship, and teaching pertaining to women, gender, or gender inequities are devalued, discouraged, or altogether thwarted" is the subject of *Antifeminism in the Academy* (Kolodny 9). Unlike sexual harassment, usually directed at individual women, intellectual harassment is broad based and collective: the structures of the academy serve to maintain institutional practices and policies that find women pooled in low-paying, labor-intensive, "soft" disciplines where student contact and service work are both expected and devalued. Tenure and promotion policies, underrepresentation in administration, allocation of resources, teaching loads, and research agendas find women and minorities "working in the ivory basement," often with little institutional recourse for complaint or redress (Benokraitis). Despite the "ivory tower" metaphor, the academy is "divided by each of the diversities— race, ethnicity, gender, class, age, sexual orientation, or handicap—insidiously or overtly replicating the social [world] and its hierarchies" (Fay 280).

If women and minorities find themselves at the bottom of academic hierarchies, then women and minorities who do performance work, especially feminist performance, are doubly marginalized (Langellier, Carter, and Hantzis). Performance work in the academy does not garner institutional support, especially when compared with the more visible, more valued work of publishing. Across the academy, the highest publication rates are in the natural sciences; the lowest publication rates are in the arts and humanities (Zimber). Despite the disciplinary trends, publication in performance studies continues to be seen as the sine qua non of academic success, phrased as an "us against them" battle: "For the past seventy-five years, arguments about our scope, our methods, our objectives, and certainly our name have consistently come with the territory. As ever, the side that prevails will be the side that works the hardest and publishes the most, and the side that loses can take comfort in the certainty that this too shall pass" (Gray 263). This picture is a bleak one, and I take little comfort in Paul Gray's certainty or in his conception of winners and losers in the academy.

But feminist performance work manages to survive, even in the hostile territory of the academy, not unlike radical feminist Kay Leigh Hagan's question, "Can orchids grow in the arctic?" "Possibly," she answers her own question, "providing a woman has adequate resources and information and she prepares herself appropriately for the relentless hostility of the arctic climate. So button up your overcoats" (60–61).

In this essay, I would like to set aside the many debates about autobiographical performances, personal narrative, and autoethnography to examine the ways in which these performance scripts and their personas serve as resources and information for women in the academy. I may be bending a strict definition of mentoring to make these scripts fit the bill, but I see too many parallels between mentoring and the work of these performances to ignore their implications. Implicit in the late Nancy Woodhull's functional approach to feminism, "Do something to help another woman every day," is an imperative for each of us to work to empower women (Tannen). Mentoring in the academy is an empowering act—for both mentor and protégé; the act of writing and performing women's lives is also empowering—for both performer and audience.

While Bryant Alexander maintains that many "performers of autobiography [use] the pedagogy of performance to inform and engage" (99), the information about women in the academy taught in these performances is a special knowledge and a special engagement. Academic feminists in the 1990s increasingly turned to autobiography and memoir to capture their lives and to teach subsequent generations of women about the academy (see Nancy Miller). Lynne Segal writes: "What the feminist academic memoir brings to [the academy] is a focus on the personal. Ironically, the more some women seem to be winning old gender battles, narrowing the gender differences affecting their daily lives, the stronger the affirmation of women's unique affiliation to personal life" (6).

Feminist mentoring models are very much about bridging the professional and the personal, and about empowering women in the adverse climate of the academy. These performance scripts and their attendant essays do all this work—an audience at a time, and a reader at a time.

ON MENTORS AND MOUNTAINS IN THE ACADEMY

Mentoring has traditionally been defined as a one-on-one, on-going relationship between mentor and protégé within an organizational setting. The goal is to provide support, guidance, and counsel for junior members, easing upward mobility and facilitating success. As I survey the literature on mentoring, books, photocopied articles, highlighters, and Post-It notes form a mountain on my desktop. And I'm struck, throughout my reading, by how well the scripts in this book give body and voice to the research conclusions. I move from "career knowledge" and "psychosocial functions" of mentoring (Kram *Mentoring;* Kram and Isabella), to the stages of mentoring relationships (Kram "Phases"), to the benefits to the mentor, mentee, and to the institution (Kram and Isabella). My favorite list comes from Newby and Heide, who claim that benefits to the mentor include curiosity, work control, job complexity, cooperation, challenge, competence, and confidence. I would venture, as well, that all of these benefits accrue from production and performance work, the intense joy and agony of mounting a show.

But I pore over the articles, the research, the mountain-become-molehill that specifically deals with women. The research on women mentoring women does not contradict any of these research findings, but instead adds to mentoring duties. That is, women should be mentored with acknowledgment of career patterns different from men—late entry, interruption, and lack of opportunity (Noe); with special attention to balancing career and family goals (DiBenedetto and Tittle; O'Connell, Betz, and Kurth); and with specific attempts to countermand society's reluctance to perceive women as competent, productive scholars (Chandler). Confidence and competence are "special mentoring needs" of women (Ragins).

Feminist models of mentoring attempt to reconstruct and to redistribute power between the mentor and protégé. In Mary Ann Cain's description of her relationship with her advisor, she says, "Naming my relationship with Lil is difficult, but for now I will call it a partnership, one based in mutuality—of learning, trust, risk, care, and challenge" (113). Christy Chandler argues that "nonhierarchical support networks, not based on disparate status as in the traditional mentoring model, may embody a more feminist construct for promoting women in academia" (94). Marie Wunsch describes a mentoring program for women faculty at the University of Hawaii: "Rather than emphasize the hierarchical, we sought strategies to stress the egalitarian and to position the pairs to gain reciprocal benefits" (3).

As I survey my mountain of information, I am most troubled not by the conclusions but by what I read between the lines. Both models of mentoring—traditionally white male models and feminist models that attempt to account for differences—conceive of power in very different ways. In traditional male models of mentoring, the successful mentor is somehow omniscient: he knows all, sees all, and simply imparts that knowledge and vision to the mentee. Career knowledge and psychosocial support are twin gifts from a benevolent god. Indeed, when mentoring goes "wrong," power—its abuse, its disparity—is often mentioned as an important factor (Auster; Braun).

The work of women mentoring women is evident in all the performance scripts collected here. But the benevolent omniscience of male-centered models of mentoring and the egalitarian mutuality of some feminist models do little service to the power of the woman performer as mentor on stage. Instead, like Jill Dolan, I like to think of these mentoring performances as different manifestations of power. That is, Jill Dolan's eloquent conception of the powerful woman performer also applies to the woman mentor in the academy: "I still find radical her power to know, intellectually and psychophysically, how to wield the authority of stage presence, how to control the seductions inherent in the frame, and how to speak the language so that authority, seduction, and language mean something different about the status of women in culture" (1). The intellectual and psychophysical knowledge imparted throughout these scripts is very much about the frame of the academy and "speaking" subjects therein. These performance scripts teach and guide in their specificity of event and in their power of individual voice and body. As Patricia Hill Collins says of blueswoman Koko Taylor, "The songs she writes permit a vast array of individual women to locate themselves [in her world] without having to abstract themselves from their personal lives" (in Davis 56–57).

The tensions between location and abstraction, between public and personal, between the individual and the social are reconciled, if only for the time it takes for the curtain to drop or the paragraph to end, in the performance scripts collected here. I found myself located, for the time it took to read these scripts, in very different worlds, but their struggles became perspectives on my struggles in bridging the personal and the professional and in conducting feminist research.

MENTORING THE PROFESSIONAL AND
THE PERSONAL

In male-models, the work of an effective mentor is twofold. The mentor imparts career knowledge and psychosocial support. Marie Wunsch defines the latter as enhancing "the protégé's sense of competence and ability to define and clarify identity which confirm effectiveness in a professional role" (2). For professional women in the academy, however, such clarity between the professional and the personal is dubious. Indeed, in refusing to partition professional lives from personal lives, Jacqueline Taylor, Tami Spry, Linda Park-Fuller, and Joni L. Jones all speak to the intersection of professional and personal for its "truth." That is, not only are they inseparable, but the academy works very hard to make it hard for professional women to balance competing demands on their time and energies.

The academy still retains the illusion that the life of the scholar-teacher is a male one: "Prior to the contemporary women's movement, many male professors produced while their wives enabled them to do so without distractions. A professorship was often a two-person operation, with two people, in different ways, supporting one career" (Coiner 199). Constance Coiner writes that the academy has too long functioned on a "polite code of silence" that makes family, and its demands, unspeakable in the academy (199). Taylor's script, "On Being an Exemplary Lesbian," not only breaks this code of silence but also brings the lesbian family into the academy. She refuses to separate the professional from the personal, weaving the multiple roles of mother, professor, partner, administrator throughout the script. Taylor's "identity" as exemplar, certainly not without its performance pressures and downside, is a lesson to audience members who struggle to "define and clarify" professional identity roles. Taylor's clarity—as professional and as parent—comes not from partitioning roles but from constantly using one set of life experiences to inform the others, in turn teaching women in the academy not to separate their strengths.

The backdrop of homophobia in the academy, and the cultural disdain for gay parenting, is manifested in the classroom as Taylor faces "an extremely polite and restrained group of women." The solemnity of four-year-old Lucy bestowing her handmade necklaces on her mothers on their anniversary—"This is for you . . . and this is for your partner"—strikes at the heart of the cultural script that writes lesbian mothers as unfit. The act of writing and performing the personal as the professional is indeed political. Taylor breaks academic codes of silence about family, about lesbian partnerships, and about mothering—deftly, humorously, poignantly, and with an acute critical awareness of her performance of synecdoche as she stands center stage for all lesbians. All feminist mentors in the academy take this risk: standing for success and imparting "wisdom" that is not omniscient, but hard-fought and earned. Taylor brings "a sense of calmness, stability, and regularity" (Pistole 33) to her performance of mothering in the antifamily, antigay academy. As front-stage exemplar, she shares her back-stage strategies.

Competence, in professional roles, is a constant battle for women in the academy, and is part and parcel of the "psychosocial support" provided by the effective feminist mentor. The voice of self-doubt, a running interior monologue for many women in the academy, is bolstered by institutional practices. Increased scrutiny, performance pressure, social isolation, and stereotypes all contribute to women and minorities having "to perform better than men to be perceived as equal to men" (Collins, Chrisler, and Quina 51). Competence, however, is often performed as seeming to be "in control." Coiner writes, "One of the unspoken requirements for tenure is for junior faculty to appear to be coping well with their myriad responsibilities. At faculty meetings and social gatherings, it behooves us to look relaxed and on top of things rather than frenzied, fatigued, malcontent. . . . It's time for people to be honest about the tremendous emotional cost of women's—and men's—professional advances" (48). If Taylor's script evidences professional and personal front-stage confidence, then Tami Spry's essay and script speak of the downsides of "control": "if you were not in control, you risked people seeing your weaknesses and vulnerabilities." Spry takes us backstage in her honest portrayal of the emotional cost of professional development, especially when "professional" is an "exhausting artifice . . . of heels, hose, suit, and power hair." For Spry, "the dynamics of professional status and impression management caused weird collisions with the already personally and culturally fractured self created out of notes and memory of going mad." Spry's tattoo, like Silja J. A. Taivi's own self-marking, offers women, in a world with few opportunities for self-creation, one of the few concrete ways to exert control over our lives. Taivi writes (almost prophetically when applied to Spry's script), "No journey in a woman's life is more significant than that which questions and challenges her sense of self, allowing truisms of identity to be reshaped or to crumble and be rebuilt" (217–18). Spry's honesty about backstage costs—how expensive such crumbling and rebuilding really is—makes the frontstage academy a more livable place.

"Women need to know about other women's experiences in negotiating the male-centered academic environment and to observe survivors as role models," writes Marie Wunsch (3). Surviving the academy seems the small message in Linda Park-Fuller's breast cancer survival story, "A Clean Breast of It." And yet the academy, her role as teacher and the pressures upon her, is the constant backdrop of the lessons her body teaches her. Park-Fuller describes herself at the beginning of the script as leading a "successful life": "But under the surface, there was a lot of stress and fear. I had become obsessed with the details of everything I did, and had lost sight of the larger view. I was afraid that I might not always be able to keep all the balls in the air—afraid that I might not do something well enough, or *on time*, you know? So I had become something of a perfectionist." In "Mothering in the Academy," Diana Hume George writes a beautifully evocative account of her own work as a creative writing teacher in the academy, and the ways in which the maternal figure, as mentor, is a double-edged sword. She writes, "The women writers who do produce [in the academy] pay tremendously high personal and professional prices. . . . [T]he pressures on her and the expectations she has on herself, and that her students (and often her colleagues) also share unconsciously, are very like the demands of motherhood that Tillie Olsen addressed in *Silences*" (229). Not only does Park-Fuller continue to teach while undergoing chemotherapy (no mother, after all, can afford to be ill or unavailable), she fulfills all the responsibilities of the end-of-the-semester chaos: "It was the week before finals and you know what that's like on a college campus—I was grading papers, and meeting with students who had questions, and making out exams, and writing recommendations for graduating seniors, and generally looking forward to a summer that I would spend just trying to heal." As Tillie Olsen wrote, "Women are traditionally trained to place others' needs first, to feel these needs as their own (the 'infinite capacity'); their satisfaction to be in making it possible for others to use their abilities" (17).

While Park-Fuller maintains, "I'm still struggling with perfectionism," her script shows that the academy was a place where others, for once, put *her* first. "I had so much support from my friends and colleagues . . . my students. . . . A woman from Yale called me—she was the mother of a teacher in our art department who knew I was having surgery." These informal networks, as women reach out to each other and for each other in times of crisis, are exemplary of the refusal to separate the professional from the personal. Indeed, when Park-Fuller lists all the things she still wants to do, after her initial diagnosis (learning to clog, to play the guitar, to love—herself and others—unconditionally), I immediately noticed the "professional" absences: writing that journal article, editing that chapter; reading that newest book. Still, Park-Fuller plays the guitar in her survival story, and plays well, incorporating one personal "to-do" into her professional one-woman show.

Joni L. Jones's "sista docta," over and over again, demonstrates the emotional and intellectual tolls the academy exacts on women of color, and the script, almost line for line, parallels the research on African American mentoring: women of color are few and far between in senior positions in academia; feelings of isolation and tokenism abound; and the mentoring load, service responsibilities, and committee work for these women is monumental—often to the detriment of research and publication that would lead to their own advancement in rank and power (Benjamin; Gloria; Hine; Wiley).

"Career knowledge," in the functional approach to mentoring, is the information needed to do the job, the "how to" nuts and bolts of day-to-day academic work. Jones's script makes clear that academic work, for African American women, is not limited to teaching and research. According to Lois Benjamin, service—not just to the department and to the university, but to the African American community—is an obligation white academics do not bear. Alberta M. Gloria writes, "How could I say no to my community, to those who helped me get to this position in higher education, and to those who were seeking guidance and answers about academia? I was the only woman faculty of color; who else would say yes?" (37).

In Jones's script, "the machine" gives voice to the many pulls at her time and energy and makes abundantly clear the burden of service work for women of color. As the academy desperately tries to balance racial and gender numbers on committees (despite the inequity of these numbers across the university), Jones's voice mail is full of requests for her presence and expertise. The stage directions, calling for Jones to jog in place throughout the messages, is physical testimony to the limits of time and energy, not to mention the fact that she gets "nowhere" for her efforts. Through apt understatement, Jones brings home the point: "The eventual sweat and exhaustion are an important commentary on being a sista docta."

The advice to women of color offered in mentoring research is dis-

heartening at best. It alternates between (1) seek out the few women of
color (and add to their load!) and (2) develop peer support groups (Chandler; Morgan). Both suggestions put the onus on the woman of color to
help herself, not to mention perpetuate a system that overburdens and
stymies the few available mentors. Jones's much more helpful advice,
however, is offered throughout the script as both "career knowledge" and
"psychosocial support" to her audience. The section "self-defense" is pertinent and applicable to all of us. "Be careful. Your misunderstandings are
dangerous" gives us a valuable script for confronting every day acts of
racism. The "HBCU" is outed for its institutional sexism and homophobia, the faculty party for its racism and male myopia, the academy for its
failure to walk (in statistics) its talk. Through it all, however, Jones maintains, "I believe that the work can be transformative." She provides yet another model of success in the academy—one that presents the battles, not
as hard won, but as ongoing.

Successful mentoring can be transformative. Taylor, Spry, Park-
Fuller, and Jones all testify to the ongoing struggles of the feminist academic—as exemplar, as professional, as teacher, as role model. Their own
transformations, their own negotiations among multiple identities and
responsibilities, are lessons to all women in the academy: "The stories
women chose to tell about the difficulties encountered, because of their
sex, in their professional lives have force and resonance because those stories are not experienced in isolation" (Kolodny 17). And I would add,
these stories take their force and resonance from their refusal to separate
the professional from the personal, to blend the two for their "truths," in
turn combating the isolation of women in the academy.

MENTORING FEMINIST THEORY AND RESEARCH

Feminist theory and feminist research in the academy face obstacles from
without and from within. From without, any movement that speaks for
the disenfranchised is viewed with suspicion. For academic feminists, it's
a hard realization that "some of the most basic tenets of feminist consciousness—that women define themselves, that they assert their rights as
human beings—remain contested notions" (Ferguson, Katrak, and
Miner 59). To build feminist theory and conduct feminist research in such
a climate adds to its difficulty. From within feminism, its many branches
and agendas find harsh political divisions and ideological contretemps. If
indeed, as Lynne Segal argues, the academy is the last bastion of femi-

nism, then I worry that we're setting ourselves up for failure. But the performances of Laila Farah, Linda M. Montano, and Terry Galloway all
demonstrate that the building of feminist theory and the practice of feminist research need not succumb to this doomsday vision of the future. Research agendas that reconcile theory with practice, academic feminism
with feminist activism, and performance as a lived, and political, practice
combine to provide hope and sustenance for feminist performance work.

Laila Farah models a survival story of the difficulty of conducting research on the daily lives of third world women. Research agendas in the
academy have always been political; feminist research is even more so, and
feminist research in the name of social justice for women is a third nail in
the coffin of academic success. The studies on research areas are depressing: women's and minority issues are thought to be "on the periphery of
traditional disciplinary concerns," and the gatekeepers—editors and re-
viewers—"often do not see the importance of such work. [Their] judg-
ments set the parameters of discussion and debate in their fields"
(Chrisler 112). When they are published, men are less likely to cite these
works than works by men (Ferber).

Conducting feminist action research, in spite of its marginalization
and because of its importance to women's lives, is a resistant act in the
academy. But resistance, as Farah tells us, "had nothing to do with revolution; it had everything to do with living." Living and claiming identity
while "balancing on the hyphen," Farah quickly acknowledges "the privilege of [her] position as a dual-national academic." She then balances this
privilege with the acutely felt responsibility of "the role of cultural critic
in the name of social justice, of cultural, social, and political awareness, to
present a community of women who wish to celebrate their tactics of survival, resistance, and cultural membership." Privilege and responsibility
are the twofold enactments of the feminist mentor in the academy.

Lynne Segal paints a sad picture of feminism at the millennium as
"bitter tension between feminist activism and academic feminisms—
often misleadingly reduced to clashes between the economic versus the
cultural; maldistribution versus misrecognition" (5). Farah's work as an
academic and activist demonstrates this need not be a clash. This script
reveals, carefully and lovingly, the intertwining of the economic and the
cultural, distribution of resources and recognition of roles, the "hands" of
women and "the shaping of the world." Farah's place on the "border" between nations is also an analogy for women in the academy: she demonstrates how the feminist academic bridges theory and practice, research

and activism, first world and third world, crossing borders to mentor women studying women.

Bridging theory and practice is still another tension for feminists in the academy. Linda M. Montano's "Death in the Art and Life of Linda M. Montano" is a script that bridges theories of cultural constructions of death with the material practices of "the final closure." That she frames this performance script as part of her "critical theory, publish-or-perish bug" is a nicely ironic play on academic death, and her own seven-year stay at the University of Texas art department. Montano is doing theory with a "difference," one little recognized or valued in the academy. Katie King describes the many forms "theory" can take: "Active thinking, speaking, conversation, action grounded in theory, action producing theory, action suggesting theory, drafts, letters, unpublished manuscripts, stories in writing and not, poems said and written, art events like shows, readings, enactments, zap actions like ACT UP" (89). Montano's "performance slide lecture," as "a nice invitation to chaos and layering," crosses so many artistic forms and formats that the theory built here is difficult to label, not unlike King's list above, and certainly falls outside malestream research. But the work "allow[s] for cultural, symbolic, and personal connections" that simply wouldn't be possible with traditional methods of academic knowledge production, and the power of her performance work lies in these multiple connections.

Most importantly, the connection between the academy and political work is made in Montano's performance script. Like Deborah L. Siegel, I refuse "the narrow parameters of the frequently invoked binarism in which academic work is condemned as an elitist expression of the ivory tower and set in opposition to the 'real' political work going on in the 'outside' world" (49). The bridges between the personal and the professional, theory and practice, academic work and political work are made throughout the script. She paints the cultural curves of death as performed across cultures, but offers advice for its performance in U.S. contemporary culture as well. Montano's "Death Notes," with the preface, "These are some of the things I learned," will stay with me, as equipment for living with death. I can think of no better way to bridge all the tensions above.

Terry Galloway's "The Performance of Drowning" details her entree into the world of performing, but it also introduces desire as a deeply felt, if yet amorphous cognitive concept for the young persona of the script. The Deep End Instructor, aptly labeled not only for her job but also for the depth of Galloway's nascent yearning, teaches an important lesson about the birth of desire. In the academy, desire, love, sexual tension are often unspoken but omnipresent, built into the relationships between teachers and students, between women helping each other in the arctic climate.

We don't often use the word love in the academy. On second thought, I suppose we do: "I love the works of Butler!" "My passion is for teaching!" But the words of desire are rerouted to, encased in, acceptable intellectual pursuits. Jane Gallop's book, *Feminist Accused of Sexual Harassment*, talks of the other route—physical desire, sexual relations—in the context of the academy during the 1970s: "Whereas my adolescent boy-craziness had filled me with romantic fantasies of love, when I thought about the women at the meetings, I burned to touch their bodies. I walked around that year constantly in heat, energized for political activity and schoolwork; I learned that desire, even desire unacted upon, could make you feel very powerful. And the space where I learned desire—where it filled me with energy and drive—I call feminism" (4–5). So too Galloway's desire is unacted upon: "I knew that I could probably get up from that cot and go down the hall to the Deep End Instructor's room. . . . She might even let me under the covers and maybe even stroke my back until I slept or just passed out from the sexual tension. But I didn't dare." "Thrown into the arms of theatre," propelled by the "guilt and exhilaration" of a co-constructed performance, Galloway and the Deep End Instructor act, across different bodies, across different physical abilities, sharing the unspoken secret, not of desire, but of performance. Performing desire, despite Galloway's insistence, "I was a kid. I didn't care about complexities," is always complex. Like Judith Butler's contention that performances are repetitive displays that expose the artificiality of gender's construction, Galloway's own realization exposed the artificiality of her own performance. But a deeper construction presents itself as an epiphany, one that, unlike Gallop, Galloway does not experience as empowerment—this culture's constructions of body, physicality, and its performances: "toward beautiful completion, flawless efficiency, perfection of form, or, at the very least, some kind of solid utilitarian usefulness." Embedded in this construction of ability is the too little theorized notion that disability is a continuum along which power is distributed (Linton), and disabled women suffer even more than disabled men from failing to meet culture's demand for perfect, idealized bodies (Wendell).

The power of performance also operates on a continuum. From Farah's in-between-ness to Montano's "Death Notes," these are all very much about Galloway's performance epiphany: "how to give up, give in, be perfectly drawn down." All these performers survive—for now—and all teach us how to live with, and perform, ourselves.

SUBJECTHOOD AND WOMEN'S PERFORMANCE

Theorists, teachers, and performers of personal narrative find much to valorize and to critique in the current state of the art. Eric Peterson and Kristin Langellier propose context, and not just text, as central to a serious consideration of methodology in studying the production of personal narrative. Craig Gingrich-Philbrook posits solo performance between epistemic and aesthetic notions of rhetoric. And Bryant Alexander proposes "generative autobiography" as a composition strategy for performance as one way to theorize the "narrator in autobiographical performance as something other than an heroic autonomous subject" (110).

My approach has been both to sidestep and to incorporate those concerns. I have chosen to feature "context," with the academy as the implicit or explicit backdrop for the scripts, to better showcase the political nature of the academy and the negotiations within it. The latest statistics show that 63.7 percent of full-time university professors are male (Zimber). While the chances of this arctic climate changing soon are slim, the examples of women mentoring each other in the academy occur daily. Clearly, as a way of "knowing" and a "politics of location," the rhetoric of these performance scripts is very much about teaching the womanly art of survival in the academy. None of the scripts here create "a heroic autonomous subject," but instead the heroism of the women created in these scripts and essays is of the quiet, connected, and divided kind. Declaration of subjecthood, let alone heroism, is secondary to survival in the academy for women.

Critiques of the autonomous subject in Western thought are now familiar ground in feminist thought (Spivak; Butler; Barrett and Phillips). But feminism is still caught in debates about subjecthood that attempt to account for the many absences in ethnocentric, ahistorical, and universal constructions of the subject. Absences like "body, relationality, contingence, and an inescapable intimacy or mutual imbrication between self and other (although here questions of asymmetry are never far away)" (Kilby and Lury 253). Performance of women's autobiography is one efficacious tenet in the debates on subjecthood. Performance surely includes and accounts for body and the multiple messages created in and by the performer's presence on stage; for relationality and its narrative and staged contours; for contingence and the possibilities, and inevitability, of change; for intimacy and imbrication as the stories of self and others are given shape and meaning on stage.

"Questions of asymmetry," unequal power relations and their multiple manifestations, are at the heart of performance of subjectivity. Placing oneself and one's story center stage is a powerful act, but the ethical performer understands that the relationship to the audience is not a "power over" relationship, but a "power with" productivity. The constructions of self performed in these scripts—as embodied, as relational, as contingent, as intimate and imbricated—argue in their specificity of voice and experience for a construction of subjecthood that is never reducible to essentialized notions of agency, to formulaic structures of heroism, to happily-ever-after closure. At the same time, the constructions of self performed in these scripts do evidence an agency, a heroism, a closure—but with a difference. "Marginalized subjectivities," the catchphrase for those denied subjecthood in traditional Western conceptions, move from margin to center (stage) in performance. And therein lies the irony of subjectivity for women's autobiographical performances: at once a speaking subject, the stories of survival critique the very structures that deny subjecthood to women. Performance then creates the hothouse conditions, in the arctic, that enable orchids to thrive.

Women mentoring women, or growing "orchids in the arctic," is just one perspective for these performance scripts. The academy is both a microcosm of the larger culture and a window from which to view it. As microcosm, these scripts portray cultural and personal issues relevant for all women: workplace politics, homophobia, cancer, depression, mental crisis, family connections and losses, ethnic and racial bonds, desire—all the ongoing constructions of our selves, our bodies, and our relationships. As a window, the academy is a location for reflection, for empowerment, and for transformation, especially because the view can be so disheartening. Taking these scripts to the "streets," as all of these performers have done, changes the landscape of the academy and the view from its window. These new vistas, strewn with orchids, are quite remarkable for the performing subjects created there.

Works Cited

Alexander, Bryant Keith. "*Skin Flint (or, The Garbage Man's Kid)*: A Generative Autobiographical Performance Based on Tami Spry's *Tattoo Stories*." *Text and Performance Quarterly* 20 (2000): 97–114.

Auster, Donald. "Mentors and Proteges: Power-dependent Dyads." *Sociological Inquiry* 54, no. 2 (1984): 142–53.

Barrett, Michelle, and Anne Phillips, eds. *Destablizing Theory: Contemporary Feminist Debates.* Cambridge: Polity Press, 1992.

Benjamin, Lois, ed. *Black Women in the Academy: Promises and Perils.* Gainesville: University Press of Florida, 1997.

Benokraitis, Nijole V. "Working in the Ivory Basement: Subtle Sex Discrimination in Higher Education." In *Career Strategies for Women in Academe: Arming Athena*, edited by Lynn H. Collins, Joan C. Chrisler, and Kathryn Quina, 3–36. Thousand Oaks, Calif.: Sage, 1998.

Braun, R. "The Downside of Mentoring." In *Women in Higher Education: Changes and Challenges*, edited by Lynne B. Welch, 191–98. New York: Praeger, 1990.

Butler, Judith. *Gender Trouble.* New York: Routledge, 1990.

Cain, Mary Ann. "Mentoring as Identity Exchange: Conflicts and Connections." *Feminist Teacher* 8, no. 3 (1994): 112–14.

Chandler, Christy. "Mentoring and Women in Academia: Reevaluating the Traditional Model." *NWSA Journal* 8, no. 3 (1996): 79–86.

Chrisler, Joan. "Teacher Versus Scholar: Role Conflict for Women?" In *Career Strategies for Women in Academe: Arming Athena*, edited by Lynn H. Collins, Joan C. Chrisler, and Kathryn Quina, 107–27. Thousand Oaks, Calif.: Sage, 1998.

Coiner, Constance. "Silent Parenting in the Academy." In *Listening to Silences: New Essays in Feminist Criticism*, edited by Elaine Hedges and Shelley Fisher Fishkin, 197–224. New York: Oxford University Press, 1994.

Collins, Lynn H., Joan C. Chrisler, and Kathryn Quina, eds. Introduction to *Career Strategies for Women in Academe: Arming Athena*, 3–36. Thousand Oaks, Calif.: Sage, 1998.

Davis, Angela Y. *Blues Legacies and Black Feminism.* New York: Pantheon, 1998.

DiBenedetto, Barbara, and Carol Kehr Tittle. "Gender and Adult Roles: Role Commitment of Women and Men in a Job Family Trade-Off Context." *Journal of Counseling Psychology* 37 (1990): 41–48.

Dolan, Jill. *Presence and Desire: Essays on Gender, Sexuality, Performance.* Ann Arbor: University of Michigan Press, 1993.

Fay, Elizabeth A. "Dissent in the Field; Or, a New Type of Intellectual?" In *Working-Class Women in the Academy: Laborers in the Knowledge Factory*, edited by Michelle M. Tokarczyk and Elizabeth A. Fay, 276–91. Amherst: University of Massachusetts Press, 1993.

Ferber, M. A. "Citations and Networking." *Gender and Society* 2 (1998): 82–89.

Ferguson, Moira, Ketu H. Katrak, and Valerie Miner. "Feminism and Antifeminism: From Civil Rights to Culture Wars." In *Antifeminism in the Academy*, edited by VèVè Clark, Shirley Nelson Garner, Margaret Higonnet, and Ketu H. Katrak, 350–66. New York: Routledge, 1996.

Gallop, Jane. *Feminist Accused of Sexual Harassment.* Durham, N.C.: Duke University Press, 1997.

George, Diana Hume. "How Many of Us Can You Hold to Your Breast?: Mothering in the Academy." In *Listening to Silences: New Essays in Feminist Criticism*, edited by Elaine Hedges and Shelley Fisher Fishkin, 225–44. New York: Oxford University Press, 1994.

Gingrich-Philbrook, Craig. "Autobiographical Performance and Carnivorous Knowledge: Rae C. Wright's *Animal Instincts.*" *Text and Performance Quarterly* 18 (1998): 63–79.

Gloria, Alberta M. "Searching for Congruity: Reflections of an Untenured Woman of Color." In *Career Strategies for Women in Academe: Arming Athena,* edited by Lynn H. Collins, Joan C. Chrisler, and Kathryn Quina, 36–39. Thousand Oaks, Calif.: Sage, 1998.

Gray, Paul H. "On Naming the Rose: A Response." *Text and Performance Quarterly* 10 (1990): 262–63.

Hagan, Kay Leigh. *Fugitive Information: Essays from a Feminist Hothead.* San Francisco: Pandora, 1993.

Heilbrun, Carolyn G. *Writing a Woman's Life.* New York: Norton, 1988.

Hine, D. C. "The Future of Black Women in the Academy: Reflections on Struggle." In *Black Women in the Academy: Promises and Perils,* edited by Lois Benjamin, 327–39. Gainesville: University Press of Florida, 1997.

Kilby, Jane, and Celia Lury. "Subject Matters." In *Transformations: Thinking through Feminism,* edited by Sara Ahmed, Jane Kilby, Celia Lury, Maureen McNeilo, and Beverley Skeggs, 253–58. New York: Routledge, 2000.

King, Katie. "Producing Sex, Theory, and Culture: Gay/Straight Remappings in Contemporary Feminism." In *Conflicts in Feminism,* edited by Marianne Hirsch and Evelyn Fox Keller, 82–101. New York: Routledge, 1990.

Kolodny, Annette. "Paying the Price of Antifeminist Intellectual Harassment." In *Antifeminism in the Academy,* edited by VèVè Clark, Shirley Nelson Garner, Margaret Higonnet, and Ketu H. Katrak, 3–33. New York: Routledge, 1996.

Kram, Kathy E. *Mentoring at Work: Developmental Relationships in Organizational Life.* Glenview, Ill.: Scott Foresman, 1985.

———. "Phases of the Mentor Relationship." *Academy of Management Journal* 26 (1983): 608–25.

Kram, Kathy E., and Lynn A. Isabella. "Mentoring Alternatives: The Role of Peer Relationships in Career Development." *Academy of Management Journal* 28 (1985): 110–32.

Langellier, Kristin, Kathryn Carter, and Darlene Hantzis. "Performing Differences: Feminism and Performance Studies." In *Transforming Visions: Feminist Critiques in Communication Studies,* edited by Sheryl Perlmutter Bowen and Nancy Wyatt, 87–124. Cresskill, N.J.: Hampton, 1993.

Linton, Simi. *Claiming Disability: Knowledge and Identity.* New York: New York University Press, 1988.

Miller, Nancy. "Review Essay. Public Statements, Private Lives: Academic Memoirs for the Nineties." *Signs: Journal of Women in Culture and Society* 22 (1997): 981.

Morgan, J. "Women Leaders of Color Call for Coalition and Unity to Advance Concerns." *Black Issues in Higher Education* 10, no. 4 (1993): 22–23.

Newby, T. J., and A. Heide. "The Value of Mentoring." *Performance Improvement Quarterly* 5, no. 4 (1992): 2–15.

Noe, Raymond A. "Women and Mentoring: A Review and Research Agenda." *Academy of Management Review* 13, no. 1 (1988): 65–78.

O'Connell, Lenahan, Michael Betz, and Suzanne Kurth. "Plans for Balancing Work and

Family Life: Do Women Pursuing Nontraditional and Traditional Occupations Differ?" *Sex Roles* 20, no. 1/2 (1989): 35–45.

Olsen, Tillie. *Silences*. New York: Delacorte Press/Seymour Lawrence, 1978.

Peterson, Eric E., and Kristin M. Langellier. "The Politics of Personal Narrative Methodology." *Text and Performance Quarterly* 17 (1997): 135–52.

Pistole, M. Carole. "Mentoring Women's Academic Careers: Using a Family Model to Enhance Women's Success." *Initiatives* 56, no. 2 (1994): 29–36.

Ragins, Belle Rose. "Barriers to Mentoring: The Female Manager's Dilemma." *Human Relations* 42 (1989): 1–22.

Segal, Lynne. *Why Feminism? Gender, Psychology, Politics*. New York: Columbia University Press, 1999.

Siegel, Deborah L. "The Legacy of the Personal: Generating Theory in Feminism's Third Wave." *Hypatia* 12, no. 3 (1997): 46–75.

Spivak, G. *In Other Worlds: Essays on Cultural Politics*. London: Methuen, 1987.

Taivi, Silja J. A. "Marked for Life: Tattoos and the Redefinition of Self." In *Adios, Barbie: Young Women Write about Body Image and Identity*, edited by Ophira Edut, 211–18. Seattle, Wash.: Seal Press, 1998.

Tannen, Deborah. "In Memory of Nancy Woodhull." *American Journalism Review*, May 1997, 17.

Wendell, Susan. *The Rejected Body: Feminist Philosophical Reflections on Disability*. New York: Routledge, 1996.

Wiley, Ed. "Ability to Manage Students and Collegial Expectations Key in Black Faculty Success." *Black Issues in Higher Education* 9, no. 21 (1992): 11–13.

Wunsch, Marie. "Giving Structure to Experience: Mentoring Strategies for Women Faculty." *Initiatives* 56, no. 1 (1994): 1–9.

Zimber, Linda J. "Background Characteristics, Work Activities, and Compensation of Faculty and Instructional Staff in Postsecondary Institutions: Fall 1998." Washington, D.C.: U.S. Department of Education. National Center for Education Statistics, 2001. Available online at http://nces.ed.gov.

Contributors

Elizabeth Bell, associate professor of communication at the University of South Florida, is coeditor of *From Mouse to Mermaid: The Politics of Film, Gender, and Culture* (Indiana University Press, 1995). She has published essays on the performance of gender and cultural politics in various journals.

M. Heather Carver is assistant professor of theatre at the University of Missouri at Columbia. She has published articles on women's autobiographical performance and has presented her work at several national conferences and performance festivals. She is currently working on a book about the Hollywoodization of women's autobiographical texts. Her essay "Delivering Twins: A Performative Excursion" appears in *The Green Window: Proceedings of the Giant City Conference on Performative Writing* (Southern Illinois University, 2001).

Eileen C. Cherry is a performance scholar, arts activist, and writer. She serves as playwright for "The People Keep on Comin'," a performance ethnography for young audiences produced by Metro Theatre Company of Saint Louis. She has held faculty appointments at DePaul University, Columbia College Chicago, and Northwestern University.

Laila Farah is assistant professor of women's studies at DePaul University. Her publications consider feminist performance and the performance of third world texts. She has held guest artist residencies at Dartmouth College, Brandeis University, and Hamilton College.

Carolyn Gage is the author of more than forty musicals, dramas, and one-act plays. She has written the first book of monologues and scenes for lesbian actors and the first book on lesbian theatre production. Her one-woman show *The Second Coming of Joan of Arc* received first-class production in Brazil, where it was the hit of the 2000–2001 season, seen by over two hundred thousand people. Gage has been a guest lecturer at Bates College and she tours to colleges and universities offering lectures and workshops on nontraditional roles for women. Her catalogue is online at www.carolyngage.com.

Terry Galloway is a performance artist whose work has been featured at P.S. 122, the Edinborough Festival in Scotland, the WOW Cafe, and the Women's Project in New York, among many other venues. The author-performer of three one-woman shows, *Out All Night and Lost My Shoes* (Apalachee Press), *Heart of a Dog* (Yale Performing Arts Journal Press), and *Lardo Weeping*, Galloway has received grants from the National Endowment for the Arts, Texas Institute of Letters, and the Pew Charitable Trusts. She has been a visiting artist at the California Institute of the Arts, Florida State University, and the University of Texas at Austin. She divides her time between Tallahassee, Florida, where she works with the Mickee Faust Club, an alternative cabaret theatre, and Austin, Texas, where she is the artistic director for the Actual Lives Disability Project.

Joni L. Jones, associate professor of performance studies in the Department of Theatre and Dance and associate director of the Center of African and African American Studies at the University of Texas at Austin, is an artist-scholar who is currently engaged in performance ethnography and videography around the Yoruba deity Osun. Her articles on performance and identity have appeared in *Text and Performance Quarterly*, *The Drama Review*, *Theatre Topics*, and *Black Theatre News*. She is a performer with international local acting credits, and the recipient of professional acting awards. She is also the proud mother of an eighteen-year-old daughter.

Carol Hanbery MacKay, professor of English at the University of Texas at Austin, is the editor of *Dramatic Dickens* (1989) and the author of *Soliloquy in Nineteenth-Century Fiction: Consciousness Creating Itself* (1987). She is a scholar of Victorian fiction, women's studies, and women's autobiography, and her interests span literary and performance studies. Her most recent book, *Creative Negativity: Four Victorian Exemplars of the Female Quest* (Stanford University Press, 2001), proposes a working template for female creative activity in the Victorian period.

Lynn C. Miller is associate professor of theatre and dance (performance studies) at the University of Texas at Austin. She has published essays on Gertrude Stein's work in performance, on women's performance art, and on autobiographical performance. She is coeditor of *The Green Window: Proceedings of the Giant City Conference on Performative Writing* (Southern Illinois University Press, 2001) and author of the novel *The Fool's Journey* (Winedale Publishing, 2002). She currently tours solo performances of Gertrude Stein, Katherine Anne Porter, and Edith Wharton.

Linda M. Montano, an innovative performance artist, does work informed by her Roman Catholic roots, by Eastern meditation practices (including Zen Buddhism, Tibetan Buddhism, Hinduism), and by the visual arts. She teaches workshops at the Art/Life Institute in Kingston, New York, and is the author of *Art in Everyday Life* (1980) and *Performance Artists Talking in the Eighties* (University of California Press, 2000). For more information see www.bobsarts.org.

Linda Park-Fuller is an assistant professor of performance studies in the Hugh Downs School of Communication at Arizona State University. An active director and performer, Park-Fuller has directed more than twenty stage productions; "A Clean Breast of It" has been toured nationally at more than fifty venues. She received the 1999 Leslie Irene Coger Award for Distinguished Performance from the National Communication Association. She has published essays on autobiographical performance in *Text and Performance Quarterly*.

Elyse Lamm Pineau is an associate professor of speech communication (performance studies) at Southern Illinois University. She has published essays on Anaïs Nin and autobiographical performance and has performed Nin at various performance festivals and conferences.

Catherine Rogers received her M.F.A. in playwriting from the University of Texas at Austin, where she was a Michener Fellow at the Texas Center for Writers. Currently a playwright in New York, Rogers has had her plays produced around the country, most recently at the Cleveland Public Theatre's New Play Festival and the Women's Project in New York City.

Tami Spry is professor of speech communication (performance studies) at Saint Cloud State University. A teacher, director, and performer of women's autobiography and personal narratives, she has performed her solo and published work at performance festivals, universities, and conferences nationally. She is currently working with Chilean and Peruvian shamans on the dialectics of spirituality and performance.

Jacqueline Taylor is director of the DePaul Humanities Center and professor of communication. She has served in a number of administrative roles at DePaul University, including director of Women's Studies, department chair, and associate dean. She is the author of *Grace Paley: Illuminating the Dark Lives* (University of Texas Press, 1990). Along with her current work on autobiographical performance, she is writing a memoir with the working title of *Waiting for the Call*.

Stacy Wolf is associate professor of theatre and dance at the University of Texas at Austin. She is the author of *A Problem like Maria: Gender and Sexuality in the American Musical* (University of Michigan Press, 2002), and has published essays on theatre audiences and on pedagogy. Wolf also works as a director and a dramaturge, and she is the current editor of *Theatre Topics*.

Wisconsin Studies in Autobiography

William L. Andrews
General Editor

Robert F. Sayre
The Examined Self: Benjamin Franklin, Henry Adams, Henry James

Daniel B. Shea
Spiritual Autobiography in Early America

Lois Mark Stalvey
The Education of a WASP

Margaret Sams
Forbidden Family: A Wartime Memoir of the Philippines, 1941–1945
Edited, with an introduction, by Lynn Z. Bloom

Charlotte Perkins Gilman
The Living of Charlotte Perkins Gilman: An Autobiography
Introduction by Ann J. Lane

Mark Twain
*Mark Twain's Own Autobiography: The Chapters from the
 North American Review*
Edited, with an introduction, by Michael Kiskis

Journeys in New Worlds: Early American Women's Narratives
Edited by William L. Andrews

American Autobiography: Retrospect and Prospect
Edited by Paul John Eakin

Caroline Seabury
The Diary of Caroline Seabury, 1854–1863
Edited, with an introduction, by Suzanne L. Bunkers

Marian Anderson
My Lord, What a Morning
Introduction by Nellie Y. McKay

American Women's Autobiography: Fea(s)ts of Memory
Edited, with an introduction, by Margo Culley

Frank Marshall Davis
Livin' the Blues: Memoirs of a Black Journalist and Poet
Edited, with an introduction, by John Edgar Tidwell

Joanne Jacobson
Authority and Alliance in the Letters of Henry Adams

Cornelia Peake McDonald
A Woman's Civil War: A Diary with Reminiscences of the War, from March 1862
Edited, with an introduction, by Minrose C. Gwin

Kamau Brathwaite
The Zea Mexican Diary: 7 Sept. 1926–7 Sept. 1986
Foreword by Sandra Pouchet Paquet

Genaro M. Padilla
My History, Not Yours: The Formation of Mexican American Autobiography

Frances Smith Foster
Witnessing Slavery: The Development of Ante-bellum Slave Narratives

Native American Autobiography: An Anthology
Edited, with an introduction, by Arnold Krupat

American Lives: An Anthology of Autobiographical Writing
Edited, with an introduction, by Robert F. Sayre

Carol Holly
*Intensely Family: The Inheritance of Family Shame and the Autobiographies
of Henry James*

People of the Book: Thirty Scholars Reflect on Their Jewish Identity
Edited by Jeffrey Rubin-Dorsky and Shelley Fisher Fishkin

G. Thomas Couser
Recovering Bodies: Illness, Disability, and Life Writing

José Angel Gutiérrez
The Making of a Chicano Militant: Lessons from Cristal

John Downton Hazlett
My Generation: Collective Autobiography and Identity Politics

William Herrick
Jumping the Line: The Adventures and Misadventures of an American Radical

Women, Autobiography, Theory: A Reader
Edited by Sidonie Smith and Julia Watson

Carson McCullers
*Illumination and Night Glare: The Unfinished Autobiography of
    Carson McCullers*
Edited by Carlos L. Dews

Marie Hall Ets
Rosa: The Life of an Italian Immigrant

Yi-Fu Tuan
Who Am I?: An Autobiography of Emotion, Mind, and Spirit

Henry Bibb
The Life and Adventures of Henry Bibb: An American Slave
With a new introduction by Charles J. Heglar

Suzanne L. Bunkers
Diaries of Girls and Women: A Midwestern American Sampler

Jim Lane
The Autobiographical Documentary in America

Sandra Pouchet Paquet
Caribbean Autobiography: Cultural Identity and Self-Representation

Voices Made Flesh: Performing Women's Autobiography
Edited by Lynn C. Miller, Jacqueline Taylor, and M. Heather Carver